CW01645089

NICEIC

ECA
Representing the best in electrical engineering and building services

Site Guide

for Electrical Installations
(for installations up to 100 A and including solar photovoltaic microgeneration)

2nd Edition

IET WIRING REGULATIONS
UPDATED TO:
17TH EDITION
BS 7671:2008
Amd 3: 2015

Acknowledgements

Certsure

Certsure LLP is a limited liability partnership between the Electrical Safety First and the Electrical Contractors' Association (ECA) registered in England and Wales. Its brands include NICEIC the UK's leading voluntary regulatory body for the electrical contracting industry, which has been assessing the electrical competence of electricians for over fifty years and currently maintains a roll of over 26,000 registered contractors. It also includes ELECSA, who provide inspection, assessment and certification services to contractors working with electrical and renewable technology installations in private dwellings.

Certsure products are delivered through the NICEIC and ELECSA brands. The products include, amongst others:

- The NICEIC Approved Contractor Scheme, a scheme for electrical contractors undertaking design, installation, commissioning and maintenance of electrical installations to *BS 7671*.
- The ELECSA and NICEIC Part P Domestic Installer Scheme, which registers installers to Full Scope or Defined Competence for domestic electrical installation work in accordance with Part P of the Building Regulations in England and Wales.
- The Microgeneration Certification Scheme (MCS), developed to assess businesses installing microgeneration technology and is designed to protect the consumer.
- The Green Deal Scheme, for energy saving improvements to dwellings and other buildings.

Electrical Safety First

Electrical Safety First (formerly the Electrical Safety Council) is an independent charity committed to reducing deaths and injuries through electrical accidents at home and at work.

Electrical Safety First is supported by all sectors of the electrical industry, approvals and research bodies, consumer interest organisations, the electricity distribution industry, professional institutes and institutions, regulatory bodies, trade and industry associations and federations, trade unions and local and central government.

The Electrical Contractors' Association

The Electrical Contractors' Association (ECA) is the leading trade association for contractors involved in electrical engineering projects in England, Northern Ireland and Wales.

Published by:

Certsure LLP, Warwick House, Houghton Hall Park, Houghton Regis, Dunstable, Bedfordshire LU5 5ZX

Tel: 0870 013 0458 Fax: 01582 556024 Website: www.certsure.com

ISBN: 978-1-906091-66-8 EAN: 9781906091668 Sap code: 5617

All rights reserved. No part of this publication may be reproduced in any form, stored in a retrieval system or transmitted in any form or by any means – electronic, mechanical, photocopying or recording – without the prior permission of Certsure LLP. Certsure LLP and any contributor believe that the guidance and information contained in this book is correct, but all parties must rely on their own skill and judgement when making use of it. Neither Certsure LLP nor any contributor assumes any liability to anyone for any loss or damage caused by any error or omission in this book, whether such error or omission is the result of negligence or any other cause. Where reference is made to legislation, it is not to be considered as legal advice. Any and all such liability is disclaimed to the extent allowed by the law.

Published by Certsure LLP © Certsure LLP (January 2015)

Contents

Page

Contents

Published by Certsure LLP © Certsure LLP (January 2015)

Published by Certsure LLP © Certsure LLP (January 2015)

Contents

Page

Published by Certsure LLP © Certsure LLP (January 2015)

Contents

Published by Certsure LLP © Certsure LLP (January 2015)

Contents

Page

Published by Certsure LLP © Certsure LLP (January 2015)

Contents

Published by Certsure LLP © Certsure LLP (January 2015)

Chapter 1

Introduction

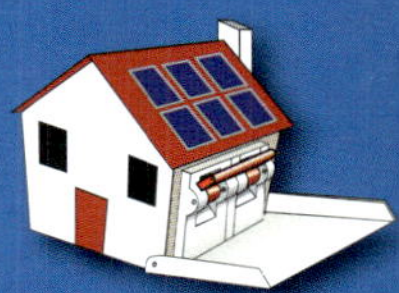

Introduction

1.1 Scope

This Guide is intended for contractors that carry out electrical installation work in locations such as dwellings, offices and shops with a single-phase or three-phase electrical supply rated up to 100 A.

It provides information and guidance relating to the design, construction, inspection, testing and certification of electrical installation work carried out in smaller premises, and is intended to promote good practice and aid understanding of the fundamental concepts of protection for safety. The guidance is based on the requirements of *BS 7671: 2008* (as amended) *Requirements for Electrical Installations*, and references to Regulation numbers are to those contained in that Standard.

This Guide is intended to complement other authoritative guidance published by the NICEIC, ELECSA and other reputable bodies.

1.2 Statutory and non-statutory requirements

1.2.1 Health and Safety at Work etc Act 1974

The Health and Safety at Work etc Act 1974 (HSW Act) is the primary piece of legislation dealing with occupational health and safety in the United Kingdom.

This is an enabling Act, a provision in law that confers on appropriate officials – in this case the Health and Safety Executive – the power to implement or enforce the law.

The HSW Act sets out the general duties that employers have towards employees and members of the public, and that employees have to themselves and to each other.

The principle of *'so far as is reasonably practicable'* may be applied to some of these duties. This principle is considered further in Section 1.3.1 of this Guide along with the principle of *absolute duty*. In the case of offences under the HSW Act, a person is deemed guilty until proven innocent, which is the opposite of the presumption of innocence that exists in 'criminal' law. This means that a person charged with a health and safety offence must demonstrate that they took the relevant precautions in relation to the duties placed on them by the HSW Act.

Published by Certsure LLP © Certsure LLP (January 2015)

1.2.2 Electricity at Work Regulations 1989

The Electricity at Work Regulations 1989 (EWR) is a Statutory Instrument made under the Health and Safety at Work etc. Act 1974 (HSW Act).

A statutory instrument is a form of subordinate or secondary legislation, which is made under an enabling Act.

Statutory instruments are classified, according to their subject matter, as being local or general in application. The requirements contained in the EWR are *generally applicable*. That is to say, they apply (with very few exceptions) wherever work is carried out on, or close to, live conductors.

The provisions contained within a statutory instrument must be complied with; they are not optional or preferred conditions.

EWR were introduced to require precautionary measures to be taken against the risk of death or personal injury caused by electricity when carrying out work activities.

EWR contains 33 regulations, of which 12 are applicable to mines only. A brief summary of the general regulations is provided below.

Regulation 2 defines a number of terms used within the Regulations, including *danger; electrical equipment; and injury.*

Regulation 3 requires employers and employees to comply with 'the provisions contained within EWR in so far as they relate to matters within (their) control'. The nature of these duties is expanded on in the Health and Safety Executive (HSE) publication *Memorandum of guidance on the Electricity at Work Regulations 1989* (HSR25), which is considered further in Section 1.3.1 of this Guide.

Regulation 4 gives requirements relating to the construction, use and maintenance of systems, and the electrical equipment therein, and is reproduced below:

> 1) All systems shall at all times be of such construction as to prevent, so far as is reasonably practicable, danger.
>
> 2) As may be necessary to prevent danger, all systems shall be maintained so as to prevent, so far as is reasonably practicable, such danger.

3) Every work activity, including operation, use and maintenance of a system and work near a system, shall be carried out in such a manner as not to give rise, so far as is reasonably practicable, to danger.

4) Any equipment provided under these Regulations for the purpose of protecting persons at work on or near electrical equipment shall be suitable for the use for which it is provided, be maintained in a condition suitable for that use, and be properly used.

Regulation 5 is concerned with the strength and capability of equipment with regard to its use under normal, transient and prospective fault conditions.

Regulation 6 relates to the construction and protection of electrical equipment against the adverse or hazardous environments to which electrical equipment might reasonably be exposed in use. This is of relevance to the use of the International Protection (IP) code described in *BS EN 60529: 1992* (as amended).

Regulation 7 requires conductors that may give rise to danger to be covered by insulation and where necessary be provided with other means of protection; or be so placed to prevent so far as is reasonably practicable, danger.

Regulation 8 is concerned with the provision of earthing or other precautions to prevent danger.

Regulation 9 deals with the integrity (that is, the continuity) of referenced conductors.

Regulation 10 requires all joints and connections to be mechanically and electrically suitable for use.

Regulation 11 requires means of protecting against excess of current to be provided.

Regulation 12 calls for the provision of secure means of isolation to any electrical equipment – that is, whole installations, or one or more circuits, or individual items as necessary to prevent danger.

Regulation 13 states that:

Adequate precautions shall be taken to prevent electrical equipment, which has been made dead in order to prevent danger while work is carried out on or near that equipment, from becoming electrically charged during that work if danger may thereby arise.

Published by Certsure LLP © Certsure LLP (January 2015)

Regulation 14 prescribes three conditions which must all be satisfied before a person may be involved in work on or near live conductors. The conditions are:

a) it is unreasonable in all the circumstances for it to be dead; **and**

b) it is reasonable in all the circumstances for him to be at work on or near it while it is live; **and**

c) suitable precautions (including where necessary the provision of suitable protective equipment) are taken to prevent injury.

Regulation 15 requires the provision of adequate working space, means of access, and lighting where electrical equipment is situated.

Regulation 16 requires persons to be competent to prevent danger or injury and is worthy of repeat here:

> No person shall be engaged in any work activity where technical knowledge or experience is necessary to prevent danger or, where appropriate, injury unless he possesses such knowledge or experience, or is under such degree of supervision as may be appropriate having regard to the nature of the work.

The issue of competency is considered further in Section 1.3.1 of this Guide.

1.2.3 Construction (Design and Management) Regulations 2007

The Construction (Design and Management) Regulations apply generally to all construction work, including that relating to the electrical installation if the construction work is likely to exceed 30 calendar days or 500 person days (regulation 2).

Regulations 5 and 6 require co-operative and co-ordinated planning and management of construction work activities to ensure, so far as is reasonably practicable, the health and safety of persons directly involved in, or likely to be affected by, the construction work.

Regulation 9 requires the client (as defined) to take reasonable steps to ensure that, in any project:

> Construction work can be carried out, so far as is reasonably practicable, without a risk to health and safety
>
> The requirements of Schedule 2 relating to welfare facilities are met
>
> A structure constructed for use as a workplace has been designed taking account of the relevant requirements of the Workplace (Health, Safety and Welfare) Regulations 1992.

Regulation 10 relates to the timely provision by the client of pre-construction information.

Regulation 14 states that where a project is notifiable, the client must appoint a CDM co-ordinator (as defined) who is suitably competent (see also regulation 4).

Regulation 17 (3) requires the client to take reasonable steps, on completion of the construction phase, to ensure that the health and safety file remains available for inspection by anyone who might need it in order to meet their obligations under any relevant statutory provisions. Further, this regulation requires that the health and safety file is updated whenever necessary.

Regulation 20 (2) makes it a requirement for the CDM co-ordinator to prepare a 'Health and safety file' and to review and update the file throughout the construction of the installation.

1.2.4 Provision and Use of Work Equipment Regulations 1998

The Provision and Use of Work Equipment Regulations require that work equipment, including installations, is so constructed (or adapted) so as to be suitable for the purpose for which it is provided.

Equipment must be inspected after installation and before use, at suitable intervals and after exceptional events e.g. fire, flooding, mechanical damage. Potentially dangerous machinery must be guarded. Where necessary, logs must be maintained and adequate training given to operators.

Published by Certsure LLP © Certsure LLP (January 2015)

1.2.5 Electricity Safety, Quality and Continuity Regulations 2002 (as amended)

The main purpose of the Electricity Safety, Quality and Continuity Regulations is to provide for the safety of the electricity supply distribution system, that is, for the safety of the general public and of persons working on the system. As the title implies, the Regulations also have requirements for power quality and supply continuity. There are many references to *BS 7671*. The regulations require distributors, prior to connection of new properties, to obtain confirmation that the installation to be connected complies with the requirements of *BS 7671* (regulations 9(4) and 25(2)).

Regulation 24 (4) requires the distributor to make available an earth connection for new supplies, unless inappropriate for reasons of safety. In the UK this is almost always achieved by the provision of a PME earthing facility.

Regulation 27 (3) recognises that, depending upon the distance from the substation transformer, the characteristics of the distribution network and the loading on the system, the voltage and the frequency of the supply at the consumers' supply terminals will vary. In the case of a low voltage supply clause 3 (b) limits the permitted variation in voltage at the consumers' supply terminals to plus 10 % and minus 6 % of the declared voltage.

Regulation 28 requires the distributor to provide on request a written statement of:

a) the maximum prospective short-circuit current at the supply terminals;

b) for low voltage connections, the maximum earth loop impedance of the earth fault path outside the installation;

c) the type and rating of the distributor's protective device or devices nearest to the supply terminals;

d) the type of earthing system applicable to the connection; and

e) the number of phases, frequency and voltage.

1.2.6 The Building Regulations

England and Wales. The Building Regulations 2010

The Building Regulations 2010 (Statutory Instrument 2010 No. 2214) are made under powers provided in the Building Act 1984 and currently apply in England and Wales, but not Scotland or Northern Ireland.

The purpose of the Building Regulations is to provide for the health and safety of people in and around buildings and also provide for matters such as energy conservation and access and use.

In the Building Regulations the term "building work" means:

a) the erection or extension of a building,

b) the provision or extension of a controlled service or fitting in or in connection with a building,

c) the material alteration of a building, or a controlled service or fitting,

d) work required by regulation 6 (requirements relating to material change of use),

e) the insertion of insulating material into the cavity wall of a building,

f) work involving the underpinning of a building.

Schedule 1 of the Building Regulations describes the requirements relating to building work and material change of use as described in Regulations 4 & 6. These requirements are divided into the following parts:

Part A (Structural safety)

Part B (Fire safety)

Part C (Resistance to contaminants and moisture)

Part D (Toxic substances)

Part E (Resistance to sound)

Part F (Ventilation)

Part G (Sanitation, hot water safety and water efficiency)

Published by Certsure LLP © Certsure LLP (January 2015)

Part H (Drainage and waste disposal)

Part J (Heat producing appliances)

Part K (Protection from falling)

Part L (Conservation of fuel and power)

Part M (Access to and use of buildings)

Part N (Glazing safety)

Part P (Electrical safety)

To provide the construction industry with guidance on how these requirements of the Building Regulations can be met, for each of the parts previously listed, the Department for Communities and Local Government (DCLG) publishes a series of Approved Documents.

The Approved Documents may be downloaded free-of-charge from

www.planningportal.gov.uk/buildingregulations/approveddocuments/

Two editions of Approved Document P, dealing with electrical safety, are available:

- the 2006 Edition,
- the 2013 Edition, which applies to work in England from 6 April 2013.

It should be noted that the power to make Building Regulations for Wales has been transferred to Welsh Ministers from 31st December 2011. The Building Regulations 2010 and related guidance such as the Approved Documents published prior to that date will continue to apply in Wales until Welsh Ministers decide that changes should be made. As a result of this transfer of power, for electrical installations in dwellings, the approved document used in England is different to that used in Wales. In England, the 2013 edition of Approved Document P is used whilst, in Wales, apart from 'excepted energy buildings[1]', the 2006 edition is used.

[1]Excepted energy buildings, as defined in *The Welsh Ministers (Transfer of Functions) (No. 2) Order 2009*, are energy infrastructure buildings and, for these buildings, the 2013 edition of Approved Document P is applicable.

Introduction

Although there are significant differences between the Approved Documents used in England and Wales both approved documents:

1. Limit the scope of Part P to electrical installations in dwelling-houses, flats and certain common areas and business premises associated with the dwelling house or flat.
2. Contain statements to the effect that electrical installation work should be designed and installed in accordance with *BS 7671*. Both editions of Approved Document P require all electrical installation work to be inspected and certified in accordance with the requirements of *BS 7671*.

However, in terms of the types of work that is classified as being 'notifiable electrical installation work' and the category of person permitted to inspect and test notifiable work there are important differences between the approved documents used in England and Wales. In approved document P the term 'notifiable electrical installation work' means electrical installation work that must be either certified by the building control body or certified by a person authorised by the applicable approved document, who will then forward a copy of the electrical installation certificate to the building control body. After completion of the notifiable electrical installation work, whichever procedure is followed, the occupier of the building should receive a copy of a Building Regulations Compliance Certificate.

Notifiable work - Wales

Section 0 of Approved Document P: 2006 provides details of notifiable work and these details are summarised below. The requirements for work in kitchens, special locations and special installations are different from the requirements for the general areas of the dwelling.

Notes:

1. A kitchen (as defined in Section 0 of Approved Document P: 2006 is a location containing a sink and food preparation facilities).
2. Special locations, as given in Table 2 of Approved Document P: 2006, are locations containing a bath tub, shower basin, swimming pool, paddling pool and a hot air sauna.

Published by Certsure LLP © Certsure LLP (January 2015)

3. Special installations are installations that, due to the nature of the installation, additional dangers exist. These are described in Table 2 of Approved Document P: 2006 and are described in the following section.

The electrical installation work that is currently notifiable in Wales is as follows:

Anywhere within or attached to a dwelling:

- a complete new installation (a full rewire),
- replacing a consumer unit,
- the installation of:
    - a new circuit,
    - the power or control wiring for a new central heating system,
    - a special installation as given in Table 2 of Approved Document P: 2006 - are electric floor and ceiling heating systems, garden lighting and power installations, a solar photovoltaic power supply system, a small scale generator or an extra-low voltage lighting installations, (other than a pre-assembled, CE marked lighting sets).

Within a kitchen or special location:

The work described in the previous section, plus:

- any alteration or addition to an existing circuit for the addition of adding lighting points, socket-outlets or a fused-spur,
- the supply to another location, such as a conservatory and attached garages.

Within a special location

- Installation of telephone or extra-low voltage wiring and equipment for the purposes of communications, information technology, signalling, control or similar.

Notifiable work - England

When compared with the description of the electrical installation work that is notifiable in Wales (based on the 2006 edition of Approved Document P), the list of the electrical installation work that is currently notifiable in England (based upon the 2013 edition of Approved Document P) is, as shown in the following section, less comprehensive.

The electrical installation work that is currently notifiable in England is as follows:

Anywhere in a dwelling or its surroundings:

- installation of a new circuit,
- replacement of a consumer unit.

Within a special location:

- any alteration or addition to an existing circuit.

As described in Approved Document P: 2013, special locations in dwellings are rooms containing a bath or shower, swimming pool or a sauna heater. For a room containing a bath or shower, an alteration or addition to an existing circuit is notifiable only where carried out in the space surrounding a bath or shower (as illustrated in Fig 1.1), rather than the whole room volume, which is the case for rooms containing a swimming pool or sauna heater.

Certification of notifiable work

The 2006 edition of Approved Document P permits the certification of notifiable work to be carried out by either:

1. an installer who is registered with a Part P competent person self-certification scheme such as the ones offered by NICEIC or ELECSA, or
2. a building control body.

In addition to the two methods of inspection and testing of notifiable work permitted by the 2006 edition of Approved Document P, the 2013 edition of this document permits certification by a registered third part certifier. However, due to concerns regarding the safety of the installation, operators of many self-certification schemes, including NICEIC and ELECSA, do not operate a 3rd party certification scheme.

Published by Certsure LLP © Certsure LLP (January 2015)

Fig 1.1 Illustration for notifiable work in a room containing a bath or shower in accordance with Approved Document P: 2013

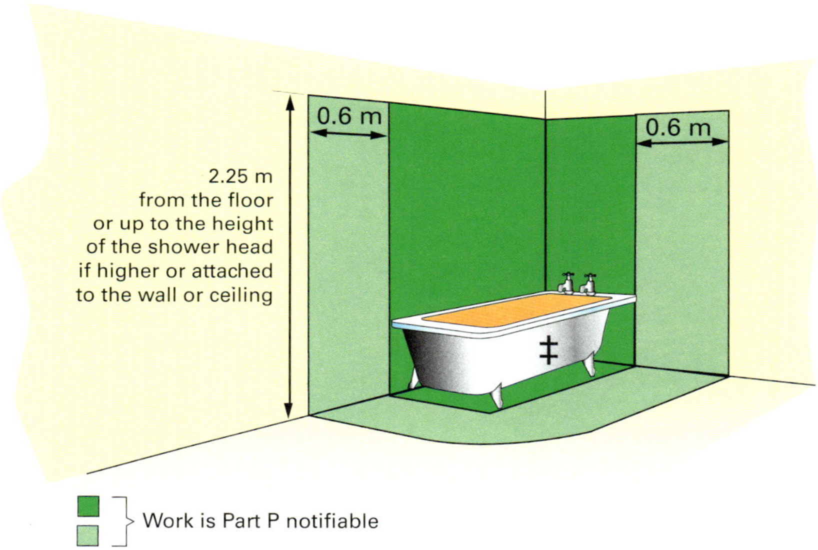

‡ Where there is no bath tub or shower tray, the space extends horizontally from the centre point of the shower head where it is attached to the wall or ceiling to a distance of 1.2 metres.

The 2013 edition of Approved Document P advises that to comply with the Building Regulations, depending upon the nature of the work being undertaken, it may be necessary to comply with other approved documents and provides the following examples:

Part A (Structural): depth of chases in walls, and the size of notches in floors and roof joists

Part B (Fire safety): Fire safety of certain electrical installations; provision of fire alarms and fire detection systems; fire resistance of service penetration through floors, walls and ceilings

Part C (Resistance to contaminants and moisture): resistance of service penetrations to rainwater and contaminants such as radon

Part E (Resistance to sound): soundproofing of service penetration

Part F (Ventilation): dwelling ventilation rates

Part L (Conservation of fuel and power): energy efficient lighting

Part M (Access to and use of buildings): height of socket-outlets and switches

Further information on how the Building Regulations effect the work of an installation electrician can be found in the in the ELECSA/NICEIC publication 'A short guide to the Building Regulations'. Within this guide advice on how to comply with Part A (Structure) is provided in Section 11.6

The responsibility for complying with the Building Regulations rests with the person carrying out the building work, which can include plumbing and electrical installations. The person carrying out the electrical installation is personally responsible for compliance. Persons employing others to carry out work should confirm who has responsibility for compliance with the Building Regulations.

Should there be any non-compliance; the owner of the building may be served with the enforcement notice if the work does not comply with the Building Regulations.

Scotland. Building (Scotland) Regulations 2004

The Building (Scotland) Regulations 2004 (Statutory Instrument 2004 No. 406) are made under powers provided in the Building (Scotland) Act 2003. This Act gives Scottish Ministers the power to make building regulations to provide for the health, safety, welfare and convenience of persons using buildings and of those who may be affected by buildings or matters connected with buildings such as how they are used by others. The Building Regulations also seek to promote the conservation of fuel and power and encourage sustainable development.

Two Technical Handbooks have been produced by Scottish Ministers to provide guidance on how to comply with the standards set in the Building (Scotland) Regulations 2004; one for domestic buildings and one for non-domestic buildings.

The handbooks consist of the following sections:

0 General

1 Structure

2 Fire

3 Environment

Published by Certsure LLP © Certsure LLP (January 2015)

4 Safety

5 Noise

6 Energy

7 Sustainability

It is worth noting at this point that a dwelling may include surgeries, consulting rooms and the like having a floor area not exceeding 50 m^2 forming a part of a dwelling and which are used by the occupier of the dwelling for professional or business purposes (Section 0.2.2 of the domestic technical handbook refers).

Where a building has mixed domestic and non-domestic usage, the relevant part(s) of the appropriate technical handbook should be applied. Where a particular building or part thereof might be considered to fall into more than one category, the building should be designed to meet the more stringent of the recommendations (see Section 0.1.6. of the Domestic Handbook).

The handbooks and associated appendices may be downloaded, free-of-charge, from the Scottish Government website given below:

www.scotland.gov.uk/Topics/Built-Environment/Building/Building-standards/techbooks

1.2.7 *BS 7671*

BS 7671: 2008 Requirements for Electrical Installations, also known as the *IET Wiring Regulations Seventeenth Edition*, contains requirements for the design, erection and verification of most types of general electrical installation (Regulation 110.1 refers).

Given the ever increasing complexity of electrical installations, it is frequently necessary to also take into account the requirements and recommendations contained within other British Standards, Codes of Practice and the like.

Certain electrical installations of a more specialised nature, such as those in aircraft, ships and trains; public systems for electrical distribution; and within a general installation, including lightning protection systems, lifts and the electrical equipment of machines, are not covered by *BS 7671* but rather by other British Standards (Regulation 110.2 refers).

Although the requirements of *BS 7671* are non-statutory, compliance with them may be cited as evidence in a court of law to claim compliance with a statutory requirement (see Regulation 114.1). The Health and Safety Executive (HSE) states in a note within the introduction of *BS 7671* that they (HSE) consider installations which conform with the relevant parts of *BS 7671* as being likely to achieve conformity with the relevant parts of the *Electricity at Work Regulations 1989*.

1.3 Guidance

1.3.1 Health and Safety Executive

HSR25 - Memorandum of guidance on the Electricity at Work Regulations 1989

This Health and Safety (HSE) publication provides clear, concise guidance on the general regulations contained within the Electricity at Work Regulations 1989 and is essential reading for any persons involved in electrical installation work in the UK. It is now downloadable – free of charge – from the HSE website.

Anyone who is involved with electricity, whether working directly on electrical systems, installations or equipment, or using electrically operated equipment, is classed as a *Duty Holder*. As has already been stated in Section 1.2.2 of this Guide, regulation 3 of EWR requires duty holders to comply with the provisions contained within EWR in so far as they relate to matters within their control.

Depending on the particular regulation concerned, the regulations in EWR 1989 impose one of two levels of duty upon persons working on, or in close proximity to, electrical systems (as defined in regulation 2 of EWR 1989) or parts thereof, namely:

- absolute, or
- so far as is reasonably practicable.

Absolute duty

This means that the requirements of a regulation must be met regardless of the cost, time or effort incurred in so doing. Regulation 29 offers a defence where criminal proceedings have been brought against a person or persons considered to have failed in their absolute duty. The defence puts the onus on the person(s) so accused to

Published by Certsure LLP © Certsure LLP (January 2015)

demonstrate that 'they took all reasonable steps and applied due diligence to avoid' committing an offence.

Unless stated otherwise, the requirements of a particular regulation are absolute.

Reasonable practicability

Where embodied in a regulation, reasonable practicability allows a balance to be struck between, on the one hand, the level of risk reduction considered acceptable and, on the other, the cost, time and effort of so doing.

In order to apply reasonable practicability, it will be necessary for a risk assessment to be performed and it should be remembered that this risk assessment could be the subject of scrutiny in the event of an accident or incident occurring.

Competence

Regulation 16 requires persons to be competent to prevent danger and injury. It should be noted that this competence requirement applies not only to those persons involved in work activities on or near electrical installations and equipment, but also to those employed in a managerial, design or supervisory capacity whose actions and decisions might put themselves or, more likely, others at risk of danger or injury.

HSR25 makes it clear that the intention of regulation 16 is 'to ensure that persons are not placed at risk due to a lack of skills on the part of themselves or others' when dealing with electrical equipment.

Regulation 16 cites technical knowledge and experience as being appropriate indicators of competence and continues to state that in some cases an appropriate degree of supervision may be necessary. Although the successful completion of a particular qualification does not of itself indicate an individual's competence, it might act as a suitable indicator of such. Similarly, having a number of years of relevant work experience does not mean that a person is competent, but it might do so.

Typically, a person will be deemed competent at a particular work activity or range of work activities on account of the relevant training and experience that has been accumulated over time.

Published by Certsure LLP © Certsure LLP (January 2015)

Introduction

Even where a company employs qualified and experienced personnel, there will be occasions when unfamiliar equipment and/or working practices may be encountered that will require further training to be provided. Furthermore, whilst staff undergo such training and become familiar with the equipment and/or practice in question, supervision may well be necessary. Supervision by a competent person can be an appropriate means of allowing those who are not yet fully competent (such as trainees) to gain valuable work experience in a safe manner. It can also permit persons who are not competent, such as painters decorating an electrical switchroom, to work in close proximity to electrical equipment without risk of danger or injury. In such circumstances *BS 7671* would consider them to be *instructed persons* (as defined).

A person carrying out inspection and testing activities must be competent in such work in terms of their experience and training, and where necessary any shortfall in either of these factors may be addressed by the provision of appropriate supervision.

In Northern Ireland the Electricity at Work Regulations (Northern Ireland) 1991 apply. The Health and Safety Executive for Northern Ireland (HSENI) has produced the *Memorandum of Guidance on the Electricity at Work Regulations (Northern Ireland) 1991* to give guidance on these Regulations.

GS38 - Electrical test equipment for use by electricians

This HSE publication gives guidance on the following in connection with the selection and use of voltage test lamps and voltage detectors:

- causes of accidents,
- requirements for test probes and leads,
- systems of work,
- examination of equipment.

Published by Certsure LLP © Certsure LLP (January 2015)

Precautions to be taken during testing

The key recommendations of GS 38 are as follows.

i) Test probes should have finger barriers to prevent hands inadvertently slipping and allowing accidental contact with live parts.

ii) The tips of the probes should be insulated such that no more than 4 mm of the tip remains exposed.

iii) Wherever practicable – that is, where this will not interfere with the correct use of the test lamp or voltage detector, no more than 2 mm of tip should be exposed, or probes fitted with spring loaded insulated screening should be used.

iv) Leads should be adequately insulated and identified.

v) Leads should also be sufficiently flexible and of length suitable for their purpose, that is, neither too long nor too short.

vi) Where the leads are not permanently attached to the instrument, there should be no accessible live parts in the event of a lead becoming detached in use.

vii) In the case of voltage test lamps, the leads (and therefore the person using the instrument) should be protected by either:

- a high breaking capacity (HBC) fuse of rating not exceeding 500 mA, or
- a current limiting resistor and a fuse.

viii) In the case of voltage detectors, the current that may pass through the instrument is limited by the internal circuit design, protective impedance and current limiting resistors built into the probes.

ix) The maximum voltage and, where applicable, any short time rating should be clearly shown on voltage test lamps and voltage detectors.

Other guidance

The HSE publish guidance on a wide range of topics which are of relevance to those involved in electrical installation work including the following.

- Simple guide to the Provision and Use of Work Equipment Regulations 1998
- Safe use of work equipment. Approved Code of Practice and Guidance (L22)
- A short guide to the Personal Protective Equipment at Work Regulations 1992 (L25).

1.3.2 Electrical Safety First

Electrical Safety First formerly known as the Electrical Safety Council produces, in association with other industry bodies, a range of technical and best practice guidance for the electrical industry, as well as information on electrical product safety.

Of particular interest to installation electricians are the Best Practice Guides and the questions and answers produced by the Electrical Installation Forum.

Best Practice Guides

There are currently eight Best Practice Guides:

No 1 Replacing a consumer unit in domestic premises, where lighting circuits have no protective conductor

No 2 Guidance on the management of electrical safety and safe isolation procedures for low voltage installations

No 3 Connecting a micro-generation system to a domestic or similar electrical installation (in parallel with the mains supply)

No 4 Electrical installation condition reporting: Classification Codes for domestic and similar electrical installations

Published by Certsure LLP © Certsure LLP (January 2015)

No 5 Electrical installations and their impact on the fire performance of buildings

Part 1 - Domestic premises: Single family units (houses, flats, maisonettes, bungalows)

No 6 Consumer unit replacement in domestic or similar premises

No 7 Test instruments for electrical installations: Accuracy and consistency

No 8 Selection and use of plug-in socket-outlet test devices.

All of the above are freely available from the ESC website at

www.electricalsafetyfirst.org.uk/electrical-professionals/best-practice-guides/

Electrical Installation Forum

The Electrical Installation Forum (EIF) comprising of technical representatives from a wide range of industry bodies, and hosted by the Electrical Safety First, produces guidance for electrically competent persons on a range of technical issues that have been raised in enquiries to the bodies contributing to the forum.

Topics relating to new work, additions and alterations, certification and reporting, and periodic inspection and testing have been discussed with the resulting guidance made freely available from the Electrical Safety First website

www.electricalsafetyfirst.org.uk/electrical-professionals/wiring-regulations/

Other guidance

The Electrical Safety First, with the co-operation and assistance of relevant industry partners, has produced guidance on matters such as downlighters and fire safety, electrical safety for landlords and electrical safety for those involved in the construction industry. This guidance is also downloadable, free-of-charge, from the Electrical Safety First website.

1.3.3 Institution of Engineering and Technology

Guidance notes

The IET publishes a series of eight Guidance Notes on particular aspects of *BS 7671*.

Other guidance

The IET also publishes a series of smaller guides. These either relate to *BS 7671* or to the content of other standards relating to, for example, emergency lighting, fire alarm systems and the building regulations that might be of interest to those involve in electrical installation work.

1.3.4 NICEIC and ELECSA

NICEIC and ELECSA have produced a wide range of publication relating to electrical installation work. Included in these publications are the popular Short Guide series which deal with specific topics, a number of Learning Guides designed to assist electricians further develop their technical skills, and Snags and Solutions which provide guidance on practical problems which may occur on site and guides to Initial and Periodic Verification.

Details of NICEIC and ELECSA publications can be found in the electrical section of NICEIC Publications at NICEIC Direct.
http://www.niceicdirect.com/epages/NICShop.sf or the corresponding ELECSA page at **http://www.elecsa.co.uk/shop/elecsa/productselection.aspx**

Published by Certsure LLP © Certsure LLP (January 2015)

Chapter
2

The service position and system types

© Certsure LLP (January 2015)

The service position and system types

2.1 The service position

The consumer's electrical installation begins at the outgoing terminals of the electricity supplier's meter, or isolator if one has been provided. All equipment upstream of these terminals, including the meter itself, is the property of the meter operator, electricity supplier or electricity distributor.

The electricity supply to the dwelling is subject to the statutory requirements of the *Electricity Safety, Quality and Continuity Regulations 2002* (as amended).

2.2 System types and earthing arrangements

Within the scope of this Guide, the electrical system, which comprises the electricity supply and the whole of the consumer's electrical installation, will be one of three distinct types: TN-S, TN-C-S or TT. The system type will determine the earthing arrangements for the installation and influence its design.

TN-S, TN-C-S and TT systems each have different regulatory requirements in respect of protection against electric shock, protection against overcurrent, and isolation and switching. It is therefore essential in terms of safety that the electrical designer and electrical contractor responsible for an installation know with certainty the type of system of which the installation forms part. For this reason, Section 312 of *BS 7671* requires the type of system to be assessed.

These three types of system are distinguished from one another by the specific methods used to earth the source of supply and the installation, and also by whether the neutral and protective functions of the system are performed by separate conductors, a combined conductor, or a mixture of the two (in different parts of the system).

For all three system types mentioned above:

- at least one point of the source of supply is directly connected to Earth (i.e. the neutral of a single-phase transformer or the star point of a three-phase transformer),
- the neutral and protective conductors of the installation are separate throughout the installation.

Published by Certsure LLP © Certsure LLP (January 2015)

Further information regarding systems and their earthing arrangements may be obtained from the electricity distributors via the Energy Networks Association (**www.energynetworks.org**).

For a TN-S system, the neutral conductor and the protective conductor are separate in the supply.

For a TN-C-S system, the neutral conductor and the protective conductor are combined into one conductor in the supply (a PEN conductor).

For a TT system, no protective conductor is available with the supply, or if a protective conductor is available, it is not used for the electrical installation (as might be the case for some special installations or locations covered within Part 7 of *BS 7671*), and the installation is earthed by means of an installation earth electrode.

Table 2.1 summarises the earthing arrangements for the three types of system and Figs 2.1, 2.2 and 2.3 illustrate diagrammatically the three system types.

Table 2.1 System types and earthing arrangements

System type	Supply		Installation		Available means of earthing
	Supply neutral conductor[1]	Supply protective conductor[1]	Installation neutral conductor[1]	Installation protective conductor[1]	
TN-S	S	S	S	S	Distributor's earthing terminal
TN-C-S	C	C	S	S	Distributor's earthing terminal
TT	S	N/A	S	S	Consumer's installation earth electrode

1: S = Separate, C = Combined, N/A = Not Available

2.2.1 TN-S

In the TN-S system, the exposed-conductive-parts of the installation are connected to the earthed point of the source of energy, and separate conductors are employed for the neutral and protective functions throughout the supply and consumer (installation) sides of the system.

The protective conductor between the source and the ends of the electricity distributor's lines on the consumer's premises is commonly provided by means of the lead sheath or wire armouring of the supply cable, although a separate conductor is sometimes provided for this purpose. A split-concentric cable can also be used for this purpose.

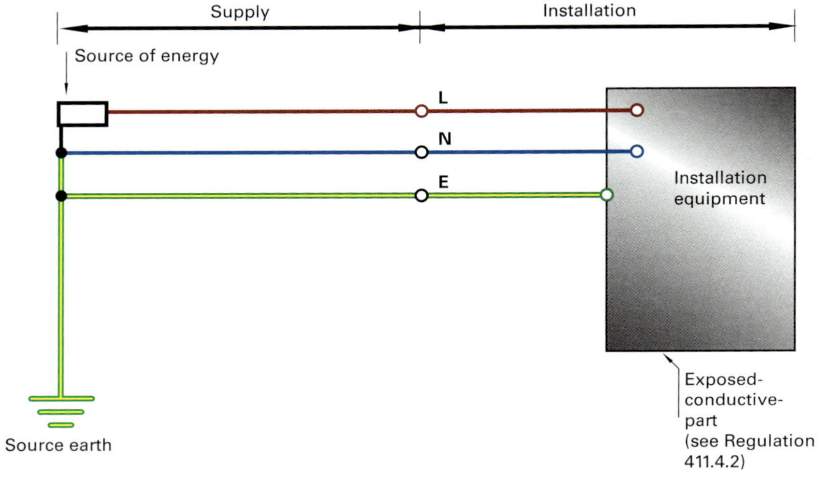

Fig 2.1 TN-S system (single-phase)

2.2.2 TN-C-S

In the TN-C-S system, the exposed-conductive-parts of the installation are connected to the earthed point of the source of energy. In addition, the neutral and protective functions are combined in a single conductor between the source and distributor's intake cut-out, beyond which separate protective and neutral conductors are provided. The most common TN-C-S system is where the combined neutral and protective conductor in the supply is earthed at multiple points.

This type of distribution is known as Protective Multiple Earthing (PME), and has been used by electricity distributors for most of the new low voltage supplies they have installed since the mid 1970s. The Combined Neutral and Earth (CNE) conductor (also known as a PEN conductor) of the distributor's lines is connected to Earth at several points in accordance with the Electricity Safety, Quality and Continuity Regulations 2002, thereby providing low resistance connections between all parts of that conductor and earthed point of the supply.

 Published by Certsure LLP © Certsure LLP (January 2015)

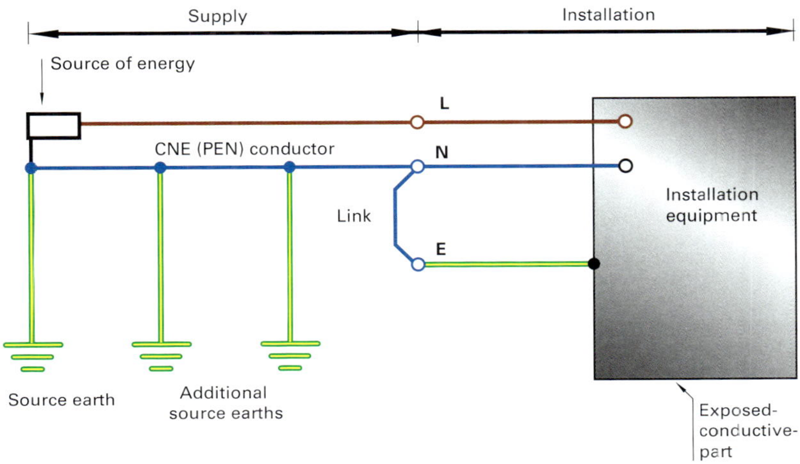

Fig 2.2 TN-C-S system (single-phase)

2.2.3 TT

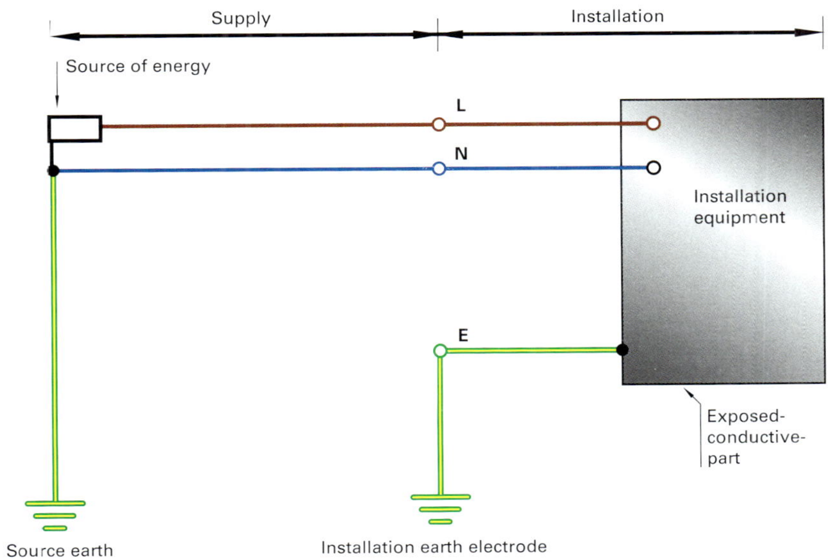

Fig 2.3 TT system (single-phase)

It should be noted that the supply to an installation which forms part of a TT system **may or may not** include a protective conductor. That is to say, the supply could consist of line and neutral conductors only, or it could include a protective conductor. The important thing to appreciate is that, where the installation is to form part of a TT system, the exposed-conductive-parts of the installation must be connected to the installation earth electrode, and **not** to the supply protective conductor (if any).

TT systems are often employed where the electricity distributor is unable on technical or safety grounds to offer an earthing facility for the installation, such as for premises in areas of low population density where the network does not have the necessary multiple earthing.

Published by Certsure LLP © Certsure LLP (January 2015)

Chapter 3

Earthing and bonding

3.1 Supply system earthing

3.2 Installation earthing

3.3 Means of earthing

3.4 The intake position

3.5 Responsibility for providing, assessing and verifying the means of earthing

3.6 Main protective bonding

3.7 Supplementary bonding

3.8 Earthing arrangements where an installation contains equipment having high protective conductor currents

3.1 Supply system earthing

Irrespective of system type (TN-S, TN-C-S or TT), the supply to an electrical installation is earthed at its source of energy, for the purpose of safety and for referencing supply voltages.

Normally, the neutral (or star) point of the source transformer secondary winding is connected to the general mass of earth (Earth), via a source earth electrode. The provision and maintenance of source earthing is normally the responsibility of the owner of the source of energy, usually the electricity distributor.

3.2 Installation earthing

Electrical installation earthing is the connection of the exposed-conductive-parts of an electrical installation to an appropriate means of earthing. It is applicable in installations where protection against electric shock is provided by Automatic Disconnection of Supply (ADS), as is the case in the majority of domestic installations in the United Kingdom.

The purpose of electrical installation earthing is to allow earth fault current to flow in order to operate the protective device for protection against electric shock, thereby providing automatic disconnection.

The principal components of the earthing system of an electrical installation are the:

- circuit protective conductors,
- Main Earthing Terminal (MET),
- earthing conductor of the electrical installation, and
- means of earthing.

These are shown diagrammatically in Fig 3.1, which depicts one of the most commonly-used types of electrical system, a TN-C-S system with Protective Multiple Earthing (PME) applied.

The supply network is shown on the left-hand side of the diagram, and the installation on the right.

Published by Certsure LLP © Certsure LLP (January 2015)

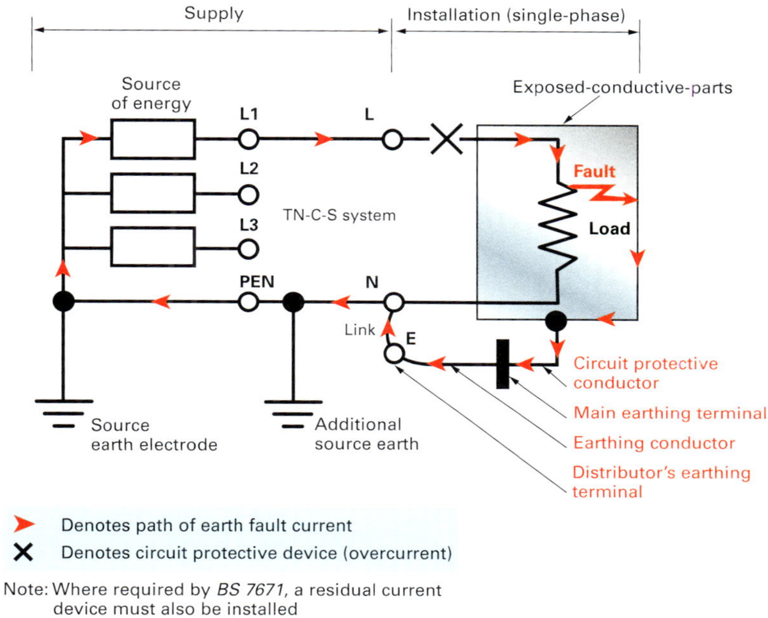

Fig 3.1 Electrical equipment earthing showing the earth fault current path for a typical TN-C-S system with Protective Multiple Earthing (PME) applied.

The installation shown in Fig 3.1 has an earth fault, the path of the fault current being represented by the red arrows. The loop impedance of this path should not exceed the maximum ohmic value permitted by Section 411 of *BS 7671*, according to the type and rating of the protective device installed to provide automatic disconnection of the circuit in question under earth fault conditions.

Provided this loop impedance requirement is met, then automatic disconnection can be expected to occur within the maximum time permitted by *BS 7671* in the event of an earth fault of negligible impedance.

As shown in Fig 3.1, the appropriate means of earthing for an electrical installation forming part of a TN-C-S system with PME applied is a facility provided by the electricity distributor. This includes a PME earthing terminal connected by the distributor to the combined protective and neutral (PEN) conductor of the supply. For electrical installations forming parts of other types of system, different means of earthing are applicable. For example, the appropriate means of earthing for an installation forming part of a TT system is an installation earth electrode, as shown in Fig 3.2.

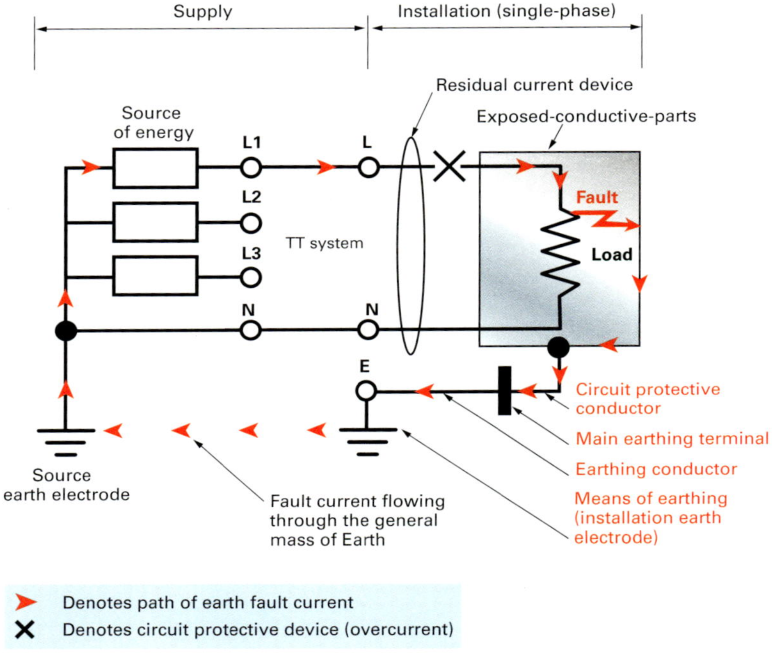

Fig 3.2 Electrical equipment earthing showing the earth fault current path for a typical TT system.

In a TT system, the path of the earth fault current includes the source earth electrode. This illustrates an additional purpose of source earthing in a TT system – to provide a path for earth fault current and protective conductor current to return to the source of energy.

3.3 Means of earthing

A means of earthing is an arrangement through which a connection is made to the general mass of Earth for the exposed-conductive-parts of an installation. The exposed-conductive-parts are connected to the means of earthing via the earthing conductor and Main Earthing Terminal (MET) of the installation (see Fig 3.3).

Published by Certsure LLP © Certsure LLP (January 2015)

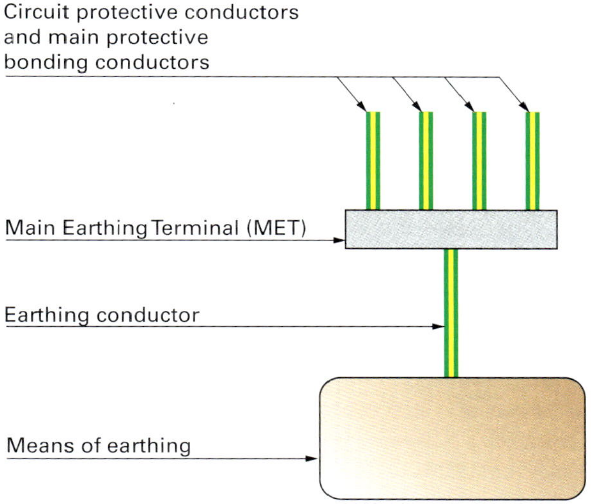

Fig 3.3 The means of earthing for an installation in relation to the earthing conductor and main earthing terminal.

The particular means of earthing for an installation depends largely on the type of system of which the installation forms part. For an installation forming part of a TT system, the means of earthing is an installation earth electrode. For an installation connected to an electricity distributor's network and forming part of a TN-S or TN-C-S system, the means of earthing is normally provided by the electricity distributor. In such a case, the particular means will depend upon the composition of the distributor's supply lines.

Regulation Group 542.1 requires the Main Earthing Terminal (MET) to be connected to Earth by one of the following means, as appropriate to the type of system:

- for a TN-S system, the MET of the installation must be connected to the earthed point of the source of energy. Part of the connection may be formed by the distributor's lines and equipment,
- for a TN-C-S system where Protective Multiple Earthing (PME) is provided, means must be made for the MET of the installation to be connected by the distributor to the neutral of the source of energy,

- for a TT system, the MET must be connected via the earthing conductor to an installation earth electrode complying with Regulation Group 542.2.

The main features of each of the different means of earthing are detailed in Table 3.1, including references to the use of facilities provided by the electricity distributor where appropriate.

Table 3.1 Main features of the means of earthing for each type of system.

System type	Means of Earthing (main features)	Remarks
TN-S	Connection of the MET of the installation to the earthed point of the source of energy via a separate protective conductor. Where a distributor provides the low voltage supply, this connection is via the distributor's supply lines, normally using: • the metallic sheath or armour of the supply cable, or • the protective conductor of a split -concentric supply cable, or • a separate protective conductor (for example, of an overhead line).	Connection to a protective conductor of a distributor's supply cable or overhead line may be carried out only with the express permission of, and by a method approved by, the distributor. Many distributors will provide, on request, an earthing terminal connected to the protective conductor of their supply cable or overhead line. The MET of the electrical installation is to be connected to this terminal by means of the earthing conductor.
TN-C-S (e.g. where protective multiple earthing (PME) is provided)	Connection of the MET of the installation to the earthed neutral of the source of energy via the combined neutral and earth PEN* conductor of the distributor's low voltage supply lines, normally using: • the PEN conductor of the supply cable, or • the PEN conductor of the overhead line.	The distributor provides an earthing terminal connected to the PEN conductor of the supply cable or overhead line. The MET of the installation is to be connected to this terminal via the earthing conductor.
TT	Connection of the MET to the installation earth electrode.	The installation earth electrode forms part of the installation.

* Note: Electricity distributors sometimes use the term 'CNE' (Combined Neutral and Earth) instead of 'PEN', for a combined protective and neutral conductor.

Published by Certsure LLP © Certsure LLP (January 2015)

3.4 The intake position

Fig 3.4, Fig 3.5, and Fig 3.6 give diagrammatic representations of the interface between the distributor's and the consumer's electrical equipment for TN-S, TN-C-S and TT systems, respectively. Typical arrangements for both overhead and underground supplies are shown.

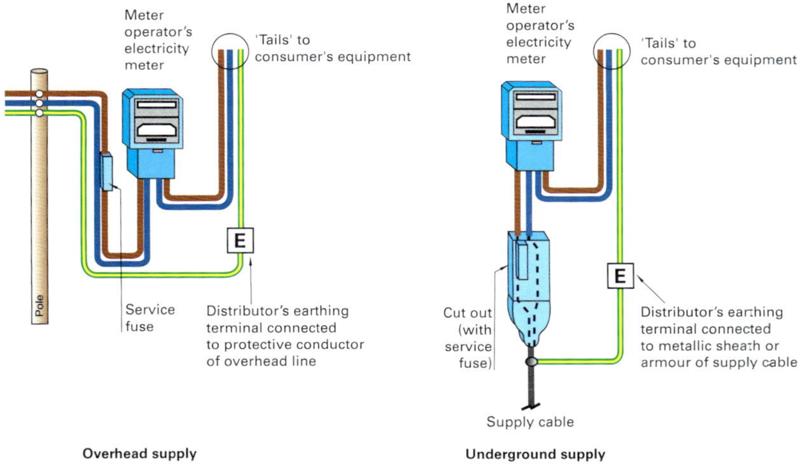

Fig 3.4 TN-S system.

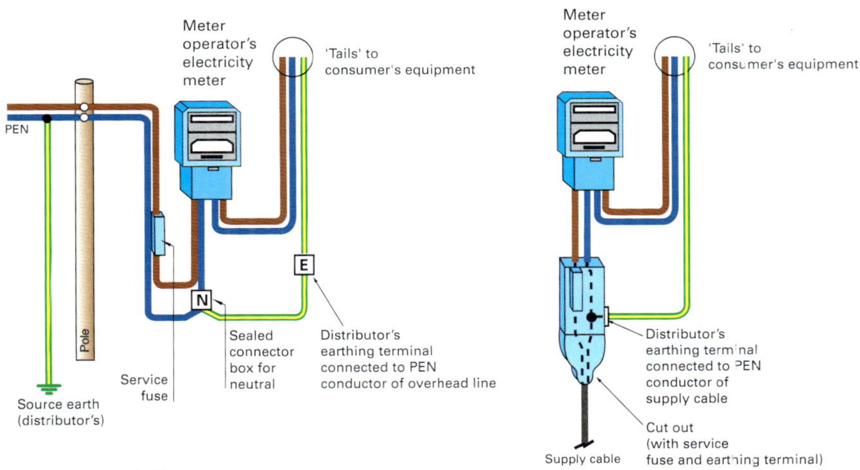

Fig 3.5 TN-C-S system.

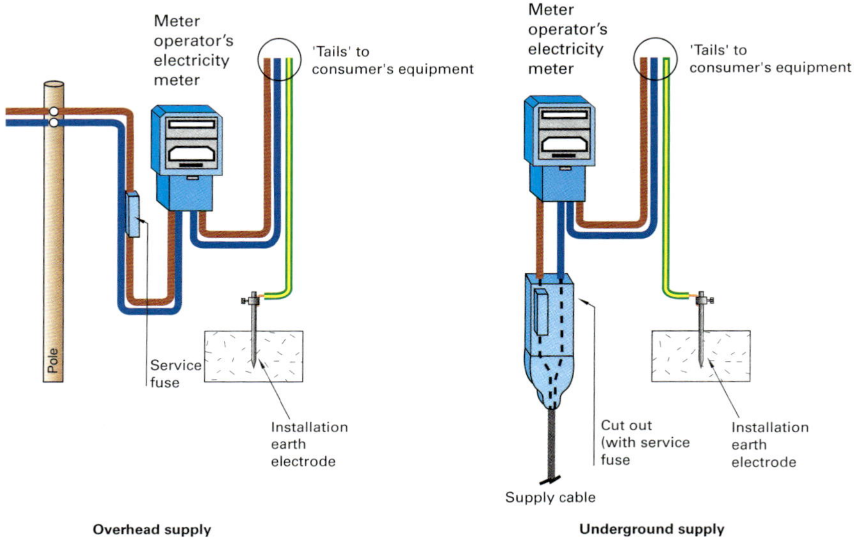

Fig 3.6 TT system.

3.5 Responsibility for providing, assessing and verifying the means of earthing

Electricity distributors will make available, in many instances, a means of earthing for an electrical installation. However, ensuring an installation is adequately connected with Earth is always the responsibility of the installation owner, who usually delegates the task to an electrical contractor. For first-time supplies, the electricity distributor is obliged under the *Electricity Safety, Quality and Continuity Regulations 2002* to make available an earthing facility for the consumer's installation, unless there are reasons of safety which preclude such a provision.

The designer of an electrical installation, or of any alteration or addition to an installation, is responsible for assessing the intended means of earthing, by inspection, testing and, where appropriate, enquiry to the distributor, to ensure that it is suitable for the needs of the installation in terms of safety (Regulations 132.16 and 313.1).

Published by Certsure LLP © Certsure LLP (January 2015)

It should never be assumed that what may seem to be an existing earthing facility, such as an earthing terminal apparently connected to the supply cable sheath or supply neutral, is an effective means of earthing. Appropriate verification must always be carried out.

3.6 Main protective bonding

Protective bonding is an indispensable part of the most commonly used protective measure against electric shock, Automatic Disconnection of Supply (ADS). Such bonding is therefore required in every electrical installation where one or more circuits relies on ADS.

An extraneous-conductive-part is defined in *BS 7671* as:

> A conductive part liable to introduce a potential, generally Earth potential, and not forming part of the electrical installation.

Regulation 411.3.1.2 requires that, in each installation, protective bonding conductors complying with Chapter 54 should connect extraneous-conductive-parts of that installation, including

- water installation pipes,
- gas installation pipes,
- other installation pipework and ducting,
- central heating and air conditioning systems,
- exposed metallic structural parts of the building

to the Main Earthing Terminal. It should be noted, that the items listed above do not always fall within the definition of extraneous-conductive-part, nor is the list exhaustive.

Where appropriate, it will be necessary to connect a lightning protection system to the protective equipotential bonding in accordance with *BS EN 62305*.

BS 7671 also requires main protective bonding to be connected to any metallic sheath of a telecommunication cable. However, the consent of the owner or operator of the cable must be obtained before so doing.

Where an installation serves more than one building, such as a house with a detached garage, the above requirements apply to each building.

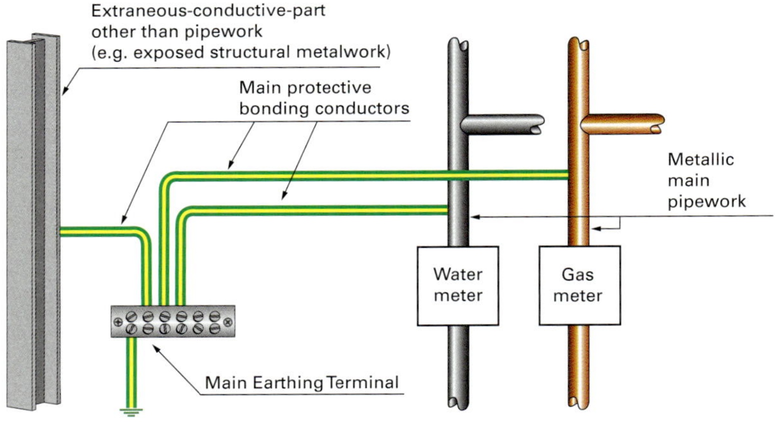

Fig 3.7 An example of the application of the requirements of Regulation 411.3.1.2 for protective equipotential bonding.

Extraneous-conductive-parts may be connected to the Main Earthing Terminal either individually, collectively (by a so-called 'common' protective bonding conductor, which loops from one extraneous-conductive-part to another), or in groups (each group employing a common protective bonding conductor).

Where a common protective bonding conductor is used, special attention is required for connections along the run, in order to avoid inadvertent loss of bonding to one or more extraneous-conductive-parts; typically, this may be achieved by the use of a continuous and unbroken conductor.

Protective bonding conductors in PME-supplied installations may have to carry sustained currents under certain distribution network conditions, which may raise the temperature of the bonding conductors. Where PME conditions apply, the electricity distributor may have particular requirements for protective bonding conductors, above and beyond those of *BS 7671*. Most electricity distributors publish notes of guidance and/or drawings to explain any such requirements, which they will issue to electrical installation designers and contractors on request. Information may also be obtained from the trade association of electricity distributors, the Energy Networks Association (**www.energynetworks.org.uk**).

Published by Certsure LLP © Certsure LLP (January 2015)

A protective bonding conductor should be identified with the colour combination green-and-yellow (Regulation 514.4.2). In addition, as is the case for any conductor, a protective bonding conductor has to be identifiable during inspection, testing, repair and alteration of the installation (Regulation 514.1.2). Each such conductor must therefore be marked or labelled to indicate its function, and to identify the item(s) to which it connects (e.g. water service) unless this information is clear from the arrangement of the conductor, such as from its position or from the terminals to which it connects.

Protective bonding conductors must be adequately supported (Regulation 522.8.5) independent of non-electrical services such as pipework (Regulation Group 528.3 refers). Attention must also be paid to the ability of protective bonding conductors to withstand external influences such as mechanical damage (Section 522), and any anticipated factors that are likely to result in deterioration (Regulation 543.3.1). The requirements for the minimum permitted cross-sectional area (csa) of a main protective bonding conductor are given in Regulation 544.1. Protective bonding conductors that are buried in the ground are, additionally, subject to the requirements of Regulation 542.3.1 for earthing conductors.

Where *PME conditions do not apply*, Regulation 544.1.1 requires a main protective bonding conductor to have a csa of not less than half that required for the earthing conductor of the installation and not less than 6 mm^2. The csa need not exceed 25 mm^2 if the main bonding conductor is of copper or, if of other metals, a csa affording equivalent conductance.

Where PME conditions apply, Regulation 544.1.1 requires the protective bonding conductors to be selected based upon the csa of the neutral conductor of the supply using Table 54.8 of *BS 7671*. Table 3.2 is partially based on information given in Table 54.8.

 © Certsure LLP (January 2015)

Table 3.2 Minimum protective bonding conductor csa in relation to the neutral of the supply where PME conditions apply

csa of the supply neutral conductor		Minimum csa required for a main protective bonding conductor		
Copper conductor 1	Aluminium conductor 2	Copper conductor 3	Steel wire armouring 4	Aluminium strip armouring 5
(mm^2)	(mm^2)	(mm^2)	(mm^2)	(mm^2)
35 or less	58 or less	10	80	16
over 35 up to 50	over 58 up to 83	16	128	26
over 50 up to 95	over 83 up to 159	25	200	41
over 95 up to 150	over 159 up to 253	35	280	57
over 150	over 253	50	400	81

* Note: Local electricity distribution network conditions may require a larger main protective bonding conductor csa than listed in columns 3, 4 or 5.

The requirement of Regulation 544.1.1 also applies to the earthing conductor of the installation. This is because the earthing conductor also performs the function of a main protective bonding conductor (see Regulation 542.3.1) and so, where PME conditions apply, the csa of the earthing conductor must be not less than the minimum required for its function as an earthing conductor and for its function as a main protective bonding conductor.

The note in Table 3.2, to the effect that an electricity distributor may require a larger conductor means that the data in the table should be used as a guide only, and that the specific requirements of the relevant electricity distributor should always be determined when considering the selection of protective bonding conductors where PME conditions apply.

It is important to appreciate that the 'supply neutral conductor' referred to in Table 3.2 is the neutral conductor of the electricity distributor's low voltage network (otherwise known as the combined protective and neutral (PEN) conductor). It is NOT the neutral conductor on the consumer's side of the supply terminals, which may have a smaller csa.

Published by Certsure LLP © Certsure LLP (January 2015)

Table 3.3 The requirements of *BS 7671* for minimum main protective bonding conductor sizes where PME conditions DO NOT apply.

csa of main line and neutral conductors, e.g. meter tails (Note: 1) 1	Minimum csa required for a copper earthing conductor not buried in ground or buried with both corrosion and mechanical protection (Notes: 2 & 3) 2	Minimum csa required for a main protective bonding conductor (Note: 4)	
		Copper conductor 3	Steel wire armouring 4
(mm^2)	(mm^2)	(mm^2)	(mm^2)
4 or 6	6	6	24
10	10	6	40
16 or 25	16	10	64
50	25	16	100
70	35	25	140

* Note:
1) The distributor may specify a minimum line and neutral conductor size in relation to cut-out fuse rated current.
2) The minimum earthing conductor sizes in column 2 have been selected in relation to the line conductor sizes in column 1, in accordance with Table 54.7 of *BS 7671*. Alternatively, however, the minimum earthing conductor size may be calculated in accordance with Regulation 543.1.3 (adiabatic equation).
3) Buried copper earthing conductors without mechanical protection are subject to a minimum size of 16 mm^2 where protected against corrosion or 25 mm^2 where not protected against corrosion.
4) The minimum main protective bonding conductor sizes in columns 3 and 4 have been chosen on the basis of the earthing conductor sizes in column 2, In accordance with the relevant requirements of Regulation 544.1.1.

Regulation 544.1.2 of *BS 7671* requires the main protective bonding connection to any gas, water or other service to be made as near as practicable to the point of entry of that service into the premises. Where there is an insulating section or insert at that point, or there is a meter, the regulation further requires that the connection is made to the consumer's hard metal pipework (not to a lead pipe or a flexible pipe for example) and before any branch pipework. Where practicable, the connection should be made within 600 mm of the meter outlet union or at the point of entry of the service to the dwelling if the meter is external. Where an electrical installation serves more than one building, such as a dwelling and a remote garage, these requirements should be applied at each building.

Earthing and bonding

Where a semi-concealed meter box is fitted, the gas service pipe (as defined in *BS 6891: 2005* (as amended) – *Installation of low pressure gas pipework up to 35 mm (R1 1/4) in domestic premises (2nd family gas). Specification*) – terminates at the meter outside the premises.

From the meter, the gas installation pipe (as defined) may then enter the premises at low level, such as below floor boards, or buried in concrete flooring or screed.

It is generally preferable for a suitable bonding connection to be made inside the premises, but this may not always be practicable.

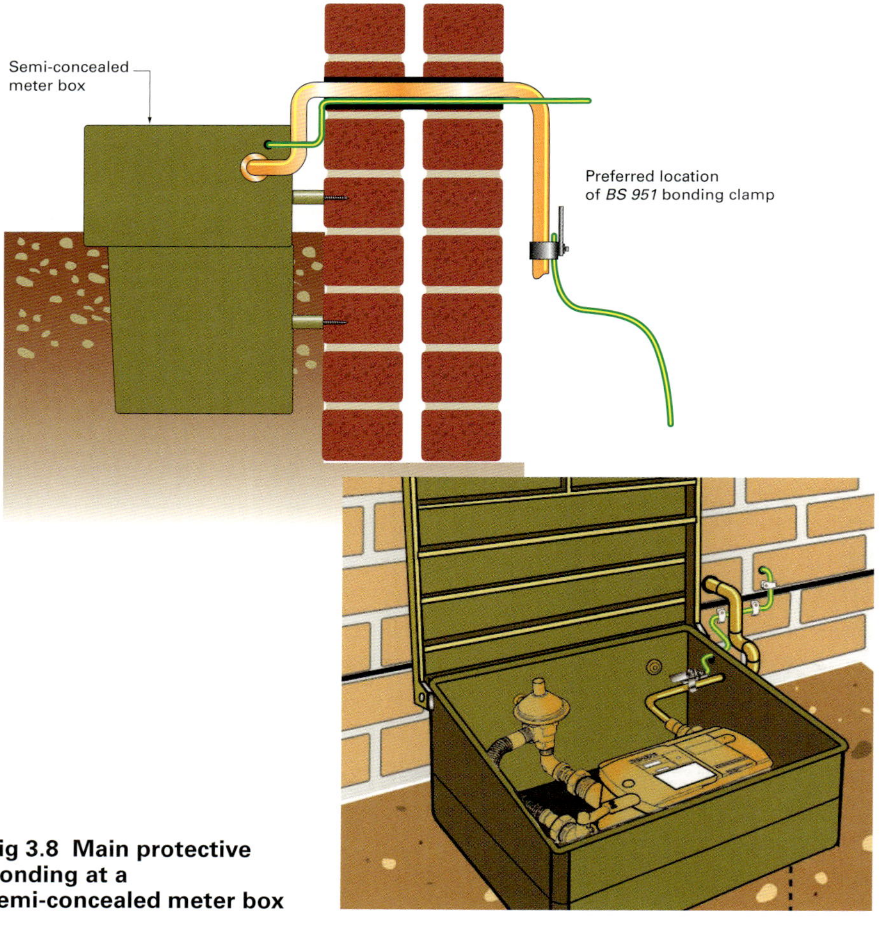

Fig 3.8 Main protective bonding at a semi-concealed meter box

Published by Certsure LLP © Certsure LLP (January 2015)

In such situations, the most practical solution is often to make the bonding connection inside the meter box itself, by means of a *BS 951* earthing and bonding clamp, fitted to the gas installation pipework where this is of the hard metal type, as shown in Fig 3.8.

The protective bonding conductor should be passed through the pre-drilled hole in the right hand side of the meter box, and a 'Safety Electrical Connection – Do Not Remove' label should also be attached (Regulation 514.13.1). Where a pre-drilled hole does not exist it is permitted for the bonding conductor to be installed alongside the gas pipe through an appropriately sealed sleeve. However it is installed, the bonding conductor and its connection should not interfere with the integrity of the meter box.

The length of protective bonding conductor external to the box, before it passes through a hole in the external wall above the damp proof course, should be as short as possible. Like any other conductor, it should be properly supported by, for example, clipping to wall surfaces. The protective bonding conductor is permitted to run through the sleeve with the gas installation pipe as shown in Fig 3.9, but it is essential that the sleeve is appropriately sealed with a non-setting, fire resistant compound, around both the gas installation pipe and the cable.

Certain older style semi-concealed gas meter boxes have an adaptor located in the side wall of the box and an earth tag washer is normally provided for connection of the bonding conductor. In such cases, a *BS 951* earthing and bonding clamp is not required. However, an earthing and bonding connection label in accordance with Regulation group 514.13 will still be required.

Fig 3.9 A more detailed view.

Older style semi-concealed gas meter box

Earthing and bonding

Protective bonding connections to metal pipework should normally be made using clamps complying with *BS 951*: 2009 *Electrical earthing. Clamps for earthing and bonding. Specification*, as shown in Fig 3.10 although other types of clamp may be used provided that the integrity of the connection meets all relevant requirements of *BS 7671*.

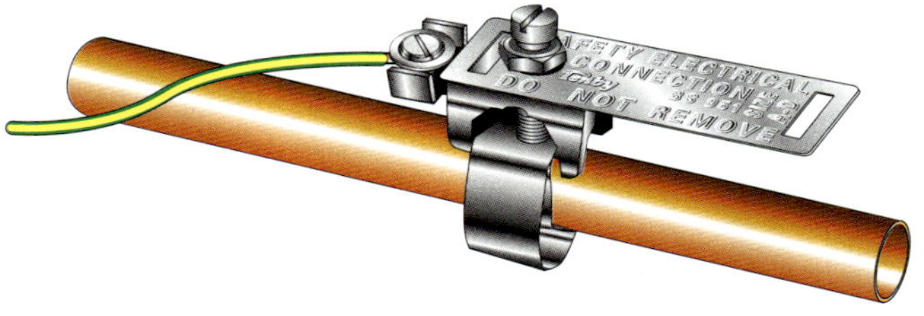

Fig 3.10 BS 951 earthing clamp.

Earthing and bonding clamps should be selected to suit both the pipe diameter and the conductor size. Other suitable means of connection will be required when connecting to extraneous-conductive-parts other than pipes, such as structural steelwork.

Where a common bonding conductor loops in and out to connect to an extraneous-conductive-part, the conductor should be left unbroken at the connection. This is so that the continuity to other items connected to the bonding conductor will not be lost if the connection becomes detached (for example, as a result of work being carried out to pipework, Regulation 528.3.3 refers).

A permanent label bearing the words 'Safety Electrical Connection — Do Not Remove' (see Fig 3.11) should be installed in a visible position at or near the point of connection of every protective bonding conductor to an extraneous-conductive-part, and at the main earthing terminal where this is separate from the consumer unit or main switchgear (Regulation 514.13.1 refers).

Fig 3.11 Warning label required at earthing and bonding connections.

Published by Certsure LLP © Certsure LLP (January 2015)

3.7 Supplementary bonding

Supplementary equipotential bonding ('supplementary bonding' for short) is a complementary measure for fault protection, which is required by *BS 7671* in certain situations. Supplementary bonding involves connecting together the conductive parts of electrical items and non-electrical items, such as those shown in Fig 3.12, to prevent the occurrence of a dangerous voltage between them under earth fault conditions.

BS 7671 calls for supplementary bonding to be provided:

- for certain types of special installations or locations covered by Part 7 of the Regulations
- where the conditions for automatic disconnection in case of a fault of Regulation Group 411.3.2 **cannot** be fulfilled by an overcurrent device - which is not likely to be the case in a dwelling.

Those instances of increased shock risk that require supplementary bonding in a dwelling are typically locations containing swimming pools and other basins. It should be noted that supplementary bonding will be required in some cases in locations containing a bath or shower (Regulation 701.415.2 refers). See Chapter 12 of this Guide for guidance regarding special locations.

Where supplementary bonding is required, Regulation 415.2 requires it to connect together all simultaneously accessible exposed-conductive-parts of equipment and extraneous-conductive-parts (including, where appropriate, the main metallic reinforcement within reinforced concrete forming part of the structure). The equipotential bonding should also be connected to the protective conductors of all equipment forming a part of the installation including the earthing contacts of socket-outlets, as illustrated in Fig 3.12.

In addition, where supplementary bonding is required because the location falls within the scope of Part 7 of *BS 7671* (Special Installations or Locations), the relevant regulations in Part 7 may require items additional to those referred to in Regulation 415.2 to be connected together by the supplementary bonding. For example, for a location containing a bath or shower, the terminal of the protective conductor of each circuit supplying Class I **and** Class II equipment is included amongst the items that must be connected together by supplementary bonding, as required by Regulation 701.415.2.

 © Certsure LLP (January 2015)

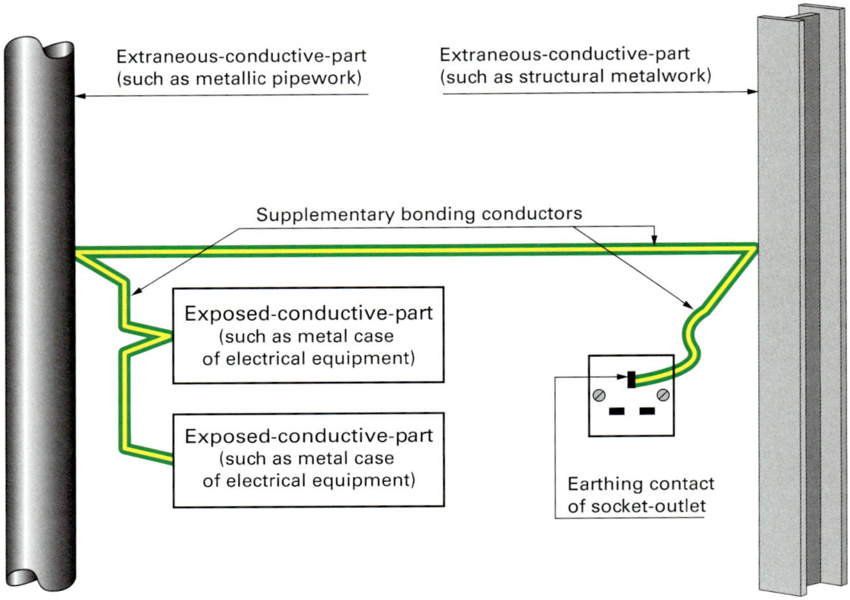

Fig 3.12 Example of items to be connected together where supplementary bonding is required.

Single-core, non-flexible, copper cable having a green-and-yellow covering is commonly used for supplementary bonding. However, this is not the only type of conductor that may be used. For example, a protective conductor forming part of a sheathed cable (such as 'twin & earth') or flexible cable may be employed as a supplementary bonding conductor. This is subject to all the relevant requirements of *BS 7671* being met, including that the cross-sectional area of the conductor must be sufficient for such use (see Table 3.4) and for use as the circuit protective conductor where the conductor also performs that function.

Regulation 543.2.1 permits the use of other types of conductor as a supplementary bonding conductor. The types of conductor which may be used include metallic parts of wiring systems and extraneous-conductive-parts, or a combination of these, provided that all the relevant requirements of *BS 7671* are met. For example, parts of a metal pipework system such as that for cold water, hot water or heating, may provide permanent and reliable electrical continuity for supplementary bonding

Published by Certsure LLP © Certsure LLP (January 2015)

purposes, to the standard required by Section 543. Note, however, that the following must NOT be selected as a bonding conductor (Regulation 543.2.3 refers):

- gas or oil pipes,
- flexible or pliable conduit,
- support wires,
- any constructional parts that are deemed to be subject to mechanical stress in normal usage.

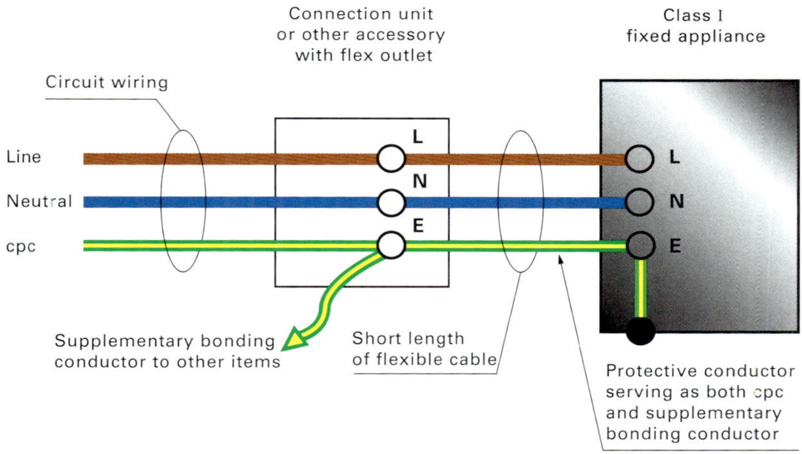

Fig 3.13 Use of cpc in a short length of flexible cable for supplementary bonding.

Fig 3.13 shows the application of the requirements of Regulation 543.2.1, for a situation where supplementary bonding is required to a Class I fixed appliance supplied via a short length of flexible cable from an adjacent connection unit or other accessory incorporating a flex outlet. Regulation 544.2.5 allows the circuit protective conductor (cpc) within the flexible cable to be used to provide the supplementary bonding connection to the exposed-conductive-parts of the appliance, from the earthing terminal in the connection unit or other accessory where the supplementary bonding conductor to other items is terminated.

The cross-sectional area (csa) of supplementary bonding conductors must be not less than that necessary to satisfy the 544.2 Regulation Group, as shown in Table 3.4.

 © Certsure LLP (January 2015)

Table 3.4 Minimum csa of copper conductors required for supplementary bonding.

Regulations	Bonding conductor connecting			
	Mechanically protected[1]	Two exposed-conductive-parts	An exposed-conductive-part and an extraneous-conductive-part	Two extraneous-conductive-parts
544.2	✓	csa ≥ csa of smaller cpc	csa ≥ csa of cpc	csa ≥ 2.5 mm²
	✗	csa ≥ 4 mm²	csa ≥ 4 mm²	csa ≥ 4 mm²

Note 1: Where sheathed* or otherwise provided with mechanical protection (e.g. by enclosure in conduit etc).
* The covering (insulation) of a single-core non-sheathed cable (eg to *BS 6004* or *BS 7211*) is not a sheath.

Regulation 415.2.2 imposes a limit on the ohmic value of the resistance (R) of a supplementary bonding conductor that connects exposed-conductive-parts and extraneous-conductive-parts, as given in the following equation:

$$R \leq \frac{50}{I_a}$$

Where I_a is the operating current of the protective device.

For an RCD, I_a is the rated residual operating current $I_{\Delta n}$. For an overcurrent protective device I_a is the minimum current which disconnects the circuit within 5 s.

Meeting these requirements for resistance (R) is unlikely to be a problem in practice in most domestic premises.

As with all conductors, supplementary bonding conductors must be adequately supported. Attention must also be paid to their ability to withstand external influences such as mechanical damage (Section 522 refers), and any anticipated factors likely to result in deterioration (Regulation 543.3.1).

Published by Certsure LLP © Certsure LLP (January 2015)

As with every other type of electrical connection, supplementary bonding connections and joints are required to have durable electrical continuity and adequate strength (Regulation 526.1). In addition, Regulation 526.3 requires, with certain exceptions, that every connection and joint is accessible for inspection, testing and maintenance.

Supplementary bonding connections to metal pipework should normally be made using bonding clamps complying with *BS 951* (see Fig 3.10). Clamps should be selected to suit both the pipe diameter and bonding conductor size. Other suitable means of connection will be required where connecting to extraneous-conductive-parts other than pipes, such as structural steelwork.

A permanent label as required by Regulation 514.13.1, bearing the words 'Safety Electrical connection — Do Not Remove', must be permanently fixed in a visible position at or near the point of connection of every bonding conductor to an extraneous-conductive-part (see Fig 3.11).

To counter a popular misconception: there is no requirement in *BS 7671* to provide supplementary bonding between a metallic kitchen sink and associated pipework. However, where a metallic waste pipe that meets the definition of an extraneous-conductive-part serves the sink, a main protective bonding conductor would be required to connect it to the MET.

3.8 Earthing arrangements where an installation contains equipment having high protective conductor currents

The earthing requirements for the installation of equipment having high protective conductor currents given in Regulation Group 543.7 are summarised in Table 3.5 overleaf.

Earthing and bonding

Table 3.5 Earthing requirements for equipment having high protective conductor currents

Ref	Application	Additional protective conductor connection requirements (alternatives)	Regulation
1	Connection of equipment having protective conductor current exceeding 3.5 mA but not exceeding 10 mA.	Permanent connection to installation wiring.	543.7.1.101
		Connection by means of *BS EN 60309-2* a plug and socket	
2	Connection of equipment having protective conductor current exceeding 10 mA.	Permanent connection to installation wiring. Protective conductor selected in accordance with Regulation 543.7.1.103 (see Ref 3)	543.7.1.102
		Flexible cable with *BS EN 60309-2* plug and socket. Csa of protective conductor of flexible cable not less than: • 2.5 mm² for plugs rated at 16 A, or • 4 mm² for plugs rated above 16 A, or • csa of line conductor.	
		Protective conductor complying with Section 543 with earth monitoring system to *BS 4444*.	
3	Final circuit or distribution circuit supplying one or more items of equipment, the total protective conductor being likely to exceed 10 mA (provision of high integrity protective connection)	A single protective conductor of csa not less than 10 mm², complying with Regulations 543.2 (types of protective conductor) and 543.3 (preservation of continuity).	543.7.1.103 and 543.7.1.104
		Single copper protective conductor of csa not less than 4 mm², complying with 543.2 (types of protective conductor) and 543.3 (preservation of continuity), enclosed to give additional protection against mechanical damage, such as in flexible conduit.	
		Two individual protective conductors, which may be of different types, such as a metallic conduit and an additional conductor enclosed within. Each must comply with Section 543 (Protective conductors). The ends of the two protective conductors must be terminated independently of each other at all connection points throughout the circuit, such as distribution board, junction boxes and socket outlets. (Regulation 543.7.1.104 refers). If both protective conductors are incorporated in a multicore cable, total csa of all the conductors, including live conductors, to be not less than 10 mm². One protective conductor may be formed by metallic sheath, armour or braid of the cable, provided this complies with Regulation 543.2.5.	
		Protective conductor complying with Section 543 with earth monitoring system to *BS 4444*.	
		Connection of the equipment to the supply by double wound transformer or equivalent, such as a motor alternator set. See Regulation 543.7.1.103(v) for detailed requirements.	

Published by Certsure LLP © Certsure LLP (January 2015)

Ref	Application	Additional protective conductor connection requirements (alternatives)	Regulation
4	Final circuit intended to supply two or more items where total protective conductor current in normal service is likely to exceed 10 mA (provision of high integrity protective connection).	Ring final circuit with a ring protective conductor. Spurs, if provided, require high integrity protective conductor connection complying with the requirements of Regulation 543.7.1 (see Ref 3).	543.7.2.101
		A radial final circuit with a single protective conductor, provided that also: • the protective conductor is connected as a ring, or • a separate protective conductor is provided at the final socket-outlet by connection to the metal conduit or ducting, or • in the case where a number of similar radial circuits supply socket-outlets in adjacent areas, a second protective conductor may be provided at the final socket-outlet on one circuit by connection to the protective conductor of the adjacent circuit. The circuits must be fed from the same distribution board, have identical means of short circuit and overcurrent protection and circuit protective conductors of the same csa.	
		Other circuits complying with the requirements of Regulations 543.7.1.101 to 543.7.1.104 (see Refs 1, 2 and 3).	

IET WIRING REGULATIONS
UPDATED TO:
17TH EDITION
BS 7671:2008
Amd 3: 2015

Other publications which have been updated to reflect the latest requirements of *BS 7671*: 2008 (Amendment 3): 2015 include -

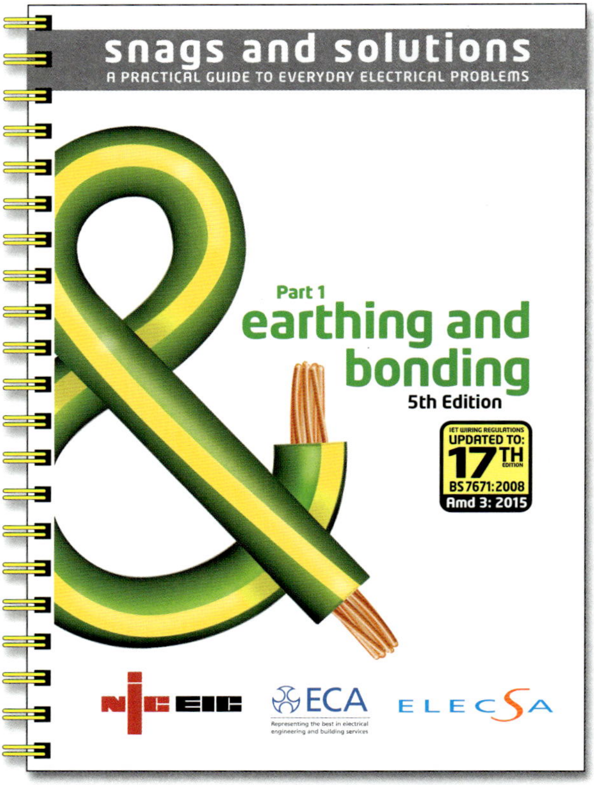

To order this or any other publication contact

NICEIC customers:	0843 290 3485	www.niceicdirect.com
ELECSA/ECA customers:	0333 321 8225	www.elecsa.co.uk

Published by Certsure LLP © Certsure LLP (January 2015)

Protective devices

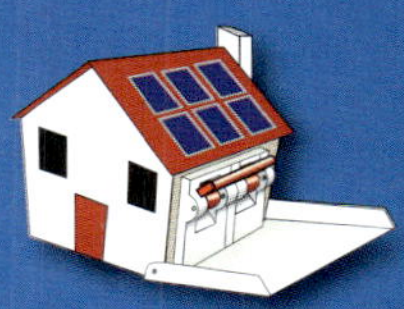

 © Certsure LLP (January 2015)

4.1 Introduction to protective devices

The following protective devices are commonly available.

- Fuses to *BS 88-2*
- Fuses to *BS 88-3*
- Fuses to *BS 1362*
- Circuit-breakers to *BS EN 60898* (as amended)
- Residual current operated circuit-breakers without integral overcurrent protection (RCCB) to *BS EN 61008*
- Residual current operated circuit-breakers with integral overcurrent protection (RCBO) to *BS EN 61009*

The following protective devices are no longer in production but are likely to be encountered in some existing domestic premises.

- Rewireable (semi-enclosed) fuses to *BS 3036*
- Cartridge fuses to *BS 1361*
- Miniature circuit-breakers (MCB) to *BS 3871*.

All the above will be discussed in this Chapter.

BS 7671 now contains requirements relating to overvoltage control. These are also considered in relation to domestic and similar premises.

4.2 Cartridge fuses

4.2.1 *BS 88*

Cartridge fuses to *BS 88-2* are widely used as circuit protective devices in commerce and industry, less so in housing.

There are a number of types of *BS 88* fuse (see Fig 4.1). The general requirements for *BS 88* fuses are now specified in *BS 88-1* (also known as *BS EN 60269-1*), and the supplementary requirements for *BS 88* fuses intended for specific conditions of use or applications are covered in the subsequent Parts of the *BS 88* series.

Published by Certsure LLP © Certsure LLP (January 2015)

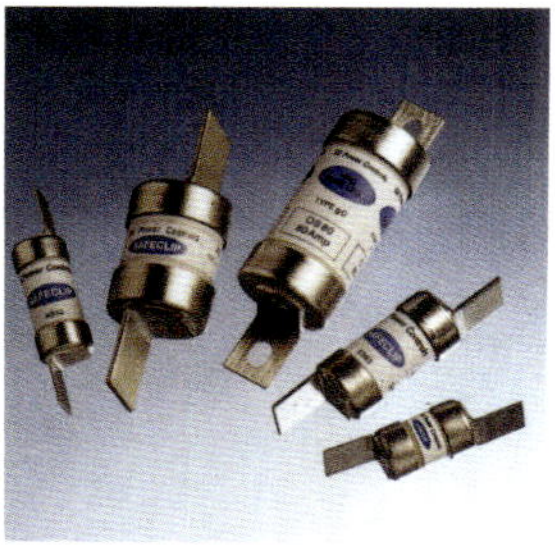

Fig 4.1 ***BS 88-2*** **fuses**

Photograph courtesy of GE power controls

BS 7671 contains information relating to the maximum permitted earth fault loop impedance and time/current characteristics for *BS 88-2* fuse system E (bolted), and G (clip-in), which are suitable for use by authorised persons, and to *BS 88-3* fuse system C (cylindrical type), which may be used or replaced by unskilled persons, such as householders.

Fuse system C type fuses are sub-divided into two types - Type I and Type II. Details of these are given in Table 4.1 below:

Table 4.1 Information relating to *BS 88-3* system C fuses.

Type	Rated current	Rated voltage	Rated breaking capacity
I	≤ 45 A	230 V	16 kA
II	≤ 100 A	400 V	31.5 kA

4.2.2 *BS 1361*

Up until the publication of Amendment No 1 to the 17th Edition of the Wiring Regulations, *BS 7671* contained data relating to cartridge fuses conforming to *BS 1361*. Broadly speaking this type of fuse has been replaced by those to *BS 88-3* fuse system C, described above.

There are two basic types of *BS 1361* fuse - Type I and Type II. Type I fuses are intended for use in distribution boards where the fuses might be replaced by the consumer. Type II fuses are primarily intended for use as distributor's cut-out fuses, installed in distributor's service units in domestic and similar premises.

 © Certsure LLP (January 2015)

Fig 4.2 Cartridge fuses to *BS 1361*.

Photograph courtesy of Hager Powertech Ltd

Table 4.2 Information relating to *BS 1361* fuses.

Type	Rated current	Rated voltage	Rated breaking capacity
I	5 to 45 A	240 V	16 kA
IIa	60 A and 80 A	415 V	31.5 kA
IIb	80 A and 100 A		

BS 1361 fuses are colour-coded as follows:

- 5 A – white
- 15 A – blue
- 20 A – yellow
- 30 A – red
- 45 A – green.

4.2.3 *BS 1362*

Cartridge fuses conforming to *BS 1362* have a rated voltage of 240 V and are suitable for use in low voltage single-phase a.c. circuits of nominal frequency 50 or 60 Hz. They are general-purpose fuses intended for domestic and similar purposes, primarily in plugs complying with *BS 1363*, although not exclusively so. *BS 1362* cartridge fuses are, for example, commonly used in fused connection units.

The rated current (I_n) allocated by the manufacturer may be any value up to and including 13 A, although the preferred values in *BS 1362* are 3 A and 13 A.

Cartridge fuses to *BS 1362* are required to be colour coded according to their rated current, and be marked with their rated current value.

Published by Certsure LLP © Certsure LLP (January 2015)

Where a fuse is used to provide protection against fault current only, for example to protect the flexible cable to an appliance with integral overload protection, the fault clearance time under both short-circuit and earth fault conditions has to meet the requirements of Regulation 434.5.2.

For overload current protection, the rated current of a fuse is to be selected to meet the requirements of Section 433 of *BS 7671*.

Where overload current protection is afforded by a *BS 1362* cartridge fuse, there tends to be a need for the circuit conductors to be of a larger cross-sectional area than required for most other types of overcurrent protective device used. This is because of the need to comply with condition (iii) of Regulation 433.1.1, which requires that the current causing effective operation of the protective device (I_2), does not exceed 1.45 times the lowest of the current-carrying capacities I_z of any of the conductors of the circuit.

BS 1362 cartridge fuses should be indelibly marked with the following information.

- Manufacturer's name or identifying mark
- British Standard Number
- Rated current in amperes.

The fuse-link barrel should also be colour coded according to rated current as follows: brown for 13 A fuses, red for 3 A fuses and black for all other current ratings (such as 2 A, 4 A, 5 A and 10 A).

4.3 Semi-enclosed fuses to *BS 3036*

Requirements applicable to rewireable (semi-enclosed) fuses are specified in *BS 3036: 1958 (2007) Semi-enclosed electric fuses*.

Whilst data relating to semi-enclosed fuses, more commonly known as rewireable fuses, is still given in *BS 7671*, these fuses are no longer in general production. However, details are given relating to *BS 3036* fuses in this Guide as they are likely to be encountered in many existing domestic premises for a considerable period of time to come.

Historically, rewireable fuses were a popular choice for protection against overcurrent and/or for fault protection. One reason for this was that the fuse element (a length of suitable tinned copper wire) was inexpensive to replace.

This rewireable feature is also a disadvantage because of the risk of the fuse-element (the wire) being replaced inadvertently, or in some cases deliberately, with a fuse element of a higher fusing current or worse still by any number of other readily available conductive materials. The circuit then has inadequate protection against overcurrent and against fault conditions (where the device is intended to provide such protection).

BS 7671 recognises the risk of the fuse-element being replaced with one with a higher fusing current and requires, in Regulation 533.1.1.3, that rewireable fuses, where selected, are to be fitted with a fuse element in accordance with the manufacturer's instructions, or in the absence of such instructions, to be fitted with a single element of tinned copper wire of the appropriate diameter in accordance with Table 53.1 of *BS 7671*.

There are three basic types of *BS 3036* fuse, categorised according to duty. These categories of duty are S1A, S2A and S4A. Each category is applicable to particular standard sizes of fuse. Table 4.3 identifies the three categories and their associated rated breaking capacities and gives details of available rated currents ratings (I_n).

Table 4.3 Categories, rated breaking capacities and rated currents of *BS 3036* fuses.

Category of duty	Rated breaking capacities (kA)	Number of sizes	Standard rating, I_n						
			5 A	15 A	20 A	30 A	45 A	60 A	100 A
S1A	1[1]	6	✓	✓	✓	✓	✓	✓	
S2A	2[2]	7	✓	✓	✓	✓	✓	✓	✓
S4A	4[3]	4				✓	✓	✓	✓

The rated breaking capacity of *BS 3036* fuses is low in comparison to that of some other protective devices. However, where *BS 3036* fuses (as with any other protective device) of rated current up to and including 45 A are contained within a consumer unit conforming to *BS EN 60439-3: 1991* (as amended), the whole assembly is considered to be conditionally rated at 16 kA (Annex ZA of that standard refers).

Published by Certsure LLP © Certsure LLP (January 2015)

The rated current (I_n) of a fuse applies to specific ambient temperature conditions. Where the ambient temperature conditions vary significantly from the ambient air temperature specified in *BS 3036*, correction factors may have to be applied.

For overload current protection, the rated current of a fuse should be selected to meet the requirements of Section 433 of *BS 7671*.

In addition to providing overcurrent protection, a fuse can be used as part of the protective measure of Automatic Disconnection of Supply (ADS). In such cases, the value of the earth fault loop impedance (Z_S) of the associated circuit is to comply with the requirements of Regulation Groups 411.4 (TN Systems), 411.5 (TT Systems) and 411.7 (FELV circuits), respectively, according to the type of system earthing.

Manufacturers of fuses to *BS 3036* were required by that Standard to produce time/current characteristics for their fuses and to make copies of these available on request.

BS 3036 defines the fusing factor of a fuse covered by that standard as: 'The ratio, greater than unity, of the minimum fusing current to the current rating of a fuse', and is not to exceed 2.0.

BS 7671 recognises that the minimum fusing current, I_2 for a *BS 3036* fuse can be as high as 2.0 I_n and advises that, where such a fuse is used for overload current protection, compliance with Regulation 433.1.1 is afforded where the rated current, I_n of the fuse is selected such that it does not exceed 0.725 times the current-carrying capacity I_z of the lowest rated conductor in the circuit protected (Regulation 433.1.101 refers).

This is because, where I_n is equal to 0.725 I_z, and I_2 = 2.0 I_n, then by substitution I_2 = 2 x 0.725 I_z, giving I_2 = 1.45 I_z.

 © Certsure LLP (January 2015)

4.4 Circuit-breakers

4.4.1 *BS EN 60898*

Circuit-breakers to *BS EN 60898-1: 2003 – Circuit-breakers for overcurrent protection for household and similar installations. Circuit-breakers for a.c. operation* (see Fig 4.3). are widely used as final circuit protective devices in distribution boards, consumer units and control panels. This Guide gives information on the main characteristics of such circuit-breakers as far as fault protection, protection against overcurrent, and isolation and switching are concerned.

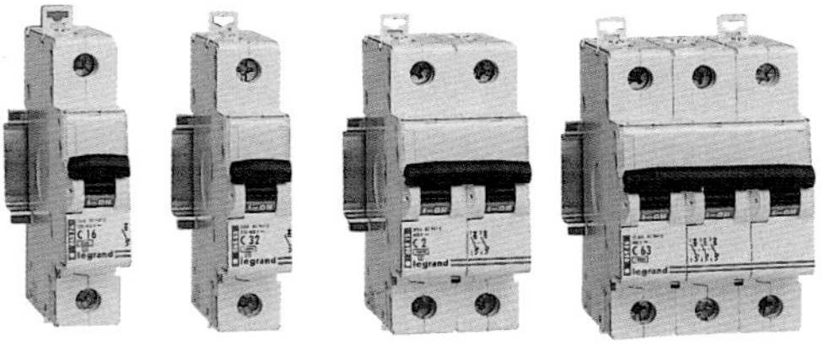

Fig 4.3 Typical circuit-breakers to *BS EN 60898*.

The preferred values of rated current given in *BS EN 60898-1* are 6, 8, 10,13, 16, 20, 25, 32, 40, 50, 63, 80, 100 and 125 A. Rated current, I_n, is the current that a circuit-breaker is designed to carry for long periods (weeks, months or even years) at a specified reference ambient air temperature, normally of 30 °C.

Circuit-breakers conforming to *BS EN 60898-1* are classified into three distinct 'Types'; Type B, Type C and Type D, according to their instantaneous tripping current. Instantaneous tripping current is the minimum value of current causing a circuit-breaker to operate automatically without intentional time delay - that is, within a time not exceeding 0.1 s (100 ms). The limiting value of earth fault loop impedance (Z_s) for a circuit-breaker for fault protection, as given in Table 41.3 of *BS 7671*, is based on the instantaneous tripping current of the device.

BS EN 60898-1 permits instantaneous tripping to begin to occur at a value of fault current, expressed as a multiple of the rated current (I_n), within a range of values for each circuit-breaker type. The standard ranges are shown in Table 4.4, although manufacturers may design circuit-breakers to operate instantaneously within smaller ranges of current, falling within the standard ranges.

Published by Certsure LLP © Certsure LLP (January 2015)

Table 4.4 Instantaneous tripping

Circuit-breaker type	Standard range	
B	above 3 I_n	up to and including 5 I_n
C	above 5 I_n	up to and including 10 I_n
D	above 10 I_n	up to and including 20 I_n

The standard ranges of instantaneous tripping current are also shown in graphical form in Fig 4.4, which is a representation of the time/current characteristics of Type B, C and D circuit-breakers.

Generally, in order to meet the requirements of *BS 7671* for automatic disconnection to occur within a prescribed time limit (such as, say, 0.2 s or 1 s, as appropriate) under earth fault conditions, the prospective earth fault current must be not less than the upper value of the range of instantaneous tripping currents for the circuit-breaker concerned.

For example, on the basis of the standard ranges of current referred to in Table 4.4 and Fig 4.4, the prospective earth fault current for a 32 A Type B circuit-breaker is required to be not less than 160 A (that is, 5 x I_n). Correspondingly, prospective earth fault currents of not less than 320 A and 640 A, respectively, are required for instantaneous tripping of 32 A Type C and D circuit-breakers.

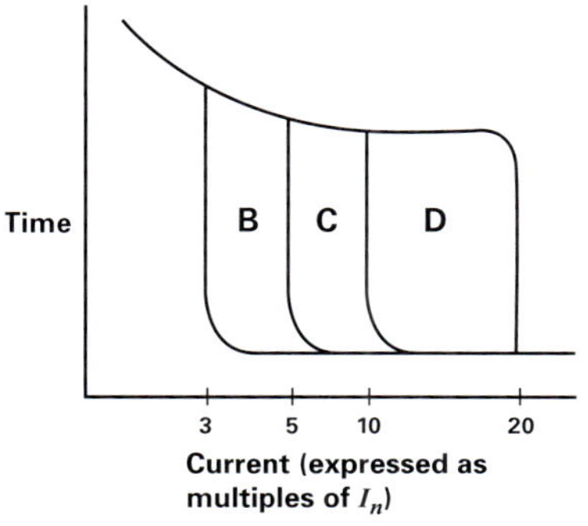

The higher the prospective fault current that is required to cause instantaneous tripping, the lower the limiting earth fault loop impedance (Z_s) needs to be. This can be seen from the limiting values of earth fault loop impedance given in Table 41.3 of *BS 7671*, for Types B, C and D circuit-breakers, and in the other similar tables, such as Table 41.6 for reduced low voltage circuits.

Fig 4.4 Graphical representation of time/current characteristics of Type B, C and D circuit-breakers (including the ranges of current within which instantaneous tripping begins to occur)

 © Certsure LLP (January 2015)

Protective devices

Due to the particular time/current characteristics of a circuit-breaker, values of earth fault loop impedance even marginally exceeding the limiting values in the above tables of *BS 7671* may result in greatly increased disconnection times which would not be acceptable for fault protection.

As it cannot be predicted where in the range a circuit-breaker will trip, the limiting values of earth fault loop impedance for *BS EN 60898* circuit-breakers, in Table 41.3 are based on the upper range values of current indicated by Table 4.4 earlier. The limiting values are derived by the method given in the introduction to Appendix 3 of *BS 7671* (Time/current characteristics of overcurrent protective devices).

Manufacturers of *BS EN 60898* circuit-breakers sometimes publish, in relation to their own circuit-breakers only, limiting values of earth fault loop impedance higher than the corresponding limiting values given in Table 41.3 of *BS 7671*. This is because, as indicated earlier in this chapter, manufacturers are free to design circuit-breakers to operate instantaneously within ranges of current smaller than, but falling within, the standard ranges given in Table 4.4.

Furthermore, some manufacturers of *BS EN 60898* circuit-breakers publish limiting values of earth fault loop impedance to facilitate tripping in a time of up to 5 s (i.e. in addition to limiting values of earth fault loop impedance based on instantaneous tripping current). This is because the characteristics of the circuit-breakers concerned can be such as to allow tripping other than instantaneously without the risk of a greatly increased disconnection time.

The rated short-circuit capacity (I_{cn}) of a circuit-breaker conforming to *BS EN 60898* is the value of the ultimate short-circuit capacity assigned by the manufacturer.

A circuit-breaker also has a corresponding service short-circuit capacity I_{cs}, which is either equal to or lower than the rated short-circuit capacity (I_{cn}), depending on the I_{cn} of the device.

The difference between the two short-circuit capacities principally relates to the condition, after being short-circuit type-tested, of a circuit-breaker whose service short-circuit capacity (I_{cs}) is lower than its rated short-circuit capacity (I_{cn}), as follows.

- After type-testing at the service short-circuit capacity (I_{cs}), the circuit-breaker is required to be fully serviceable and the operating characteristics must remain unchanged.

Published by Certsure LLP © Certsure LLP (January 2015)

- After type-testing at the rated short-circuit capacity (I_{cn}), the operating characteristics of the circuit-breaker may have changed.

Thus, where a circuit-breaker has cleared a short-circuit fault or earth fault at a prospective current in excess of its rated value of I_{cs}, the device is likely to be unfit for continued service and should be replaced.

Of the two short-circuit capacities (I_{cs} and I_{cn}), only the rated short-circuit capacity (I_{cn}) is required to be marked on a circuit-breaker. This is shown within a rectangle, as illustrated in Fig 4.5. The example indicates a rated short-circuit capacity of 6000 A.

6000

Fig 4.5 Example of marking that denotes the rated (ultimate) short-circuit capacity (I_{cn}).

Within the scope of this Guide, the preferred values of rated short-circuit capacity (I_{cn}) given in *BS EN 60898-1* are 1500 A, 3000 A, 4500 A, 6000 A and 10000 A.

The ratio between the service short-circuit capacity and the rated short-circuit capacity is a factor, k, given in Table 18 of *BS EN 60898-1*, which for ease of reference has been reproduced in this Guide.

Table 4.5 Short-circuit capacities according to of *BS EN 60898-1: 2003*

I_{cn}	k
≤ 6 000 A	1
> 6 000 A ≤ 10 000 A	0.75*
> 10 000 A	0.5**

* Maximum value of I_{cs} : 6000 A
** Maximum value of I_{cs} : 7500 A

4.4.2 *BS 3871*

Although *BS 3871: Part 1: 1965 - Specification for miniature and moulded case circuit-breakers. Miniature air-break circuit-breakers for a.c. circuits* was withdrawn in July 1994, *BS 3871* MCBs may still be encountered when carrying out work in existing installations.

The short-circuit capacity of a *BS 3871* MCB is indicated by a Capital 'M' followed by the rated duty in kilo-amps (kA). For example, if the short-circuit capacity of a particular MCB was 3000 A this would be identified as M3 on the circuit-breaker.

BS 3871 MCBs were available in a range of types according to their instantaneous tripping current, as given in Table 2 of that standard, and shown in Table 4.6, below.

Table 4.6 Instantaneous tripping current by type for *BS 3871* MCBs

MCB type	Instantaneous tripping current	
1	above 2.7 I_n	Up to and including 4 I_n
2	above 4 I_n	Up to and including 7 I_n
3	above 7 I_n	Up to and including 10 I_n
4	above 10 I_n	Up to and including 50 I_n
B	above 3 I_n	Up to and including 5 I_n
C	above 5 I_n	Up to and including 10 I_n
D	above 10 I_n	Up to and including 20 I_n

4.5 Residual current devices

A Residual current device (RCD) monitors the algebraic sum of the currents in the line and neutral conductors (the residual current) at the point where it is installed in a circuit, and mechanically interrupts the circuit when this sum exceeds a preset value (the rated residual operating current, $I_{\Delta n}$).

Published by Certsure LLP © Certsure LLP (January 2015)

The following definition is given in Part 2 of *BS 7671*.

Residual current device (RCD). A mechanical switching device or association of devices intended to cause the opening of the contacts when the residual current attains a given value under specified conditions.'

The term RCD therefore includes:

- RCCB (residual current operated circuit-breaker without integral overcurrent protection),
- RCBO (residual current operated circuit-breaker with integral overcurrent protection),
- SRCD (socket-outlet incorporating an RCD),
- Portable RCD - an RCD formed of a suitable association of devices including current transformers, a residual current sensor, a test button and a circuit-breaker.

4.5.1 RCCBs to *BS EN 61008* and *BS 4293*

A residual current operated circuit-breaker without integral overcurrent protection (RCCB) is **not** designed to perform the function of protection against overcurrent (overload current or fault current).

A circuit, controlled by an RCCB must therefore be provided with a means for protection against overcurrent, such as suitable circuit-breakers or fuses.

RCCBs should comply with *BS EN 61008-1: 2004 - Specification for residual current operated circuit-breakers without integral overcurrent protection for household and similar uses (RCCBs) – Part 1: General rules.*

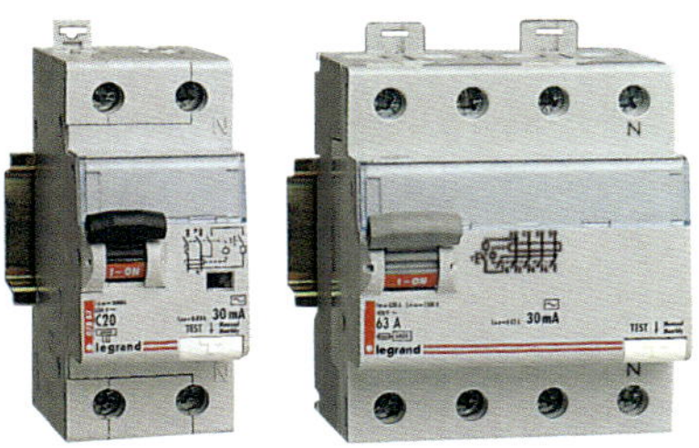

Fig 4.6 RCCBs for DIN rail mounting for use in an enclosure such as consumer unit.

Photograph courtesy of Legrand Electric Ltd

Although *BS 4293: 1983 Specification for Residual current-operated circuit-breakers* was withdrawn in December 2009, *BS 4293* RCDs might still be encountered when carrying out work in existing installations. For this reason, information relating to the requirements for their testing is included in Section 16.3.10 of this Guide.

4.5.2 RCBOs to *BS EN 61009*

A residual current operated circuit-breaker with integral overcurrent protection (RCBO) is designed to perform the function of protection against overcurrent, as well as that of an RCD.

RCBOs are often used as circuit protective devices in consumer units and distribution boards (see Fig 4.7).

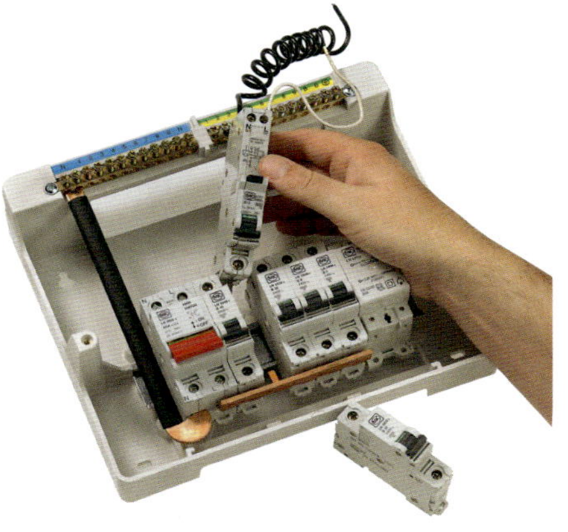

Fig 4.7 RCBO being installed into a consumer unit

Photograph courtesy of MK Electric Ltd

RCBOs should comply with *BS EN 61009-1: 2012 Residual current operated circuit-breakers with integral overcurrent protection for household and similar uses (RCBOs) — Part 1: General rules*

Published by Certsure LLP © Certsure LLP (January 2015)

4.5.3 Classification of RCDs (RCD type)

When used to describe the operating characteristics of an RCD, the term 'type' relates to the frequency and shape of current waveform for which tripping is assured.

In alternating current circuits, particularly those supplying electronic equipment, even though the voltage is a sine wave, the current flowing in the circuit can be non-sinusoidal and may have a d.c. component. In domestic installations the increased use of electronic devices, in particular the use of electric vehicle charging systems and inverters in micro-generators systems means that many circuits now draw non-sinusoidal current.

When RCDs of the type designed to operate with a sinusoidal current are used in circuits supplying electronic equipment that draw a non-sinusoidal current then the RCD may not function satisfactorily.

To provide installers of RCDs with guidance as to the ability of an RCD to function satisfactorily when carrying current with specified waveforms, product standard committees have developed a number of standard performance criteria known as type tests. These performance criteria are used to confirm the performance of the RCD is of a certain 'type'; the 'type' being indicated by using the classifications AC, A, B or F. The British Standard applicable to Type B and F RCDs is *BS EN 62423: 2012*.

For each of the standard RCD 'types', in addition to providing description of the current waveforms for which tripping is assured Fig 4.8 shows the symbols used to provide the user with a visual indication of the particular current waveforms.

Type AC RCDs, the type of RCD used in most electrical installations, may not operate satisfactorily when used in circuits supplying electronic equipment. For example Sections 710 (Medical locations), Section 712 (Solar photovoltaic power supply systems) and Section 722 (Electric vehicle charging installations) of *BS 7671* all include requirements for the use of RCDs other than type AC.

TYPE		Operation is assured for
AC		• residual sinusoidal alternating currents, whether suddenly applied or slowly rising.
A		• as for type AC and, in addition, residual pulsating direct currents and residual pulsating direct currents superimposed on a smooth direct current of 6 mA.
B	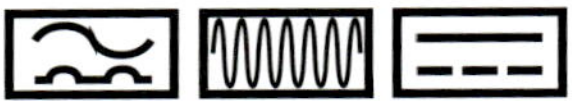	• as for type A, and in addition: residual sinusoidal alternating currents up to 1000 Hz, residual alternating currents superimposed on a smooth direct current of 0.4 times the rated residual operating current, residual pulsating direct currents superimposed on a smooth direct current of 0.4 times the rated residual operating current and residual direct currents which may result from rectifying circuits.
F		• as for type A, and for residual currents from mixed frequencies up to 1000 Hz

Fig 4.8 Suitability of various types of RCD

Published by Certsure LLP © Certsure LLP (January 2015)

4.5.4 RCD protected socket-outlets

SRCDs should comply with *BS 7288: 1990 Specification for Socket-outlets incorporating residual current devices (SRCDs).*

The use of an SRCD does not preclude the need to provide RCD protection to the final circuit supplying the SRCD where this is required by *BS 7671* (such as for the purposes of Regulation 522.6.102 or 522.6.103, relating to cables concealed in a wall or partition, or for one of the other purposes mentioned in Table 4.7 of Section 4.5.4 of this Guide.

Fig 4.8 Examples of SRCDs (socket-outlets with RCDs)

Photograph courtesy of Legrand Electric Ltd

4.5.5 Typical applications for RCDs in domestic premises

Table 4.7 overleaf summarises the typical applications and rated residual currents for RCDs as required by *BS 7671* that are applicable to installations in domestic and similar premises.

Table 4.7 Applications for RCDs in domestic premises.

Application	Requirement	Relevant *BS 7671* Regulation(s)
Additional protection (against electric shock) – General, ADS	$I_{\Delta n}$ = 30 mA	411.3.3; 415.1.1; 415.1.2
Fault protection shock – General, ADS, in TN system	As required in order to achieve required disconnection time i.e. $I_{\Delta n}$ = 30; 100; 300; 500 mA	411.4.9
Fault protection – General, ADS, in TT system Note: RCD protection is preferred for fault protection in TT systems (411.5.2 refers)	As required in order to achieve required disconnection time, and to ensure that $R_A \times I_{\Delta n} = 50$ V	411.5.3
Additional protection – cables without mechanical protection concealed in walls and partitions	$I_{\Delta n}$ = 30 mA	522.6.201; 522.6.202
Additional protection – all low-voltage circuits either serving the location containing a bath or a shower or passing through zones 1 or 2 but not serving the location	$I_{\Delta n}$ = 30 mA	701.411.3.3
Additional protection – all circuits of a sauna (except sauna heater unless specifically stated as being required by the manufacturer)	$I_{\Delta n}$ = 30 mA	703.411.3.3
Additional protection of circuit supplying equipment of floor and ceiling heating systems of Class II construction or equivalent insulation	$I_{\Delta n}$ = 30 mA	753.415.1

Published by Certsure LLP © Certsure LLP (January 2015)

Table 4.7 (continued) Applications for RCDs in domestic premises.

Application	Requirement	Relevant *BS 7671* Regulation(s)
Solar photovoltaic installations	Where the inverter does not provide simple separation and RCD protection is required to provide either fault protection or additional protection a Type B RCD required. (Where the inverter is not able to feed fault current into the electrical installation a Type B device is not required)	712.411.3.2.1.2
Electric vehicle charging installations	Every charging point to be individually protected by a 30 mA RCD that shall interrupt all live conductors. The RCD shall be a Type A device unless the current has a d.c. component exceeding 6 mA when the RCD should be Type B device.	722.531.2.101

4.6 Overvoltage protection and surge protective devices (SPDs)

Section 443 of *BS 7671* is concerned with protection against overvoltages of atmospheric origin or due to switching actions. Amongst other things, it contains methodologies for determining whether overvoltage protection measures are required for an installation, based on factors such as its usage and occupancy, its geographical location, and the means by which a supply is delivered to the premises or around the installation.

Section 443 does not consider direct lightning strikes on the low voltage lines of the public supply network or to the electrical installation (See Regulation 443.1.1).

Where the low voltage system supplying an installation has no overhead lines, and there are no low voltage overhead lines within the installation, *BS 7671* does not require protection against overvoltages of atmospheric origin to be provided so long as the equipment within the installation has an impulse withstand voltage in accordance with that of the appropriate category given in Table 44.3 of *BS 7671* (Regulation 443.2.1 refers).

Table 4.8 gives a summary of the equipment impulse withstand categories and the corresponding minimum impulse withstand voltages.

When applying the requirements of Section 443, a suspended cable that has insulated conductors and an earthed metallic covering is not considered to be an overhead line; it is considered to be equivalent to an underground cable.

Table 4.8 Summary of impulse withstand categories and voltages

Impulse withstand category	Summary of the category	Examples of equipment likely to be found in domestic or similar premises	Minimum impulse withstand voltage required (kV)*
IV	Equipment likely to be located on the supply side at the origin of the installation	Energy meters Service cut-outs	6
III	Equipment forming part of the fixed installation	Consumer units Circuit-breakers Fixed equipment	4
II	Mobile equipment having some degree of protection against transient overvoltages, typically connected via plug and socket-outlet	Household white goods and appliances Portable power tools	2.5
I	Mobile equipment having a reduced impulse withstand voltage and designed to be connected to circuits to which transient overvoltage limitation measures have been applied	Household white goods and appliances Portable power tools	1.5

* For installations falling within the scope of this Guide, the nominal voltage of the installation is assumed to be 230/240 V.

Published by Certsure LLP © Certsure LLP (January 2015)

Where the requirement of Regulation 443.2.1, discussed previously, does not apply (that is where there is a low voltage overhead line in the supply to, or within, the installation, Section 443 contains two methods by which the need to provide SPDs can be assessed.

- AQ criteria method (based on the number of thunderstorm days per year).
- Risk assessment method.

4.6.1 AQ criteria method

This method can be applied where an installation is either supplied by a low voltage system that contains overhead lines, or the installation itself contains overhead lines.

If the installation is geographically placed such that it is likely to be exposed to **not** more than 25 thunderstorm days per year (external influence category AQ1), nc additional protection against overvoltage is required where the equipment within the installation meets the relevant impulse withstand voltage stated in Table 44.3 of *BS 7671* and as summarised in Table 4.8 of this Guide (Regulation 443.2.3 refers).

If the installation is geographically placed such that it is likely to be exposed to **more than** 25 thunderstorm days per year (AQ2), protection against overvoltage of atmospheric origin should be provided. The protection level of any SPD provided for this purpose should not exceed the level for overvoltage category II (Regulation 443.2.3) – which is 2.5 kV for installations having a nominal voltage of 230 V.

4.6.2 Risk assessment method

This method recognises five consequential levels of protection, in which the consequences considered relate to:

1. human life (continuity of operation of medical equipment etc)
2. public services (effects on transport infrastructure, public services and the like)
3. commerce and industry (loss/disruption of business activities)
4. groups of individuals (in large residential and public buildings
5. individuals (small to medium sizes residential buildings etc) (Regulation 443.2.4).

Levels 1, 2 and 3 above fall outside the scope of this Guide and so are not considered any further.

Regulation 443.2.4. gives a formula that can be applied to designs for installations falling within levels 4 and 5 to determine whether overvoltage protection is required for a particular property.

Most domestic premises in the United Kingdom will not require the installation of SPDs.

 Published by Certsure LLP © Certsure LLP (January 2015)

Chapter 5

Protection against electric shock

Published by Certsure LLP © Certsure LLP (January 2015)

Protection against electric shock

5.1 General

The fundamental rule of protection against electric shock is that:

- live parts, such as energised conductors, must not be accessible and
- conductive parts which are accessible, such as metal enclosures of equipment or metal pipes, must not be live.

The two conditions, above, must be achieved both in normal (no fault) conditions and under single fault conditions (such as a fault between a live conductor and a metal casing).

Protection under normal conditions is achieved by basic protection.

Basic protection is defined as:

- protection against electric shock under fault-free conditions and is provided to protect persons or livestock coming into direct contact with live parts.

A live part is defined as:

- a conductor or conductive part intended to be energised in normal use, including a neutral conductor but, by convention, not a PEN conductor.

Figs 5.1 and 5.2 illustrate a person coming into contact with live parts.

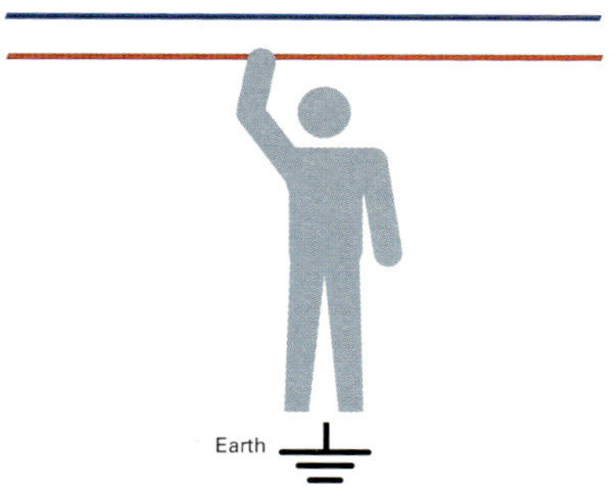

Fig 5.1 A person coming into contact with a live conductor whilst in contact with Earth

Fig 5.2 A person coming into contact with live conductors at different potentials

Published by Certsure LLP © Certsure LLP (January 2015)

Fault protection provides protection for persons or livestock coming into contact with exposed-conductive-parts which have become live under single fault conditions. An exposed-conductive-part is defined as 'a conductive part of equipment which can be touched and which is not a live part but which may become live under fault conditions.' Fig 5.3 illustrates how a person could receive an electric shock under single fault conditions.

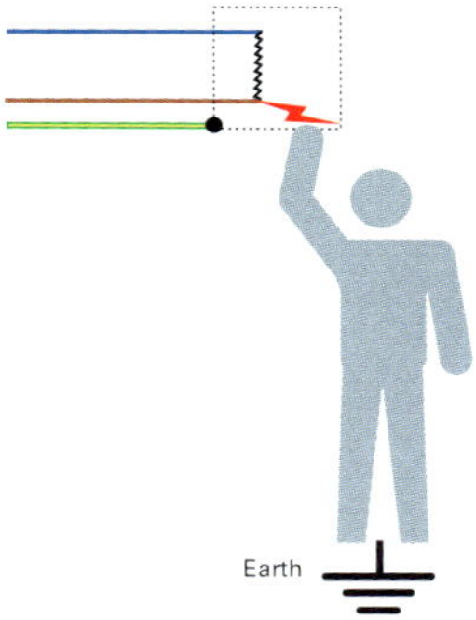

Fig 5.3 Single fault conditions.

The person in Fig 5.3 is in contact with the metal enclosure of an item of Class I electrical equipment which has become live under earth fault conditions. The potential of the metal enclosure is higher than that of the main earthing terminal of the installation (and that of Earth), because of a potential difference created by the passage of earth fault current through the impedance of the circuit protective conductor.

The protective measures of ADS, double or reinforced insulation, electrical separation to supply a single item of current-using equipment and extra-low voltage provided by separated extra-low voltage (SELV) or protective extra-low voltage (PELV) are recognised in *BS 7671* (Regulation 410.3.3 refers) with the measure of ADS being the measure that is employed in almost every electrical installation.

A protective measure, such as Automatic Disconnection of Supply (ADS) or double or reinforced insulation must consist of a provision for basic protection and a provision for fault protection.

In the case of ADS, basic protection is provided by insulation and/or barriers and enclosures while fault protection is provided by protective earthing, protective bonding and automatic disconnection in the case of a fault (see Regulation 411.1). As can be seen, the basic and fault protective provisions are independent.

In the case of reinforced insulation, basic protection and fault protection are both provided by the reinforced insulation between live and accessible parts (Regulation 412.1.1 (ii)).

5.2 Provisions for basic protection

Basic protection, or protection against direct contact with live parts, provides protection under normal conditions and is provided by insulation and/or barriers or enclosures.

Where insulation provides basic protection it must completely cover the live part. Such insulation must only be able to be removed by destruction, for example, by stripping the insulation from an insulated conductor prior to its termination (Regulation 416.1 refers).

Where barriers or enclosures provide basic protection they must:

- provide a degree of protection of at least IPXXB or IP2X, with permitted exceptions for access and replacement of parts (See Regulations 416.2.1 and 416.2.4),
- provide a degree of protection of IPXXD or IP4X for any readily accessible horizontal top surface (Regulation 416.2.2),
- be firmly secured in place and have sufficient stability and durability taking into account the external conditions (Regulation 416.2.3).

5.3 Protective measure: Automatic disconnection of supply (ADS)

The protective measure of ADS is employed in almost every electrical installation and consists of basic protection, fault protection and, for some circuits and locations, additional protection.

- Basic protection is provided by basic insulation of live parts and/or by barriers or enclosures (See 5.2 above).

Published by Certsure LLP © Certsure LLP (January 2015)

- Fault protection is provided by protective earthing, protective equipotential bonding and automatic disconnection in the event of a fault (Regulation 411.1) and is discussed further later in this chapter.
- Additional protection by one or more RCDs having a rated residual operating current ($I_{\Delta n}$) not exceeding 30 mA must be provided for specified circuits (see Regulation Group 522.6, Regulations 411.3.3, 701.411.3.3 and 703.411.3.3 for example).

5.3.1 Protective earthing

Protective earthing requires all exposed-conductive-parts to be connected to a protective conductor which in turn is connected to the Main Earthing Terminal and hence, via the Earthing Conductor to the means of earthing. In addition, a protective conductor must be run to and terminated at each point in the wiring and at each accessory except a lampholder having no exposed-conductive-parts and suspended from such a point. (Regulation 411.3.1.1 refers).

5.3.2 Protective equipotential bonding

In each installation, protective equipotential bonding conductors (formerly referred to as main bonding conductors) complying with Chapter 54 are required to connect extraneous-conductive-parts, including those listed below, to the main earthing terminal:

- water installation pipes,
- gas installation pipes,
- other installation pipework and ducting,
- central heating and air conditioning systems,
- exposed metallic structural parts of the building.

Any connection of a lightning protection system to the protective equipotential bonding should be carried out in accordance with *BS EN 62305*.

Where an installation serves more than one building, such as a dwelling with a detached garage with lighting and socket-outlets, the requirements for protective equipotential bonding must be provided in both buildings (the dwelling and the garage) where applicable.(Regulation 411.3.1.2 refers.)

 © Certsure LLP (January 2015)

5.3.3 Automatic disconnection in case of a fault

The impedance of the earth fault loop and the characteristics of the relevant protective device must be co-ordinated such that when an earth fault occurs, the fault current is of sufficient magnitude to operate the circuit protective device, such as a fuse, circuit-breaker or RCD to automatically disconnect the supply to the faulty circuit within a prescribed time.

A protective device such as a fuse, circuit-breaker or RCD is to be provided and the circuit designed such that the device operates and disconnects the circuit in the event of a fault of negligible impedance between a line conductor and an exposed-conductive-part or a protective conductor.

The disconnection must occur within the times stated in Table 5.1.

Table 5.1 Maximum disconnection times (where U_0 is greater than 120 V and less than or equal to 230 V)

	Final circuit not exceeding 32 A	Final circuit exceeding 32 A	Distribution circuit
TN system	0.4 s	5 s	5 s
TT system	0.2 s	1 s	1 s

With reference to Table 5.1, where in a TT system disconnection is achieved by an overcurrent protective device and protective equipotential bonding is connected to all the extraneous-conductive-parts within the installation in accordance with Regulation 411.3.1.2, the maximum disconnection times applicable to a TN system may be used.

In a TN system the characteristics of the protective devices and the circuit impedances are required to fulfil the following requirement (Regulation 411.4.5):

$$Z_S \times I_a \leq U_0 \times C_{min}$$

where:

Z_S is the impedance in ohms (Ω), the fault loop comprising:

- the source,
- the line conductor up to the point of the fault, and

Published by Certsure LLP © Certsure LLP (January 2015)

- the protective conductor between the point of the fault and the source.

I_a is the current in amperes (A) causing the automatic operation of the disconnecting device within the time specified in Table 5.1

U_0 is the nominal a.c. rms or d.c. line voltage to Earth in volts (V).

C_{min} is the minimum voltage factor.

Table 5.2 indicates where maximum values for earth fault loop impedance for a U_0 of 230 V can be found in *BS 7671*.

Table 5.2 Locations of maximum earth fault loop impedance values within *BS 7671* with respect to required disconnection time.

Required disconnection time (s)	Protective device type	Table Number within the 411.4 Regulation group
0.4	*BS 88-2* fuse systems E and G *BS 88-3* fuse system C *BS 3036* *BS 1362*	41.2
0.4 to 5	*BS EN 60898* circuit-breaker *BS EN 61009* RCBO	41.3
5	*BS 88-2* fuse systems E and G *BS 88-3* fuse system C *BS 3036* *BS 1362*	41.4

In a TT system every exposed-conductive-part should be connected to a common earth electrode via the Main Earthing Terminal, (Regulation 411.5.1 refers).

If two or more protective devices are in series, the exposed-conductive-parts may be connected to separate earth electrodes corresponding to each protective device. It should be noted that any simultaneously accessible exposed-conductive-parts must be connected to the same earthing system (Regulation 411.3.1.1 refers).

The preferred protective device for fault protection is an RCD (Regulation 411.5.2) but where an RCD is used, as it will be in most cases, overcurrent protection must nonetheless be provided by a fuse or a circuit-breaker, or, alternatively a residual current operated circuit-breaker with integral overcurrent protection (RCBO) may be employed.

Where an RCD is used for fault protection, the following conditions are to be fulfilled for the circuit in question (Regulation 411.5.3 (i) refers):

- the required disconnection time will be achieved, that is:
  - 0.2 s maximum for a.c. final circuits not exceeding 32 A (Regulation 411.3.2.2), or
  - 1 s maximum for a.c. distribution circuits and final circuits exceeding 32 A (Regulation 411.3.2.4),
- $R_A \times I_{\Delta n} \leq 50$ V

Where:

R_A is the sum of the resistances of the earth electrode and the protective conductor connecting it to the exposed-conductive-parts (in ohms)

$I_{\Delta n}$ is the rated residual operating current of the RCD.

Maximum values for earth fault loop impedance for RCDs which do not have time delay are given in Table 41.5 of *BS 7671*.

5.3.4 Additional protection by RCD

BS 7671 recognises this measure as reducing the risk of electric shock in the event of the failure of

- basic protection, and/or
- fault protection or
- the carelessness of users of the installation.

The measure must not be used as the sole means of protection against contact with live parts (Regulation 415.1.2 refers) and so a protective measure such as ADS must always be provided.

Regulation 410.3.2 states that additional protection by means of an RCD having a rated residual operating current ($I_{\Delta n}$) not exceeding 30 mA is specified as part of a protective measure under certain conditions of external influences, such as:

- where cables are concealed in walls and partitions (see Regulations 522.6.201 and 522.6.202),

Published by Certsure LLP © Certsure LLP (January 2015)

- in certain special locations as given in the corresponding Part 7, such as circuits supplying equipment in bathrooms (Section 701).

Where a person makes contact with a live part of a circuit to which this type of protection is provided, and such contact results in a current to Earth of not less than the rated residual operating current of the RCD ($I_{\Delta n}$), the RCD disconnects the supply to the circuit. Note that the RCD cannot detect the current flowing through the body of a person making contact between line and neutral conductors only, and will therefore provide no protection in this circumstance.

The requirements for the rated residual operating current ($I_{\Delta n}$) and operating time of the RCD are given in Regulation 415.1.1. The device is required to have an $I_{\Delta n}$ not exceeding 30 mA and an operating time not exceeding 40 ms at a residual current of 5 $I_{\Delta n}$.

With certain exceptions, additional protection by the use of an RCD is required to be provided for every socket-outlet rated at 20 A or less and for mobile equipment rated at 32 A or less for use outdoors (Regulation 411.3.3 refers).

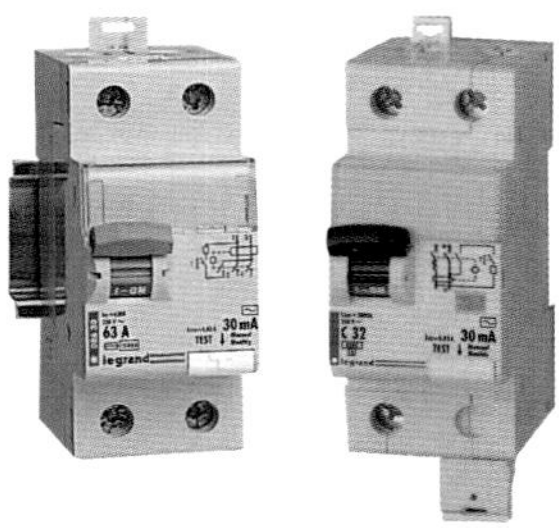

Fig 5.4 Typical forms of RCDs used to provide additional protection

Photograph courtesy of Legrand Electric Ltd.

For the following conditions Regulation 411.3.3 permits socket-outlets to be exempt from the requirement for RCD protection.

1. For installations other than those in a dwelling, where a documented risk assessment demonstrates that RCD protection is not necessary.
2. Where a specifically labelled or otherwise suitably identified socket-outlet that has been provided for the sole purpose of connecting a particular item of equipment. An example would be a single socket-outlet installed to supply a chest freezer provided the socket was installed very close to or behind the freezer (suitably identified by position) or labelled 'Chest freezer only'.

5.4 Protective measure: Double or reinforced insulation

Double or reinforced insulation is a protective measure in which either basic protection is provided by basic insulation, and fault protection is provided by supplementary insulation, or both basic and fault protection are provided by reinforced insulation between live parts and accessible parts (Regulation 412.1.1).

Double or reinforced insulation is intended to prevent the appearance of a dangerous voltage on the accessible parts of electrical equipment through a fault in the basic insulation. There is no provision for the connection of exposed metalwork of the equipment to a protective conductor, and there is no reliance upon the earthing arrangements in the fixed wiring of the installation.

The protective measure of double or reinforced insulation is generally applicable in all situations.

In the case of an installation in a domestic premises, double or reinforced insulation will not be the main protective measure and will be applied in addition to ADS for a circuit or part thereof, or for an item of current-using equipment such as a luminaire. Indeed its use as the sole protective measure in premises, such as domestic installations, not under effective supervision is precluded by Regulation 412.1.3.

It is likely that most equipment providing this protective measure will comprise type-tested items bearing the symbol shown in Fig 5.5.

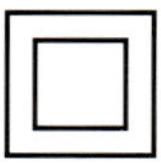

Fig 5.5 Class II equipment should be identified by the Class II construction mark.

A wiring system is considered to meet the requirements of Regulation Group 412.2 for basic and fault protection if:

- the rated voltage of the cable is not less than the nominal system voltage and at least 300/500 V, and

Published by Certsure LLP © Certsure LLP (January 2015)

- adequate mechanical protection of the basic insulation of the cable has been provided by one or more of the following:
  - the non-metallic sheath of the cable, or
  - non-metallic trunking or ducting or non-metallic conduit (see Regulation 412.2.4.1).

5.5 Protective measure: Electrical separation

There are two main principles underlying protection by electrical separation:

- neither the source of the supply,
- nor any live parts of the separated circuit should be connected to any other circuit or to Earth.

Thus, in the event of a single fault to an exposed-conductive-part of equipment in the separated circuit, fault protection is afforded because there is no path for fault current to return to the source.

Electrical separation is a protective measure in which:

- barriers or enclosures provide basic protection, and
- simple separation of the separated circuit from other circuits and from Earth provides fault protection. That is, basic insulation provides the required separation between circuits or between a circuit and Earth. (Regulation 413.1.1 refers).

Unless the particular requirements of Regulation Group 418.3 are met with regard to factors such as provision of warning notices, basic and fault protection, and earthing and bonding arrangements, this protective measure is limited to the supply of one item of current-using equipment supplied from one unearthed source with simple separation.

For an installation in a dwelling, the only likely application of the use of electrical separation is a shaver supply unit complying with *BS EN 61558-2-5*.

Shaver supply units to *BS 3535* may still be found in older installations and may remain in service subject to their remaining in a sound, serviceable condition.

Fig 5.6 illustrates a person holding an electric shaver, in contact with a metal radiator. Because electrical separation has been utilised as the protective measure, there can be no potential difference across that person. Where a shaver supply unit incorporates a metal plate, this normally is required to be earthed.

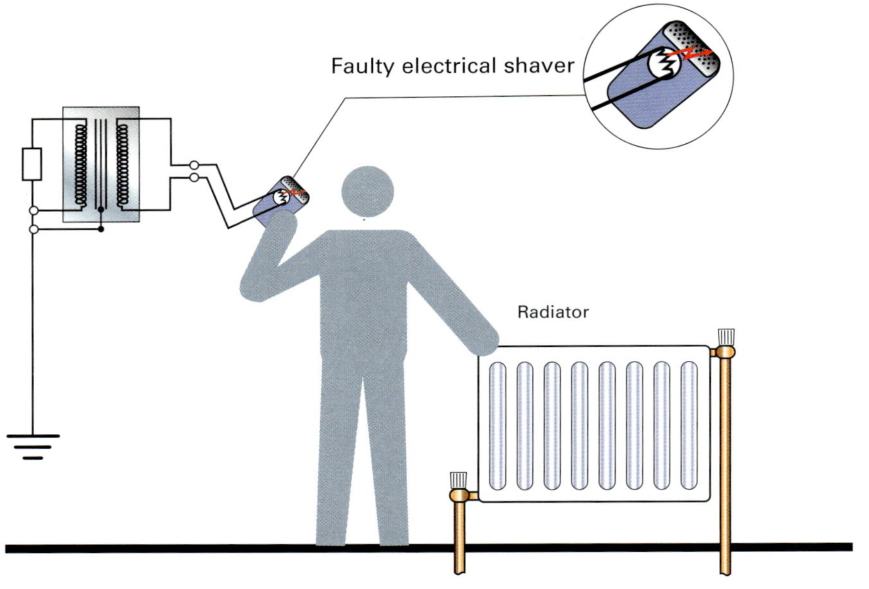

Fig 5.6 Electrically separated shaver socket-outlet

5.6 Protective measure: Extra-low voltage provided by SELV or PELV

Section 414 of *BS 7671* contains the requirements for extra-low voltage provided by SELV or PELV, which are summarised below.

A SELV system is an extra-low voltage system electrically separated from Earth and from other systems. To this end the live parts of a SELV system must have:

- basic insulation between live parts and other SELV or PELV circuits,
- basic insulation between live parts and Earth, and

Published by Certsure LLP © Certsure LLP (January 2015)

- protective separation from live parts of any other systems by means of double or reinforced insulation, or basic insulation and protective screening for the highest voltage present. (Regulation 414.4.1 refers).

A PELV system meets all the requirements for a SELV system except those relating to electrical separation from Earth.

Protection by extra-low voltage provided by SELV or PELV requires all of the following.

- Limitation of voltage in the SELV or PELV system to the upper limit of voltage Band I (50 V a.c. or 120 V d.c.).
- Protective separation of the SELV or PELV system from all circuits other than SELV and PELV circuits.
- Basic insulation between the SELV or PELV system and other SELV or PELV systems.
- For SELV systems only, basic insulation between the SELV system and Earth.

Extra-low voltage is generally considered insufficient to present a hazard of electric shock (as defined) in dry situations where the person protected has a body resistance within normal limits. In certain locations, including those containing a bath or shower, the requirements of Part 7 limit the value of the extra-low voltage to lower than 50 V a.c. or 120 V d.c.

If the nominal voltage of a SELV or PELV circuit exceeds 25 V a.c. or 60 V d.c., or if the equipment will be immersed, basic protection must be provided by insulation, or barriers or enclosures.

5.6.1 Requirements for basic protection and fault protection

Basic protection and fault protection are provided subject to all of the listed conditions being met.

- The nominal voltage cannot exceed the upper limit of voltage Band I.
- The supply is from a permitted source (see Section 5.6.2 of this Guide).
- The following requirements applicable to SELV or PELV circuits are met. (Regulation 414.2 refers).

If the system is supplied from a higher voltage system by equipment which provides at least simple separation between that system and the extra-low voltage system but which does not meet the requirements for a SELV and PELV source, the requirements for FELV may be applicable. In such cases, the system does not meet the requirements for SELV or PELV and therefore must not be used in an application where use of these systems is required.

5.6.2 Sources for SELV and PELV

The following sources may be used for SELV and PELV systems.

- A safety isolating transformer in accordance with *BS EN 61558-2-6*.
- A source of current providing a degree of safety equivalent to that of the safety isolating transformer such as a motor-generator with windings providing equivalent isolation.
- An electrochemical source (e.g. a battery) or another source independent of a higher voltage circuit (e.g. a diesel-driven generator).
- Certain electronic devices complying with appropriate standards, where provisions have been taken to ensure that, even in the case of an internal fault, the voltage at the outgoing terminals cannot exceed 50 V a.c. or 120 V d.c. Higher voltages at the outgoing terminals are, however, permitted if it is ensured that, in case of contact with a live part or in the event of a fault between a live part and an exposed-conductive-part, the voltage at the output terminals is immediately reduced to 50 V a.c. or 120 V d.c. or less.
- A mobile source supplied at low voltage, e.g. a safety isolating transformer or a motor-generator, shall be selected and erected in accordance with the requirements for protection by the use of double or reinforced insulation.

Sources for the supply of SELV and PELV circuits must comply with the above requirements and this is to ensure that there is no possibility of a dangerous voltage occurring in a SELV or PELV circuit due to an internal fault in the source. For example, an insulation breakdown in a step-down transformer could raise the voltage of the secondary circuit to a dangerous level.

Published by Certsure LLP © Certsure LLP (January 2015)

Such danger is prevented by using a safety isolating transformer complying with *BS EN 61558-2-6*, or one of the other sources, listed previously in this section. Fig 5.7 shows a suitable transformer together with circuit configuration and identifying symbol.

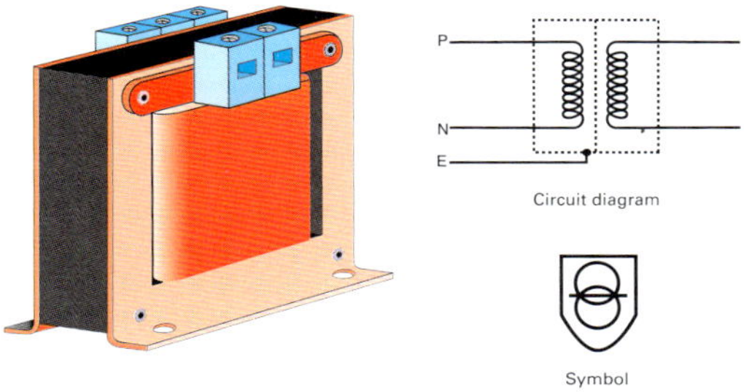

Fig 5.7 Safety isolating transformer complying to *BS EN 61558-2-6*.

SELV and PELV circuit wiring is electrically (and often physically) separated from the wiring of higher voltage systems. This is to minimise the possibility of introducing a higher voltage into a SELV or PELV circuit in the event of an insulation failure in a conductor of a higher voltage circuit.

To further reduce the risk of electric shock, conductors and exposed-conductive-parts of a SELV system are not connected to Earth or to other systems.

BS 7671 requires further protection in locations of increased shock risk, including bathrooms, rooms containing a shower, and swimming pools. Such protection may include limiting the nominal voltage to a value not exceeding 25 V a.c. r.m.s or 60 V ripple-free d.c. (or in some cases an even lower limit), and the provision of insulation, barriers or enclosures for protection against contact with live parts.

In some locations of increased shock risk, such as certain zones of swimming pools, SELV is the only protective measure against electric shock permitted by *BS 7671*.

The wiring systems of SELV or PELV circuits are required to have protective separation from the live parts of other circuits, which must have at least basic insulation, and this separation must be achieved by one of the following arrangements.

- SELV and PELV circuit conductors enclosed in a non-metallic sheath or insulating enclosure in addition to basic insulation.

- SELV and PELV circuit conductors separated from conductors of circuits at voltages higher than Band I by an earthed metallic sheath or earthed metallic screen.
- Circuit conductors at voltages higher than Band I may be contained in a multi-conductor cable or other grouping of conductors if the SELV and PELV conductors are insulated for the highest voltage present.
- The wiring systems of other circuits are in compliance with the requirements of Regulation 412.2.4.1 for double or reinforced insulation.
- Physical separation.

5.6.3 Accessories

A socket-outlet or luminaire supporting coupler in a SELV or PELV circuit must be dimensionally incompatible with those used for any other system in use in the same premises (see Regulation 414.4.3). Additionally Regulation 414.4.4 states that plugs and socket-outlets in a SELV system must not have a protective conductor contact.

5.6.4 Additional requirements for SELV circuits.

Exposed-conductive-parts of a SELV circuit must not be connected to Earth, or to protective conductors or to exposed-conductive-parts of another circuit.

If exposed-conductive-parts of a SELV circuit could come into contact, either fortuitously or intentionally, with the exposed-conductive-parts of other circuits, the requirements of the protective measure SELV will not have been met and protection against electric shock will no longer depend solely on protection by SELV, but also on the protective measures applied to the circuit to which the latter exposed-conductive-parts are related.

5.7 Additional protection

Additional protection is required, in many cases, to supplement the selected protective measure under certain conditions of external influences and in certain special locations (see Part 7 of *BS 7671*). The additional protection required may be either provided by:

- an RCD, or
- supplementary equipotential bonding.

Published by Certsure LLP © Certsure LLP (January 2015)

5.7.1 RCDs

RCDs having a rated residual operating current ($I_{\Delta n}$) not exceeding 30 mA and an operating time not exceeding 40 ms at a residual current of 5 $I_{\Delta n}$ can be installed to provide additional protection in the event of failure of the provision for basic protection and/or the provision for fault protection or the carelessness of users in a.c. systems. (Regulation 415.1.1 refers).

However, the use of such devices is not recognised as a sole means of protection and does not obviate the need to apply one of the recognised protective measures (Regulation 415.1.2).

5.7.2 Supplementary equipotential bonding.

Where supplementary equipotential bonding is installed it must include all simultaneously accessible exposed-conductive-parts of fixed equipment and extraneous-conductive-parts.

Such bonding must be connected to the protective conductors of all equipment of the installation or part thereof or location including those connected to socket-outlets where installed.

The resistance R between simultaneously accessible exposed-conductive-parts and extraneous-conductive-parts should fulfil the following condition in an a.c. system:

$$R \leq \frac{50\,V}{I_a}$$

Where

I_a is the operating current in amperes of the protective device.

If the protective device is an RCD, I_a is the rated residual operating current ($I_{\Delta n}$). If the protective device is a fuse or circuit-breaker it is the current that causes operation in 5 s. (Regulation 415.2.2 refers).

IET WIRING REGULATIONS
UPDATED TO:
17TH EDITION
BS 7671:2008
Amd 3: 2015

Other publications which have been updated to reflect the latest requirements of *BS 7671*: 2008 (Amendment 3): 2015 include -

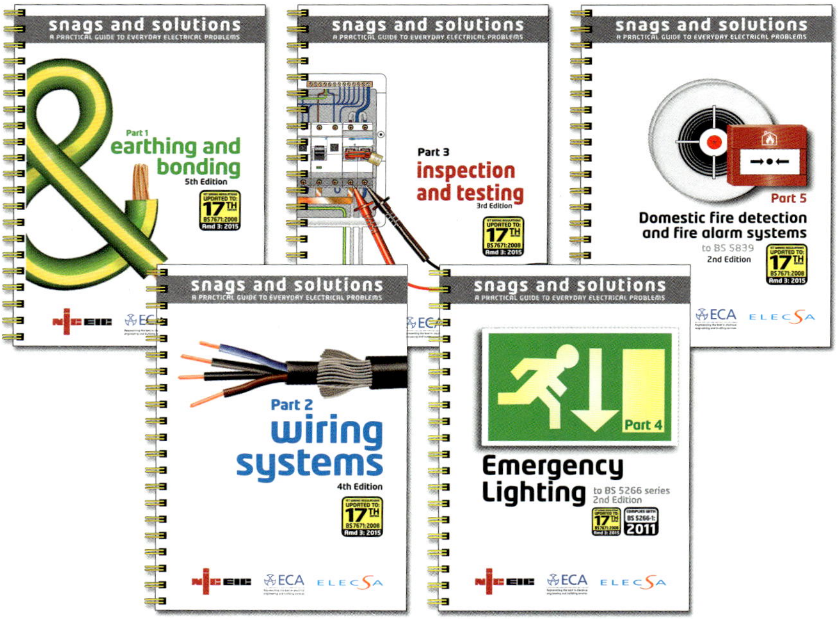

To order this or any other publication contact

NICEIC customers:	0843 290 3485	www.niceicdirect.com
ELECSA/ECA customers:	0333 321 8225	www.elecsa.co.uk

Published by Certsure LLP © Certsure LLP (January 2015)

Chapter 6

Consumer unit and distribution board arrangements

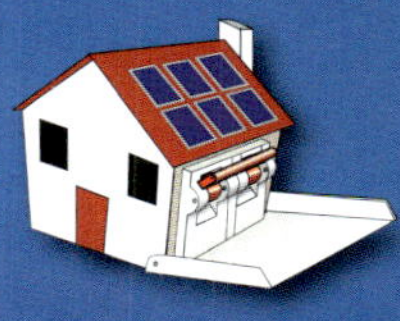

Published by Certsure LLP © Certsure LLP (January 2015)

6.1 Introduction

This chapter explains the requirements of *BS 7671* affecting the choice of consumer unit.

A consumer unit is a particular type of distribution board designed for use in domestic and similar installations. A consumer unit should meet the requirements of *BS EN 60439-3: 1991* (as amended) *Low-voltage switchgear and controlgear assemblies. Particular requirements for low-voltage switchgear and controlgear assemblies intended to be installed in places where unskilled persons have access to their use. Distribution boards.*

Consumer units may be designed for either surface or flush fitting, and prior to the introduction of Amendment 3 could have either a metal or plastic casing and front cover. Traditionally consumer units have been designed for either surface or flush fitting, with either a metal or plastic casing and front cover. However, Regulation 421.1.201, introduced by Amendment 3, requires that in addition to complying with the requirements of *BS EN 61439-3*, consumer units and similar switchgear assemblies used in domestic premises shall either have their enclosures manufactured from non-combustible material or be enclosed in a cabinet constructed of non-combustible material complying with Regulation 132.12. A note to Regulation 421.1.201 states that a ferrous metal such as steel is an example of a non-combustible material. To allow manufacturers of consumer units to make the necessary changes to their manufacturing processes the date for the implementation of Regulation 421.1.201 is January 2016.

The effect of the introduction of Regulation 421.1.201 is that after January 2016, in domestic premises, unless housed in a cabinet constructed of non-combustible material, it is likely that only consumer units constructed of steel will be permitted. The installation of metal clad consumer units in installations forming part of a TT system is dealt with in Section 6.6 of this guide.

In its simplest form, a consumer unit comprises:

- an enclosure,
- a main switch that, when operated, disconnects both live (i.e. line and neutral) conductors (Regulation 537.1.4 refers),
- a number of protective devices such as fuses, circuit-breakers and RCDs,

 Published by Certsure LLP © Certsure LLP (January 2015)

- neutral and earth termination bars,
- interconnecting busbars/wiring.

However, and with reference to the definition of a consumer unit given in Part 2 of *BS 7671*, a consumer unit may also contain signalling devices, transformer units and the like. It should be noted that any component to be so installed should be type-tested as suitable for use within the particular make and model of consumer unit.

Many consumer units in older (pre-17th Edition) installations forming part of a TN system do not contain RCDs and where supplementary protection has been provided, the RCD is installed some way downstream of the origin of the final circuits, for example to protect individual socket-outlets likely to be used to supply portable equipment for use outdoors.

In the case of consumer units in installations forming part of a TT system, consumer units having an RCD main switch are not uncommon. Such an arrangement would be unlikely to satisfy the requirement of Regulation 314.1 (i) to minimise inconvenience in the event of a fault in anything other than the simplest of installations.

The 17th Edition saw the introduction of more instances where RCD protection will be required. This has resulted in equipment manufacturers producing consumer units that are more modular in nature and which allow for a configuration that closely meets those requirements of *BS 7671* that are applicable to a particular installation in most cases.

Starting with a basic enclosure and main switch, a consumer unit may be arranged with:

- each final circuit protected individually by an RCBO (see Section 4.5.2 of this Guide) and allowing the possibility of circuit-breaker or fuse protection for those circuits where RCD protection is not appropriate,
- a 'split' board containing two or more 2-pole RCCBs, each protecting a number of final circuit ways, which have circuit-breakers or fuses fitted to provide overcurrent protection,
- a 'split' board containing two or more 2-pole RCCBs as described above but with a number of final circuit ways not protected by the RCCBs thus allowing the possibility of fault protection by a circuit-breaker or fuse for those circuits where RCD protection is not required.

6.2 Split-load arrangements

Split-load consumer units can provide a range of circuit configurations. Where it is not necessary to provide individual RCD protection for each final circuit, a suitable split-load consumer unit enables those circuits requiring RCD protection to be provided with such protection as a group, whilst also making provision for any circuits that do not require RCD protection.

Fig 6.1 shows one such arrangement for a consumer unit for use in an installation forming a part of a TN system in which the main switch supplies two RCCBs. The final circuits of the installation are shared between the two RCCBs in a manner that would minimise disruption and avoid danger in the event of a fault.

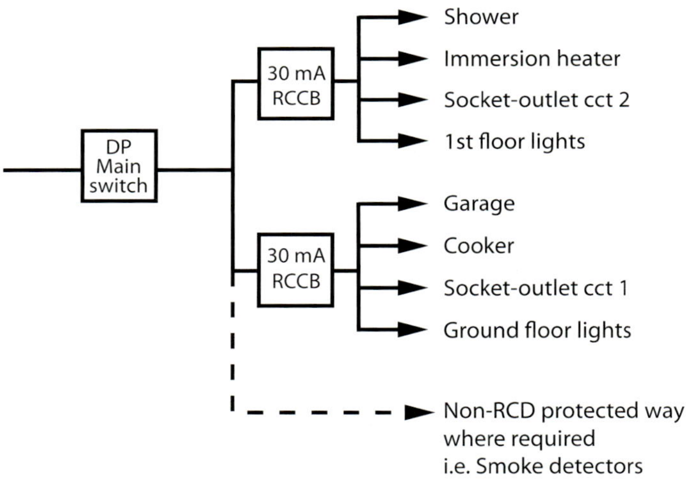

Fig 6.1 Split-load consumer unit for a domestic installation forming part of a TN system

Published by Certsure LLP © Certsure LLP (January 2015)

The broken line denotes a circuit 'way' that is not protected by an RCCB. Such an arrangement might be appropriate for, say, a supply to a chest freezer (see Regulation 411.3.3 (b) or fire detector/alarm units where the circuit has been run on the surface, or if concealed within a wall, the cable:

- incorporates an earthed metallic covering, or
- has been installed in earthed conduit, trunking or ducting, or
- otherwise sufficiently mechanically protected to prevent penetration by nails, screws or similar

(Regulations 522.6.201 to 522.6.203 refer, the requirements of which are explained further in Chapter 11 of this Guide).

It should be noted that it remains acceptable to connect fire detector/alarm units of a Grade D system to a separately electrically protected and regularly used local lighting circuit using 'soft skinned' cables such as thermoplastic insulated/sheathed cable typically used to wire the lighting and other circuits within the dwelling. (Clause 15.5 a) ii) of *BS 5839-6: 2013* refers). The rationale behind this provision is that the householder or occupier can be expected to know that the fire detector/alarm(s) are connected to the lighting circuit. As a result, any loss of supply to the detector/alarms would be unlikely to go unnoticed and the supply to them would be quickly reinstated.

Whilst, preferably, a circuit supplying fire detector/alarm units should not be protected by an RCCB, such protection should be provided where it is necessary to do so in order to meet the requirements of *BS 7671* (such as in installations forming a part of a TT system).

6.3 Advantages and disadvantages of a split-load consumer unit

A split-load consumer unit has the major advantage that it can provide a convenient means of meeting the requirements of *BS 7671* for most dwellings.

RCD protection of a group of final circuits has the disadvantage that an earth fault sufficient to operate the RCCB protecting any one circuit of the group will cause all the circuits of that group to be disconnected.

The installation designer needs to decide whether the use of a split-load consumer unit for a particular application meets with the requirements of Regulations 314.1 and 314.2. Regulation 314.1 requires every installation to be divided into circuits as necessary to avoid danger and minimise inconvenience in the event of a fault, and to facilitate safe operation, inspection, testing and maintenance. Regulation 314.2 requires, amongst other things, that due account shall be taken of the consequences of the operation of any single protective device.)

6.4 Series connected RCDs

A configuration employing a split-load consumer unit with RCDs connected in series is illustrated in Fig 6.2. Such a configuration might be found in an installation forming part of a TT system.

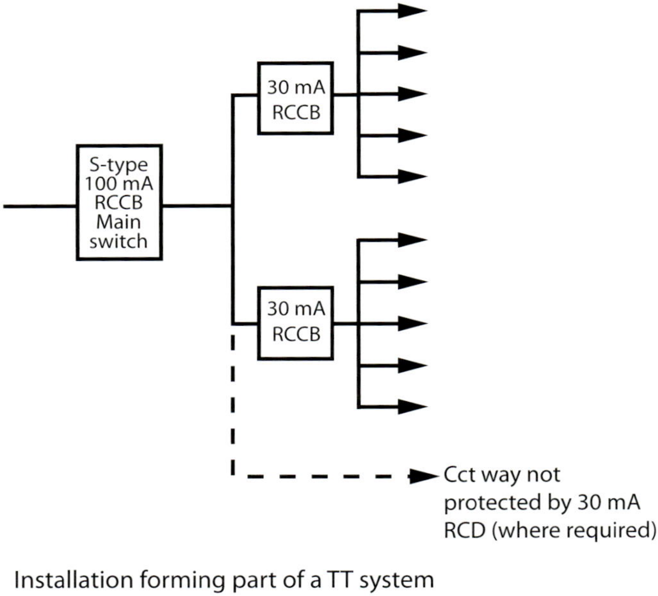

Fig 6.2 Simplified diagram of a split-load consumer unit with time-delay RCCB main-switch for use in a domestic installation forming part of a TT system

Published by Certsure LLP © Certsure LLP (January 2015)

Fig 6.3 shows a consumer unit having a main switch and a number of circuit 'ways' protected individually by RCBOs. Where RCCB protection is not appropriate (as discussed previously in Section 6.2) a particular circuit could be provided with fault protection by a circuit-breaker or fuse.

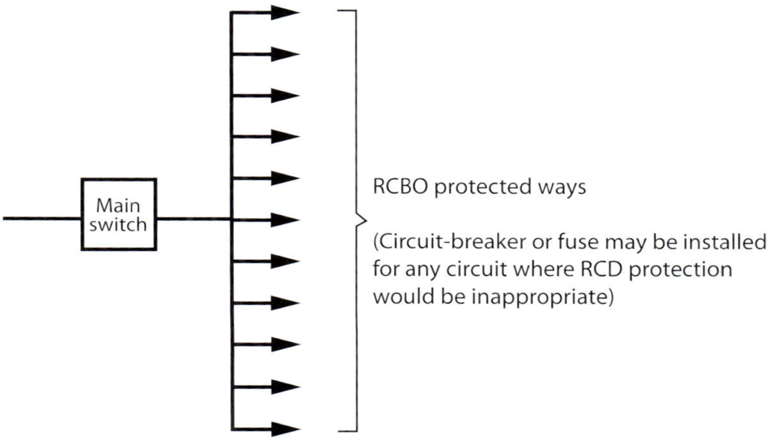

Fig 6.3 Consumer unit suitable for use with circuit-breakers, fuses and RCBOs

Given the ever reducing cost of RCBOs, the use of a consumer unit such as that shown in Fig 6.3 becomes an increasingly attractive proposition.

6.5 Discrimination between RCDs in series

On occasion, a domestic electrical installation may include RCDs connected in series, particularly where the installation forms part of a TT system. Where such RCDs provide fault protection or otherwise prevent danger, and where discrimination in their operation is necessary to prevent danger, Regulation 531.2.9 of *BS 7671* requires that their characteristics are such that discrimination is achieved.

The need for discrimination is also implicit in Regulation 314.2. The regulation requires that a separate circuit be provided for each part of an installation that needs to be separately controlled for compliance with the Regulations or otherwise to prevent danger, so that such circuits remain energised in the event of failure of any other circuit of the installation, due account being taken of the consequences of the operation of any single protective device, such as a 30 mA RCCB at the origin protecting the whole installation.

Discrimination between RCDs connected in series is required for reasons other than to prevent danger. Regulation 314.1 requires that every installation be divided into circuits as necessary, not only to avoid danger but to minimise inconvenience in the event of a fault.

Even where it is not strictly necessary to provide discrimination between RCDs to prevent danger or to minimise inconvenience, it is considered good practice to do so, not the least because it can greatly simplify identification and/or location of the device that has operated.

Where two or more RCDs are connected in series, discrimination will generally be achieved by selecting time-delayed characteristic(s) for the upstream device(s).

Discrimination between RCDs can really only be accomplished by delaying the tripping of the RCD upstream such that the downstream RCD has time to disconnect the fault before the time delay of the upstream RCD has expired.

It should be noted that RCDs used for additional protection are not permitted to have an operating time delay. Such RCDs must, as stated in Regulation 415.1.1, have a rated residual operating current (I_n) not exceeding 30 mA and have an operating time of not more than 40 ms when exposed to a residual current of 5 $I_{\Delta n}$.

Furthermore, where RCDs with a time delay are used to provide fault protection, the total operating time is not to exceed the applicable maximum disconnection times required by Chapter 41 of *BS 7671*.

British Standards *BS EN 61008-1* and *BS EN 61009-1* for residual current operated circuit-breakers with and without integral overcurrent protection, respectively, classify residual current operated circuit-breakers with time-delay as 'type S' (for selectivity).

6.6 Installations forming part of a TT system

Prior to Amendment 3, the majority of consumer units installed in domestic installations employed a plastic all-insulated enclosure. However, from 1st January 2015, to meet the requirements of Regulation 421.1.201, all consumer units in domestic premises are

Published by Certsure LLP © Certsure LLP (January 2015)

required to either have enclosures manufactured from a non-combustible material or be mounted in an cabinet constructed from a non-combustible material. It is very likely that, from 1st January 2016[1], this will result in the majority of consumer units installed in domestic installations being manufactured from ferrous metal (generally steel).

Although metal-clad consumer units are non-flammable, compared with equivalent all-insulated units, metal clad units have the disadvantage that, as illustrated by Fig 6.4, if installed in an installation forming part of a TT system, a fault between the incoming tails and the metal case will result in the metal case becoming live. This will cause all other exposed-conductive-parts connected to the main earthing terminal, to rise to a potential approaching close to that of the single phase supply to earth. Due to the high external earth fault loop impedance of a typical TT system, the service fuse may not operate and in this situation all the earthed metalwork within the installation will be at a dangerously high voltage.

Fig 6.4 Effect of fault to earth between incoming tails and the metal case of a consumer unit.

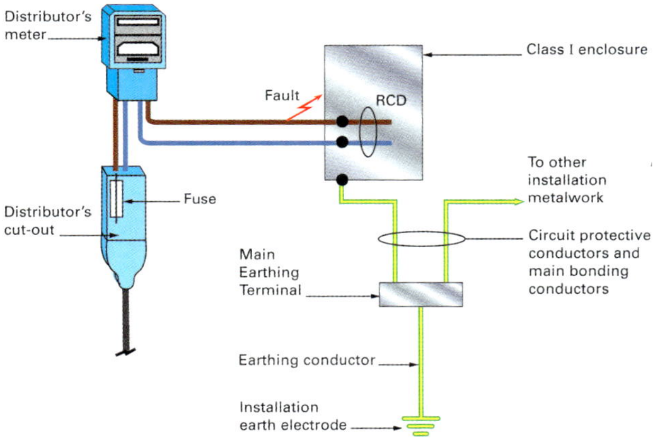

[1]Although Amendment 3 of *BS 7671* comes into effect on the 1st July 2015, to allow manufacturers of consumer units to make the necessary changes in their production processes, Regulation 421.1.201 does not come into effect until 1st January 2016.

To alleviate this danger described in the previous paragraph, Regulation 531.41 requires that for an installation which is part of a TT system and is protected by a single[2] RCD then either:

1. the RCD is placed at the origin of the installation, or
2. the part of the installation between the origin and the device (RCD in the consumer unit) complies with the requirements for the protection by the use of class II equipment or equivalent insulation.

Although it is possible to comply with the requirements of Regulation 531.41 by installing an RCD in the tails between the energy meter (or in some cases an isolating switch) and the consumer unit the most cost effective method, and the approach generally adopted, is to use thermoplastic or thermosetting insulated and sheathed meter tails taken through and insulated bushes, located where the tails enter the metallic consumer unit or protective cabinet. Details of typical insulated bushes are shown in Fig 6.5.

Fig 6.5 Insulated bushes for entries to Class I enclosures

[2]Note: Although Regulation 531.4.1 refers to an installation protected by a single RCD, the regulation also applies where an installation is protected by a number of RCDs, each of which is supplied from the origin without the intervention of another RCD.

Published by Certsure LLP © Certsure LLP (January 2015)

6.7 Protective conductor currents

The cumulative addition of protective conductor currents (commonly referred to as 'earth leakage current'), during normal operation in the individual circuits of a group of circuits protected by an RCD, can be sufficient to cause the RCD to operate. For example, where suppressors or filters such as capacitors are connected between line, neutral and circuit protective conductors, a protective conductor current will flow which can cause operation of the RCD. In such cases, the installation designer will need to decide whether the use of a split-load consumer unit for a particular application meets with the requirements of Regulation 531.2.4, which requires an RCD to be so selected and the electrical circuits so subdivided such that any protective conductor current likely to occur during normal operation of the connected load(s) does not cause unnecessary tripping of the device.

Information technology and other equipment that exhibits significant protective conductor currents are subject to the requirements of Regulation Group 543.7, the requirements of which are summarised in Section 3.8 of this Guide.

6.8 Location

The chosen location for a consumer unit must provide reasonable access to facilitate the operating of switches and protective devices, and to permit inspection, maintenance and access to all connections. Where a consumer unit is mounted in a cabinet, compartment or similar, this should be done in a way that does not impair access.

Switches and protective devices housed in a consumer unit need to be accessible to the user. It should not be necessary, for example, to make use of a ladder or other temporary platform to gain access. Where the user is likely to be elderly or infirm, access to switches and protective devices should comply with *BS 8300: 2009 + A1: 2010 - Design of buildings and their approaches to meet the needs of disabled people – Code of practice.*

6.9 Mounting height

Part M of the Building Regulations, for England and Wales, requires reasonable provision to be made for people to gain access and to use the building and its facilities. Guidance on meeting the requirements of Part M is given in Approved Document M.

Section 8 of Approved Document M, which applies to new dwellings, includes the objective of assisting people whose reach is limited to use the dwelling more easily. The document indicates that wall-mounted switches, socket-outlets and control devices should be installed at a height between 450 mm and 1200 mm above finished floor level, the dimensions taken from the bottom and top edges of the equipment respectively. Similar recommendations are given for compliance with the building regulations in Scotland and in Northern Ireland by Technical Handbooks and Technical Booklets respectively.

6.10 Dwellings liable to flooding

Guidance on installations where there is a risk of flooding is given in a publication entitled Preparing for floods, and a free electronic copy can be downloaded by visiting the Department of Communities and Local Government's website, at **www.communities.gov.uk**

When undertaking work at a dwelling at risk of flooding, items such as consumer units and energy meters (subject to agreement with the distributor) should be mounted above the expected flood level if practicable.

Published by Certsure LLP © Certsure LLP (January 2015)

Isolation and switching

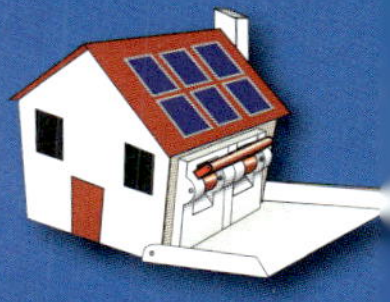

Isolation and switching

7.1 Introduction and terminology

Section 537 of *BS 7671* details the requirements for isolation and switching that should be provided for an electrical installation and the electrical equipment or machinery therein as appropriate to the particular circumstances.

The term 'isolation and switching' refers to four distinct functions, namely:

- isolation,
- switching off for mechanical maintenance,
- emergency switching, and
- functional switching.

The purpose of isolation (as defined) is to provide protection for a person engaged in work on, or near to, electrical equipment. Once equipment has been securely isolated from the source of energy and any electrical energy has been discharged, persons should be able to safely access parts that would otherwise be live, or may become live, without the risk of danger from electric shock, electric arcing and/or explosion, or electric sparking (where this may cause fire and/or explosion) or from movement of electrically powered equipment and machines.

Every circuit must be capable of being isolated from each of the live supply conductors, with certain exceptions relating to a neutral conductor (Regulation 537.1.2 refers). A neutral conductor falls within the definition of a live conductor. With permitted exceptions for TN-S and TN-C-S systems, detailed below, it should be possible to isolate the neutral conductor of every circuit from the corresponding supply conductor (see Regulations 537.2.1.1 and 537.1.2).

A means of isolating and switching the supply on load must be provided as near as practicable to the origin of every installation. The means of isolation and switching is required to be a main linked switch or a linked circuit-breaker (Regulation 537.1.4 refers).

Isolation of the neutral conductor of a circuit in TN-S or TN-C-S systems is not generally required where that conductor can be reliably regarded as being connected to Earth by a suitably low impedance. However, isolation of the neutral is still required for a main switch of a single-phase installation intended for operation by ordinary persons (as defined) (Regulation 537.1.4 refers). This will be the case for domestic installations.

 Published by Certsure LLP © Certsure LLP (January 2015)

A group of circuits may be isolated by a common means (Regulation 537.2.1.1). However, where such an arrangement is being considered, the requirements of Regulation Group 314 relating to division of an installation must be taken into account.

A common example of a single device used to isolate a group of circuits is where the main switch of a consumer unit is operated (switched off), thereby isolating all of the outgoing circuits.

The requirements for the isolation of live supply conductors at the origin, as applicable to domestic and similar premises, are illustrated in Figures 7.1 to 7.3.

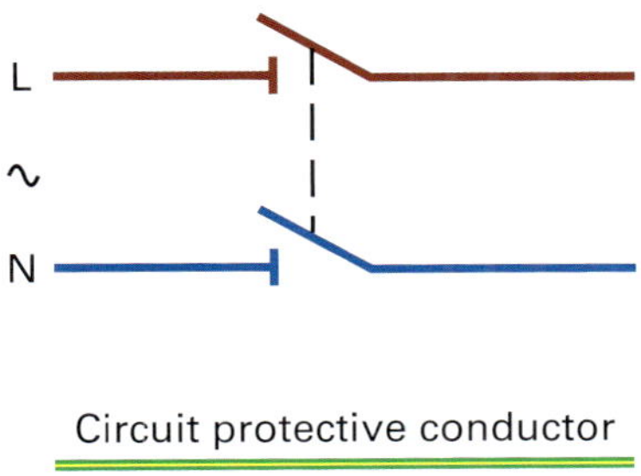

Fig 7.1 Isolation arrangement at the origin – TN-S system

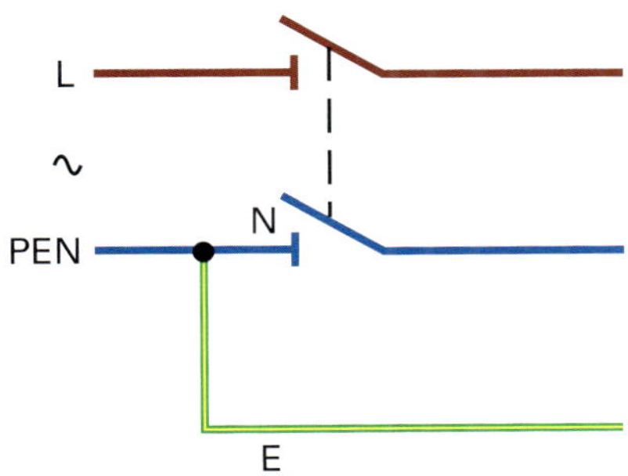

Fig 7.2 Isolation arrangement at the origin – TN-C-S system

 © Certsure LLP (January 2015)

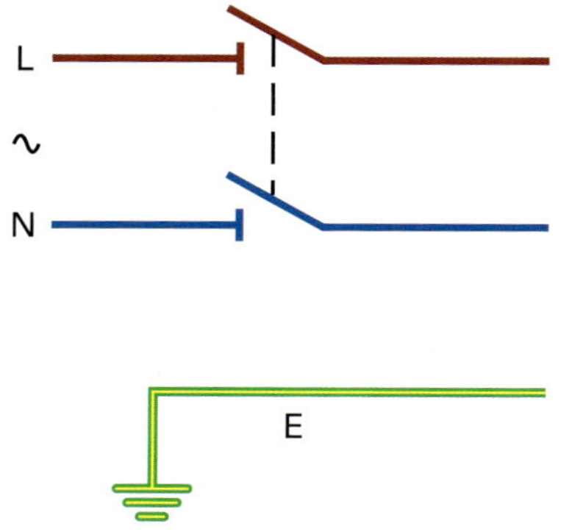

Fig 7.3 Isolation arrangement at the origin – TT system

In most installations, a circuit is formed at the origin consisting of 'meter tails' connecting to the consumer unit. For example, a single-phase domestic supply circuit may consist of either a *BS 1361* or *BS 88-3* fuse (in the service cut-out) connected by the meter tails to a consumer unit as illustrated in Figure 7.4.

Regulation 537.1.3 states that the isolation requirements for the meter tails may be met where a means of isolation meeting the requirements of Chapter 53 is provided by the distributor at the origin and said distributor agrees to its use for that purpose.

On occasion, an isolator may have been provided either as an integral part of the meter or as a separate item.

Persons working in domestic and similar premises should not attempt to access or withdraw the cut-out fuse(s) under any circumstances unless authorised to do so by the relevant distributor.

Isolation of other circuits of the installation should be achieved at the circuit protective device for the circuit(s) in question at the consumer unit.

Published by Certsure LLP © Certsure LLP (January 2015)

Note:
Do not attempt to access or withdraw the cut-out fuse unless authorised to do so by the relevant distributor

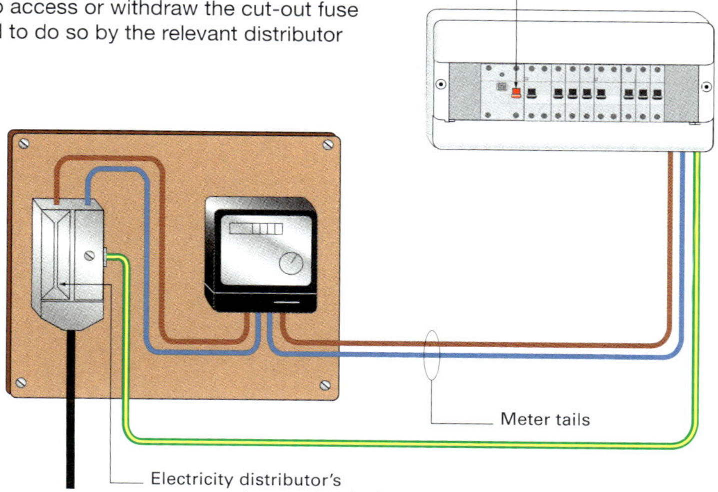

Fig 7.4 Means of isolation for meter tails

7.2 Installations supplied from more than one source

Where an installation is supplied from more than one source, a main switch (a means of isolation and switching the supply on load) must be provided for each source of supply. Such situations may arise in dwellings that have small-scale embedded generators, such as solar photovoltaic systems and domestic combined heat and power units. Additionally, where an installation has more than one supply, Regulations 514.15.1 and 537.1.6 require a durable warning notice to be permanently fixed and so placed as to warn any person seeking to isolate the installation of the need to operate the isolation and switching device for each source of supply.

Any device used for isolation must be non-automatic (Regulation 537.1) - that is, requiring manual operation. Further, any device used for isolation should be suitably positioned or durably marked such that the installation or the circuit that it isolates is clearly identifiable (Regulation 537.2.2.6).

7.3 Remote isolation

Where an isolating device for a particular circuit is located remotely from the location in which work activities will be carried out, provision must be made such that the means of isolation can be secured in the open position (Regulation 537.2.1.5 refers). The securing arrangement and the procedures put in place for its release must be such that closing of the means of isolation is not possible until it is safe to do so. Where the provision for securing in the open position takes the form of a lock or a removable handle, the key or handle is to be non-interchangeable with any others used for similar purposes within the installation.

7.4 Isolating devices

The particular requirements of *BS 7671* applicable to the devices providing isolation are summarised in Table 7.1 and further discussed in this chapter.

Table 7.1 Summary of requirements for isolation

Requirement	Regulations
Device to isolate all live supply conductors (with certain permitted exceptions)	537.1.2; 537.2.1.1; 537.2.2.1
A multipole device is preferable where multipole isolation is needed	537.2.2.5
Manual operation	537.1
The disconnection and separation is to be secure and the device is unlikely to intentionally re-close	537.2.1.2; 537.2.2.3
Isolation externally visible or clearly and reliably indicated	537.2.2.2
Permitted devices	Table 53.4; 537.2.2.5
Unsuitable devices	Table 53.4; 537.2.2.1
Marking	537.2.2.6
Discharge of stored energy	537.2.1.4
Provision for disconnection of the neutral conductor	537.2.1.7

Published by Certsure LLP © Certsure LLP (January 2015)

Devices for isolation, which must be suitable for manual (non-automatic) operation, are required to isolate all live supply conductors from the circuit concerned, except in TN-S or TN-C-S systems, where the neutral conductor need not be isolated or switched if it can be reliably regarded as being connected to Earth by a suitably low impedance. This exception does not apply to the main switch of household and similar premises where the means of isolation may be used by ordinary persons (as defined) (Regulation 537.1.4).

Where multipole isolation is required, it is preferable for the means of isolation to be a multipole isolating device. However, single-pole devices such as fuses or links situated adjacent to each other are permitted (Regulation 537.2.2.5 refers).

A device for isolation must be selected, and/or installed in such a way, as to prevent unintentional closure such as may be caused by mechanical shock, accidental knocks or vibration (Regulations 537.2.1.2 and 537.2.2.3 refer).

The position of the contacts or other means of achieving isolation are to be either externally visible or clearly and reliably indicated. Furthermore, the isolated position is to be indicated only when the specified isolation has been fully attained in each pole (Regulation 537.2.2.2 refers).

A plug and socket-outlet or similar device such as a luminaire support coupler may be selected for use as a means of isolation.

It should be noted that circuit-breakers, switches and other devices might **not** meet the requirements for a disconnector such that they are suitable as a means to provide isolation. It is important that such devices are not used for isolation purposes unless they meet the requirements of a disconnector as defined in Part 2 of *BS 7671*.

Table 53.4 of *BS 7671* provides guidance on the selection of devices in terms of their suitability to perform the functions of isolation, emergency switching and functional switching.

Some product standards, for example *BS EN 60947-3*, require the product to be marked with a symbol to indicate its suitability for isolation. Examples of the symbols used for some of the more common means of isolation are shown in Fig 7.5. The left hand column of the chart shows devices suitable for no-load isolation. The right hand column shows devices suitable for on-load making, breaking and isolating.

Isolating	Making, breaking and isolating
Disconnector 	Switch-disconnector 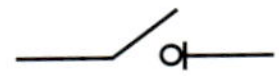
Disconnector-fuse 	Switch-disconnector-fuse 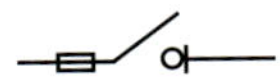
Fuse-disconnector 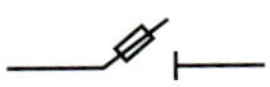	Fuse-switch-disconnector 

Fig 7.5 Symbols used for some of the more common means of isolation

Semiconductor devices must not be selected for the purposes of isolation (Regulation 537.2.2.1 refers).

7.5 Switching off for mechanical maintenance

Switching off for mechanical maintenance is provided for the benefit of persons who are not necessarily electrically-skilled and may not necessarily be competent to avoid the dangers which electricity may create. Great care must be taken, in the design and implementation of measures for switching off for mechanical maintenance, to ensure that they provide safe working conditions, particularly where non-electrically skilled persons are likely to be undertaking the maintenance.

7.6 Emergency switching

In domestic installations, there is generally no requirement to install devices such as emergency stop buttons. However, installers should be aware that even though *BS 7671* does not permit *BS 1363* plugs and socket-outlets to be selected as a means of providing emergency switching (Regulation 537.4.2.8), in an emergency such as a fire involving deep fat fryers or tumble dryer, the user may use a *BS 1363* plug and socket-outlet to disconnect the equipment.

 Published by Certsure LLP © Certsure LLP (January 2015)

When installing socket-outlets that may, in an emergency, be used to disconnect equipment such as that previously described, the installer should ensure that the socket-outlets are positioned so that, when the equipment is in use, the socket-outlets are readily accessible to the user.

7.7 Functional switching

A functional switching device should be provided for each part of a circuit that needs to be controlled independently of other parts of the installation (Regulation 537.5.1.1 refers). Regulation 537.5.1.3 states that all items of current-using equipment requiring control should be controlled by a functional switching device that is appropriate in relation to particular circumstances. In the case of appliances, the device for functional switching may be, and often is, an integral part of the appliance.

A single functional switch may be used to control several items of equipment where those items are intended to operate simultaneously, such as a lighting switch configured to control multiple downlighters in a single room.

Where there is possibility of confusion, a functional switch should be labelled to indicate its purpose. For example, where a functional switch controls a water heater in another part of the house or that otherwise might not readily be associated with the switch, the switch should be labelled to indicate its purpose. Where the purpose of a functional switch is clearly evident, a label need not be provided to indicate its purpose.

Functional switching is provided for the users of electrical installations for normal operating purposes to control items of current-using equipment. The equipment may be controlled either individually or in groups (see Figure 7.6).

Fig 7.6 Familiar functional switches

Photograph courtesy of Legrand Electric Ltd.

Isolation and switching

The functional switching/control of equipment may be either manual or automatic. A time switch is an example of an automatically-operated functional switch (see Figure 7.7).

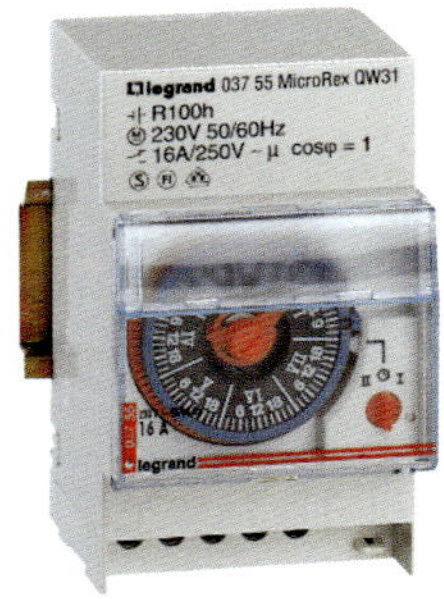

Figure 7.7 A time switch meets the definition of a functional switch

Photograph courtesy of Legrand Electric Ltd.

Examples of functional switches include:

- a switch in a socket-outlet,
- a contactor switching the supply to start and stop an electric motor,
- push buttons used to control a contactor or relay,
- a thermostat used to switch an immersion heater or central heating 'on' and 'off',
- a pressure switch or level switch used to control a pump,
- lighting switches and dimmers.

Functional switching devices are generally required to be capable of switching the load 'on' and 'off'. All functional switching devices are required by Regulation 537.5.2.1 to be suitable for the most onerous duty intended, and should be selected to have a utilisation category appropriate to the type of load being switched.

Published by Certsure LLP © Certsure LLP (January 2015)

Opening contacts are not essential

Functional switching devices do not necessarily have contacts that open and close. Rheostats, potentiometers, and semiconductor devices that control current electronically, such as a wall mounted dimmer switch, may be used as functional switching devices.

Disconnectors (no-load isolators), fuses and links are not considered to be suitable devices for functional switching and are not to be used for this purpose (Regulation 537.5.2.3 refers).

A plug and socket-outlet having a rated current not exceeding 32 A may be used for functional switching in a.c. circuits. (Table 53.4 of *BS 7671* refers).

Table 53.4 contains a note advising that circuit-breakers and RCDs are circuit-protective devices and as such they are not intended for frequent load switching. However, for the purposes of isolation or emergency switching the infrequent switching of circuit-breakers is acceptable. Where a more frequent duty is required manufacturer's instructions should be consulted and where necessary an alternative device provided.

IET WIRING REGULATIONS
UPDATED TO:
17TH EDITION
BS 7671:2008
Amd 3: 2015

Other publications which have been updated to reflect the latest requirements of *BS 7671*: 2008 (Amendment 3): 2015 include -

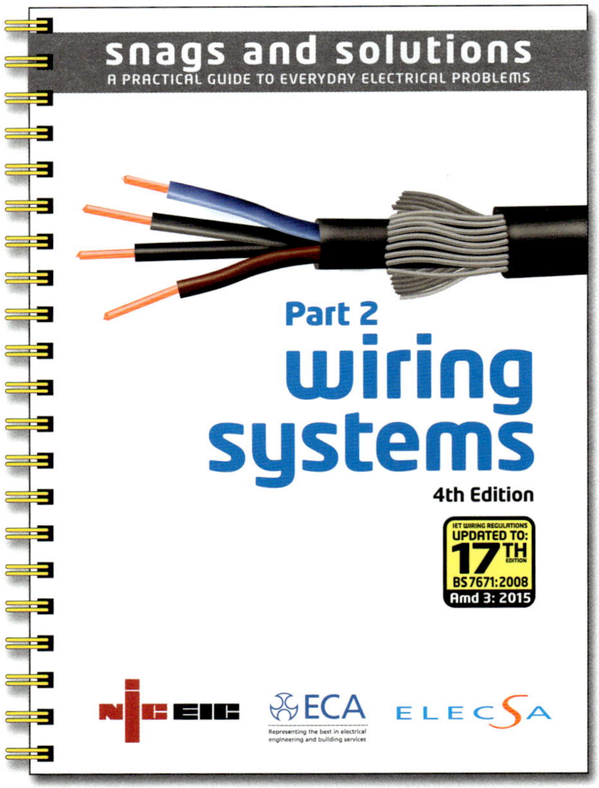

To order this or any other publication contact

NICEIC customers:	0843 290 3485	www.niceicdirect.com
ELECSA/ECA customers:	0333 321 8225	www.elecsa.co.uk

Published by Certsure LLP © Certsure LLP (January 2015)

Chapter

8

Identification and labelling

Identification and labelling

8.1 Introduction and general requirements

Labelling provided for identification, information or warning purposes should be clearly legible and durably marked. Any inscription on an item of equipment or a label should remain legible for the lifetime of the installation. For example, inscriptions might be engraved or embossed into suitable material, although other suitable methods of marking are not precluded.

In general, labels must be sized such that they are clearly visible from the normal viewing position. Any labels affixed to, or adjacent to, an item of equipment should be permanent.

Many labels may have black letters on a white background, but where identification of a device for isolation and switching forms part of a safety sign, or provides clarifying information supportive of a safety sign, then the label should comply with, and be colour-coded in accordance with, *BS ISO 3864-1:2011 Graphical symbols. Safety colours and safety signs. Design principles for safety signs and safety markings.*

For example, notices warning of the need to operate appropriate isolating devices and identifying their location should have black lettering on a yellow background. Fire equipment signs should have white lettering, and where necessary white directional arrows, on a red background. Additionally, the requirements of the *Health and Safety (Safety Signs and Signals) Regulations 1996* must be met, where applicable.

Labels should be fixed to equipment such as switchgear or controlgear by suitably secure means such as screws, rivets or adhesive. The means of fixing a label to an item of equipment should always be selected such that the integrity of the ingress protection of the enclosure is not compromised.

Consideration should always be given to the effects of environmental conditions such as heat, water, pollution or corrosive substances, when determining whether a label may be considered to be durably marked and permanent.

The following are examples of informative labels required by *BS 7671*.

- Periodic inspection and testing (date of last inspection and recommended date of next inspection)
- Identification of switchgear and controlgear

Published by Certsure LLP © Certsure LLP (January 2015)

- Location of means of isolation and switching
- Identification of source(s) of supply
- Identification of circuit protective devices
- Identification of current-using equipment
- Warning of dual supply where an installation includes a generating set such as a solar photovoltaic (pv) system or a wind-powered generator.

Any items of switchgear and controlgear are required to be provided with a label or some other suitable means of identification, to indicate their purpose, except where the purpose of the switchgear or controlgear is obvious (Regulation 514.1.1 refers).

8.2 Conductors

Changes to the colour identification of conductors in fixed wiring were introduced by Amendment No 2 to *BS 7671: 2001* on 31 March 2004. The new colours were the European harmonized colours. Installations commencing on site after 31 March 2006 were required to comply with Section 514 of *BS 7671* as amended and, as appropriate, cores to be identified with the harmonized colours. Installations commencing on site after 31 March 2004 and before 1 April 2006 were required to be installed in accordance with Amendment No. 2: 2004 or Amendment No 1: 2002 of *BS 7671: 2001*; that is they may use the harmonized colours or the old colours but not both. This section of this Guide is based on the use of the harmonized colours.

8.2.1 Single-phase installations

The line conductors of single-phase circuits should be identified by the colour brown. A neutral conductor, where identified by colour, must be identified by the colour blue (Regulation 514.4.1 refers). Protective conductors must be identified by the green-and-yellow colour combination specified in Regulation 514.4.2; that is, one colour covering not more than 70 % and the other colour covering at least 30 % of the coloured surface area.

8.2.2 Identification of switch-wires

Where a two-core and earth cable with a brown and a blue conductor is used for the wiring to a lighting switch, both the brown and blue conductors are used as line conductors, and so the blue conductor must be suitably identified at its terminations. Such identification will normally be accomplished by using brown sleeving at BOTH ends of the conductor (See Fig 8.1). Alternatively, a cable with both cores in brown may be used for such a purpose.

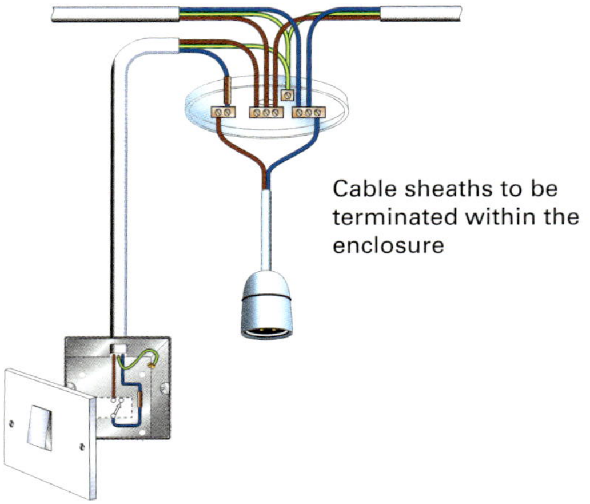

Fig 8.1 Identification of a one-way switch-wire

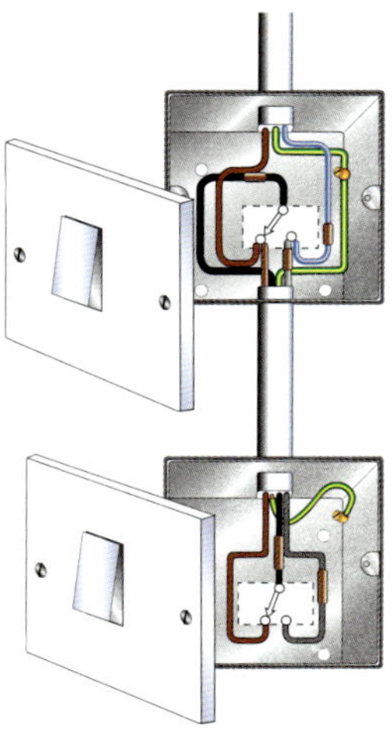

Where a flat three-core and earth cable with cores coloured brown, black and grey is used to connect two-way or two-way and intermediate lighting switches, all three conductors are line conductors, and so the black and grey conductors must, once again, be suitably marked typically by brown sleeving (see Fig 8.2).

Fig 8.2 Two-way switching

Published by Certsure LLP © Certsure LLP (January 2015)

8.2.3 Extensions, alterations or repairs to an existing single-phase installation

An extension, alteration or repair to an existing single-phase installation originally wired using an older cable colour coding system should be wired using the colours brown, blue, and green-and-yellow for the line, neutral and protective conductors respectively.

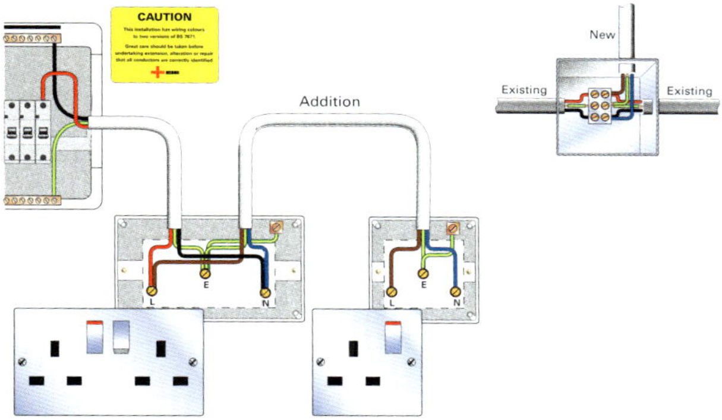

Fig 8.3 Requirements for a single-phase installation

For a single-phase installation, the extension, alteration or repair can then be considered to be unambiguously marked, and further marking at the interface between old and new wiring is not necessary, provided both of the following conditions are met (Regulation 514.1.3 refers).

- The existing cables are correctly identified by the colours of red for line conductor and black for neutral conductor.
- The new cables are correctly identified by the colours of brown for line conductor and blue for neutral conductor.

8.2.4 Identification of conductors – warning notice at the consumer unit or distribution board

If an extension, alteration or repair is made to an installation such that both brown and blue, and red and black, cable cores are present, a warning notice must be affixed at or near the appropriate distribution board or consumer unit (Regulation 514.14.1 refers).

Fig 8.4 Identification warning notice of conductor colours

8.2.5 Three-phase installations

The circuits of a new three-phase installation should be wired in the colours of brown, black and grey for the line conductors, and blue for the neutral conductor. The protective conductors remain green-and-yellow (see Fig 8.5). For single-phase circuits, the line conductors should be brown, irrespective of the supply phase to which they are connected.

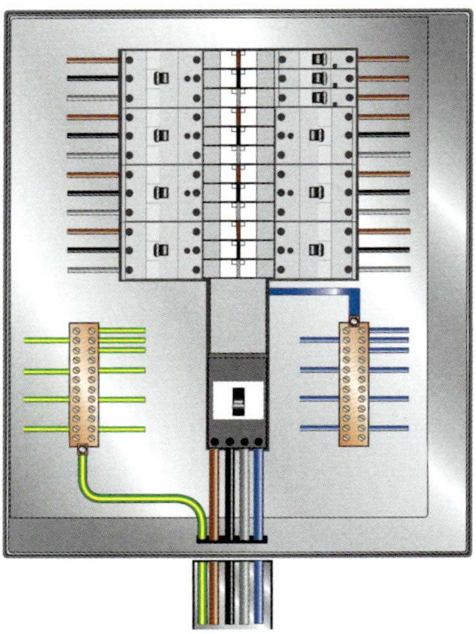

Fig 8.5 Identification requirements for three-phase installations

An extension, alteration or repair to an existing installation should be wired in the colours of brown, black, grey and blue, and green-and-yellow, as applicable (see Fig 8.6).

Published by Certsure LLP © Certsure LLP (January 2015)

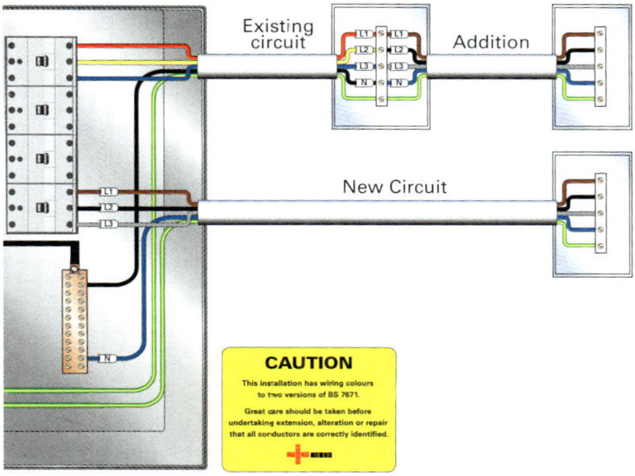

Fig 8.6 Extensions, alterations or repairs to an existing 3-phase installation

At the wiring interface(s) where an extension, alteration or repair is made with cable in the new colours to a three-phase installation wired in the old colours, unambiguous identification is required at the interface. Neutral conductors, where identified by colour, must be identified by the colour blue. Old and new line conductors should be fitted with sleeves marked L1, L2 and L3, and neutral conductors should be fitted with sleeves marked N to avoid any possibility of confusion (see Fig 8.7).

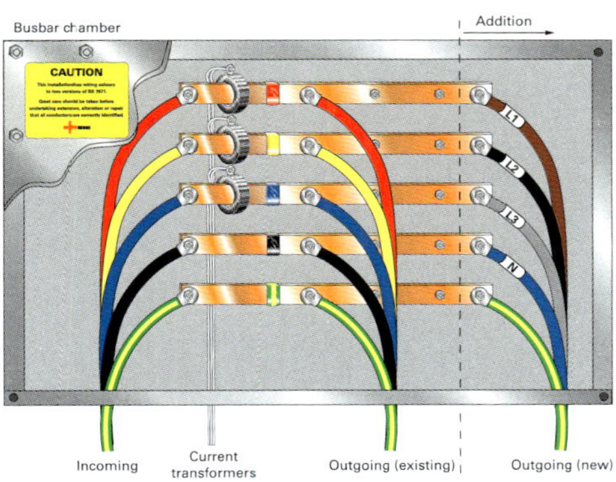

Fig 8.7 Three-phase busbar

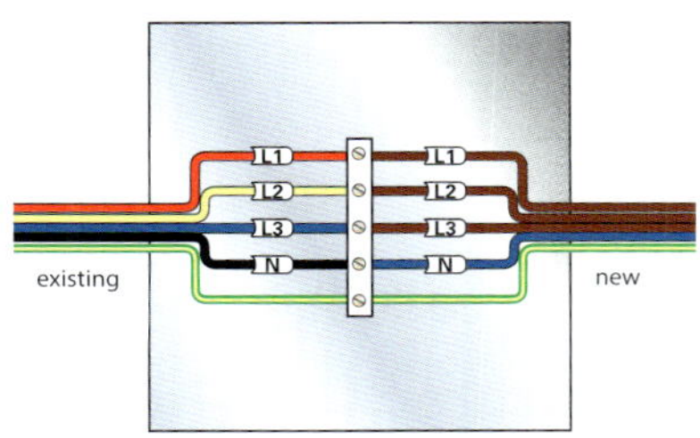

Fig 8.8 Alphanumeric identification

A permitted alternative arrangement is to use three single cores with insulation of the same colour, but unambiguous identification must be provided at the terminations. This could be achieved by using numbering or lettering (see Fig 8.8).

 © Certsure LLP (January 2015)

8.2.6 Summary of conductor identification

Fig 8.9 summarises the permitted cable colours for a.c. low voltage and extra-low voltage conductors.

Function	Colour	Alpha numeric
Protective conductors	Green-and-yellow	
Functional earthing conductor	Cream	
a.c. power circuit[1]		
Line of single-phase circuit	Brown	L
Neutral of single- or three-phase circuit	Blue	N
Line 1 of three-phase circuit	Brown	L1
Line 2 of three-phase circuit	Black	L2
Line 3 of three-phase circuit	Grey	L3
Control circuits, ELV and other applications		
Line conductor	Brown, Black, Red, Orange, Yellow, Violet, Grey, White, Pink, or Turquoise	L
Neutral or mid-wire[4]	Blue	N or M

NOTES: [1] Power circuits include lighting circuits.
[2] An earthed PELV conductor is blue.

Fig 8.9 Summary of permitted means of conductor identification

8.3 Protective devices

Regulation 514.8.1 requires protective devices to be arranged and identified so that the circuit protected will be easily recognised. Manufacturers of consumer units and distribution boards usually provide a space for circuit labels either adjacent to each protective device or inside the external cover. Circuit identification must be written clearly and should provide sufficient information to ensure that it will not be confused with any other circuit on the distribution board. A circuit chart should also be provided.

Published by Certsure LLP © Certsure LLP (January 2015)

8.4 Charts, diagrams, tables and circuit information

Regulation 514.9.1 requires a legible diagram, chart or table or equivalent form of information to be provided within or adjacent to each distribution board (including consumer units). This requirement may be met by using the NICEIC Circuit Details label which may be attached to the front of the consumer unit. (see Fig 8.10)

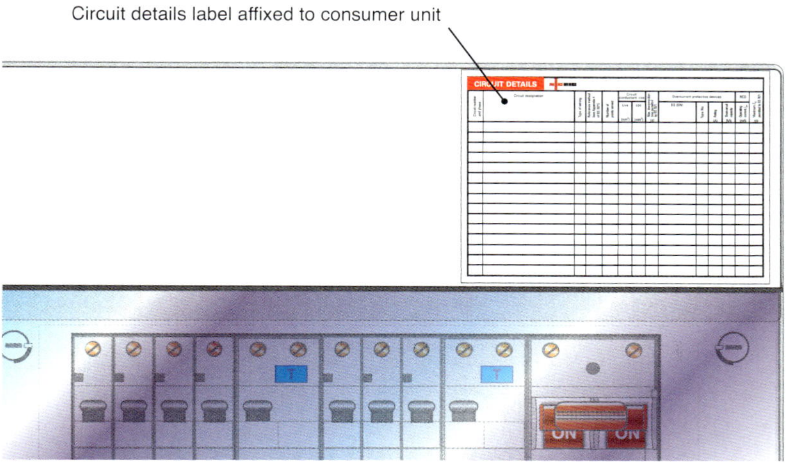

Fig 8.10 Use of NICEIC circuit details label

8.5 Voltage

Where the nominal voltage to earth (U_0) exceeds 230 V and the presence of such a voltage would not normally be expected, a warning notice is to be provided, indicating the maximum voltage present (Regulation 514.10.1). The notice is to be so arranged that before access is gained to a live part a warning of the maximum voltage to earth present is clearly visible.

8.6 Isolation

A notice of durable material is to be fixed in each position where there are live parts that are not capable of being isolated by a single device (Regulation 514.11.1 refers). Unless there is no possibility of confusion due, for example, to the close proximity of an isolator to the equipment that it controls, the location of each isolator (or disconnector) is to be clearly identified.

 © Certsure LLP (January 2015)

8.7 Periodic inspection and testing

A notice should be affixed at the origin of each installation stating:

> **IMPORTANT**
>
> **This installation should be periodically inspected and tested and a report on its condition obtained, as prescribed in the IET Wiring Regulations BS 7671 Requirements for Electrical Installations.**
>
> **Date of last inspection.......................**
>
> **Recommended date of next inspection...........................**

Fig 8.11 Periodic inspection and testing notice

The notice should include the date of the last inspection and the recommended date for the next inspection (Regulation 514.12.1 refers).

8.8 RCD test button

Regulation 514.12.2 requires a label having the wording shown below to be placed in a prominent position at, or close to, the origin of the installation.

> This installation, or part of it, is protected by a device which automatically switches off the supply if an earth fault develops. Test quarterly by pressing the button marked 'T' or 'Test'. The device should switch off the supply and should then be switched on to restore the supply. If the device does not switch off the supply when the button is pressed, seek expert advice.

Fig 8.12 RCD test button notice

Such a notice may also be fixed in close proximity to an RCD, wherever located within the installation.

Published by Certsure LLP © Certsure LLP (January 2015)

8.9 Earthing and bonding connections

In accordance with Regulation 514.13.1, a permanent label to *BS 951* with the words "Safety Electrical Connection - Do Not Remove" (see Fig 8.13) must be permanently fixed in a visible position at or near:

- the point of connection of every earthing conductor to an earth electrode, and
- the point of connection of every bonding conductor to an extraneous-conductive-part, and
- the main earth terminal, where separate from main switchgear.

A suitable label complying with *BS 951* is normally supplied with each earthing and bonding clamp conforming to that standard. Where such a clamp is used, the label should normally be fitted to the clamp in accordance with the manufacturer's instructions.

Earthing and bonding connections made by means other than a *BS 951* clamp will require a separate label, meeting the requirements of Regulation 514.13.1, to be fixed adjacent to each connection.

Fig 8.13 'Safety Electrical Connection - Do Not Remove' notice

Illustration reproduced by courtesy of Tenby Industries Ltd

Aluminium may be susceptible to electrolytic corrosion in damp conditions when in contact with dissimilar metals. Risk of electrolytic corrosion will be reduced if aluminium labels are not placed in contact with dissimilar metals.

8.10 Alternative supplies

As required by Regulation 514.15.1, where an installation includes a generating set such as a solar photovoltaic system or a generating boiler, that is used as an additional source of supply in parallel with the distributor's supply, warning notices should be affixed at the following locations in the installation:

- at the installation's origin,
- at the meter position, where this is remote from the origin,
- at the consumer unit or distribution board to which the generating set is connected,
- at all points of isolation of all sources.

The warning notice is required to have the wording given in Fig 8.14.

Fig 8.14 Warning label required where installation has alternative supplies

8.11 Circuits having a high protective conductor current

Regulation 543.7.1.105 requires information to be provided at the consumer unit to identify any circuits that have a high protective conductor current.

8.12 Presence of solar photovoltaic (solar PV) systems

A label should be affixed to any junction boxes forming a part of a solar PV installation warning that parts within the boxes may remain live after isolation from the PV convertor (Regulation 712.537.2.2.5.1 refers).

Published by Certsure LLP © Certsure LLP (January 2015)

Chapter 9

Distribution circuits

9.1 Introduction

9.2 Load centres and supplies to other buildings

9.3 Assessment of current demand

9.4 Voltage drop

9.5 Disconnection times

9.6 Recording of circuit details

Published by Certsure LLP © Certsure LLP (January 2015)

9.1 Introduction

A distribution circuit is a circuit that supplies a distribution board or other switchgear and does not extend directly to current-using equipment or a means of connection for such equipment.

An example of a distribution circuit that may be encountered in a domestic installation is a supply to another building, such as, for example, a detached garage.

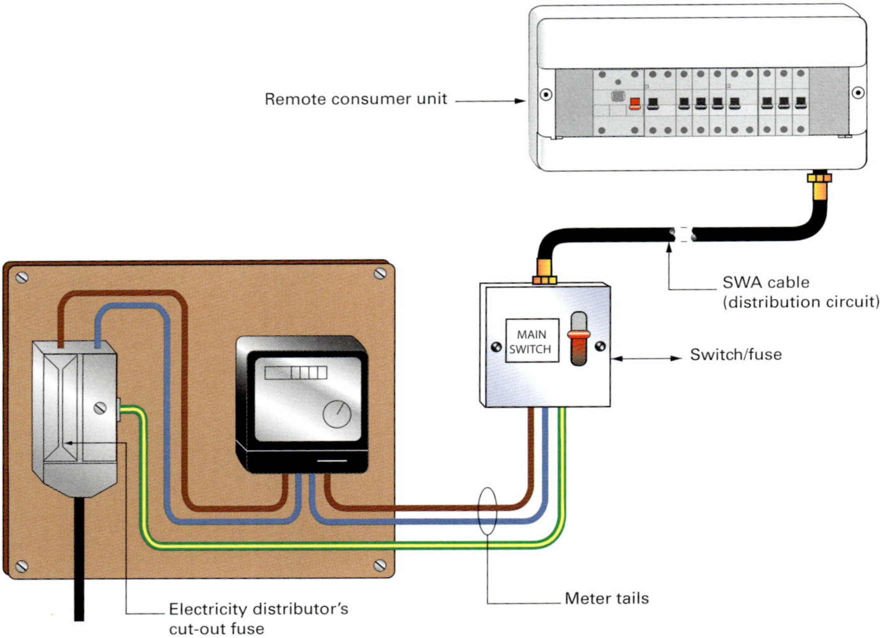

Fig 9.1 Example of a distribution circuit

9.2 Load centres and supplies to other buildings

The circumstances relating to distribution circuits in electrical installations in dwellings are diverse, and it is not possible to identify examples for all such circumstances. However, the following two examples may serve to provide an indication where such circuits may be used to advantage.

Published by Certsure LLP © Certsure LLP (January 2015)

- A distribution circuit feeding a distant internal distribution board or consumer unit from a switch-fuse or circuit-breaker at the origin of the installation. The use of such a circuit may be advantageous where the electrical loads are some considerable distance from the origin.
- A distribution circuit feeding a detached building located at some distance from the intake position in the dwelling.

It is a requirement of Regulation 411.3.1.2 that in each installation, main protective bonding conductors complying with Chapter 54 connect extraneous-conductive-parts to the main earthing terminal. This regulation also requires that where an installation serves more than one building, main protective bonding conductors must connect to the extraneous-conductive-parts in each building. A detached garage would be one example of such a building.

The significance of Regulation 411.3.1.2 in the context of a building that is supplied via a distribution circuit is that the protective conductor associated with the distribution circuit supplying such another building also serves as a main protective bonding conductor and should have a cross-sectional area complying with Regulation 544.1.1. For an installation where PME conditions do not apply (TN-S or TT system), the copper equivalent cross-sectional area of the main protective bonding conductors must be not less than half that required for the earthing conductor of the installation, subject to a minimum of 6 mm^2. The cross-sectional area need not exceed 25 mm^2 where the bonding conductor is of copper.

Where PME conditions apply (TN-C-S system) if:

- metallic gas, water or other pipes extend to other buildings, or
- the building supplied by a distribution circuit contains extraneous-conductive-parts (such as metallic structure in contact with Earth).

Then, except where the next paragraph applies, the associated protective conductor of the distribution circuit must have the cross-sectional area not less than that required by Table 54.8 of *BS 7671* in relation to the neutral conductor of the distributor's supply cable. So for supply neutral conductors with a copper equivalent cross-sectional area of not more than 35 mm^2, the minimum cross-sectional area of copper main protective bonding conductors need not exceed 10 mm^2).

 © Certsure LLP (January 2015)

Alternatively, the earthing system for the remote building could be segregated from the PME earthing terminal and connected to an installation earth electrode forming part of a TT earthing system, all other requirements of *BS 7671* for a TT system being met. Reference should also be made to Chapter 3 of this Guide, which looks at requirements for earthing and bonding in greater detail.

9.3 Assessment of current demand

The current demand of a distribution circuit supplying a number of final circuits may be assessed by applying the allowances for diversity given in Table H2 of *IET Guidance Note 1* to all the equipment supplied by the distribution circuit.

Alternatively, where a diversity factor is known from experience of a particular type of installation, the current demand of a distribution circuit may be calculated by applying a diversity factor to the sum of the connected loads.

Other methods of calculating the current demand of a distribution circuit may be used. Such methods are often based on known links between current demand and other criteria, such as floor area and population.

9.4 Voltage drop

Having determined the design current for a distribution circuit, a suitable conductor size must be chosen. One factor to be considered when choosing a suitable conductor size is the maximum value of voltage drop that can be permitted. Within *BS 7671* the requirements for voltage drop in a consumers' installation is given in Section 525, and guidance on complying with these requirements is given in Section 6.4 of Appendix 4. It should be borne in mind that for an installation that includes a distribution circuit supplying a final circuit, the total voltage drop will be the sum of the voltage drops of the distribution circuit and the final circuit.

Published by Certsure LLP © Certsure LLP (January 2015)

9.5 Disconnection times

For a distribution circuit, the following disconnection times are permitted for a.c. circuits supplied at a nominal voltage, (U_0), of 230 V.

Table 9.1 Disconnection times for distribution circuits

System earthing type	Maximum permitted disconnection time	Relevant Regulation in *BS 7671*
TT	1 second	411.3.2.4
TN	5 seconds	411.3.2.3

9.6 Recording of circuit details

As with all circuits, distribution circuits are required to be inspected and tested and the results recorded on the Electrical Installation Certificate (see Chapter 15).

Regulation 514.9.1 and Chapter 63 call for circuit details and test results to be provided for all circuits in an electrical installation. However, there is sometimes a tendency to overlook the provision of this information for distribution circuits (or sub-mains as they are sometimes called), where such circuits form part of the installation. The requirement to provide such information applies to distribution circuits as much as for final circuits.

One situation where this type of omission of data occurs is where a main switch, located at the origin, feeds a single distribution circuit to a remote distribution board or consumer unit (see Figure 9.1). **Without this recorded data the certification for the installation is incomplete**. This does not apply to meter tails making the short connection between the consumer unit or main switch to the electricity meter or distributor's isolator.

 © Certsure LLP (January 2015)

IET WIRING REGULATIONS UPDATED TO: 17TH EDITION BS7671:2008 Amd 3: 2015

Other publications which have been updated to reflect the latest requirements of *BS 7671*: 2008 (Amendment 3): 2015 include -

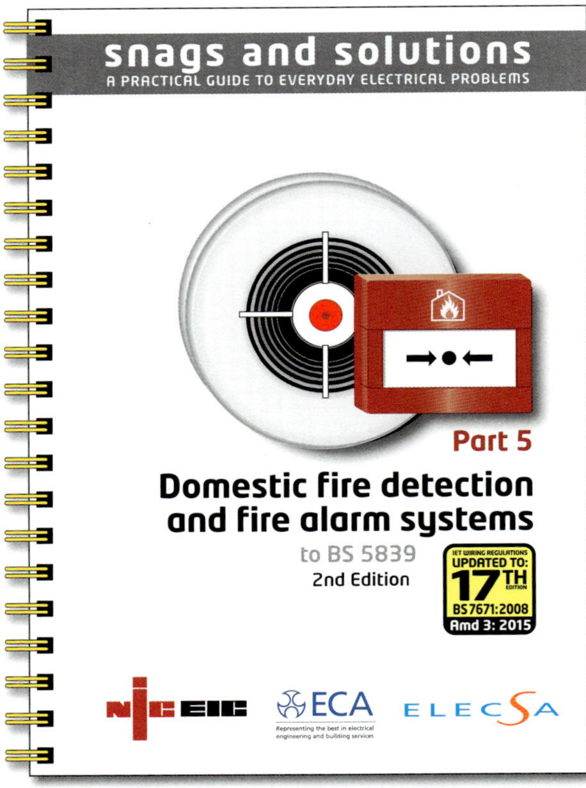

To order this or any other publication contact

NICEIC customers:	0843 290 3485	www.niceicdirect.com
ELECSA/ECA customers:	0333 321 8225	www.elecsa.co.uk

Published by Certsure LLP © Certsure LLP (January 2015)

Final circuits

Chapter 10

Published by Certsure LLP © Certsure LLP (January 2015)

10.1 Introduction

A final circuit is a circuit that connects directly to items of current-using equipment, or to a socket-outlet or connection unit or the like for the connection of current-using equipment. Information is given in this chapter on types of conventional circuit arrangements for use in household premises.

10.2 Types of conventional final circuit

10.2.1 Radial final circuit

Whilst the term radial final circuit is not defined in Part 2 of *BS 7671* it is generally considered to be a final circuit connected to the supply at one end only (see Fig 10.1).

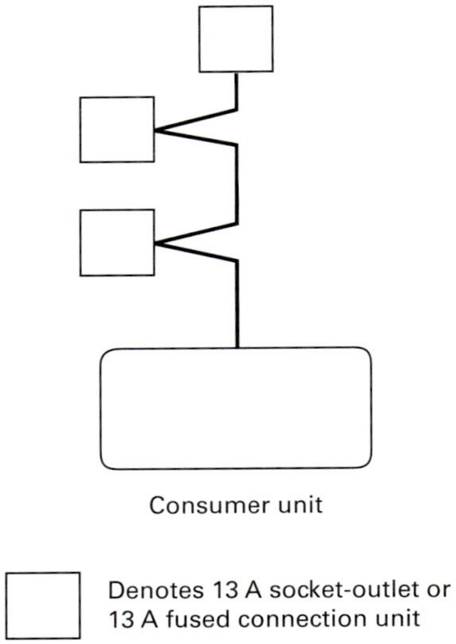

Fig 10.1 An example of a radial final circuit supplying 13 A accessories

Radial final circuits may be used to supply lighting, socket-outlets or individual items of current-using equipment such as cookers and immersion heaters.

Published by Certsure LLP © Certsure LLP (January 2015)

10.2.2 Ring final circuit

A ring final circuit starts and ends at a single 'way' within a consumer unit and so two conductors (i.e. two ends of the same conductor) will be terminated at the protective device and at the corresponding terminals on the neutral and earth bars of the consumer unit, and, except those connected to spurs, at each outlet.

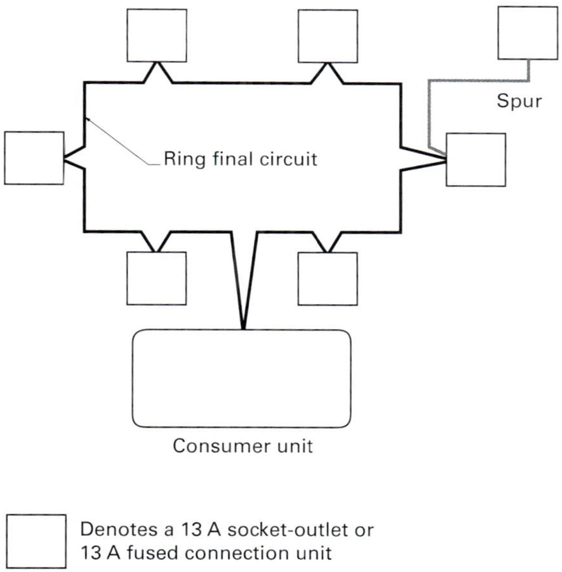

Fig 10.2 An example of a ring final circuit supplying 13 A accessories

Ring final circuits are used to supply socket-outlets and fused connection units to *BS 1363*.

10.3 Circuits supplying socket-outlets

Socket-outlets may be supplied by either a ring or a radial final circuit. In either case, a number of items of permanently connected equipment may also be supplied by the circuit. Such equipment should preferably be of a rating not exceeding 2 kW. Permanently connected equipment may be connected directly to a ring final circuit using a fused connection unit incorporating a *BS 1362* fuse (not exceeding 13 A) or a Type B or C circuit-breaker (not exceeding 16 A) complying with *BS EN 60898* or *BS EN 61009-1*, or *BS EN 60947-2*. In the case of some existing installations, Type 1, 2 or 3 MCBs complying with *BS 3871* may still be encountered (see also Chapter 4 of this Guide).

A switch should be provided where a fixed or stationary appliance that may give rise to a hazard in normal use is connected to the supply other than by a plug and socket-outlet.

Socket-outlets and fused connection units may be connected to the circuit directly or via a spur (see Section 10.3.1 below).

Regulation 411.3.3 requires that additional protection by means of an RCD with a rated residual operating current ($I_{\Delta n}$) not exceeding 30 mA and an operating time not exceeding 40 ms at a residual current of 5 $I_{\Delta n}$ must be provided for socket-outlets with a rated current not exceeding 20 A. An exception is permitted for a specific labelled or otherwise suitably identified socket-outlet provided for the connection of a particular item of equipment, such as a freezer.

The number and positions of socket-outlets should be such as to ensure compliance with Regulation 553.1.7. This regulation stipulates that where mobile equipment is likely to be used, sufficient provision, in terms of number of socket-outlets and indeed the location of such, should be made to allow mobile equipment to be fed from an adjacent and conveniently accessible socket-outlet. Due account should be taken of the length of flexible cable normally fitted to portable appliances and luminaires when considering such provision.

10.3.1 Spurs

A spur is a branch from a final circuit (Part 2 of *BS 7671* refers). A spur may be either unfused or fused.

Published by Certsure LLP © Certsure LLP (January 2015)

Unfused spur

An unfused spur consists of a conductor, of suitable current-carrying capacity, connected to the terminals of the circuit's overcurrent protective device in the consumer unit, or directly to either the terminals of an accessory such as a socket-outlet or a junction box without further overcurrent protection being provided at the point of connection.

For radial final circuits, the current-carrying capacity of conductors, corrected for the particular installation conditions, (I_z) used for an unfused spur must be least equal to the rated current (I_n) of the protective device of the circuit.

In the case of ring final circuits, copper conductors should have a minimum cross-sectional area of 2.5 mm^2. For conductors of two-core mineral insulated cables a minimum csa of 1.5 mm^2 applies.). Additionally, in either case, the current carrying capacity (I_z) of the live conductors should not be less than 20 A (Regulation 433.1.103).

Fig 10.2 shows an unfused spur taken from a ring final circuit.

Only one unfused spur, supplying either a single 1-gang or 2-gang socket-outlet, may be connected to any accessory forming a part of the circuit. This means that there will be a maximum of three conductors connected into any terminal.

In the case of a ring final circuit each unfused spur may only feed one single or one double socket-outlet, or a single item of current-using equipment.

Fused spur

A fused spur originates at a fused connection unit to *BS 1363-4*, which may be of the switched or unswitched type. Conductors used for fused spurs should have an adequate current-carrying capacity for the connected load. The fused spur is protected by a cartridge fuse to *BS 1362*. The rating of a fuse protecting a fused spur is determined from the total current demand of the spur, up to a maximum of 13 A. The current rating of the fuse in the unit is not to exceed the effective current-carrying capacity of the cable forming the spur.

The number of socket-outlets supplied by a fused spur is unlimited. However, an assessment should be made to ensure that the current demand of the equipment, connected via the socket-outlets forming part of the fused spur, does not exceed the rating of the fuse in the connection unit in normal use.

 © Certsure LLP (January 2015)

10.4 Permanently connected loads

A radial circuit dedicated to a particular load is generally provided where the operating current of the load is such that it would dominate a circuit. For example, in most cases, a fixed electric heater rated at about 2 kW or more is served by a dedicated circuit. Where a number of items of current-using equipment are served by a common circuit, disconnection of all the items will occur if the circuit protective device operates. Where disconnection of an item of equipment under such circumstances is likely to cause inconvenience or danger, a dedicated circuit should be provided for that equipment so that disconnection occurs only in the event of a fault attributable to that equipment or its associated circuit.

10.5 Lighting circuits

10.5.1 Introduction

Amendment 3 to *BS 7671: 2008* introduced changes in how the regulations relating to certain types of lighting installations are arranged within *BS 7671*. Prior to the introduction of this amendment all regulations relating exclusively to the particular requirements of luminaires and lighting installations were included in Section 559 (Luminaires and lighting installations). However, due to the increased level of danger associated with certain types of lighting installations, Amendment 3 now classifies outdoor lighting installations and extra-low voltage lighting installations as special installations and in addition to the general requirements of *BS 7671*, are subject to the requirements of Sections 714 and 715 respectively.

In this Guide, in order to avoid fragmentation, the requirements of Section 714 (Outdoor lighting installations) are included in the lighting section of Chapter 13 (Electrical equipment outside the dwelling) and the requirements of Section 715 (Extra-low voltage lighting installations) are included in Section 10.5.4 of this chapter.

Lighting in household premises should be served by one or more designated radial final circuits, according to the size and layout of the property. It could be argued that, where practicable, more than one lighting circuit should be provided, even in small premises, so as to avoid the loss of all lighting should one circuit be disconnected due to the operation of its circuit protective device.

 Published by Certsure LLP © Certsure LLP (January 2015)

Similarly, it might be desirable for areas such as a hallway and stairs to be served by separate circuits so that some lighting for the stairs is still available should one of the circuits be disconnected.

Regulation 559.5.1 lists acceptable means of final connection that should be provided at each lighting point. In domestic premises this final connection is likely to be made via a ceiling rose, a batten lampholder or a pendant set, or by direct connection to the terminals of a luminaire.

Each radial final circuit for lighting connects a number of such lighting points to the circuit overcurrent protective device within a consumer unit or a distribution board (see Fig 10.3).

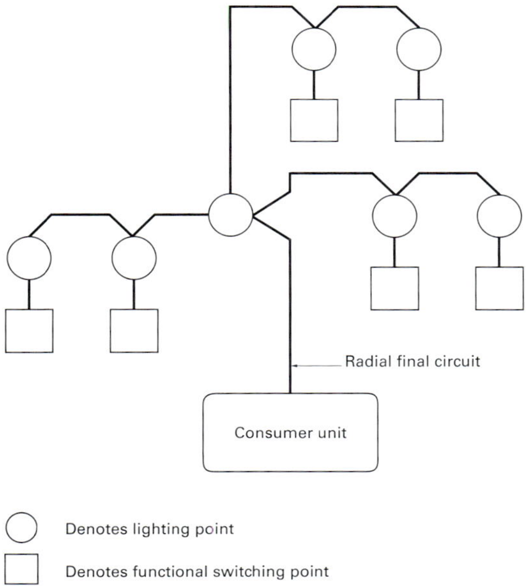

Fig 10.3 A typical radial final circuit supplying lighting

10.5.2 Ceiling roses

Ceiling roses are used to connect a flexible cable from a suspended luminaire (a pendant luminaire) to the fixed wiring installation. A typical arrangement using a ceiling rose is shown in Fig 10.5.

Fig 10.4 shows a pendant set which comprises a ceiling rose and a lampholder connected by a length of flexible cable.

Where a luminaire is installed suspended by a pendant set, the method of fixing the ceiling rose to the fabric of the building should be capable of carrying a mass of not less than 5 kg, and must be in accordance with the manufacturer's instructions. The weight of the luminaire and its accessories must be compatible with the mechanical capability of the ceiling or suspended ceiling or supporting structure where installed (Regulation 559.5.2 refers).

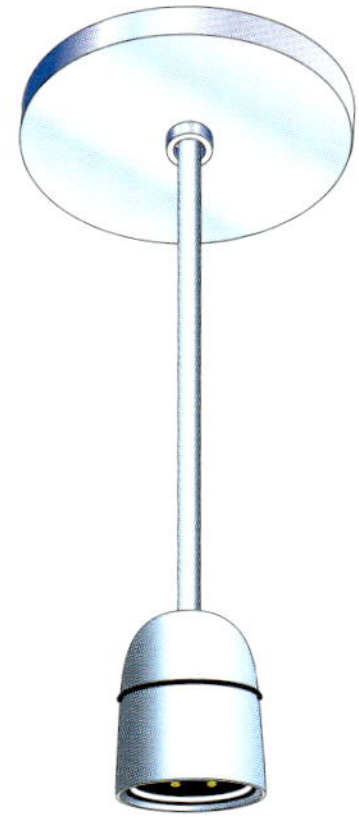

Fig 10.4 Typical pendant arrangement

Where ceiling roses are used, Regulation 559.5.1.201 requires that only one outgoing flexible cable be connected to each ceiling rose, except where the ceiling rose is specifically designed for more than one such pendant connection. Any cable between the fixing means and the luminaire must be installed so that any expected stresses in the conductors, terminals and terminations will not impair the safety of the installation. (Regulation 559.5.2).

It should be noted that Regulation 559.5.1.200 precludes the use of ceiling roses in circuits that normally exceed 250 V in operation. Ceiling roses complying with *BS 67* have maximum current and voltage ratings of 6 A and 250 V respectively, and are intended for use in final circuits having a rating not exceeding 16 A where the ceiling rose has screw-type supply terminals (see Figure 10.5), or not exceeding 10 A where the supply terminals of the ceiling rose are the screwless type.

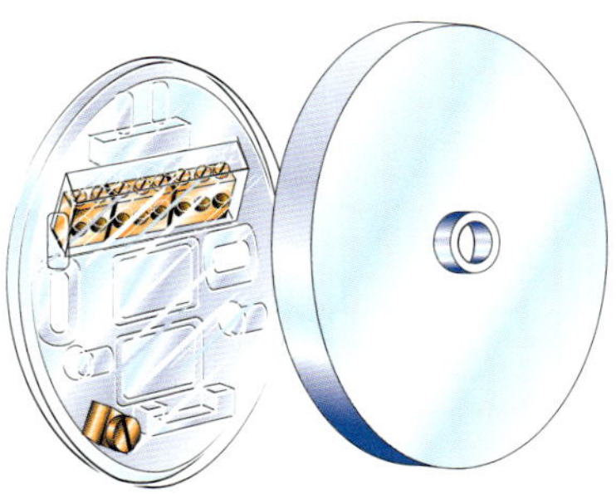

Fig 10.5 Typical ceiling rose with screw-type supply terminals

Published by Certsure LLP © Certsure LLP (January 2015)

10.5.3 Luminaire supporting couplers

Where there is a requirement for a luminaire to be easily disconnected from the fixed wiring installation, for maintenance or cleaning purposes for example, this may be achieved by using a luminaire supporting coupler (LSC) (see Fig 10.6) as the means of connecting the luminaire to the fixed wiring system.

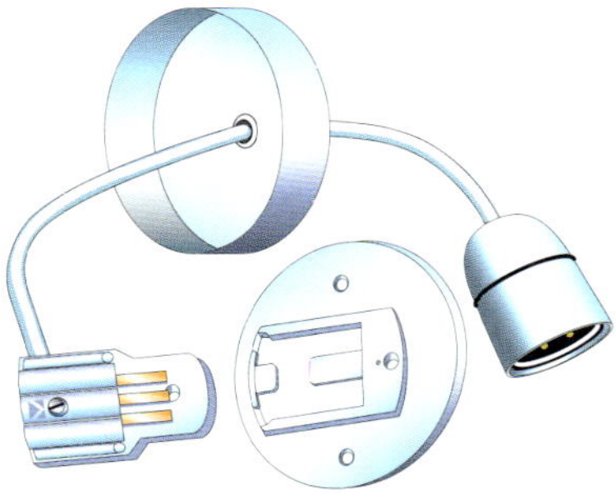

Fig 10.6 Typical luminaire supporting coupler (LSC)

Each LSC comprises an LSC outlet for fixed mounting and connection to the fixed wiring installation, and an LSC plug which is either connected to the flexible cable of a luminaire, or which is a component part, or an integral part, of the luminaire.

Not all LSCs are interchangeable; that is, the plug of one LSC may not be compatible with the outlet of another. Where there is a requirement for interchangeability so that, for example, a complete luminaire may be quickly unplugged and replaced or moved to another position, an LSC complying with *BS 7001* should be used.

LSCs complying with *BS 7001* are of a standardised format and are interchangeable, irrespective of the manufacturer, whereas those complying with *BS 6972* are not necessarily so.

Ceiling roses to *BS 67*, commonly used in household premises, and luminaire supporting couplers to *BS 6972* or *BS 7001* have a rated current not exceeding 6 A, and lighting circuits for household premises are generally protected by an overcurrent protective device with a rated current or current setting (I_n) of 6 A. For the purposes of designing the lighting circuits of domestic premises, and in the absence of more specific information, each lighting point may be considered to have a rating of 100 W. Therefore a lighting circuit having a nominal voltage of 230 V and having a 6 A protective device is able to supply at least 13 lighting points (6 A x 230 V = 1380 W).

 © Certsure LLP (January 2015)

Where luminaires incorporating discharge lamps (such as compact fluorescent) are used, account should be taken of the load of their control gear and the transient and harmonic currents produced, when assessing the load of the lighting circuit.

The design of lighting circuits must incorporate the means to switch individual luminaires or groups of luminaires on and off according to their location (Regulations 537.5.1.1 and 537.5.1.3 refer). The switching arrangement (whether one-way, two-way or intermediate) should be so placed to be readily accessible at the points of access to the area being illuminated.

With reference to Table 52.3 of *BS 7671*, the minimum conductor size for a radial final circuit for lighting, protected by an overcurrent protective device with a rated current or current setting (I_n) of 6 A, is 1 mm^2 for thermoplastic (PVC) or thermosetting insulated cables with copper conductors.

The flexible cable between the ceiling rose or similar and the lampholder is permitted to have a minimum cross-sectional area of 0.75 mm^2 (see Regulations 433.3.1(ii), 524.1 and Table 52.3). This flexible cable should preferably have 90 °C thermoplastic insulation.

As for any other circuit, the voltage drop between the origin of the installation and the terminals of the luminaire needs to be checked in order to verify compliance with Regulation Group 525 and Appendix 12 of *BS 7671*.

For 70 °C thermoplastic (pvc) insulated and sheathed flat cable with protective conductor, examples of the maximum circuit cable length, consideration having been given to voltage drop (amongst other things), are given in Appendix A of this Guide.

10.5.4 Extra-low voltage lighting installations

Extra-low voltage (ELV) lighting installations, which typically are used to supply extra-low voltage LED or tungsten halogen lighting, are subject to the requirements of Section 715. When dealing with extra-low voltage lighting installations, it should be remembered that the content of Section 714 modifies or is additional to the content of Parts 1 to 6 of *BS 7671* which means that, where relevant, the content of Section 559 still applies to the extra-low voltage lighting installations.

Section 715 applies to lighting installations supplied from a source with a maximum rated voltage of 50 V a.c. or 120 V d.c. (Regulation 715.1 refers).

Published by Certsure LLP © Certsure LLP (January 2015)

For safety reasons, Section 715 permits the extra-low voltage system used to supply the lighting installation to be either separated extra-low voltage (SELV) or protective extra-low voltage (PELV). However, functional extra-low voltage (FELV) is not to be used (Regulation 715.411.7.200 refers).

Where extra-low voltage luminaires are installed without provision for the connection of a protective conductor, they should only be installed as part of a SELV system. (Regulation 715.414 refers).

As shown by Fig 10.7, some extra-low voltage systems employ, on the output of the transformer, uninsulated conductors and, for this arrangement, the maximum operating voltage is reduced to 25 V a.c. or 60 V d.c. (Regulation 715.414 refers).

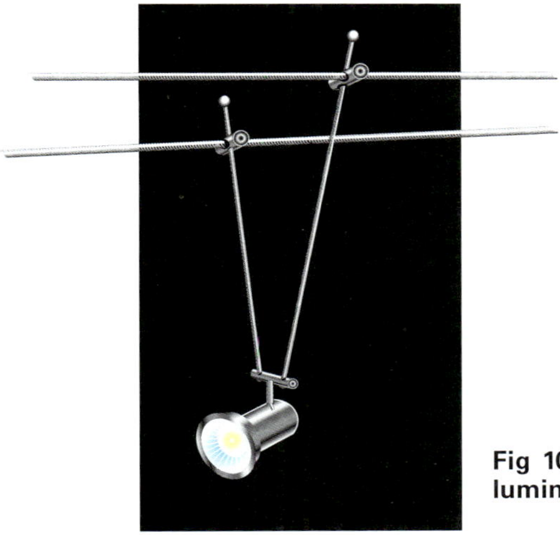

Fig 10.7 Suspended extra-low voltage luminaire with uninsulated conductors

In ELV lighting systems the LED lighting systems and some tungsten halogen systems operate using an extra-low voltage supply which is produced by either a transformer or electronic converter conforming to the appropriate British Standard specified in Regulation 715.414. The transformer or converter is normally supplied by a standard 230 V mains supply (see Fig 10.8). Transformers can only provide an a.c. supply whereas electronic converters, depending upon their design, can provide either an a.c. or d.c. supply. An electronic converter has the additional advantage that when there is a change in either the current taken by the lamp(s) or in the input voltage, the electronic converter will try to keep the voltage to the lamps at the rated value.

 © Certsure LLP (January 2015)

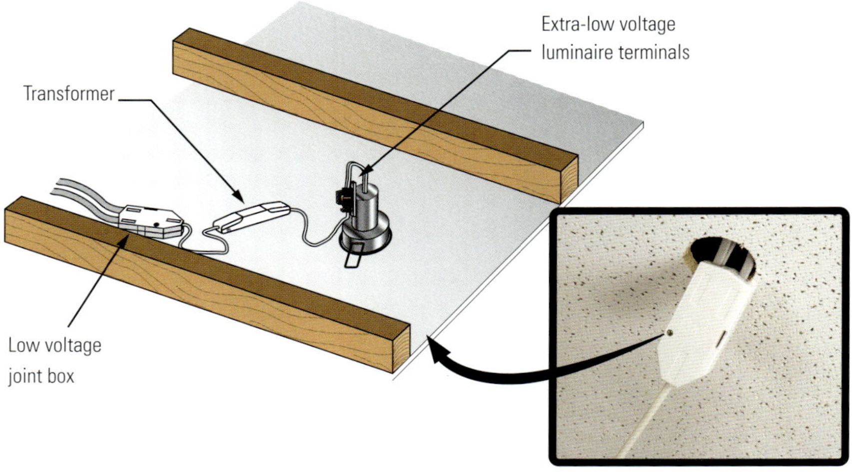

Fig 10.8 Typical installation of an extra-low voltage luminaire in a suspended ceiling

As listed in Table 55.2 of *BS 7671* the symbols for a short-circuit proof safety isolating transformer and an electronic convertor, for use in an ELV lighting installation are shown in Fig 10.9.

a) Symbol for short-circuit proof safety isolating transformer

b) Symbol for electronic converter for use in an ELV lighting installation

Fig 10.9 Symbols for short-circuit proof safety isolating transformer electronic converter for use in ELV lighting installations

Published by Certsure LLP © Certsure LLP (January 2015)

If a short-circuit occurs across the output of a transformer, there is the possibility that the heat generated by the short-circuit current can be the cause of a fire. To protect against such an event Regulation 715.422.106 requires the transformer/converter used to supply an extra-low voltage lighting system should either employ a fail-safe overcurrent protective device that meets all the features described in Regulation 715.422.107.2 or be short-circuit proof (be able to withstand the effects of a short circuit).

Where, to protect against the effects of short circuit, the transformer employs an overcurrent protective device, Regulation 715.430.104 limits the use of self-resetting overcurrent protective devices to transformers up to 50 VA. For overcurrent protective devices protecting transformers above this rating, once the device has operated, it must be manually reset.

The likelihood of a short-circuit occurring is particularly high for extra-low voltage systems that use uninsulated conductors on the secondary side of the transformer. Where both live conductors are uninsulated Regulation 715.422.107.1 requires that, either:

- they should be provided with a protective device complying with the requirements of Regulation 715.422.107.2, or
- the system should comply with *BS EN 60598-2-23*, or
- the maximum rating of the transformer or convertor should not exceed 200 VA.

Other regulations relating to protection against thermal effects and the impact upon the fire performance of the building can be found in Regulations 421.1.2, 421.1.4 and Section 527.

Regulation 715.521.1 permits a wide range of wiring systems to be used for ELV lighting systems. Track systems and systems where the lamp is suspended from bare conductors allow the position of the lamps to be altered.

Where a system using bare conductors is installed it is not permissible to utilise metallic structural parts of the building or parts of furniture as live conductors. Where parts of the ELV lighting installations are accessible, the maximum temperature limits given in Table 42.1 of *BS 7671* should not be exceeded.

 © Certsure LLP (January 2015)

Where uninsulated live conductors are used the following requirements apply:

i) the nominal voltage does not exceed 25 V a.c. or 60 V d.c.,

ii) the cross-sectional area of the conductor is not less than 4 mm^2 (see Table 10.1), and

iii) the conductors are not placed directly on combustible material.

In addition, where bare conductors are used, in order to prevent a short-circuit in the section between the transformer and the short-circuit protection device, at least one conductor and its terminal should be insulated.

Regulation 715.521.107 contains requirements for the use of suspended ELV lighting systems. Included in this Regulation are the following requirements:

i) where the ELV system is suspended, the suspension devices must be able to support five times the weight of the ELV luminaire and its lamp and not less than 5 kg,

ii) where the suspended system is fixed to the walls or ceilings by distance cleats the installation should be accessible throughout its length,

iii) the use of insulation piercing type connectors is prohibited.

Operating at extra-low voltage means that the cable between the transformer or converter and the lamps can carry a comparatively high current. Irrespective of the lamp rating or the type of lamp Regulation 715.524.200 specifies the minimum cross-sectional area of the live conductors. These minimum values are reproduced in Table 10.1.

Table 10.1 Minimum cross-sectional area of extra-low voltage conductors (copper)

Extra-low voltage conductors	Minimum csa
General	1.5 mm^2
Flexible cables with a maximum length of 3m	1.0 mm^2
Suspended flexible cables or insulated conductors	4.0 mm^2
Composite cables consisting of braided tinned copper outer sheath, having a material of high tensile strength inner core	4.0 mm^2

 Published by Certsure LLP © Certsure LLP (January 2015)

For extra-low voltage lighting installations, in order to comply with Regulation Group 525, the voltage drop between the transformer/electronic converter and furthest luminaire should not exceed 5% of the nominal voltage of the ELV installation; that is 0.6 V for a 12 V installation (Regulation 715.525 refers).

Regulation 715.530.3.104 requires that for ELV lighting systems protective the devices are accessible.

For installations where the luminaires of ELV lighting systems are recessed into suspended ceilings and the control gear and wiring is concealed above the ceiling (as shown in Fig 10.8), following the operation of the protective device accessing the protective device can be problematic. Regulation 715.530.3.104 requires that where the control gear for ELV lighting is located above a false ceiling, information regarding the presence and location of the protective devices is provided.

Regulation 715.530.3.104 also requires that:

i) where the identification of a protective device for a circuit is not immediately evident, a sign or diagram, located close to the protective device, shall identify the circuit and its purpose,

ii) the SELV sources, protective devices and similar equipment shall be permanently connected, adequately supported and mounted in such a way that mechanical stress on the terminations is avoided, and

iii) the SELV sources and their protective devices shall be installed in such a way that overheating of the SELV sources and their protective devices due to thermal insulation is avoided.

To enable effective isolation where an ELV lighting system is fed from several transformers connected in parallel, the primary circuits shall be permanently connected to a common isolating device (Regulation 715.536.1.1 refers).

10.6 Voltage drop

Where a circuit is supplied from a distribution board that is not at the origin of the installation, the total voltage drop between the origin of the installation and the load end of the circuit is equal to the sum of the voltage drops in the distribution circuit and the circuit concerned (normally a final circuit). For a single-phase installation in domestic premises, this is a straightforward arithmetic sum and requires no further explanation.

The requirements of Regulation Group 525 of *BS 7671* are deemed to be satisfied if (as given in Section 6.4 of Appendix 4 in *BS 7671*) the voltage drop between the origin of the installation and either the fixed current using equipment or the terminals of a socket-outlet does not exceed 5% of the nominal voltage and in the case of lighting circuit does not exceed 3% of the nominal voltage.

Published by Certsure LLP © Certsure LLP (January 2015)

Chapter 11

Factors relating to installation of wiring systems and cables

Published by Certsure LLP © Certsure LLP (January 2015)

11.7 Connections

11.7.1 General

11.7.2 Fundamental requirements

11.7.3 Selection of means of connection and termination

The material of the conductor and its insulation

The number and shape of the wires forming the conductor

The cross-sectional area of the conductor

The number of conductors to be connected together

The temperature attained by the terminals in normal service

Soldered connections

Provision of adequate locking arrangements

External influences

11.7.4 Enclosure of connections

11.7.5 Protection against electric shock

Basic protection

Fault protection

11.7.6 Accessibility of connections

11.7.7 Protective conductor connections involving the metal sheath or armouring or metal enclosure

11.8 Cable supports

11.8.1 General

11.8.2 Surfaces in contact with a cable

11.8.3 Suitability for external influences

11.8.4 Avoidance of electrolytic corrosion

11.8.5 Enclosure of non-sheathed cables

Vertical runs of trunking or ducting exceeding 5 m in length

Vertical runs of conduit exceeding 5 m in length

Vertical runs of cable supported from the top

11.8.6 Cables resting without fixings

11.8.7 Spacing between supports

11.8.8 Cable supports and wiring systems in escape routes

Published by Certsure LLP © Certsure LLP (January 2015)

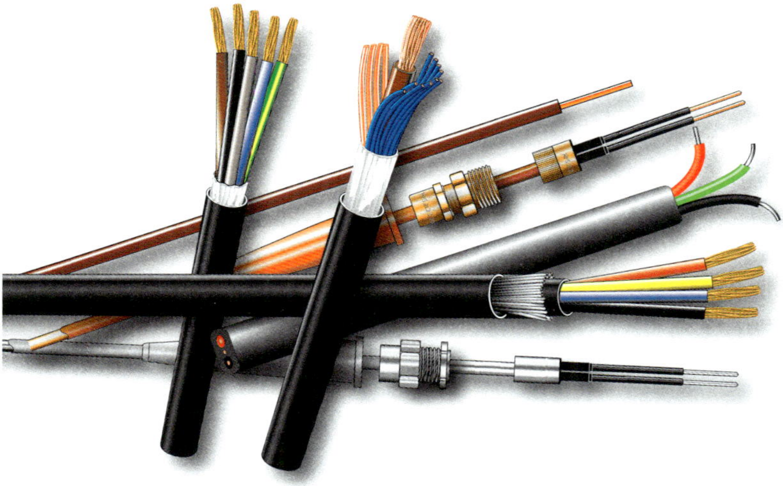

11.1 Wiring systems - Types

To comply with the requirements of Regulations 511.1 and 511.2, wiring systems must utilise cables complying with the relevant requirements of an applicable British Standard or Harmonised Standard. Where equipment is used which does not comply with a relevant British Standard or Harmonised Standard or it is used outside the scope of its standard, the designer of the electrical installation must verify that the equipment provides the same degree of safety as that afforded by compliance with the Regulations.

Any prefabricated wiring systems employed should comply with *BS 8488: 2009 (2010) – Prefabricated wiring systems intended for permanent connection in fixed installations – Specification.*

Regulation 512.1.1 requires that every item of equipment (including cables) to be suitable for the nominal voltage (U_0) of the installation and cable manufacturers always state the voltage grade for particular types of cables. Conduit wiring cables (such as 6491X) are 450/750 V grade. Flat twin and earth wiring cables (such as 6242Y) are designated 300/500 V grade.

11.2 Applications of cables for fixed wiring

Table 11.1 provides information about a range of cables in common use by electrical installation contractors.

Table 11.1 The range of cables in common use

Type of cable	Uses	Comments
Thermoplastic (pvc), thermosetting or rubber insulated non-sheathed	In conduits and cable trunking	Intermediate support may be required on long vertical runs 70 °C maximum conductor temperature for normal wiring grades – including thermosetting types (Note 4) Cables run in pvc conduit are not permitted to operate with a conductor temperature greater than 70 °C (Note 4)
Flat thermoplastic (pvc) or thermosetting insulated and sheathed	General indoor use in dry or damp locations. May be embedded in plaster On exterior surface walls, boundary walls and the like Overhead wiring between buildings (Note 6) Underground in conduits and pipes In building voids or ducts formed of building fabric	Additional mechanical protection may be necessary where exposed to mechanical stresses Protection from direct sunlight may be necessary. See Note 4 Unsuitable for embedding directly in concrete May need to be hard drawn (HD) copper conductors for overhead wiring (Note 6)
Split-concentric thermoplastic (pvc) insulated and sheathed	General	Additional mechanical protection may be necessary where exposed to mechanical stresses Protection from direct sunlight may be necessary. Black sheath colour is better for cables in sunlight
Mineral insulated	General	With overall pvc covering where exposed to the weather or risk of corrosion, or where installed underground, or in concrete ducts
Thermoplastic (pvc) or XLPE insulated, armoured, thermoplastic sheathed	General	Additional mechanical protection may be necessary where exposed to mechanical stresses Protection from direct sunlight may be necessary. Black sheath colour is better for cables in sunlight
Screened multicore cables having low emission of smoke and corrosive gasses when affected by fire, to *BS 8436*	General use for use in walls, partitions and building voids	Care should be exercised during installation to avoid any damage to cable coverings

1) The use of cable covers is desirable for all underground cables which might otherwise be disturbed. Route marker tape should also be installed, buried just below ground level.

2) Cables having thermoplastic (pvc) insulation or sheath should preferably be installed only when the ambient temperature is above 0 °C, and has been for the preceding 24 hours. Where thermoplastic (pvc) cables are to be installed during a period of low temperature, precautions should be taken to avoid risk of mechanical damage during handling. A minimum ambient temperature of 5 °C is advised in *BS EN 50565* for some types of thermoplastic (pvc) insulated and sheathed cables.

3) Cables must be suitable for the maximum ambient air temperature, and must be protected from any excess heat produced by other equipment, including other cables.

4) Thermosetting cable types (to *BS 7211* or *BS 5467*) can operate with a conductor temperature of 90 °C. This must be limited to 70 °C where cables are drawn into a conduit made of thermoplastic material or where installed in a common enclosure with cables with a maximum conductor operating temperature of 70 °C. Also equipment must not be connected to conductors intended to operate at temperatures higher than 70 °C unless the manufacturer has confirmed that the equipment is suitable for such conditions. Regulation 512.1.5 refers.

5) For cables to *BS 5467, BS 6004, BS 6724* and *BS 7211* further guidance may be obtained from those standards. Additional advice is given in *BS EN 50565-1: 2014 Electric cables. Guide to use for cables with a rated voltage not exceeding 450/750 V (U_0/U). General guidance.*

6) Cables used for overhead wiring between buildings must be able to support their own weight and any imposed wind loading and any ice or snow loading. A catenary support is normally used.

Published by Certsure LLP © Certsure LLP (January 2015)

11.3 Installation methods

The basis for determining the current-carrying capacity of cables is set out in Appendix 4 of *BS 7671*. The value of tabulated current-carrying capacity for a particular cable is dependent upon the chosen Installation Method, and this is reflected in the data of current-carrying capacities.

Table 4A2 lists the Installation Methods for which consideration has been given to current-carrying capacities in Appendix 4 of *BS 7671*. Reference Methods are installation methods where a determination (by test or calculation) has been made of current-carrying capacity in more specific circumstances.

Table 11.2 identifies some common installation and reference methods.

Table 11.2 Some common installation and reference methods for thermoplastic cables used in dwellings

Installation description	Installation method	Reference method
Non-sheathed cables in conduit in a thermally insulated wall having an inner skin of thermal conductance not less than 10 W/m^2K	1	A
Multicore cable in conduit in a thermally insulated wall having an inner skin of thermal conductance not less than 10 W/m^2K	2	A
Multicore cable direct in a thermally insulated wall having an inner skin of thermal conductance not less than 10 W/m^2K	3	A
Multicore cable in conduit on a wooden or masonry wall, or spaced less than 0.3 times the conduit diameter from it	5	B
Single-core or multicore cables fixed on (clipped direct), or spaced less than 0.3 times the conduit diameter from a wooden or masonry wall	20	C
Non-sheathed (50) or sheathed (51) cables in flush cable trunking in the floor	50, 51	B
Non-sheathed (52) or sheathed (53) cables in flush cable trunking	52, 53	B
Single-core or multicore cables direct in masonry having a thermal resistivity not greater than 2 K.m/W without added mechanical protection	57	C
Single-core or multicore cables direct in masonry having a thermal resistivity not greater than 2 K.m/W with added mechanical protection such as capping	58	C
Non-sheathed (59) cables or multicore (60) cables in conduit in masonry of thermal resistivity not greater than 2 K.m/W	59, 60	B
Flat twin and earth cable clipped direct to a wooden joist , or touching the plasterboard ceiling surface, above a plasterboard ceiling with thermal insulation of thickness **not** exceeding 100 mm having a minimum U value of 0.1 W/m^2K	100	Table 4D5
Flat twin and earth cable clipped direct to a wooden joist , or touching the plasterboard ceiling surface, above a plasterboard ceiling with thermal insulation of thickness **exceeding** 100 mm having a minimum U value of 0.1 W/m^2K	101	Table 4D5
Flat twin and earth cable in a stud wall with thermal insulation having a minimum U value of 0.1 W/m^2K with the cable **touching** the inner wall surface, or **touching** the plasterboard ceiling surface , and the inner skin having a minimum U value of 10 W/m^2K	102	Table 4D5
Flat twin and earth cable in a stud wall with thermal insulation having a minimum U value of 0.1 W/m^2K with the cable **not** touching the inner wall surface	103	Table 4D5

Where a cable is installed in contact with thermal insulation, its current-carrying capacity might be reduced by as much as 50 % of its tabulated value, depending on the particular circumstances.

The data in Table 4D5 of *BS 7671* indicates that the current carrying-capacity (Reference Method C – clipped direct) of 70 °C thermoplastic (PVC) insulated and sheathed cables will be reduced by approximately 25 % where the same cable is installed to Reference Method A (enclosed in conduit in an insulated wall). For domestic lighting circuits rated at 6 A, this is unlikely to cause a problem since the smallest permitted conductor size of 1 mm^2 has a current-carrying capacity above that which is needed. However, increased cable sizes may have to be selected for circuits supplying other equipment.

For a single cable completely surrounded by thermal insulation for a length of more than 500 mm, its current-carrying capacity (clipped direct) is reduced by 50 %. Where a cable is surrounded by thermal insulation for less than 500 mm, its current-carrying capacity is reduced appropriately depending on the size of cable, the length of cable in contact with thermal insulation, and the thermal properties of the insulation. Guidance is given in Table 52.2 of *BS 7671*, which is reproduced below as Table 11.3.

Table 11.3 Derating factors to be applied where a cable is surrounded by thermal insulation

Length of thermal insulation (mm)	50	100	200	400
Derating factor	0.88	0.78	0.63	0.51

The above derating factors are appropriate for conductor cross-sectional areas up to 10 mm^2 in thermal insulation having a thermal conductivity (λ) greater than 0.04 $Wm^{-1}K^{-1}$.

Consider, for example, a 6 mm^2 70 °C thermoplastic (pvc) insulated and sheathed 'twin and earth' cable, supplying a domestic cooker, installed in the loft of a bungalow. The cable has a current-carrying capacity of 47 A at an ambient temperature of 30 °C when clipped direct, not grouped with other loaded cables, and the design current is 30 A. If the cable were surrounded with thermal insulation for more than 500 mm of its length, its current-carrying capacity would be reduced to 23.5 A. This could lead to overheating and potential danger, and possible premature ageing of cable insulation and sheath.

Published by Certsure LLP © Certsure LLP (January 2015)

Either the cable would have to be installed along a different route so that it is not surrounded by thermal insulation, or a cable having higher current-carrying capacity should be used.

It should be noted that subsequent introduction of thermal insulation in a loft where cables already exist can cause cables to overheat. The actual risk will depend on the type of cable, type and thickness of thermal insulation and the electrical loading of the cables.

It should also be noted that material used for sound insulation (e.g. in inter-floor spaces) may also be thermally insulating.

11.4 Wiring in lofts

Cables installed in a roof space may cause a tripping hazard if not correctly placed and secured. Cables could also be damaged by impact, snagging or other mechanical stresses. Cables surrounded by thermal insulation could also exceed their maximum operating temperature if not correctly selected (see Section 11.3 above).

Cables in lofts and other accessible voids should **not** be installed over joists (supporting the ceiling below) or over the low-level parts of roof trusses, except:

- in areas of the void where the cables will not be susceptible to mechanical damage, or
- where the cables are provided with adequate protection against mechanical damage.

It should be borne in mind that the joists and the like in lofts and other accessible voids are liable to being walked on (for example by persons using the space for storage or to gain access to water tanks), and to having objects placed on or moved across them (such as stored items or loose-laid boards). It is therefore necessary for cables to be positioned or protected so that they will not be damaged by adverse influences such as impact, penetration, abrasion, crushing or snagging.

Flat 70 °C thermoplastic (pvc) insulated and sheathed cable covered by Table 4D5 of *BS 7671* installed in accessible positions should be supported by clips at spacings not exceeding the appropriate value given in Table 1 of *BS EN 50565-1: 2014*. Table 11.8 of this Guide is based on some of the information within Table 1 of that standard. Refer to Section 11.8 of this Guide for further details.

 © Certsure LLP (January 2015)

In this guide advice regarding the drilling of ceiling joists can be found in Section 11.5.7 (Protection of concealed cables in floors and ceilings) and Section 11.6.1 (Penetration of elements of building construction by wiring systems).

11.5 External influences

An external influence is a factor that affects the design and safe operation of an electrical installation that relates to its use or the environment in which it is located.

A list of external influences relating to Chapter 32 (Classification of external influences) of *BS 7671* is given in Appendix 5 of that Standard.

Chapter 52 of *BS 7671*, which refers to (amongst other things) the codification of external influences developed for IEC Publication 60364-3, identifies the requirements for selection and erection of wiring systems in relation to external influences.

Protection against external influences is not restricted to completed work. For example, Regulation 522.6.1 requires that wiring systems shall be selected and erected so as to minimise mechanical damage; such as damage due to impact, abrasion, penetration, compression, or tension; during installation, use and maintenance.

Chapter 51 of *BS 7671* gives the requirements for selection and erection of equipment. In short, either equipment should, of itself, be suitable for the environment in which it is to be installed or, where this is not the case, and where appropriate, additional measures should be taken during installation to provide the necessary protection (Regulations 512.2.1 and 512.2.2 refer).

11.5.1 Ambient temperature

Ambient temperature is the temperature of the air or other medium surrounding the electrical equipment.

Component parts of the electrical installation should be designed to operate in the highest and the lowest ambient temperatures to which they are expected to be subjected where they are installed.

In the UK, ambient temperature in most electrical installations indoors is likely not to exceed 30 °C except in close proximity to heating equipment, where localised higher temperature should be expected.

Published by Certsure LLP © Certsure LLP (January 2015)

One area in domestic installations where the ambient temperature is likely to be higher than 30 °C is an airing cupboard. Only cables having a suitably high temperature rating should be connected to an immersion heater.

The current-carrying capacities of cables given in Appendix 4 of *BS 7671* are based on an ambient temperature of 30 °C. Where the ambient temperature of an installation is known or expected to be higher or lower than 30 °C, Tables 4B1 and 4B2 give rating factors to be applied to the tabulated values of current carrying-capacity.

Thermoplastic (pvc) insulated and sheathed cables, including flat cables with protective conductors, and certain other types of cable, should be installed only when the cable and the ambient temperature is above 0 °C and has been so for the previous 24 hours.

11.5.2 External heat sources

External heat sources such as sunlight and radiant heat from certain types of equipment can raise the temperature of cables and in some cases cause degradation.

Cable sheaths containing carbon black and other types of ultra-violet (UV) stabilisers are less likely to be affected by solar radiation. However, shielding is always recommended. Where radiated heat is sufficiently powerful to raise the temperature of cables above ambient temperature, a correction factor should be applied to the tabulated current carrying-capacity. See also Section 11.5.17 of this Guide.

11.5.3 Water and high humidity

A correctly selected and erected wiring system must be installed such that no damage will be caused by condensation or ingress of water during installation, use and maintenance.

Protection against the effects of condensation can be achieved by provision of suitable drainage holes in wiring accessories at low points within the installation.

Only suitably designed equipment should be exposed to rain, water spray, or immersion, and such suitability should confirmed by the manufacturer's data.

11.5.4 Solid and foreign bodies

A wiring system should be selected and erected to minimise the ingress of solid foreign bodies during installation, use and maintenance. Such ingress may be prevented during installation by the use of temporary covers.

11.5.5 Corrosive and polluting substances

Parts of the wiring system and other equipment likely to be in contact with corrosive and polluting substances must be either protected or manufactured from materials resistant to such substances.

Equipment outdoors must be resistant to corrosion and be weather resistant.

Metals liable to initiate electrolytic action should not be placed in contact with each other.

11.5.6 Impact

Wiring systems must be selected and erected so as to minimise mechanical damage e.g. damage due to impact, abrasion, penetration, compression, or tension, during installation, use and maintenance.

Additional mechanical protection should be provided to any part of the electrical installation which may be vulnerable to mechanical damage. For example, localised protection may be required to protect cables against impact from, for instance, footwear or a floor cleaning appliance.

The following sections of this guide relate to protection against impact:

11.5.7 Protection of concealed cables in floors and ceilings.

11.5.8 Protection of concealed cables in walls.

11.5.9 Protection of cables embedded in walls by wet plaster.

Regulation 522.6.200 relating to wiring systems located under a floor or above a ceiling and Regulation 522.6.201 and 522.6.202 relating to wiring systems concealed in walls can be satisfied by using one of the installation methods described in Regulation 522.6.203 and summarised in Table 11.4

Published by Certsure LLP © Certsure LLP (January 2015)

Table 11.4 Methods of installation permitted by Regulation 522.6.203

Option No.	Method of installation
i)	Incorporate an earthed metallic covering, capable of satisfying the requirements for a protective conductor, and comply with one of the following *BS 5467, BS 6724, BS 7846, BS EN 60702-1* or *BS 8436*. (Details of the metallic-covered cables that can be used to satisfy this requirement are given in Table 11.5 of this guide).
ii)	Be enclosed in earthed conduit, capable of satisfying the requirements for a protective conductor, complying with *BS EN 61386-21*.
iii)	Be enclosed in earthed trunking or ducting, capable of satisfying the requirements for a protective conductor complying with *BS EN 50085-2-1*.
iv)	Be mechanically protected in a manner sufficient to penetration of the cable by nails, screws and the like.
v)	Form part of a SELV or PELV circuit meeting the requirements of Regulation 414.4.

Meeting the requirements of Regulation 522.6.203

As permitted by Regulation 543.2.5 options (i) to (iii) of Regulation 552.6.203 allows the use of either the earthed metallic covering of a cable, an earthed conduit or earthed trunking to be used as a protective conductor. However, the protective conductor needs to be suitable for the purpose and satisfy the requirements of indents (i) and (ii) of Regulation 543.2.2, relating to electrical continuity and cross-sectional area respectively.

Regulation 522.6.203 Option i) cable incorporating an earthed metallic covering

The use of the metallic covering of a cable to satisfy option (i) of Regulation 522.6.203 is intended to ensure that it will not be possible for a nail, screw or the like to make contact with a line conductor of the cable without first coming into good electrical contact with the earthed metallic covering (by piercing). A direct path is thus provided for earth fault current to flow and cause automatic disconnection of the circuit concerned.

Those metallic-covered cables that can be used to satisfy the requirements of Regulation 522.6.203(i) are listed in Table 11.5.

 © Certsure LLP (January 2015)

Table 11.5 Type of metallic covered cables that may be used to meet the requirement of Regulation 522.6.203 option (i)

British Standard	Description of cable
BS 5467	Armoured cables having thermosetting insulation
BS 6724	Armoured cables having thermosetting insulation and low emission of smoke and corrosive gases when affected by fire
BS 7846	Armoured fire-resistant cables having thermosetting insulation and low emission of smoke and corrosive gases when affected by fire
BS EN 60702-1	Mineral insulated cables with a rated voltage not exceeding 750 V
BS 8436	300/500 V screened cables having low emission of smoke and corrosive gases when affected by fire, for use in thin partitions and building voids

Note: In order to be used to satisfy condition (i), the metallic covering of the cables listed has to be earthed. The metallic covering must also meet the requirements of Regulation 543.2.5 for a circuit protective conductor of the circuit concerned (that is, be suitable for that purpose and satisfy the requirements of indents (i) and (ii) of Regulation 543.2.4, relating to electrical continuity and cross-sectional area respectively).

Where, for example, a mineral insulated copper sheathed (MICS) cable or steel wire armoured (SWA) cable is used, the designer of the installation should confirm that the earthed metallic covering or armouring of the cable meets the requirements for a protective conductor for the circuit concerned. Regulation 543.2.5 permits the use of the metallic covering of a cable as a protective conductor provided it is suitable for the purpose and satisfies the requirements of items (i) and (ii) of Regulation 543.2.2, relating to electrical continuity and cross-sectional area, respectively.

Where screened cable to *BS 8436: 2011* is used, the requirements contained in Section 12 of that standard for the selection of protective devices and for the maximum current rating of cables must be met in addition to the requirements of *BS 7671*. These additional requirements are summarised below.

Only Type B circuit-breakers to *BS EN 60898-1* or Type B RCBOs to *BS EN 61009-1* may be used to provide overcurrent protection. Furthermore, the protective device must have the following characteristics given in Table 11.6.

 Published by Certsure LLP © Certsure LLP (January 2015)

Table 11.6 Requirements for circuit breakers and RCBOs protecting *BS 8436* cable

Conductor size (mm^2)	Maximum let-through energy, I^2t (A^2t)	Maximum* rated current (I_n) of Type B circuit-breaker or Type B RCBO
1	42000	16
1.5	42000	20
2.5 (used as part of ring final circuit wiring)	60000	32
4	60000	32

* A lower rating may be required to meet the requirements of *BS 7671* for electric shock or overcurrent protection.

These requirements are likely to be met where

- a Type B circuit-breaker to *BS EN 60898-1* or a Type B RCBO to *BS EN 61009-1* is used as the circuit protective device, provided that the device is of energy limiting Class 3. Where this is the case, this is likely to be indicated on the device (on the front of a circuit-breaker, or the side of an RCBO) as shown below.

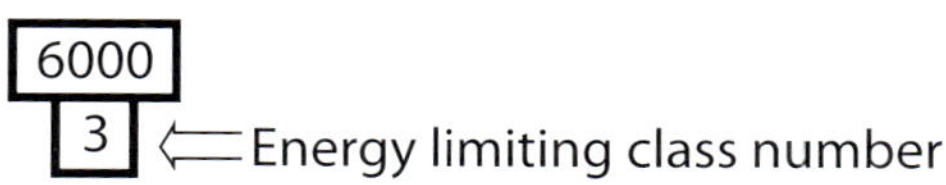

and

- the prospective earth fault current in the circuit does not exceed 5 kA (this corresponds to an earth fault loop impedance (Z_S) of not less than 0.046 W in a circuit having a nominal voltage of 230 V).

Regulation 522.6.203 Options ii) & iii) cables enclosed in earthed metallic conduit or trunking

In principle, an earthed steel conduit complying with *BS EN 61386-21* as described in condition (ii) or an earthed steel trunking or ducting complying with *BS EN 50085-2-1* as described in condition (iii) utilises the same method of protection as a cable with an earthed metallic covering and, by construction, provides a higher degree of protection against mechanical damage.

Regulation 522.6.203 Option iv) the provision of mechanical protection

Option (iv) of Regulation 522.6.203 (shown in Table 11.4) relates to the provision of additional mechanical protection of a cable sufficient to prevent penetration of the cable by nails, screws and the like. It should be noted that this condition may prove hard to achieve in practice. Regulation 522.6.203 does not require such additional mechanical protection to be earthed.

A protective plate provided to prevent penetration by such fixings (see Fig 11.1) should be at least 3 mm thick. In situations where shot fired fixings are likely to be used, even a 3 mm plate will not prevent penetration and where shot fired fixings are being employed, the use of a metal plate would not be considered to afford compliance with Regulation 522.6.203 and would therefore be unacceptable. In such a case, cables should preferably be at least 50 mm from the surface of the joist or batten. If this is not practicable, then cables should either incorporate an earthed armour or metal sheath suitable for use as a protective conductor or be enclosed in earthed steel conduit, trunking or ducting.

Some proprietary metal plates intended for fixing to the surface of a joist or batten where a cable passes through are unsuitable for such use because they are too thin to prevent a nail, screw or the like penetrating the cable, or even to make the person driving in the fixing aware of the metal plate.

Regulation 522.6.203 Option v) the use of SELV or PELV meeting the requirement of Regulation Group 414.4

Although *BS 7671* does not contain any regulations dealing specifically with the protection of extra-low voltage cables concealed in walls or flooring against impact, guidance is provided by Regulation 522.6.1. This regulation requires that all wiring systems shall be selected and erected so as to minimise damage from impact, abrasion, penetration, tension or compression during installation use or maintenance.

 Published by Certsure LLP © Certsure LLP (January 2015)

Consequently, when using SELV or PELV to satisfy the requirements of Regulation 522.6.203 the wiring must be installed in a manner that minimises the risk of mechanical damage and satisfies the requirements of Regulation 522.6.1.

11.5.7 Protection of concealed cables in floors and ceilings

Regulation 522.6.200 requires that a cable installed under a floor or above a ceiling is run in such a position that it is not liable to be damaged by contact with the floor, the ceiling or any of their fixings. The regulation also requires that where a cable has to pass through a timber joist within a floor or ceiling construction, or through a ceiling batten, the cable must either:

1. be at least 50 mm measured vertically from the top, or bottom, as appropriate, of the joist or batten,

or

2. comply with Regulation 522.6.203 (as described in Section 11.5.6.).

Fig 11.1 illustrates some of the methods of transversing joists permitted by Regulation 522.6.200.

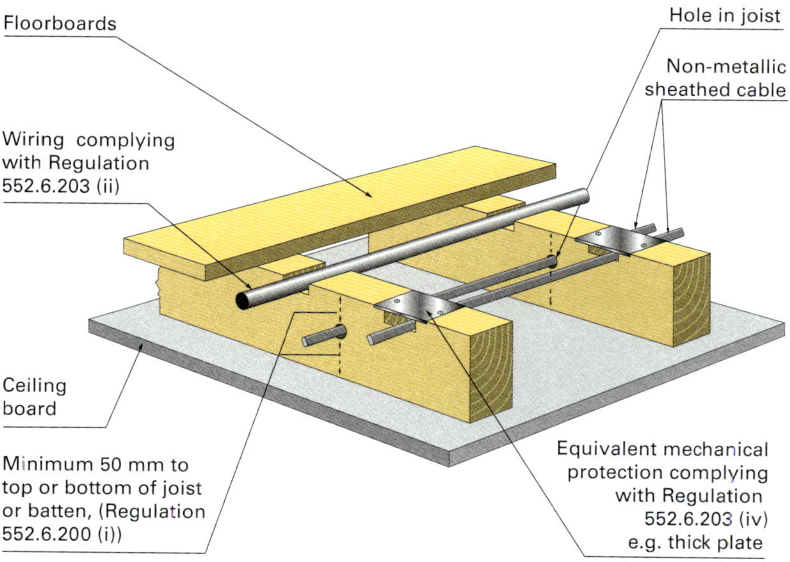

Fig 11.1 Cables in floor joists

Guidance on drilling holes and forming notches in ceiling and floor joists is included in Section 11.11.6.1 of this guide

A cable meeting the 50 mm or greater requirement of Regulation 522.6.200 will, in normal circumstances, be at a sufficient distance from the top or bottom, as appropriate, of a joist or batten to prevent a nail, screw or the like penetrating the cable. However, if the installer knows or believes that the fixings being employed in a particular instance are likely to penetrate a cable placed at 50 mm from the top or bottom of the joist, then the cable must be placed at a depth within the surface sufficient to prevent the fixings from damaging the cable. If this is not practicable then at least one of requirements of 522.6.203 must be met (Regulation 522.6.200 refers).

11.5.8 Protection of concealed cables in walls

Cables embedded in a wall or partition can be vulnerable to penetration by nails, screws and the like, which can lead to the danger of electric shock or even fire. It is therefore important that cable runs are properly planned and that the cables are installed in such a manner as to afford compliance with the requirements of Regulation Group 522.6 dealing with protection against impact.

Where a wall or partition contains significant metal parts, such as would be found in walls and partitions constructed using a metal frame, there is a danger that as the result of damage to a cable all the metalwork within the wall or partition will become live. *BS 7671* treats walls or partition containing significant metal parts differently to walls and partition constructed using traditional methods such as blockwork or timber studwork which do not contain significant metal parts.

Walls with an internal construction NOT containing significant metallic parts

Regulations 522.6.201 deals with protection against impact where a cable is run at a depth of less than 50 mm from the surface of a wall or partition, where the internal construction does not contain significant metal parts. In this situation the cable must comply with the requirements of either of the following requirements:

(i) be installed in a prescribed zone (as shown in Fig 11.2) and be provided with additional protection by means of an RCD having the characteristics specified in Regulation 415.1.1, or

Published by Certsure LLP © Certsure LLP (January 2015)

(ii) comply with Regulation 522.6.203 (as described in Section 11.5.6.).

Regulation 552.6.201 (i) describes the prescribed zones as:

a) within 150 mm from the top of the wall or partition, or
b) within 150 mm of an angle formed by two adjoining walls or partitions, or
c) either horizontally or vertically, to the point, accessory or switchgear on the surface of the wall or partition, to which the cable is connected.

Figure 11.2 provides a visual representation of these zones.

Fig 11.2 The zones detailed in Regulation 522.6.201 (i)

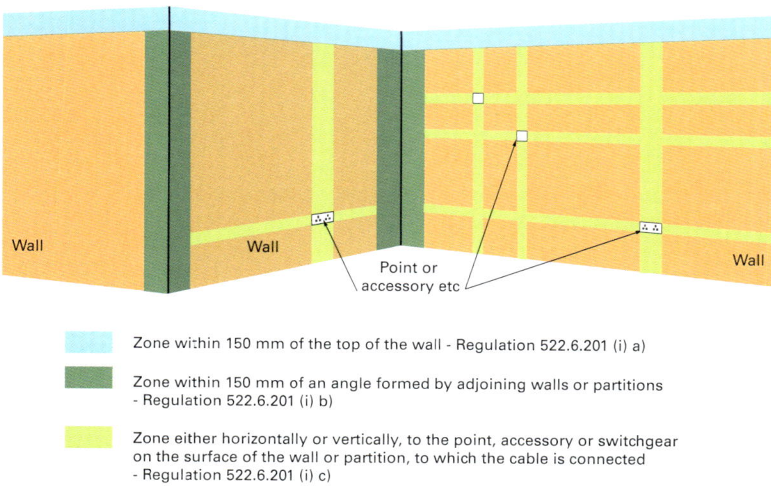

Generally, a zone created on one side of a wall or partition does not extend to the reverse side. However, where the location of the accessory, point or switchgear can be determined from the reverse side, a zone formed on one side of a wall or partition of 100 mm thickness or less extends to the reverse side. An example of this situation is shown in Fig 11.3.

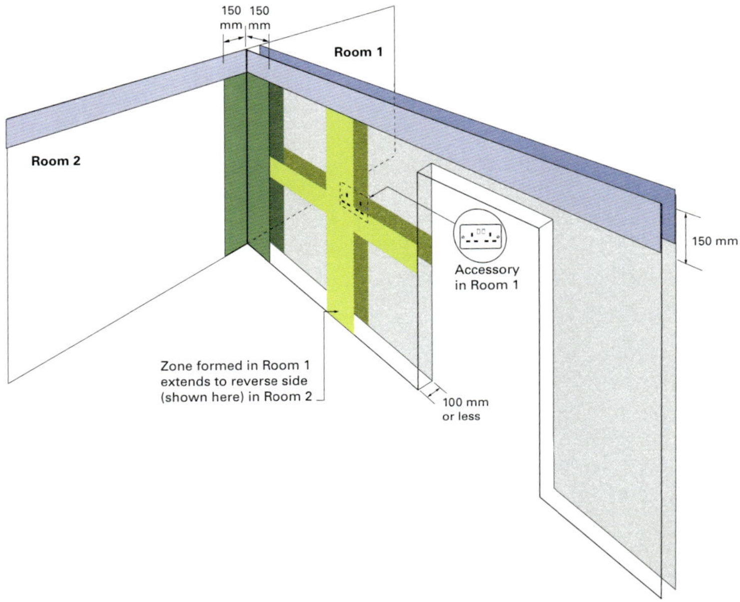

Fig 11.3 An example of where the location of an accessory can be determined from the reverse side of a wall

The presence of a doorway in Fig 11.3 means that a person intending to drive a nail, screw or the like into the wall can reasonably determine the location of the accessory from the reverse side of the wall. A mirror image of the permitted cross-shaped zone created in the room with the accessory (room 1) is therefore considered to exist in the other room. Thus, the concealed wiring connected to the accessory is permitted to be within 50 mm of surface of the reverse side of the wall (just as it is permitted to be within 50 mm of the surface with the accessory), provided it is within the mirror image zone.

Apart from where the location of accessories, switchgear and the like can be determined from the reverse side, a cable that is concealed at a depth of less than 50 mm from either side of a wall or partition has to be in at least one of the permitted zones with respect to that side.

The installation of a cable in such a zone, but passing through the box of an accessory rather than connecting to the accessory, is generally considered acceptable.

Published by Certsure LLP © Certsure LLP (January 2015)

In order to comply with the requirements of Option 1 of Regulation 552.6.20 in addition to being ran in an appropriate zone the wiring be provided with additional protection by means of an RCD having the characteristics specified in Regulation 415.1.1.

Walls with an internal construction containing significant metallic parts

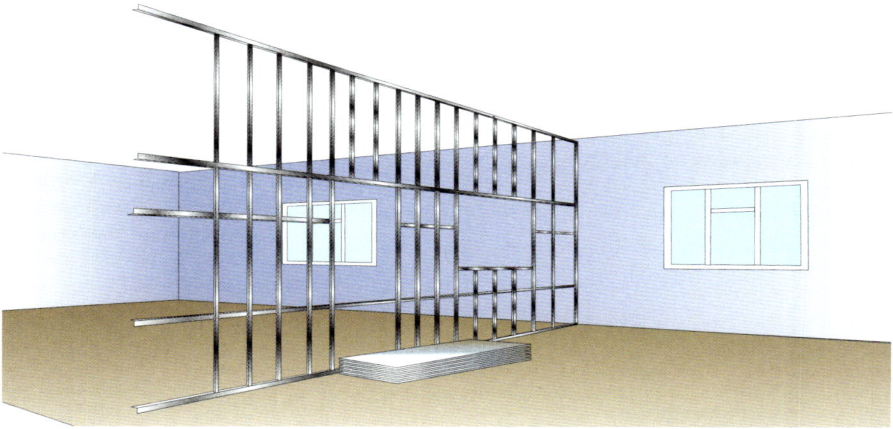

Fig 11.4 The internal construction of a metal framed partition wall

Where a cable is concealed within a wall or partition where the internal construction contains significant metal parts, such as that shown in 11.4, Regulation 522.6.202 requires that irrespective of the depth of the cable from the surface of the wall or partition, the cable shall:

i) be provided with additional protection by means of an RCD having the characteristics specified in Regulation 415.1.1, or

ii) be mechanically protected sufficiently to avoid damage to the cable during construction of the wall or partition and during the installation of the cable, or

iii) comply with requirements of Regulation 522.6.203 (as described in Section 11.5.6.).

In addition, for a cable installed at a depth of 50 mm or less from the surface of a wall or partition containing significant metal parts the requirements of Regulation 522.6.201 previously described shall also apply.

11.5.9 Protection of cables embedded in walls by wet plaster

Where cables are to be embedded in walls by 'wet' plaster, particular consideration also needs to be given to the requirements of Regulation 522.8.1, which requires a wiring system to be so selected and erected to minimise damage to the sheath and insulation during not only installation, but also during use and maintenance activities.

One obvious cause for concern when considering the installation of cables on walls that will subsequently be plastered is the possible damage to the cables that may be caused by the plasterer's trowel. A common method of protecting cables in such instances is to shield them with plastic or metallic capping, which also serves to secure the cables in place.

Whilst capping or indeed plastic conduit may be used to protect cables from damage during construction (see Fig 11.5), they do **not** provide adequate mechanical protection in service for cables located outside the zones described by Regulation 522.6.201.

Cables, concealed in plaster, may be installed outside these zones if they are protected by earthed metal conduit, as shown in Fig 11.6.

Fig 11.5 The use of cable capping

Published by Certsure LLP © Certsure LLP (January 2015)

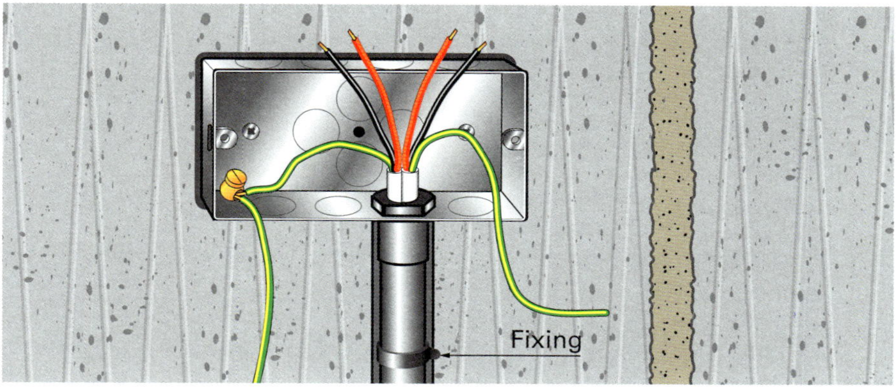

Fig 11.6 Earthed metal conduit

11.5.10 Other mechanical stresses

The following are classified in Appendix 5 of *BS 7671* as 'Other mechanical stresses' (external influence code 'AJ') and do not involve impact or vibration:

- abrasion (e.g. friction, chafing or scraping),
- compression (such as crushing),
- tension (pulling force), and
- torsion (twisting) stresses.

11.5.11 Damage caused during installation

Cables and other parts of a wiring system can easily be damaged during installation, and appropriate steps should be taken to prevent such damage. For example, the sheath of a cable may be torn or chafed where cables are being pulled through an opening in a joist or other part of a building structure, unless the opening is sufficiently large and smooth, and adequate care is exercised in the installation work. Similarly, cables already located in holes through joists may be damaged by the friction generated by other cables being pulled through the hole.

Care must be taken during the erection of conduit and trunking to ensure that there are no internal sharp edges. Internal burred metal must be removed at all joints, and bushes should be installed where cables pass through apertures in enclosures.

To protect cables from damage any containment system employed should be adequately sized and there should be adequate means of access for drawing cables in and out.

Steps should also be taken to protect cables and other parts of a wiring system from damage due to the operations of other trades, such as plastering, the boarding of ceilings, floors and walls, or 'hot' work, such as welding.

In any event, wiring systems should be protected against impact, including that which could result from the operations of other trades.

11.5.12 Means of access to withdrawable wiring systems

For a wiring system designed to be withdrawable, such as cables in a conduit or ducting system, Regulation 522.8.6 requires adequate means of access to be provided for drawing cables in and out.

In addition, where a withdrawable wiring system is buried in the structure, Regulation 522.8.2 requires the wiring system for each circuit to be completely erected between access points **before** the cables are drawn in.

The above requirements are intended to avoid damage to cables when being drawn either in or out, due to inadequate means of access. For example, cable insulation could be damaged by abrasion, or due to excessive pulling force being applied to a cable.

Excessive pulling force may also stretch the conductor of a cable thereby reducing its cross-sectional area and lead to 'hot spots', or cause one or more strands of the conductor to fracture, resulting in intermittent or permanent discontinuity.

11.5.13 Bending radii

Regulation 522.8.3 requires the radius of every bend in a wiring system to be such that the conductors or cables are not damaged.

To comply with this requirement, a cable must not be bent to a radius smaller than a given value, based on its overall diameter (see Fig 11.7). To do so may cause damage to the conductors and insulation, or to the sheath, armouring or serving (if any) of the cable during erection of the installation or at some other time, such as under fault conditions.

Published by Certsure LLP © Certsure LLP (January 2015)

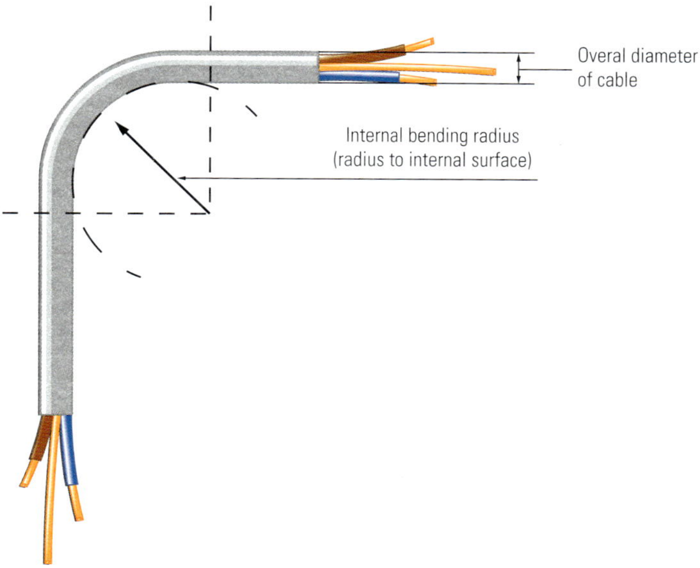

Fig 11.7 The internal bending radius and overall diameter of a cable

Regulation 522.8.3 requires the radius of every bend in a wiring system to be such that the conductors or cables are not damaged.

To comply with this requirement, a cable must not be bent to a radius smaller than a given value, based on its overall diameter. To do so may cause damage to the conductors and insulation, or to the sheath, armouring or serving (if any) of the cable during erection of the installation or at some other time, such as under fault conditions.

Regulation 522.8.3 also requires that no undue stress is placed upon terminations when cables or conductors are bent.

Table 11.7 gives the recommended minimum bending radius for many commonly employed types of non-armoured cable. The radii quoted are in accordance with the relevant British Standards or, where no such information is given in the British Standard for the cable concerned, represent accepted practice. The minimum radius dimension given in Table 11.7 relates to the surface of the cable on the inside of the bend (see Fig 11.7) and is given in terms of the overall diameter of the cable.

Table 11.7 Minimum internal radii for non-armoured cables

Cable type	Conductor material and construction	Cable overall diameter*	Factor to be applied to overall diameter of cable to determine minimum internal radius of bend	
		Non-armoured	Single-strand conductor (solid)	Multi-strand conductor
Thermoplastic (pvc) or thermosetting (XLPE or rubber)	Copper and aluminium circular and circular stranded conductors	Not exceeding 10 mm	3	2
		Exceeding 10 mm but not exceeding 25 mm	4	3
		Exceeding 25 mm	6	6
	Copper shaped conductors and solid aluminium	All	8	8

* For flat type cables the diameter refers to the major axis.

11.5.14 Flexible wiring systems

Flexible wiring systems are sometimes used for certain applications in domestic electrical installations, for example, under-cupboard and wardrobe lighting, and final connections to items of equipment that are subject to vibration or which have to be moveable (such as for maintenance).

Regulation 521.9.2 requires that where equipment is intended to be moved during use, connection should be made using flexible cables.

Where an item of stationary equipment, such as a cooker, needs to be moved temporarily on occasion to permit connection, cleaning, maintenance or the like, the connection to the fixed wiring may be made by non-flexible cables (for example 'twin and earth' type cable). However, if the equipment is subject to vibration in use, flexible cable must be used for the connection (Regulation 521.9.3 refers).

11.5.15 Presence of fauna, flora and/or mould growth

Where exposed to conditions of fauna or flora and/or mould growth that may constitute a hazard, wiring systems and other equipment of an installation are required to be appropriately selected, or special measures adopted. (Regulation Groups 512.2, 522.9 and 522.10 of *BS 7671* refer).

Published by Certsure LLP © Certsure LLP (January 2015)

The term 'fauna' (animal life) includes insects, small animals and birds. Examples of flora (plant life) include plants, trees and other forms of vegetation; mould also has to be considered.

Many electrical installations in external locations, as well as in some internal ocations (such as greenhouses), may be exposed to fauna or flora and/or mould growth that could impair safety or functionality.

As with all external influences, it is best to avoid installing electrical equipment where it will be exposed to adverse effects. For example, distribution equipment (such as switchgear and consumer units) supplying outdoor installations should, where practicable, be installed in an indoor location.

If not suitably selected or adequately protected, equipment enclosures installed in contact with the ground (or buried in it) might become infested by insects.

Luminaires and other equipment designed to be installed outdoors may not necessarily prevent the ingress of insects and should be used only in accordance with the manufacturer's instructions. Cable joints for buried cables are usually compound filled and so ingress by fauna is not possible.

Equipment enclosures provided with small holes to allow collected or condensed water to drain away should not be installed where they are liable to become infested by insects.

Damage to cables from the gnawing of rats, mice and squirrels etc. is a relatively common occurrence. There is no evidence to show that these rodents are uniquely attracted to one type of cable. All types of cable, for example thermoplastic (pvc), rubber and lead sheathed and even steel wire armoured cables, seem susceptible to attack, resulting in exposure of the conductors (Fig 11.8).

Fig 11.8 A pvc insulated and sheathed cable gnawed by mice

Factors relating to installation of wiring systems and cables

Where conductors exposed by the gnawing action are surrounded by rodents' nesting materials, which are generally combustible, there is a risk of fire. This is in addition to the obvious danger of electric shock to persons from direct contact with an exposed live conductor.

Regulation 522.10.1 requires wiring systems to be suitably resistant to damage where the presence or actions of fauna constitutes a hazard and where not suitably resistant to such effects of itself, additional protective measures should be provided to counteract adverse effects. Such measures could include:

- choice of siting/location, or
- the provision of additional protection against mechanical damage either generally or locally, or
- a combination of the above.

Therefore, where cables are installed in areas that are, or are liable to be, inhabited by rodents, such as might be found in the roof voids and cellars of certain older properties, the wiring system must be capable of resisting damage caused by gnawing.

It is advisable to employ cables or wiring systems such as the following for use in such areas:

- steel conduit, or trunking,
- mineral-insulated, metal-sheathed cables,
- steel wire armoured cables,
- thermoplastic (pvc) sheathed cables having galvanized steel braid covering,
- steel capping to protect short exposed runs of thermoplastic (pvc) insulated and sheathed cables.

Cables are less likely to be attacked by rodents where they are attached as far up a wall as possible, or, where installed in a roof void, fixed to the underside of the roof structure.

The enclosures of electrical switchgear, accessories and wiring systems (such as trunking) should be free of any openings through which rodents could gain entry to build nests and cause damage to cables or other equipment.

Cable entries to equipment, such as luminaires, must be effected through correctly selected cable entries using, if necessary, cable glands.

 Published by Certsure LLP © Certsure LLP (January 2015)

11.5.16 Solar and ultra-violet radiation

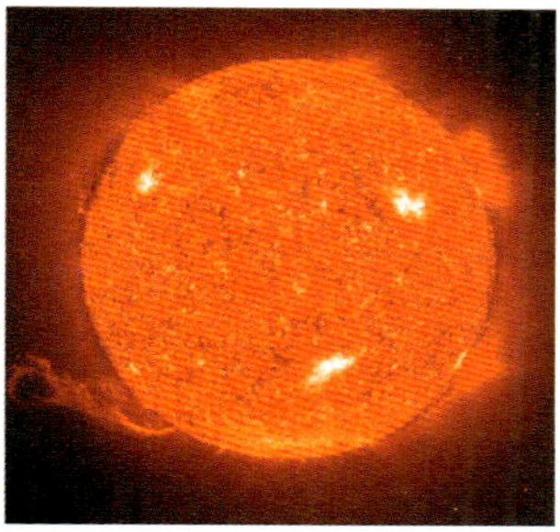

BS 7671 requires wiring systems that will be exposed to solar radiation (external influence code 'AN') to be either selected so that they are resistant to the damage from this external influence or protected from such damage (Regulations 522.2.1 and 522.11.1 refer).

Fig 11.9 Solar radiation being given off by the sun

Ultraviolet (UV) radiation can affect cable sheaths in two ways:

- degradation (splitting, etc), which may lead to danger, and
- colour fade – colour fade can occur without the loss of mechanical properties.

Black cable sheaths made of thermoplastic (pvc) or rubber (but not natural rubber) material generally contain carbon black, an ingredient that gives good resistance to both degradation and colour fade. Grey cable sheaths of such materials contain less carbon black and are therefore likely to afford less resistance to degradation and colour fade than black sheaths. Carbon black is not present in thermoplastic or rubber sheaths of colours other than black or grey but an alternative UV stabiliser is sometimes incorporated.

Black or grey low-smoke zero-halogen sheaths used for armoured cables generally contain a UV stabilizer which resists degradation and colour fade.

Where cables intended mainly for use inside buildings incorporate a low-smoke zero-halogen sheath (such as for some types of cable commonly used for fire alarm systems), the sheath is generally not UV-stabilised as standard. However, a stabiliser may be incorporated to special order. A white sheath of such a cable will normally be materially stabilized but not colour stabilized.

It is important to appreciate that cable product specifications do not stipulate that cable sheaths should be resistant to UV radiation. Therefore, where cables are to be exposed to UV radiation, it is important that the electrical installation designer confirms that the sheaths are suitable for that purpose.

As an alternative to using cables having a sheath that is resistant to UV radiation, cables may be protected by shielding them from direct sunlight.

11.5.17 Solar Gain

Solar gain effectively increases the ambient temperature. As with any increase in temperature, the effective increase in temperature due to solar gain reduces the current-carrying capacity of cables. It may therefore be necessary to use cables having either an increased conductor size or a higher rated temperature in order to provide an adequate current-carrying capacity for the needs of the installation.

The ambient temperature rating factor (C_a) used when determining the current-carrying capacity of the cables should typically be based upon 10 °C above the maximum ambient air temperature in the United Kingdom unless the cables have been shielded from direct sunlight.

Installations in locations with glass roofs (such as greenhouses and conservatories) may also be subject to increased effective ambient temperature as a result of solar gain.

11.6 Impact upon the building structure

When chasing walls or drilling holes through the structural components of a dwelling electrical contractors need to exercise care to ensure that structural integrity of the dwelling is not compromised. Failure to take the necessary care can result in the electrical contractor being liable for expensive repairs.

11.6.1 Penetration of elements of building construction by wiring systems

A cable, trunking or cable tray sometimes has to pass through an element of building construction, such as a floor, wall or beam, necessitating the formation of a notch or opening in the element. To comply with Regulation 522.8.14, no wiring system should penetrate an element of construction that is intended to be load bearing unless the load bearing ability of the element remains satisfactory after such penetration.

Published by Certsure LLP © Certsure LLP (January 2015)

For reasons of structural integrity, there may be restrictions on the dimensions or location of a notch or opening that may be formed in a load bearing element of construction. In some cases the formation of a notch or opening may be completely unacceptable. Where necessary, the advice of a suitably competent person should be obtained.

When working on domestic property electrical contractors are likely to encounter a variety of types of floor and ceiling joists, these may range from traditional solid timber joists to manufactured joists with timber or metal webs. Some preformed joists employ solid timber webs and when it is necessary to drill through this type of web it is most important to either follow the manufacturer's instructions or to take advice from a suitably qualified structural engineer.

Joists with solid timber web

Joists with open metal web

Fig 11.10 Examples of prefabricated joists

Approved Document A no longer provides guidance on the drilling of solid timber joists, instead guidance is provided by *BS EN 1995-1: 2004* (as amended). The Timber Research and Development Association is a useful source of information regarding the drilling and notching of timber structural elements (www.trada.co.uk).

It is generally accepted, within the construction industry, that when dealing with simply supported[1], solid timber joists not greater than 250 mm in depth, adherence to the following guidance means that the effect of notches and holes need not be calculated (see Fig 11.11).

[1]Simply supported means that each end of a floor or roof joist is supported.

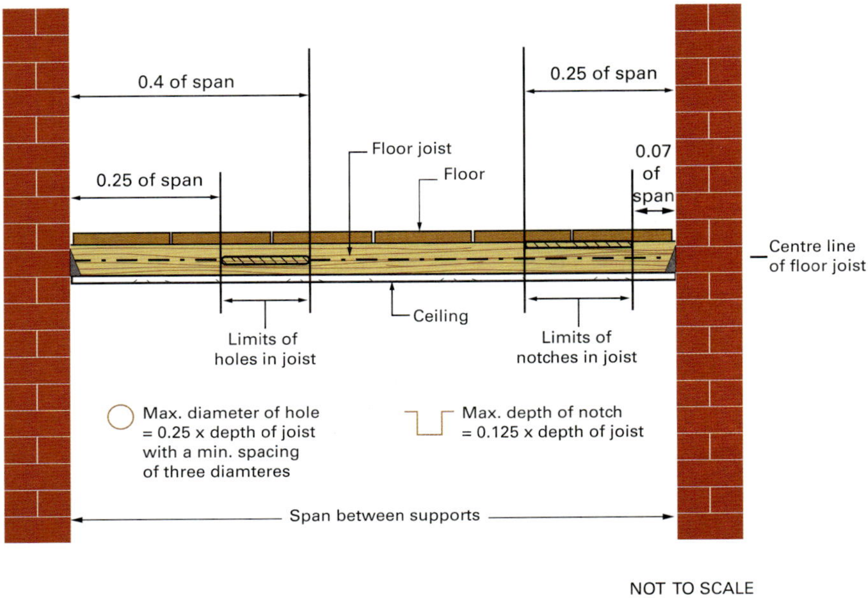

Fig 11.11 Acceptable positions for holes and notches in solid timber joists

Notches should:

- be no deeper than 0.125 times the depth of a joist; and
- not be cut closer to the support than 0.07 of the span, nor further away than 0.25 times the span.

Holes should be:

- no greater diameter than 0.25 times the depth of the joist; should be drilled at the neutral axis[2]; and
- not less than 3 diameters (centre to centre) apart; and
- located between 0.25 and 0.4 times the span from the support.

---

[2]The neutral axis of a joist lies along is the centre line of a joist and is where the joist has neither a compressive or tensional stress.

 Published by Certsure LLP © Certsure LLP (January 2015)

It should be noted that notches or holes should not be cut in roof rafters, other than at supports where the rafter may be birdsmouthed[3] to a depth not exceeding 0.33 times the rafter depth.

11.6.2 Chases in walls

The following requirements for chases in walls are given in paragraph 2C30 of Approved Document A (2004 edition, incorporating 2010 and 2013 amendments):

> **Vertical chases** should not be deeper than ⅓ of the wall thickness or, in cavity walls, ⅓ of the thickness of the leaf.
>
> **Horizontal chases** should not be deeper than ⅙ of the thickness of the wall or leaf.
>
> **Chases** should not be so positioned as to impair the stability of the wall, particularly where hollow blocks are used.

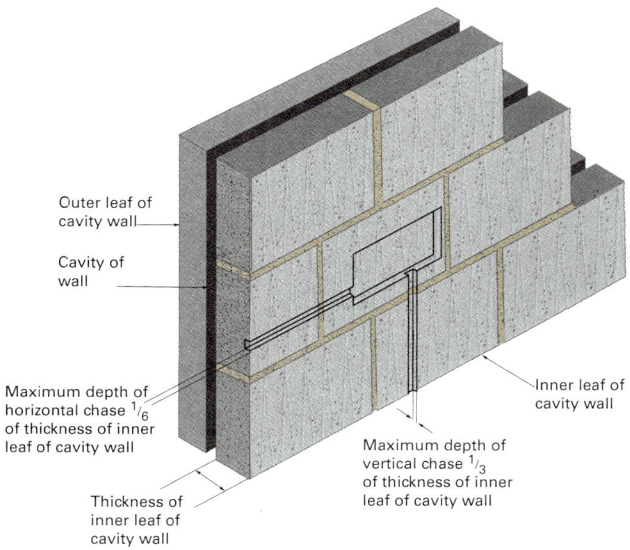

Fig 11.12 Examples of chases in the leaf of a cavity wall

[3]A woodworking joint generally used to connect a roof rafter to the top plate of a supporting wall

11.7 Connections

11.7.1 General

Electrical connections (joints and terminations) are common within installations, both in live (line and neutral) conductors and in protective conductors. The requirements relating to connections apply regardless of the voltage and therefore include extra-low voltage circuits. *BS 7671* contains a number of requirements concerning the construction of electrical connections, to protect against the following dangers which could arise from a poorly constructed connection.

- **Fire or other harmful thermal effects** (due, for example, to excessive temperature developed in a high resistance connection when it carries current, or to arcs or high temperature particles emitted from a loose connection)
- **Contact of a person or livestock with a live conductor** at a connection (direct contact). Basic protection is provided to prevent such a contact.
- **Fault conditions** (due, for example, to a high resistance or open circuit connection in a protective conductor causing the earth fault loop impedance of a circuit to exceed the maximum value required for automatic disconnection of the supply in the event of an earth fault). Fault protection is provided to prevent electric shock due to indirect contact.

11.7.2 Fundamental requirements

Every connection between conductors and between a conductor and equipment (such as switchgear, accessories or current-using equipment) is required to provide durable electrical continuity and adequate mechanical strength (Regulation 526.1 refers). These requirements are likely to be met by complying with the recommendations of this Guide.

Measures for protection against electric shock also have to be provided for connections in live conductors. Additionally, every connection in a live conductor or combined protective and neutral (PEN) conductor must be enclosed.

 Published by Certsure LLP © Certsure LLP (January 2015)

Apart from certain exemptions (listed in Regulation 526.3), all connections must be accessible for inspection, testing and maintenance.

11.7.3 Selection of means of connection and termination

A means of connection between conductors, or between a conductor and an item of equipment, may take one of many forms, depending on the requirements of a particular installation. Examples of means of connection include a terminal of an accessory or item of switchgear, a terminal of a joint box, a connector block, a soldered or compression-type ferrule, and a soldered or compression-type lug bolted to a busbar.

Whatever means of connection is employed, Regulation 526.2 requires its selection to take account, as appropriate, of:

- i) the material of the conductor and its insulation,
- ii) the number and shape of the wires forming the conductor,
- iii) the cross-sectional area of the conductor,
- iv) the number of conductors to be connected together,
- v) the temperature attained by the terminals in normal service such that the effectiveness of the insulation of the conductors connected to them is not impaired,
- v) where a soldered connection is used, the design must take account of creep, mechanical stress and temperature rise under fault current conditions (the term 'creep' refers to a gradual change of shape of material under stress.),
- vii) the provision of adequate locking arrangements in situations subject to vibration or thermal cycling.

In all cases, the limitations of equipment use specified in manufacturer's instructions must be observed.

 © Certsure LLP (January 2015)

The material of the conductor and its insulation

The material of a conductor and its insulation can influence the selection of a means of connection in various ways, some examples of which are as follows.

i) Precautions must be taken to prevent galvanic (electrolytic) corrosion where certain dissimilar metals are placed in contact with each other. For example:

- an aluminium conductor must not be placed in contact with a terminal of brass or other metal having a high copper content, unless the terminal is suitably plated (with zinc or cadmium, for example) or other suitable precautions, are taken to prevent corrosion (such as fitting a suitable ferrule to the conductor)
- where an aluminium conductor and a copper conductor are joined together, precautions (such as plating) must be taken against corrosion.

Where an aluminium conductor is to be connected to a terminal, ferrule or lug, precautions must be taken to ensure that no undue mechanical pressure can be applied to the conductor, for example by the over-tightening of a clamping screw.

Crimped ferrules or lugs should always be correctly selected for the particular cable size and conductor shape and should be compressed only with the dies and nests recommended by the manufacturer.

Conductor insulation must not be subjected to temperatures exceeding its rated value in normal service. Particular attention is needed where conductors insulated with materials of different temperature ratings, such as thermoplastic (pvc) and thermosetting (XLPE or rubber), are to be connected. For example, the rated temperature of the insulation at the joint must be not less than the highest of those for the conductor insulation, or the conductors must be sized such that their normal operating temperatures will not exceed the lowest rated temperature of any of the insulating materials.

Published by Certsure LLP © Certsure LLP (January 2015)

The number and shape of the wires forming the conductor

There are a wide range of conductor types which may need to be connected to each other or to equipment. These include (amongst others), conductors of cables (single-stranded, multi-stranded, flexible or non-flexible), braided conductors, circular rods (such as earth electrodes), and rectangular bars (such as busbars).

Whatever the number or shape of wires forming a conductor, the means of connection must be selected so as to:

- securely contain and anchor all the wires of the conductor, and
- make good electrical contact with the conductor.

The means of connection must not weaken or damage the conductors.

The cross-sectional area of the conductor

The means of connection must be suitable for the cross-sectional area of the Conductor so that:

- adequate mechanical strength is provided by the means of connection (e.g. to withstand the forces of thermal movement of the conductor),
- the conductor can be inserted into the terminal or other means of connection without using unreasonable force, and
- good electrical contact is provided between the conductor and the means of connection (for example, the terminal or other means of connection must be neither too large nor too small for the conductor, and must be correctly designed for the shape of the conductor).

Where it is necessary to reduce the cross-sectional area, or change the shape, of a conductor at the point of connection, this should be done by means of a recognised technique, such as the use of an appropriate pin connector.

The number of conductors to be connected together

BS 7671 does not place a general limit on the number of conductors that an individual terminal or other means of connection may be used to connect together. However, the number of conductors must be limited where necessary to facilitate the proper identification, inspection, testing and maintenance of the connections or conductors (Regulations 514.1.2 and 513.1 refer). Due attention should also be paid to appropriate product standards and manufacturers' instructions as required by Regulations 511.1 and 134.1.1.

The temperature attained by the terminals in normal service

For most types of equipment, the temperature attained by terminals in normal service is unlikely to impair the effectiveness of the insulation of the conductors connected to them.

Soldered connections

Soldering of lugs and ferrules to conductors, although rarely carried out nowadays, was common practice until the use of compression-type sockets became established in the 1960s. In the absence of more precise information, soldered connections or joints are limited to a maximum temperature under fault conditions of 160 °C. They are therefore unsuitable for cable installations taking full advantage of the limiting final temperatures of above 160 °C offered by cables insulated with certain materials (such as thermosetting material).

Fitting and soldering of lugs and ferrules is a skilled practice and therefore relies on a jointer's skill to produce a solid ferrule or lug without leaving cavities or poorly tinned conductor strands. Such defects can result in a high resistance connection, leading to premature failure.

Provision of adequate locking arrangements

Locknuts or other suitable locking arrangements must be provided to prevent terminal screws or other means of connection becoming loose in service where subject to vibration or thermal cycling.

 Published by Certsure LLP © Certsure LLP (January 2015)

External influences

Like any other parts of a wiring system, electrical connections must be appropriately selected and erected to be suitable for the external influences they are likely to encounter, such as the following, which are referred to in Section 522 of *BS 7671*.

- Ambient temperature (taking account of the highest and lowest local ambient temperatures).
- External heat sources (such as solar gain).
- Presence of water, high humidity or solid foreign bodies (prevention of ingress and/or accumulation, as applicable).
- Presence of corrosive or polluting substances.
- Impact.
- Other mechanical stresses (for example, where necessary to prevent damage due to snagging, connection boxes should be securely fixed, and means such as a cable clamp should be provided to prevent strain on terminations).
- Presence of flora and/or mould growth or fauna (e.g. insects or vermin).
- Radiation (solar or ultra-violet).
- Building design (e.g. structural movement).

See also Section 11.5 of this Guide.

11.7.4 Enclosure of connections

Irrespective of nominal voltage, every termination and joint in a live conductor or PEN conductor is required to be contained within an enclosure selected in accordance with Regulation 526.5. This includes connections in extra-low voltage circuits such as those supplying extra-low voltage luminaires.

The purpose of such an enclosure is to protect persons, and property against harmful thermal effects, such as arcs or high temperature particles which may be emitted from a loose connection (Regulation 421.1.3 refers). The enclosure may also provide basic protection against electric shock and protection against external influences.

 © Certsure LLP (January 2015)

11.7.5 Protection against electric shock

As for any other part of an electrical installation, a connection in a live (line or neutral) conductor must be provided with a measure of basic protection and a measure of fault protection.

Basic protection

The enclosure may often be used for basic protection. This is provided that the design of the enclosure meets the requirements of *BS 7671* for such use, such as affording an appropriate degree of protection (IP Code), and having suitable facilities (such as a screw-fixed cover) where opening of the enclosure is necessary.

Where the enclosure is not relied on for basic protection, the live parts at a connection must normally be insulated or placed behind a barrier, in accordance with the applicable requirements. It should be noted that the use of insulating tape will almost certainly **not** meet the requirements of *BS 7671* for basic protection.

Fault protection

At least one of the protective measures referred to in Regulation 410.3.3 must be provided for an electrical connection (such as Automatic Disconnection of Supply, which includes the earthing of exposed-conductive-parts of metal enclosures).

In addition, the electrical continuity of connections in protective conductors is an essential part of ensuring that the earth fault loop impedance of a circuit does not exceed the maximum value required for automatic disconnection of the supply in the event of an earth fault, and is maintained at a suitably low value.

11.7.6 Accessibility of connections

Regulation 526.3 requires every connection (with certain exceptions, listed in the regulation) to be accessible for inspection, testing and maintenance.

Except where a concealed conduit, trunking, metal armouring or metal cable sheath is used as a circuit protective conductor (cpc), the requirements of Regulation 526.3 for accessibility apply no less to a connection in a protective conductor than to a connection in any other conductor.

Published by Certsure LLP © Certsure LLP (January 2015)

11.7.7 Protective conductor connections involving the metal sheath or armouring or metal enclosure.

Subject to all the relevant requirements being met, a protective conductor may consist of a metal part of a wiring system, such as a metal sheath, armouring or screen of a cable, or a metal conduit or other enclosure or electrically continuous support system for conductors (see Regulation 543.2.2).

The electrical continuity of connections involving such parts of a wiring system is required (no less than that of the parts themselves) to be assured in such a way as to be protected against mechanical damage, chemical and electrochemical deterioration.

11.8 Cable supports

11.8.1 General

The basic requirements for the support of cables are given in Regulations 522.8.4 and 522.8.5 of *BS 7671*. In particular, cables should be supported in such a way that they will not be exposed to undue mechanical strain, including any strain caused by their own weight, and that there is no appreciable mechanical strain on the terminations of the conductors. Where a cable is supported at intervals, rather than continuously, the intervals should be appropriate to meet the above requirements for avoidance of strain.

BS 7671 does not stipulate the particular means by which cables should be supported, but leaves this to be dictated by the needs of the installation concerned. However, a number of essential requirements need to be met, some examples of which are expanded upon below.

11.8.2 Surfaces in contact with a cable

All surfaces in contact with a cable must be reasonably smooth and free from sharp corners or edges likely to damage the cable (Regulation 522.8.11). This applies to cable clips, parts of a wiring system (such as conduit and cable tray) and parts of a building (such as walls, ceilings and floors).

 © Certsure LLP (January 2015)

11.8.3 Suitability for external influences

Cable supports and their fixings, like any other parts of a wiring system, must be selected so as to be suitable for the external influences they are likely to be exposed to at their location (Section 522).

For example, where vibration is likely to occur, locking arrangements such as shakeproof washers may be required.

11.8.4 Avoidance of electrolytic corrosion

Metallic cable clips, support systems (such as cable tray), cable sheaths and armour etc. of dissimilar metals between which electrolytic corrosion is liable to occur, should not be placed in contact with each other (Regulation 522.5.2 refers). Such corrosion is possible between, for example, zinc (as used in galvanizing) and copper, especially in the presence of moisture.

11.8.5 Enclosure of non-sheathed cables

Non-sheathed cables for fixed wiring are required by Regulation 521.10.1 to be enclosed in conduit, ducting or trunking. This requirement does not apply to a protective conductor complying with Section 543 of *BS 7671*. However, where the protective conductor belongs to an a.c. circuit installed in a ferrous enclosure (such as steel conduit, trunking or ducting) the protective conductor must be installed in the same enclosure in order to meet the requirements of Regulation 521.5.1 relating to electromagnetic effects.

Vertical runs of trunking or ducting exceeding 5 m in length

For cables of any type in a vertical run of trunking or ducting exceeding 5 m in length, intermediate cable supports should be provided.

Vertical runs of conduit exceeding 5 m in length

For non-sheathed cables in a vertical run of conduit exceeding 5 m in length, precautions (such as additional cable supports) should be taken to protect the cable insulation on the bend at the top of the run against undue compression.

Published by Certsure LLP © Certsure LLP (January 2015)

Vertical runs of cable supported from the top

Where a vertical run of cable is supported from the top, such support should comprise a clip and a rounded support of radius not less than that recommended in Table 11.8. In addition, for reasons of protection against mechanical damage (Regulation Groups 522.6 and 522.8), the cable should be inaccessible and unlikely to be disturbed.

11.8.6 Cables resting without fixings

Cables resting without fixing on part of a building (such as on the top surface of a plasterboard ceiling beneath floorboards) should be located where they are inaccessible and unlikely to be disturbed.

11.8.7 Spacing between supports

BS 7671 requires the intervals between cable supports (as well as the means of support) to be such that cables do not suffer mechanical damage or strain. Table 11.8 gives suggested maximum spacings between supports for both horizontal and vertical runs of cable.

Table 11.8 Maximum spacing of supports for cables in accessible positions, the entire support being derived form the clips

Overall diameter of cable, Φ [3] (mm)	Non-armoured thermosetting cable[1]	
	Horizontal [2][4] (mm)	Vertical [2] (mm)
$0 < \Phi \le 9$	250	400
$9 < \Phi \le 15$	300	400
$15 < \Phi \le 20$	350	450
$20 < \Phi \le 40$	400	550

Notes:

1. The spacings given in this table are maxima, and for good workmanship in certain circumstances the spacings may need to be reduced.
2. For the spacing of supports of cables having an overall diameter not exceeding 40 mm.
3. For flat cables, taken as the dimension of the major axis.
4. The spacings stated for horizontal runs may be applied also to runs at an angle of more than 30° from the vertical. For runs at an angle of 30° or less from the vertical, the vertical spacings are applicable.

 © Certsure LLP (January 2015)

As *BS 7671* is principally concerned with the safety aspects of support systems, supports additional to those indicated in Table 11.8 are often needed to make the finished installation visually acceptable. Additional supports may also be needed in an installation subjected to vibration of medium or high severity, or where there is an increased risk of mechanical damage, such as by accidental snagging of the cable.

Special considerations sometimes apply to the spacing and arrangement of supports for distribution cables installed in free air, due to thermal expansion, and for the maximum lengths of span and minimum heights for overhead wiring linking buildings etc.

11.8.8 Cable supports and wiring systems in escape routes

Due to the heat generated in a fire, plastic cable ties and non-metallic conduit or trunking can fail and this can result in cables hanging, at low level, across escape routes. To minimise the likelihood of firefighters and others being entangled in cables, Regulation 521.11.200 requires that wiring systems run in escape routes shall be supported in such a way that, in the event of a fire, they will not be liable to premature collapse. Regulation 521.11.200 also states that the requirements of Regulation 422.2.1 relating to the selection of wiring systems for use in buildings where specified conditions for evacuation apply.

With the possible exception of extremely spacious homes, the requirements of Regulations 521.11.200 and 422.2.1 will not apply to many individual dwellings. However, the requirements of both these Regulation are likely to apply to the corridors, stairwells and communal areas of blocks of flats and houses in multiple occupancy.

 Published by Certsure LLP © Certsure LLP (January 2015)

Chapter 12

Special installations and locations

Published by Certsure LLP © Certsure LLP (January 2015)

 Published by Certsure LLP © Certsure LLP (January 2015)

12.1 Introduction and scope

This Chapter looks at the requirements for the following special installations or locations falling within the scope of Part 7 of *BS 7671* that may be found in domestic premises.

- Locations containing a bath or shower (Section 701).
- Swimming pools (Section 702).
- Saunas (Section 703).
- Electric vehicle charging installations (Section 722).

Section 700 of *BS 7671* explains that the requirements within Part 7 supplement or modify the general requirements found elsewhere in that standard. In the absence of any additional or modified requirements in a Part 7, the general requirements apply unchanged.

A zonal concept is applied for some of the special locations covered in this chapter, whereby the requirements for safety are based on the perceived degree of risk of electric shock at a particular point within the location.

In this Chapter the term '30 mA RCD' is often used. This term means a Residual Current Device (RCD) with a rated residual operating current ($I_{\Delta n}$) not exceeding 30 mA and an operating time not exceeding 40 ms at a residual current of 5 $I_{\Delta n}$ (Regulation 415.1.1).

Such a device is recognised in a.c. systems as providing additional protection in the event of failure of the provision for basic protection and/or the provision for fault protection or carelessness by users (Regulation 415.1.1).

The use of such devices is not recognised as a sole means of protection and does not obviate the need to apply one of the protective measures specified in Sections 411 to 414 of *BS 7671* (Regulation 415.1.2).

12.2 Locations containing a bath or shower

Locations containing a bath, shower or cabinet containing a shower and/or bath and the surrounding areas are considered to be locations where there is an increased risk of electric shock due to:

- a reduction in body resistance caused either by bodily immersion or by wet skin, and
- likely contact of substantial areas of the body with earth potential.

Consequently, a number of specific requirements are contained within Section 701 (Locations containing a bath or shower) of *BS 7671*.

In addition to the requirements given in Section 701, all other relevant sections of *BS 7671* apply to such locations, albeit supplemented and modified by Section 701.

It should be noted that the requirements of Section 701 must be applied where a bath or shower is located in a room having a different primary purpose, such as a bedroom.

12.2.1 Zones

Zone 0 as described in Regulation 701.32.2, is the interior of the bath tub or shower basin. For showers without a basin, zone 0 extends to 0.10 m vertically and to the same extent horizontally as zone 1 as described below.

Zone 1 is the three dimensional space limited by:

- The finished floor level and whichever is the higher, the horizontal plane aligning with the highest fixed shower head or water outlet or the horizontal plane lying 2.25 m above the finished floor level.
- The vertical surface:
  - a) forming the edge of the bath tub or shower basin, or
  - b) for showers without a basin, at a distance of 1.20 m from the centre point of the fixed water outlet on the wall or ceiling.

Zone 1 does not include zone 0.

The space under the bath tub or shower basin is considered to be zone 1 unless such space is accessible only with a tool, in which case it is considered to be outside the zones (Regulation 701.32.3).

 Published by Certsure LLP © Certsure LLP (January 2015)

Zone 2 is the three dimensional space limited by:

- The finished floor level and whichever is the higher, the horizontal plane aligning with the highest fixed shower head or water outlet or the horizontal plane lying 2.25 m above the finished floor level.
- The vertical surface between the boundary of zone 1 and the parallel vertical surface at a distance of 0.60 m from the zone 1 border.

For showers without a basin, there is no zone 2 but zone 1 is increased, extending 1.20 m horizontally from the fixed water outlet.

The zones are limited by walls, doors, fixed partitions, ceilings and floors where these effectively limit the extent of a zone.

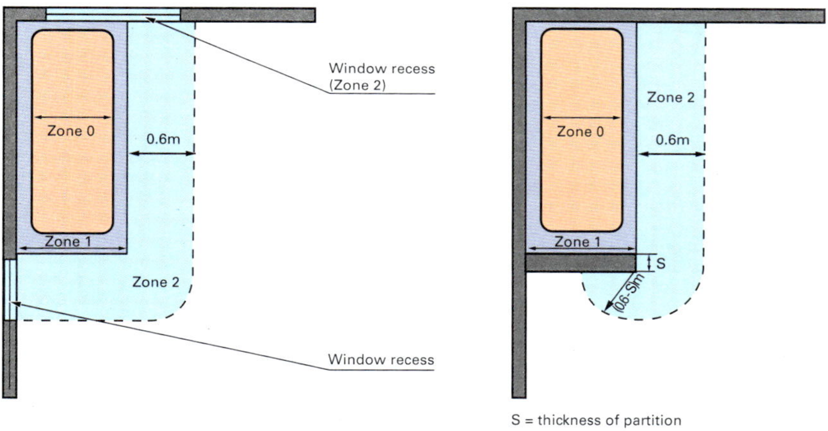

Fig 12.1 Bath tub. Plan views (with and without a permanently fixed partition) to illustrate zone boundaries

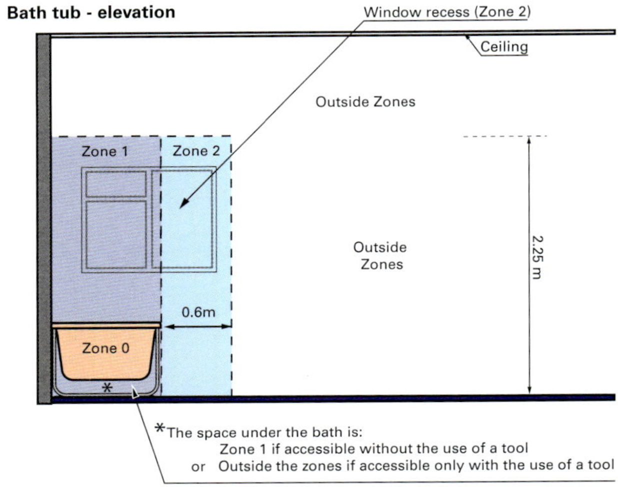

Fig 12.2 Bath tub. Elevation

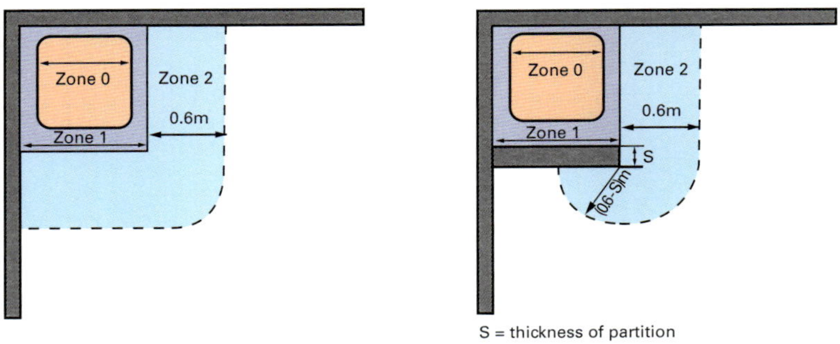

Fig 12.3 Shower basin. Plan views (with and without a permanently fixed partition) to illustrate zone boundaries

Published by Certsure LLP © Certsure LLP (January 2015)

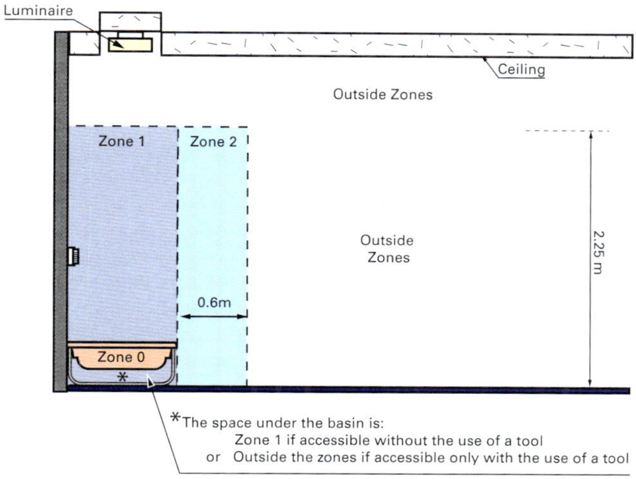

Fig 12.4 Shower basin. Elevation

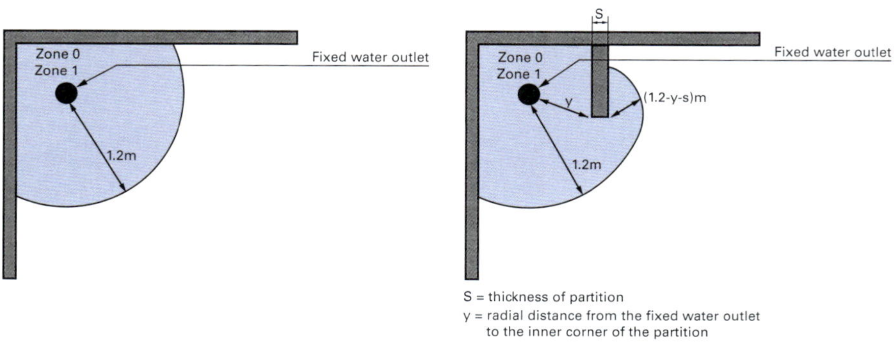

Fig 12.5 Shower, without a basin. Plan views (with and without a permanently fixed partition) having a fixed water outlet

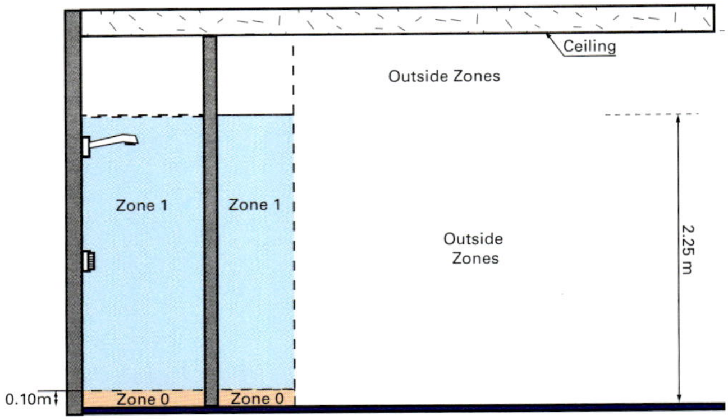

Fig 12.6 Shower without a basin. Elevation with a permanently fixed partition

12.2.2 Protection against electric shock

BS 7671 does not allow basic protection to be provided by obstacles or protection by placing out of reach anywhere within in a location containing a bath or shower (Regulation 701.410.3.5). Further, fault protection by non-conducting location or by earth-free local equipotential bonding is similarly prohibited (Regulation 701.410.3.6).

12.2.3 Additional protection

Regulation 701.411.3.3 requires that all low voltage circuits (typically 230 V) serving or passing through zones 1 or 2, but not serving the location containing a bath or shower, are required to have additional protection by one or more RCDs meeting the requirements of Regulation 415.1 (that is, having $I_{\Delta n}$ = 30 mA). This includes any circuits provided for lighting. It is the responsibility of the installation designer to configure the consumer unit and the final circuits so that all circuits extending into the location have the necessary RCD protection. The possibility of unwanted tripping must be considered and, if necessary, suitable arrangements made (Regulation Group 314 and Regulation 531.2.4 refer). See also Section 5.3.4 of this Guide.

 Published by Certsure LLP © Certsure LLP (January 2015)

12.2.4 SELV or PELV circuits

Where extra-low voltage by means of SELV or PELV is used, whatever the nominal voltage, basic protection for equipment in zones 0, 1 and 2 must be provided by basic insulation or barriers or enclosures affording a degree of protection of at least IPXXB or IP2X.

12.2.5 Supplementary equipotential bonding

Except where it is permitted to omit supplementary equipotential bonding (as discussed later in this Chapter), Regulation 701.415.2 requires the protective conductor terminals of each circuit supplying electrical equipment, whether of Class I or Class II construction, and the accessible extraneous-conductive-parts to be connected together by local supplementary equipotential bonding conductors. This is to prevent the occurrence of voltages between any such parts of a magnitude that could cause danger of electric shock.

Examples of parts commonly found in a bathroom that may come within the definition of an extraneous-conductive-part include:

- metallic pipes supplying services, and metallic waste pipes (e.g. water, gas),
- metallic central heating pipes and air conditioning systems,
- accessible metallic structural parts of the building; (metallic door architraves, window frames and similar parts are not considered to be extraneous-conductive-parts unless they are connected to metallic structural parts of the building),
- metallic baths and metallic shower basins.

All such parts, and any other parts that fall within the definition of an extraneous-conductive-part given in Part 2 of *BS 7671*, require supplementary bonding. An example of such bonding is shown in Fig 12.7.

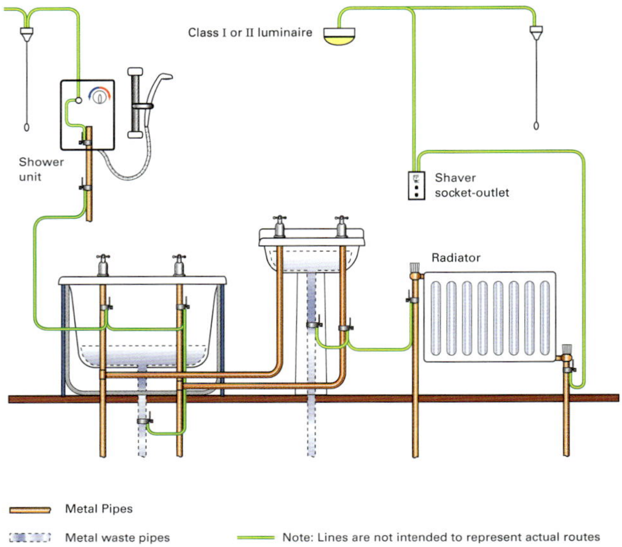

Fig 12.7 Examples of supplementary bonding applied in a location containing a bath

The requirements for supplementary equipotential bonding in a location containing a bath or shower apply only to the accessible extraneous-conductive-parts and to the protective conductor terminals of equipment.

The required supplementary bonding may be carried out either within the location containing the bath or shower or outside where it may be more aesthetically acceptable (such as in an adjoining roof void or an airing cupboard opening into, or adjoining, the room) but preferably close to the point of entry of the extraneous-conductive-parts into the room. (Regulation 701.415.2).

Metallic pipes solidly and reliably connected to each other within or adjacent to the special location (such as soldered pipes in an adjoining airing cupboard) might not need further supplementary bonding to each other.

A metallic bath generally requires supplementary bonding. Connections between hot and cold and waste pipes might only provide intermittent or fortuitous contact.

Published by Certsure LLP © Certsure LLP (January 2015)

Supplementary bonding connections, as with all electrical connections or joints, should be:

- accessible for inspection, testing and maintenance (Regulation 526.3) apart from connections or joints made in one of the ways exempted by that Regulation, and
- identified by a permanent label at the point of connection of ever bonding conductor to an extraneous-conductive-part (Regulation 514.13).

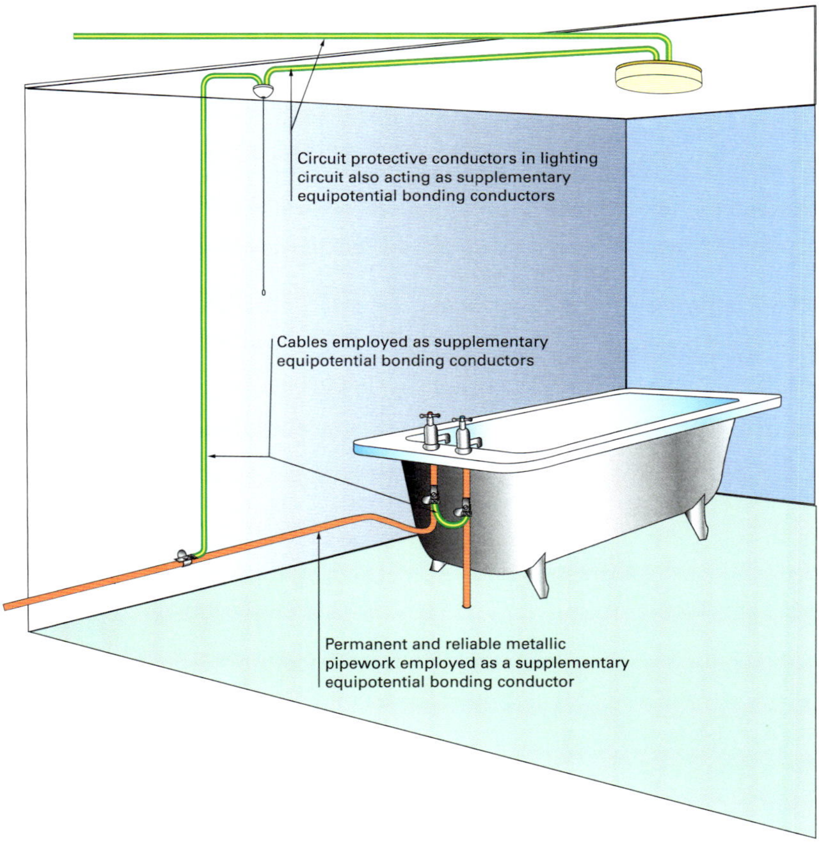

Fig 12.8 Supplementary bonding conductors in a bathroom

Omission of supplementary bonding

Where the location containing a bath or shower is in a building with a main protective equipotential bonding system in accordance with Regulation 411.3.1.2 (as should generally be the case), supplementary equipotential bonding may be omitted where **all** of the following conditions are met:

- all final circuits of the location comply with the requirements for automatic disconnection according to Regulation 411.3.2, and
- all final circuits of the location have additional protection by means of a 30 mA RCD, and
- all extraneous-conductive-parts of the location are effectively connected to the protective equipotential main bonding according to Regulation 411.3.1.2.

Note: The effectiveness of the connection of extraneous-conductive-parts in the location to the main earthing terminal may be assessed, where necessary, by the application of Regulation 415.2.2 regarding the value of resistance (Regulation 701.415.2 refers).

Permitted types of supplementary bonding conductor

By virtue of Regulation 543.2.6, certain extraneous-conductive-parts in the special location, may, at least in part, be used as supplementary bonding conductors. This is subject to the extraneous-conductive-parts satisfying all the requirements given therein. For example, the supplementary bonding conductors in a particular bathroom could comprise a combination of permanent-and-reliable metal pipework (perhaps of the central heating and water supply services), green and yellow covered copper cables and circuit protective conductors subject to their meeting the csa requirements of Chapter 54 of *BS 7671* for such use. See Fig 12.8.

The supplementary bonding connection to a fixed electrical appliance, such as an electric towel rail, may be provided by the circuit protective conductor (cpc) within a short length of flexible cable connecting the appliance to an accessory having a flex outlet (Regulation 544.2.5).

Published by Certsure LLP © Certsure LLP (January 2015)

BS 7671 does not require an additional separately run independent bonding conductor (such as a main protective bonding conductor) to link the supplementary equipotential bonding in a bathroom or shower room with the Main Earthing Terminal (MET) of the installation.

External influences

Each item of electrical equipment in a location containing a bath, shower, or cabinet containing a shower and/or bath, no less than in any other area, must be selected and erected so as to be suitable for the external influences likely to occur at the particular point of installation. Such influences are likely to include steam (leading to condensation), falling drops of water and sprays and/or jets from shower nozzles.

Shower units (incorporating an electrical instantaneous water heater), as with all equipment, must be suitable both for the zone and the conditions likely to occur.

Regulation 701.512.2 of Section 701 contains a number of requirements regarding the degree of protection against ingress of water into electrical equipment to be applied in addition to general requirements for external influences given in Regulation Group 512.2 and Section 522.

The minimum permitted degree of protection related to the zones is shown in Table 12.1.

Table 12.1 Minimum required degrees of ingress protection

Zone(s)	Minimum degree of protection[2] IP code
Zone 0	IPX7
Zones 1 and 2[1]	IPX4
Zones 1 and 2 where water jets are likely to be used for cleaning IPX5[2] purposes in communal baths or communal showers	IPX5[1]
Outside zones 0, 1 and 2	General rules (see note 2)

Note 1: Shaver supply units to *BS EN 61558-2-5* may be installed in zone 2 if located where direct spray from a shower is unlikely (Regulation 701.512.2).

Note 2: Equipment has to be suitable for the conditions likely to occur at the particular point of installation. This may mean a higher IP rating than the minimum value required by the Table.

Switchgear, controlgear and accessories

Table 12.2 identifies the switchgear, controlgear and accessories that may be installed within a particular zone in the special location (Regulation 701.512.3).

Table 12.2 Permitted equipment in the zones

Zone	Permitted equipment
Zone 0	Switches and controls incorporated in fixed current-using equipment suitable for use in the zone. Insulating pull cords of cord operated switches.
Zone 1	Switches and controls incorporated in fixed current-using equipment suitable for use in the zone. Switches of SELV circuits supplied at a nominal voltage not exceeding 12 V a.c. rms or 30 V ripple-free d.c., the safety source being installed outside of zones 0, 1 and 2. Insulating pull cords of cord operated switches.
Zone 2	Switches and controls incorporated in fixed current-using equipment suitable for use in the zone. Switches or socket-outlets of SELV circuits, the safety source being installed outside of zones 0, 1 and 2. Shaver supply units complying with *BS EN 61558-2-5* (if located where direct spray from a shower is unlikely). Insulating pull cords of cord operated switches.
Outside of zones 0, 1 and 2	The general requirements of *BS 7671* apply.

Note: Except for SELV socket-outlets complying with Section 414 and shaver supply units complying with *BS EN 61558-2-5*, socket-outlets are prohibited within a distance of 3 m horizontally from the boundary of zone 1.

A question sometimes arises of whether wall-mounted lighting switches and other such accessories are permitted in a location containing a bath or shower. Regulation 701.512.3 does not preclude the installation of such equipment outside of the zones. However, the general requirements of *BS 7671* are applicable to locations containing a bath or shower and Regulation 512.2.1 calls for every item of equipment to be of a design appropriate to the situation in which it is to be used, or its mode of installation shall take account of the conditions likely to be encountered.

Published by Certsure LLP © Certsure LLP (January 2015)

The requirements of *BS 7671* may be met by:

- installing a wall-mounted light switch with an IP rating suitable for its position within the location
- using a pull-cord switch complying with *BS EN 60669-1: 1999 (2008)* with an IP rating suitable for its position. The body of the switch must be installed outside of zones 0, 1 and 2 but the pull cord itself is permitted to enter zones 1 or 2 provided it is of insulating material.

Fixed current-using equipment

Table 12.3 identifies, with respect to the zone, the fixed current-using equipment that may be installed in a location containing a bath or shower (Regulation 701.55).

Table 12.3 Fixed current-using equipment that may be installed in a location containing a bath or shower

Zone	Permitted equipment
Zone 0	Current-using equipment that: • complies with the relevant standard **and** • is suitable for the conditions of the zone according to the manufacturer's instructions for use and mounting, **and** • is fixed and permanently connected **and** • is protected by SELV at a nominal voltage not exceeding 12 V a.c. rms or 30 V ripple-free d.c. **and** • the source is installed outside of zones 0, 1 and 2.
Zone 1	The following fixed, permanently connected current-using equipment provided it is suitable for installation in zone 1 according to the manufacturer's instructions: • whirlpool units • electric showers • shower pumps • equipment protected by SELV or PELV at a nominal voltage not exceeding 25 V a.c. rms or 60 V ripple free d.c. the safety source being installed outside zones 0,1 and 2 • ventilation equipment • towel rails • water heating appliances • luminaires
Zone 2 and outside of zones 0, 1 and 2	The general requirements of *BS 7671* apply.

Low voltage socket-outlets

Low voltage socket-outlets, such as a 13 A, 230 V socket-outlet, are not permitted within a distance of 3 m horizontally from the boundary of zone 1 in a location containing a bath or shower (see Regulation 701.512.3). The circuit supplying the socket-outlet, in common with all the low voltage circuits of the location, must have additional protection provided by an RCD meeting the requirements of Regulation 415.1.1 (see Regulation 701.411.3.3).

Shaver supply units and SELV socket-outlets

Shaver supply units complying with *BS EN 61558-2-5* may be installed in zone 2 and beyond as can SELV socket-outlets complying with Section 414. Such shaver supply units incorporate a safety isolating transformer to afford protection by electrical separation.

Shaver supply units are not normally splash-proof and whilst Regulation 701.512.3 permits their installation outside zones 0 and 1 they should be positioned well away from baths or showers.

Normal lighting switch height (that is, between 450 mm and 1200 mm above finished floor level) will usually safeguard against splashing from a wash basin.

Stationary equipment

Washing machines, tumble dryers and the like may be installed beyond zone 2 in a location containing a bath or shower supplied by a socket-outlet or fused connection unit.

However, in extreme cases, a manufacturer's agent may not be prepared to carry out servicing or maintenance on an appliance in a location containing a bath or shower until it is moved to what they consider to be a safer location, even where all the relevant electrical installation requirements of *BS 7671* have been met.

Electric floor heating systems

Regulation 701.753 states that only heating cables according to relevant product standards or thin sheet flexible heating elements according to the relevant equipment standard should be employed for electric floor heating systems in a location containing a bath or shower.

Any such heating cable or element should either have either a metallic sheath, or a metallic enclosure or a fine mesh metallic grid which should be connected to the

Published by Certsure LLP © Certsure LLP (January 2015)

protective conductor of the supply circuit, except where the protective measure of SELV is provided for the floor heating system.

This Regulation further states that the protective measure of protection by electrical separation is not permitted for floor heating systems within the location.

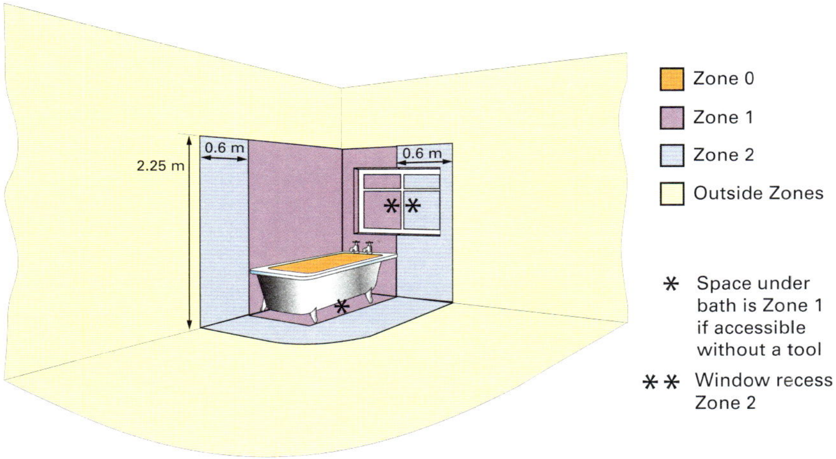

Fig 12.9 Summary of zoning requirements for a location containing a bath

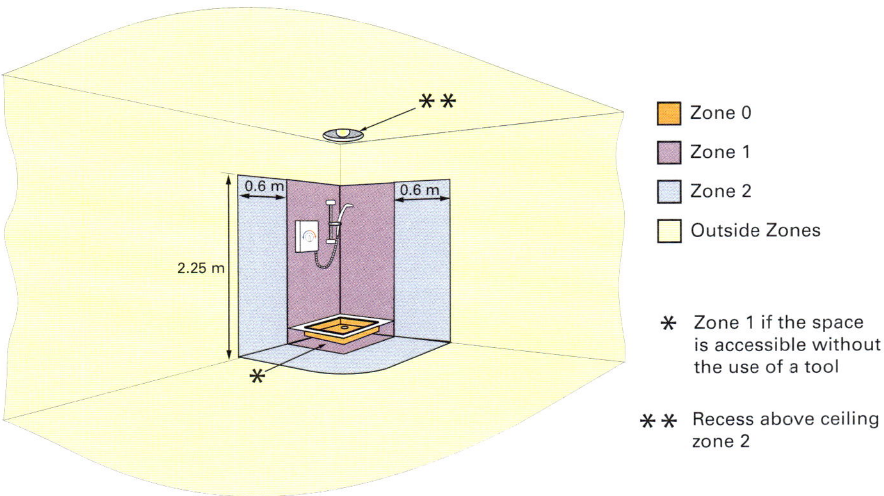

Fig 12.10 Summary of zoning requirements for a location containing a shower

ZONE	OUTSIDE NOTE 5	2 NOTE 6 IPX4 (See Note 9)	1 NOTE 6 IPX4 (See Note 9)	0 NOTE 6 IPX7 (See Note 10)
230V wall mounted plate switch		✗	✗	✗
Luminaire			Note 3	✗
SELV or PELV safety source		✗	✗	✗
Shaver supply unit		Note 2	✗	✗
Ventilation equipment			Note 3	✗
Pull cord switch mechanism		✗	✗	✗
Insulated pull cord				
SELV switches/socket-outlets		Note 8	Note 7	✗
Switches or controls in fixed current-using equipment suitable for use in the zone				
Whirlpool unit Electric shower Shower pump Ventilation equipment Towel rail Water heating appliance			Note 3	✗
Equipment, such as a fan or light, protected by SELV or PELV at a nominal voltage not exceeding 25V a.c. rms or 60V ripple-free d.c.			Note 3	✗
SELV fixed light or fan. Equipment protected by SELV at a nominal voltage not exceeding 12V a.c. rms or 30 V ripple-free d.c.				Note 4
230V socket-outlet	Note 1	✗	✗	✗

Note 1 Prohibited within a distance of 3 m horizontally from the boundary of zone 1.

Note 2 A shaver supply unit must be to BS EN 61558-2-5. The requirement for a degree of protection of a minimum of IPX4 in zone 2 does not apply to shaver units situated where direct spray from showers is unlikely.

Note 3 Equipment must be fixed, permanently connected, suitable for zone 1 according to the manufacturer's instructions.

Note 4 Equipment must be fixed, permanently connected, and suitable for zone 0 according to the manufacturer's instructions.

Note 5 The general requirements in Parts 1 to 6 of the Regulations are applicable outside of the zones including Regulation 512.2.1 which requires equipment to be of a design appropriate to the situation in which it is to be used or its mode of installation must take account of the conditions likely to be encountered.

Note 6 The general requirements in Parts 1 to 6 of the Regulations are applicable within the zones of a location containing a bath or shower but are supplemented by the additional requirements in Part 701 of BS 7671.

Note 7 SELV switches must be supplied at a nominal voltage not exceeding 12V a.c. rms or 30V ripple-free d.c. and the safety source must be outside zones 0, 1 and 2.

Note 8 SELV switches and socket-outlets permitted but the safety source must be outside zones 0, 1 and 2.

Note 9 Equipment must have a minimum protection of IPX4 (IPX5 if water jets are likely).

Note 10 Equipment must have a minimum protection of IPX7.

Note that all circuits of the location must have additional protection provided by one or more RCDs that have a rated residual operating current ($I_{\Delta n}$) not exceeding 30 mA and an operating time not exceeding 40 ms at a residual current of 5 $I_{\Delta n}$ (701.411.3.3).

Note that providing all final circuits of the location have additional protection, meet the requirements for automatic disconnection and the installation is fitted with protective main equipotential bonding, then supplementary equipotential bonding may be omitted (701.415.2).

Fig 12.11 Summary of the requirements for a location containing a bath or shower

Published by Certsure LLP © Certsure LLP (January 2015)

12.3 Swimming pools

Swimming pools, paddling pools and their surroundings are considered to be locations where there is an increased risk of electric shock due to:

- a reduction in body resistance caused either by bodily immersion or by wet skin, and
- likely contact of substantial areas of the body with earth potential.

Consequently, a number of specific requirements are contained within Section 702 (Swimming pools and other basins) of *BS 7671*. These should also be applied to the basins of any fountains if is intended or likely that they are liable be occupied by people.

The requirements for fountains not expected to be occupied by persons are not discussed in this Guide.

In addition to the requirements given in Section 702, all other relevant sections of *BS 7671* apply to such locations, albeit supplemented and modified by Section 702.

Early design collaboration and installation co-ordination are needed if significant problems are to be avoided during construction and verification of the electrical installation. Without such collaboration and co-ordination, problems may occur, for example, in relation to the installation of metallic grids in floors where necessary, the installation of supplementary bonding conductors, the positioning of electrical equipment relative to the zones referred to in this Guide, and the protection of electrical equipment against external influences.

Special requirements beyond those of *BS 7671* may apply to swimming pools for medical use, although this falls outside of the scope of this Guide.

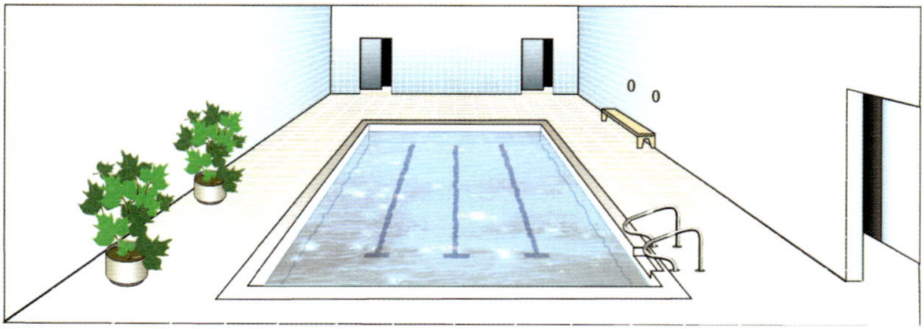

Fig 12.12 Swimming pool

12.3.1 Zones

Regulation 702.32 divides the basins of pools (and fountains intended for occupation by persons) and their surroundings into zones 0, 1 and 2 for the purposes of selecting suitable equipment and shock protection measures. The zones are explained in Table 12.4 and illustrated in Figures 12.13, 12.14 and 12.15.

Table 12.4 Zone definitions

	Zone definitions
zone 0	This zone is the interior of the basin of the swimming pool or fountain including any recesses in its walls or floors, basins for foot cleaning and water jets or waterfalls and the space below them.
zone 1	This zone is limited by: • zone 0 • a vertical plane 2 m from the rim of the basin • the floor, or the surface expected to be occupied by persons • the horizontal plane 2.5 m above the floor or the surface expected to be occupied by persons. Where the swimming pool or fountain contains diving boards, spring boards, starting blocks, chutes or other components expected to be occupied by persons, zone 1 comprises the zone limited by: • a vertical plane situated 1.5 m from the periphery of the diving boards, spring boards, starting blocks, chutes and other components such as accessible sculptures, viewing bays and decorative basins • the horizontal plane 2.5 m above the highest surface expected to be occupied by persons.
zone 2	This zone is limited by: • the vertical plane external to zone 1 and a parallel plane 1.5 m from the former • the floor or surface expected to be occupied by persons • the horizontal plane 2.5 m above the floor or the surface expected to be occupied by persons. There is no zone 2 for fountains.

Published by Certsure LLP © Certsure LLP (January 2015)

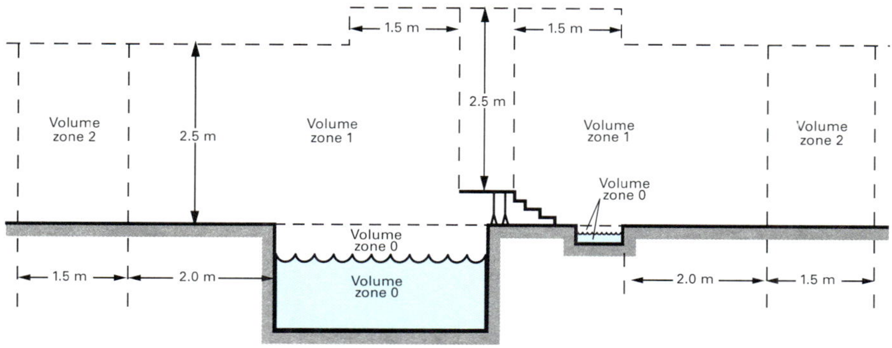

Fig 12.13 Zone requirements for swimming pools and paddling pools

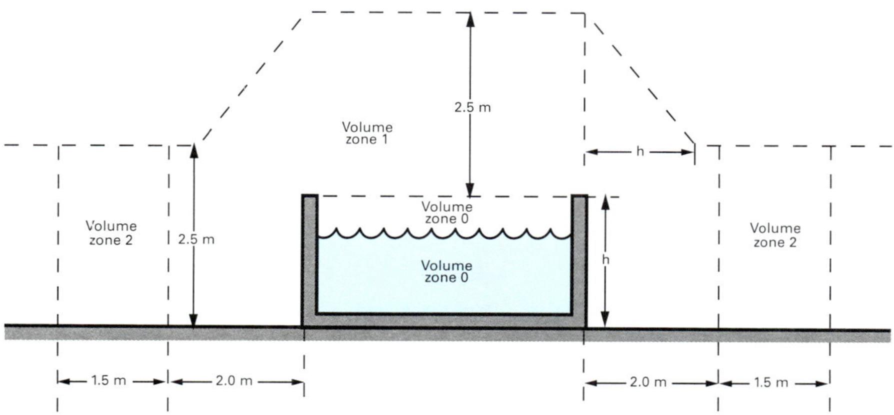

Fig 12.14 Zone dimensions for basin above ground

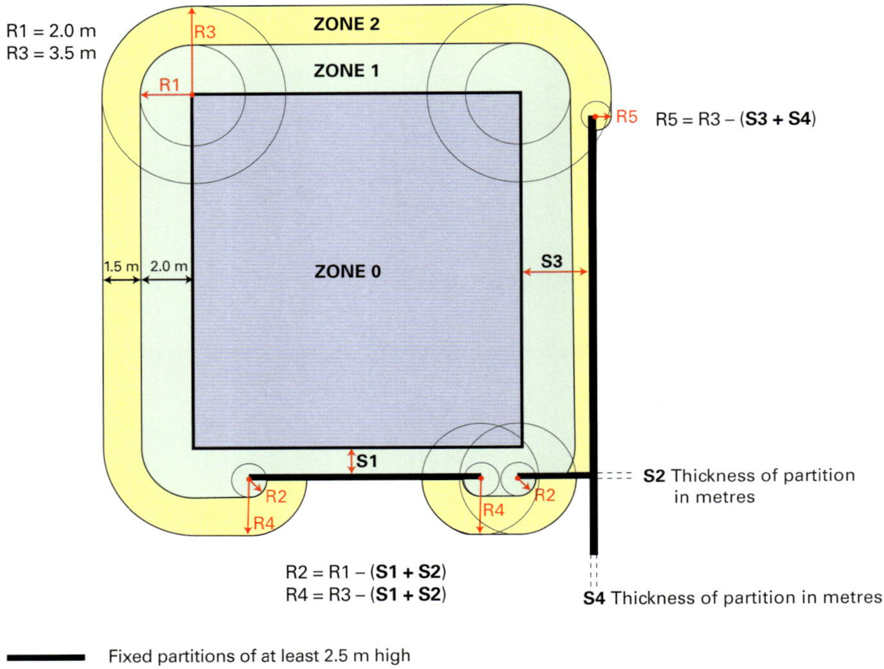

Fig 12.15 Example showing the effect of fixed partitions on zone dimensions (height of fixed partitions at least 2.5 m)

12.3.2 Protection against electric shock

BS 7671 does **not** allow basic protection to be provided by obstacles or protection by placing out of reach anywhere falling within the scope of Section 702 (Regulation 702.410.3.5 refers). Further, fault protection by non-conducting location or by earth-free local equipotential bonding is similarly prohibited (Regulation 702.410.3.6).

Published by Certsure LLP © Certsure LLP (January 2015)

Zones 0 and 1 of a swimming pool

In zone 0, and with the exception of fountains, only protection by SELV at a nominal voltage not exceeding 12 V a.c. rms or 30 V ripple-free d.c. is permitted.

In zone 1, and with the exception of fountains, only protection by SELV at a nominal voltage not exceeding 25 V a.c. rms or 60 V ripple-free d.c. is permitted.

In both cases, the source for SELV must be installed outside zones 0, 1 and 2.

Any equipment for use in the interior of basins that is only intended to be in operation when people are not inside zone 0 should be supplied by a circuit protected by:

- SELV, having the source for SELV installed outside zones 0, 1 and 2, unless the supply circuit is protected by a 30 mA RCD in which case the source for SELV may be placed in zone 2, or
- automatic disconnection of the supply using a 30 mA RCD, or
- electrical separation supplying only one item of current-using equipment, the source for which installed outside zones 0, 1 and 2, unless the supply circuit is protected by a 30 mA RCD in which case the source for electrical separation may be placed in zone 2.

A warning notice should be located at the socket-outlet used to provide the supply to such equipment and the associated control device to warn the user that this equipment should be used only when the swimming pool is not occupied by persons (see Regulation 702.410.3.4.1).

Zone 2 of a swimming pool

One or more of the following protective measures should be employed in zone 2:

- SELV, having the source for SELV being installed outside zones 0, 1 and 2, unless the supply circuit is protected by a 30 mA RCD in which case the source for SELV may be placed in zone 2, or
- automatic disconnection of supply using a 30 mA RCD,

 © Certsure LLP (January 2015)

NOTE: Where the swimming pool supply forms part of a TN-C-S system employing Protective Multiple Earth (PME) a note to Regulation 702.410.3.4.3 recommends that an earth mat or earth electrode of suitably low resistance (in the region of 20 Ω or less) is installed and connected to the protective equipotential bonding for the swimming pool.

or

- electrical separation supplying only one item of current-using equipment, the source for which installed outside zones 0, 1 and 2, unless the supply circuit is protected by a 30 mA RCD, in which case the source for electrical separation may be placed in zone 2.

SELV

Where extra-low voltage provided by SELV is used as the protective measure, basic protection must be provided by basic insulation or barriers or enclosures affording a degree of protection of at least IPXXB or IP2X whatever the nominal voltage (Regulation 702.414.4.5 refers).

12.3.3 Supplementary equipotential bonding

If there are any exposed-conductive-parts within zones 0, 1, or 2 (except exposed-conductive-parts of a SELV circuit), local supplementary bonding is required in zones 0, 1 and 2 to connect together the following:

- all extraneous-conductive-parts (which may include metal handrails, exposed structural steelwork and metal pipes etc), and
- the protective conductors of all exposed-conductive-parts within these zones.

(Regulation 702.415.2)

The connection with the protective conductor may be made in an enclosure for an accessory or in a local distribution board.

Attention should be paid to the protection of supplementary bonding conductors against mechanical damage and to the avoidance of corrosion, particularly at connections.

Connections should be accessible to permit inspection testing and maintenance (see Section 11.7.6 of this Guide).

Published by Certsure LLP © Certsure LLP (January 2015)

If a metallic grid is installed in a solid floor in zones 0, 1 or 2 (Figure 12.16), it must be connected to the local supplementary bonding. There is no absolute requirement in *BS 7671* to provide a grid, but the need for such a provision should be considered at the design stage, particularly where a solid floor may be an extraneous-conductive-part (for instance, where the floor is not electrically well insulated from Earth potential).

Two or more bonding connections should be made to the grid, preferably at diagonally opposite corners, and it should be ensured that all parts of the grid are connected together such that reliable electrical continuity is provided.

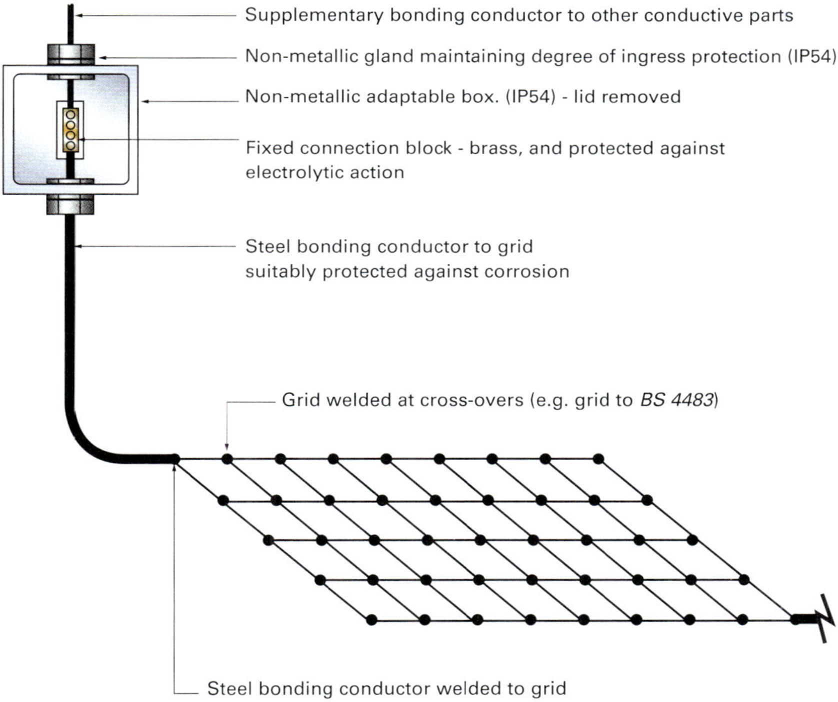

Fig 12.16 Examples of one of the connections to a metallic grid

12.3.4 External influences

Each component part of the electrical installation is to be selected and erected to comply with the requirements of Section 522 (Selection and erection in relation to external influences), taking into account all the conditions existing or likely to exist at the point of installation.

Particular areas of concern include:

- the presence of water (Regulation Group 522.3), and
- the presence of corrosive or polluting substances, such as chlorine (Regulation Group 522.5).

12.3.5 Degrees of protection of enclosures against water ingress

The degree of protection of enclosures against ingress of water should be appropriate to the zonal location of the equipment (Regulation 702.512.2).

The minimum permitted degree of protection related to the zone is shown in Table 12.5.

Table 12.5 Minimum degree of protection

Zone	Minimum degree of protection
0	IPX8
1	IPX4, IPX5 where water jets are likely to be used for cleaning
2	IPX2 for indoor pools IPX4 for outdoor locations IPX5 where water jets are likely to be used for cleaning

12.3.6 Wiring systems

Regulation 702.522.21 states that any metallic sheath or metallic covering of a wiring system situated in zones 0, 1 or 2 must be connected to the supplementary equipotential bonding. The regulation further recommends that cables should preferably be installed in conduits made of insulating material.

Within zones 0 and 1 of a swimming pool, only wiring systems necessary to supply equipment situated in these zones should be installed (Regulation 702.522.22).

Published by Certsure LLP © Certsure LLP (January 2015)

Junction boxes should not be installed within zones 0 or 1, unless wiring therein is limited to that of SELV circuits, in which case junction boxes may be installed in zone 1 (see 702.522.24).

12.3.7 Switchgear and controlgear

The requirements for switchgear and controlgear in a swimming pool are summarised in Table 12.6.

Table 12.6 Switchgear and controlgear

Zone	Requirement	Regulation
0	Switchgear or controlgear not to be installed Socket-outlets not to be installed	702.53
1	Switchgear or controlgear not to be installed Socket-outlets not to be installed For a swimming pool where it is not possible to locate a socket-outlet or switch outside zone 1, a socket-outlet or switch, preferably having a non conductive cover or coverplate, is permitted in zone 1 if it is installed outside (1.25 m) from the border of zone 0, and placed at least 0.3 m above the floor, and it must be protected by: • SELV, at a nominal voltage not exceeding 25 V a.c. rms or 60 V ripple-free d.c., the source for SELV being installed outside zones 0 and 1, or • Automatic disconnection of supply, using a 30 mA RCD, or • Electrical separation for a supply to only one item of equipment, the source for electrical separation being installed outside zones 0 and 1.	702.53
2	A socket-outlet or a switch is permitted only if the supply circuit is protected by one of the following protective measures: • SELV, the source of SELV being installed outside zones 0, 1 and 2. However, it is permitted to install the source of SELV in zone 2 if its supply circuit is protected by a 30 mA RCD, or • Automatic disconnection of supply, using a 30 mA RCD, or • Electrical separation, the source for electrical separation supplying only one item of current-using equipment, or one socket-outlet, installed outside zones 0, 1 and 2. However, it is permitted to install the source in zone 2 if its supply circuit is protected by a 30 mA RCD. The general requirements of *BS 7671* apply.	702.53

 © Certsure LLP (January 2015)

12.3.8 Current-using equipment of swimming pools

The requirements for switchgear and controlgear in a swimming pool are summarised in Table 12.7.

Table 12.7 Current-using equipment

Zone	Requirement	Regulation
0	It is only permitted to install fixed current-using equipment specifically designed for use in a swimming pool	702.55.1
1	It is only permitted to install fixed current-using equipment specifically designed for use in a swimming pool	702.55.1
2 **Outside of the zones**	The general requirements of *BS 7671* apply	

Any equipment that is only intended to be in use when people are not inside zone 0 may be employed in all zones provided that it is supplied by a circuit protected according to Regulation 702.410.3.4.

Electric heating may be embedded in the floor, provided that one or more of the following requirements of Regulation 702.55.1 is met:

- protection by SELV is provided, the source of SELV being installed outside zones 0, 1 and 2. (the source of SELV may be installed in zone 2 if its supply circuit is protected by a 30 mA RCD), or
- the heating element incorporates an earthed metallic sheath that is connected to the supplementary equipotential bonding specified in Regulation 702.411.3.3 and its supply circuit is additionally protected by a 30 mA RCD, or
- it is covered by an embedded earthed metallic grid that is connected to the supplementary equipotential bonding specified in Regulation 702.415.2 and its supply circuit is additionally protected by a 30 mA RCD.

Published by Certsure LLP © Certsure LLP (January 2015)

12.3.9 Underwater luminaires for swimming pools

Any luminaire for use submerged in the water, or in contact with the water, must be fixed and must comply with *BS EN 60598-2-18: 1994 Luminaires. Particular requirements. Luminaires for swimming pools and similar applications* (as amended).

Any underwater lighting located behind watertight portholes, and arranged to be serviced from behind, should comply with the appropriate part of *BS EN 60598* and be installed such that no intentional or unintentional conductive connection can occur between any exposed-conductive-part of the underwater luminaires and any conductive parts of the portholes (Regulation 702.55.2 refers).

12.3.10 Special requirements relating to the installation of electrical equipment in zone 1 of swimming pools

Fixed equipment designed for use in swimming pools and other basins such as filtration systems, jet stream pumps and the like supplied at low voltage may be installed in zone 1, if **all** the following requirements given in Regulation 702.55.4 are met:

a) the equipment is located inside an insulating enclosure providing at least Class II or equivalent insulation and providing protection against mechanical impact of medium severity (AG2) irrespective of the classification of the equipment, and

b) the equipment is only accessible via a hatch (or a door) by means of a key or a tool. The act of opening of the hatch (or door) should disconnect all live conductors. Further, the supply cable and the main disconnecting means must be installed such that protection of Class II or equivalent insulation is provided, and

c) the supply circuit of the equipment must be protected by:

- SELV at a nominal voltage not exceeding 25 V a.c. rms or 60 V ripple-free d.c., the source of SELV being installed outside zones 0, 1 and 2, or
- a 30 mA RCD, or
- electrical separation, the source for electrical separation supplying a single fixed item of equipment and being installed outside of zones 0, 1 and 2.

 © Certsure LLP (January 2015)

In the case of swimming pools where there is no zone 2, lighting equipment supplied by other than a SELV source at 12 V a.c rms. or 30 V ripple-free d.c. may be installed in zone 1 on a wall or on a ceiling provided that the following requirements are fulfilled:

- the circuit is protected by automatic disconnection of the supply and additional protection is provided by a 30 mA RCD, and
- the height from the floor is at least 2 m above the lower limit of zone 1.

In addition, every luminaire must have an enclosure providing Class II or equivalent insulation and providing protection against mechanical impact of medium severity.

12.3.11 Accessibility

As required by Regulation 513.1, all electrical equipment must be arranged so as to facilitate its operation and maintenance and to permit access to each connection. For example, luminaires should not be mounted directly over the water of a swimming pool unless proper arrangements are in place to gain adequate and safe access to them without undue difficulty. The facility for access must not be significantly impaired by mounting equipment in an enclosure.

12.3.12 Protective Multiple Earthing (PME)

BS 7671 does not preclude the use of the earthing facility of a PME supply (i.e. the PME earthing terminal) as the means of earthing for the electrical installation in a location containing a swimming pool or paddling pool.

However, electricity distributors are sometimes unwilling to allow such use, or may attach conditions to it. This is possibly because of complaints, received in the past, of perceived electric shock by persons in such locations, when touching exposed-conductive-parts or extraneous-conductive-parts connected to the PME earthing terminal whilst in contact with an uninsulated solid floor. Such sensation of electric shock is caused by the potential difference that can exist between the PME earthing terminal and 'true' Earth. The potential difference is due to the voltage drop in the PEN conductor, caused by load current returning to the source of supply.

Published by Certsure LLP © Certsure LLP (January 2015)

In order to avoid the risk of perceived electric shock caused by the above, it may be preferable to separate the exposed-conductive-parts and extraneous-conductive-parts in the special location from the PME earthing terminal. Often, the installation in the special location would then be arranged to form part of a TT system and would have to meet all the associated requirements of *BS 7671*, including being connected to Earth by a suitable installation earth electrode.

However, avoiding the risk of perceived electric shock by separation of the conductive parts from the PME earthing terminal, as described above, is sometimes impracticable. This is the case, for example, where the special location occupies part of a building, the electrical installation in another part of which uses the PME earthing terminal as its means of earthing. In these circumstances, exposed-conductive-parts and/or extraneous-conductive-parts in the special location might be in metal-to-metal contact with metalwork connected to the PME earthing terminal, meaning that any desired separation is not achieved.

Alternatively, exposed-conductive-parts or extraneous-conductive-parts in the special location might be simultaneously accessible with metalwork connected to the PME earthing terminal, and would therefore, be required to be electrically connected to that metalwork, due to the requirements of Regulation 411.3.1.2 (protective equipotential bonding).

Where it is necessary to use the PME earthing terminal as the means of earthing for the installation in the special location (which should only be done with the distributor's express consent), metallic floor grids connected to the local supplementary bonding should be provided in all uninsulated solid floors. In addition, the distributor may have further requirements, such as the provision of an earth electrode connected to the main earthing terminal of the installation in the special location.

12.4 Saunas

A room or cabin containing a sauna heater is considered by *BS 7671* to be a location of increased electric shock risk, as large areas of the human body are exposed and are wet due to perspiration and occasional high humidity.

Regulation 703.1 states that the particular requirements of Section 703 of *BS 7671* apply to sauna installations erected on site, whether cabins or within a room.

In the latter case the whole room is considered to be the sauna and the requirements of Section 703 need to be applied as appropriate.

The requirements of Section 703 do not apply to prefabricated sauna cabins complying with a relevant equipment standard.

Electrical installations for rooms and cabins containing sauna heaters are also subject to the general requirements of *BS 7671* (supplemented or modified where appropriate by Section 703). Where rooms and cabins containing sauna heaters form part of another special location, such as a swimming pool, it will be necessary to consider the requirements of *BS 7671* for both locations when designing the installation.

12.4.1 Temperature zones

The interior of a hot air sauna is classified into three zones (1, 2 and 3) for the purposes of protection against electric shock and selecting and erecting suitable equipment. The zones illustrated in Figure 703 of *BS 7671*, are represented in Fig 12.17.

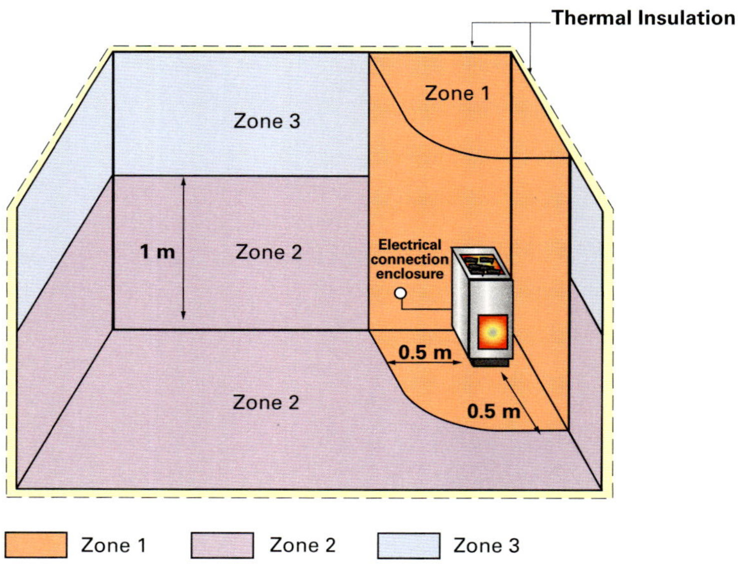

Fig 12.17 Zones of a room and cabin containing a sauna heater

Published by Certsure LLP © Certsure LLP (January 2015)

12.4.2 Protection against electric shock

BS 7671 does **not** allow basic protection to be provided by obstacles or protection by placing out of reach (Regulation 703.410.3.5). Further, fault protection by non-conducting location or by earth-free local equipotential bonding is similarly prohibited (Regulation 703.410.3.6).

12.4.3 Additional protection by RCDs

In general, additional protection must be provided for all circuits of the sauna, by the use of one or more 30 mA RCDs. However, it is not necessary to provide RCD protection for the sauna heater unless recommended by the equipment manufacturer (Regulation 703.411.3.3).

12.4.4 SELV or PELV

Where SELV or PELV is used, regardless of the nominal voltage, basic protection must be provided by basic insulation, or barriers or enclosures affording a degree of protection of at least IPXXB or IP2X (Regulation 703.414.4.5).

12.4.5 Selection and erection of equipment

The general philosophy of Section 703 is to keep all electrical equipment out of the sauna except for equipment which is absolutely necessary for the operation and use of the sauna.

Sauna heating appliances must comply with *BS EN 60335-2-53: 2011 - Household and similar electrical appliances. Safety. Particular requirements for sauna heating appliances and infrared cabins* and should be installed in accordance with the manufacturer's instructions.

All equipment in the room or cabin containing the sauna heater must have a degree of protection of at least IPX4 and if cleaning by the use of water jets may to be expected, electrical equipment must have a degree of protection of at least IPX5.

- In zone 1, only the sauna heater and equipment belonging to the sauna heater may be installed
- In zone 2, there are no special requirements relating to the heat resistance of equipment

 © Certsure LLP (January 2015)

- In zone 3,
  - the equipment should be able to withstand a minimum temperature of 125 °C, and
  - the insulation and sheaths of cables should be able withstand a minimum temperature of 170 °C.

12.4.6 Wiring systems

The wiring system should be preferably installed outside the zones of the location, that is, on the cold side of the thermal insulation. A wiring system installed on the warm side of thermal insulation in zones 1 or 3 must be heat-resisting. Where a wiring system has metallic sheathing or where metallic conduit has been employed, they should not be accessible in normal use (see Regulation 703.52).

12.4.7 Isolation, switching, control and accessories

Switchgear and controlgear forming part of the sauna heater equipment or of other fixed equipment installed in zone 2, should be installed within the sauna room or cabin in accordance with the manufacturer's instructions. Other switchgear and controlgear, provided for control of local lighting, should be installed outside the sauna room or cabin.

Socket-outlets should not be installed within the location (Regulation 703.537.5).

12.5 Lighting installations

In this guide, details of the requirements for Outdoor lighting installations and Extra-low voltage lighting installations can be found in sections 13.3.5 and 10.5.4 respectively.

12.6 Electric vehicle charging installations

Section 722 of *BS 7671*, introduced by Amendment 2 in 2013, contains additional requirements for **electric vehicle (EV)** charging installations. The requirements of Section 722 supplement or modify the general requirements contained in the parts 1 to 6 of *BS 7671*. The introduction of Section 722 resulted in a number of new terms relating to EV charging equipment being added to the definitions included in Part 2 of *BS 7671*. In this guide, when used for the first time, these terms are shown in bold.

Published by Certsure LLP © Certsure LLP (January 2015)

The requirements of Section 722 do not apply to inductive charging of electric vehicles or to installations for charging mobility scooters or similar vehicles that take a rated current of 10 A or less from the electrical installation (Regulation 722.1).

12.6.1 EV charging equipment suitable for use in domestic premises

This section of the guide will focus on the installation of single-phase charging units, of the type designed for use in domestic premises, which are typically rated at 16 A.

The batteries in an electric vehicle are charged from the electricity supply by the use of a flexible cable which is connected to the electric vehicle by means of a **vehicle coupler** (part of the charging cable) and a **vehicle connecter** (mounted on the vehicle) inlet. Regulation 722.55.201.1 requires that the vehicle coupler and vehicle connecter meet the requirements of *BS EN 62196 - Plugs, socket-outlets, vehicle connectors and vehicle inlets*. There are three designs of connector known as Type 1, Type 2 and Type 3, that meet the requirements of *BS EN 62196* and details of these are shown in Table 12.8.

Table 12.8 Types of connectors recognised by *BS 7671* for charging of electric vehicles

Type	Pictorial reference	Description
Type 1: SAE J1772	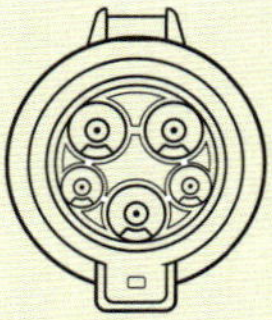	**A single-phase connector developed in the USA**
Type 2: VDE–AR–E 2623-2-2	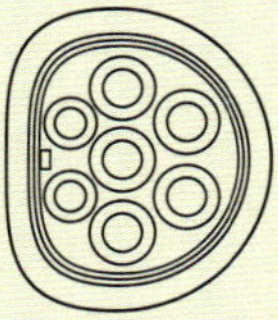	**A single-phase or three-phase connector developed in Europe.**
Type 3: EV Plug Alliance	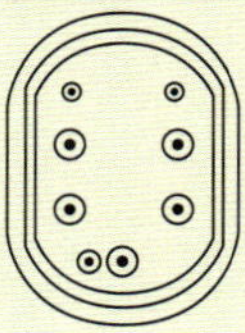	**An alternative single or three-phase connector developed in Europe. Unlike Type 1 and Type 2 connectors this connector is provided with shutters.**

 © Certsure LLP (January 2015)

The charging cable can be connected to the electrical supply by either a *BS 1363-2* or a *BS EN 60309-2* plug and socket-outlet (see Fig 12.18), supplied by a dedicated final circuit or by connection to an electric vehicle charging unit. As shown by Fig 12.19, where an electric vehicle charging unit is used the charging cable can be either permanently connected to the electric vehicle charging unit (tethered) or be connected to the charging unit via a *BS EN 62196* socket-outlet mounted on the charging unit (Regulation 722.55.201.1). It should be noted that portable socket-outlets are not permitted. Also, a socket-outlet or vehicle connector shall supply only one electric vehicle. (722.55.101.3)

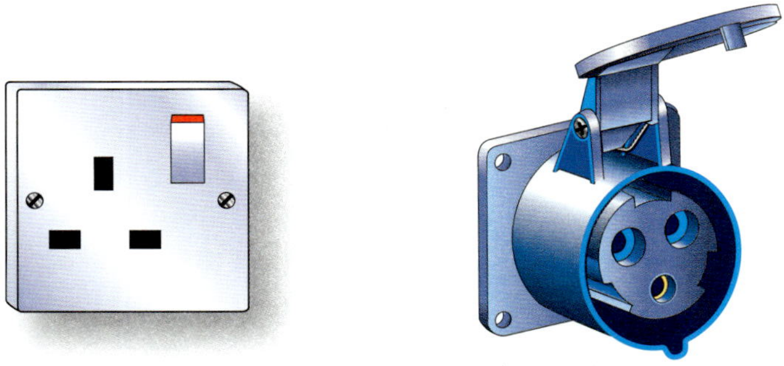

Fig 12.18 *BS 1363-2 and *BS EN 60309-2*** socket-outlets**

*Where a 13A *BS 1363-2* socket-outlet is being used, due to the likelihood of the device carrying a significant current for long periods of time, Regulation 722.55.201.1 (i) requires that the manufacturer of the socket-outlet approves its suitability for use in an electric vehicle charging system.

**Where a *BS EN 60309-2* socket-outlet is being used, to prevent contact with live parts of the socket contacts, Regulation 722.55.201.1 (ii) requires the socket-outlet to incorporate an interlock that complies with one of the two sets of requirements, described in the regulation.

Published by Certsure LLP © Certsure LLP (January 2015)

(a) **EV charging unit with a tethered charging cable**

(b) **EV charging unit incorporating a socket-outlet**

Fig 12.19 Alternative arrangements for EV charging units

Recent developments n EV charging systems have resulted in several new systems for plugs, socket-outlets and connectors being introduced. If an EV charging system including connectors not recognised by *BS 7671* is to be installed then a note should be attached to the Domestic Electrical Installation Certificate or Electrical Installation Certificate stating 'The EV charging system includes connectors not recognised by *BS 7671*: this does not imply that these connectors are unsafe.'

BS 7671 defines an **Electric vehicle charging point** as the point where the electric vehicle is connected to the fixed electrical installation. Where the charging cable belongs to the vehicle, the charging point is a socket-outlet and where the charging cable is permanently connected to the charging equipment, the charging point is the connector of the charging cable.

As electric vehicle charging technology has developed, various standard methods of charging known as **modes of charging** have been developed and Part 2 of *BS 7671* defines four modes of charging (Mode 1 to Mode 4). However, the majority of new charging equipment used in a domestic situation are likely to employ either Mode 2 or Mode 3 charging.

Mode 2 charging: uses a charging cable incorporating an in-cable control box that includes an RCD and control box to connect the EV to a socket-outlet conforming to *BS 1363-2* or *BS EN 60309-2*. The control box also includes a system for detecting safety-specific issues, including that a vehicle is plugged in and that the protective earth is connected.

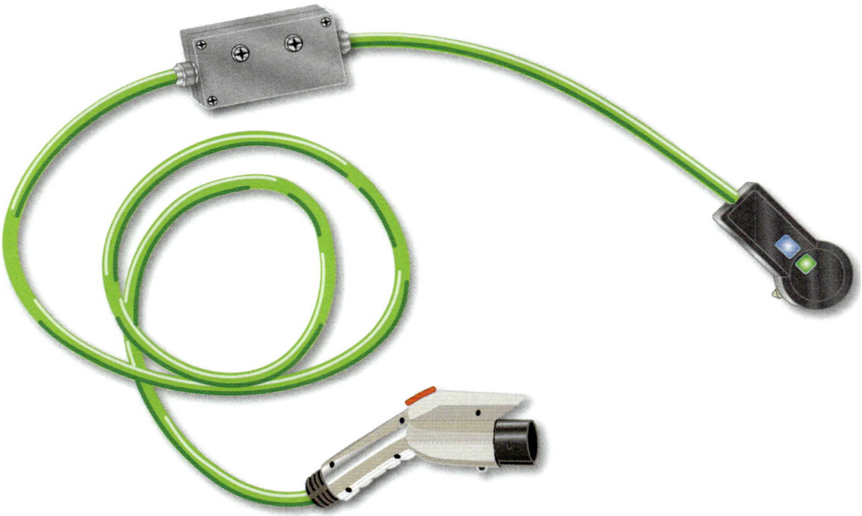

Fig 12.20 – A Mode 2 charging cable

Although some vehicle manufacturers may offer a Mode 2 charging cable at an entry level, most car manufacturers would recommend dedicated Mode 3 charging systems. However, the ability to plug into any available *BS 1363-2* 13 A socket-outlet means that some owners of electric vehicles use Mode 2 cables as standby equipment i.e. for use when the battery becomes depleted and there is no dedicated EV charging point within range.

Mode 3 charging: compared to Mode 2 charging, Mode 3 charging provides for faster charging. Although on some systems one end of the charging cable may be permanently tethered to the charging point or vehicle, others use plugs and socket-outlets complying with *BS EN 62196*. The Mode 3 charging equipment may well include an RCD and the electronics required to monitor safe operation. To enable the equipment to communicate with the vehicle, the cable and its connectors are provided with additional cable cores.

Published by Certsure LLP © Certsure LLP (January 2015)

Vehicles produced by different manufacturers may well use different connector types, and before installing electric vehicle charging equipment, as advised by a note to Regulation 722.55.201.1 to ensure that the EV charging equipment (including the charging cable) and the electric vehicle are compatible, the installer should consult the vehicle manufacturers' instructions.

12.6.2 The supply to electric vehicle charging equipment in domestic premises

Circuit design and loading allowances

Regulation 722.311 requires that a final circuit provided for the connection to electric vehicles must be dedicated to that purpose alone. Where a final circuit supplies one or more charging points, the regulation states that an allowance for diversity is not permitted.

Protective measures against electric shock

Although Regulation Group 722.4 permits a number of protective measures to be used, for EV charging equipment installed in domestic premises it is unlikely that anything other than Automatic Disconnection of Supply (as described in Section 411) will be used.

Where Protective Multiple Earthing (PME) is used

As shown in Fig 12.21, where the protective measure is automatic disconnection supply and the means of earthing is PME (i.e. a TN C S system), in the unlikely event of the combined protective and neutral (PEN) conductor supplying the installation developing an open-circuit fault, the earthed metalwork of the installation and any equipment connected to it (including any electric vehicle and its charging equipment) can rise to a dangerous voltage. This dangerous voltage can exist for long periods of time and will pose a danger to any person touching the metalwork whilst in contact directly with the general mass of Earth. In this situation, as the shock current flows in both the line and neutral conductors, there is no imbalance in the currents and an RCD will not interrupt the current.

 © Certsure LLP (January 2015)

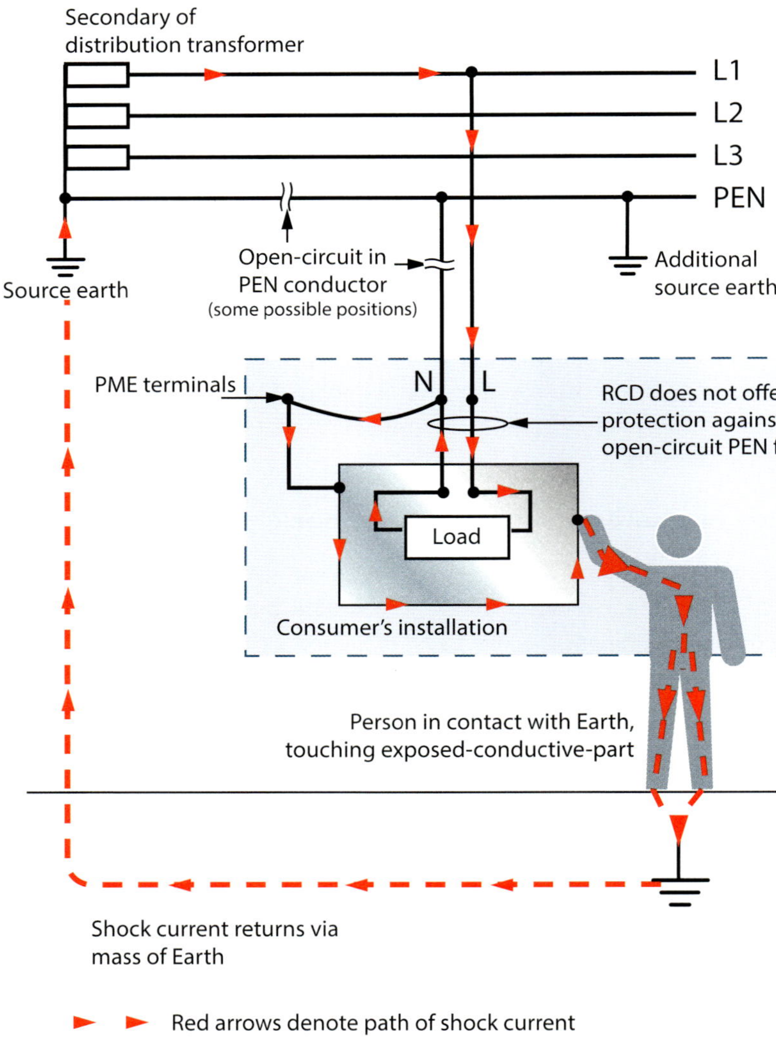

Fig 12.21 Electric shock risk due to an open-circuit fault in the supply PEN conductor

Published by Certsure LLP © Certsure LLP (January 2015)

Regulation 722.411.4.1, states that where the electric vehicle charging point is located outdoors, or might reasonably be expected to be used to charge a vehicle located outdoors and the protective measure is automatic disconnection supply a PME earthing facility is only permitted where one of the following conditions apply.

(i) The charging point forms part of a three-phase installation that also supplies loads other than for electric vehicle charging and because of characteristics of the load and the supply in the event of an open circuit fault in the PEN conductor of the supply to the installation, the voltage between the main earthing terminal and earth does not exceed 70 V. Item A722.3 of Annex A722 provides further guidance.

(ii) The main earthing terminal of the installation is connected to an installation earth electrode having a resistance to Earth not exceeding a value calculated in accordance with a formula given in Annex A722, which is sufficiently very low that in the event of an open circuit fault in the PEN conductor of the supply to the installation, the voltage between the main earthing terminal and earth does not exceed 70 V.

(iii) Protection is provided by a special type of voltage-operated earth-leakage circuit breaker (not an RCD) that disconnects the charging point from the live conductors of the supply and from protective earth under specified conditions. The device is not yet commercially available but a product standard for it is being developed (Regulation 722.411.4.1 (iii) refers).

However, Regulation 722.411.4.1 includes the following dispensation - ***The requirement to comply with (i), (ii) or (iii) need not be applied for a charging point at a dwelling if none of the three conditions is reasonably practicable***. In this context, 'dwelling' means a self-contained unit designed to accommodate a single household. It does not mean a building exclusively containing rooms for residential purposes, such as a nursing home or student accommodation or similar.

RCD protection of charging points

Where automatic disconnection of supply is used as the protective measure, Regulation 722.531.2.101 requires every charging point to be individually protected by an RCD having a rated residual operating current ($I_{\Delta n}$) not exceeding 30 mA and an operating time not exceeding 40 ms at 5 $I_{\Delta n}$. The device must disconnect all live conductors, including the neutral.

The RCD is required to be at least a type A, due to the likelihood of d.c. being present in vehicle charging current. If it is known that the d.c. component of residual current will exceed 6 mA, the RCD must be of type B to *BS EN 62423*. Types of RCD are discussed in Section 4.5.3 of this guide.

It should be noted that the use of a Mode 2 charging cable (which includes an RCD) does not meet the requirements of Regulation 722.531.2.101. However, where a EV charging unit (as shown in Fig 12.18) is used, the unit may include a suitable RCD.

Protection against external influences

Where an EV charging unit is installed outdoors, the equipment is required to be selected with a degree of protection of at least IP44.

Miscellaneous requirements

Other notable requirements of Section 722 include (amongst others):

- Emergency switching devices, where required, must be capable of breaking the full load current of the relevant parts of the installation and disconnect all live conductors. (722.537.4.101).
- Each socket-outlet must be installed in a fixed socket-outlet box or a distribution board. (722.55.201.2).
- Tethered vehicle connectors are permitted but not portable socket-outlets. (722.55.201.2).
- For charging equipment employing charging Modes 3 or 4, unless the socket-outlet or the vehicle connector has been de-energised by switched off from the supply, arrangements must be provided to prevent insertion or removal of plugs. (722.55.101.4).
- The lowest part of a socket-outlet is to be between 0.5 m and 1.5 m above the ground. (722.55.101.6).

Published by Certsure LLP © Certsure LLP (January 2015)

Chapter 13

Electrical equipment outside of the dwelling

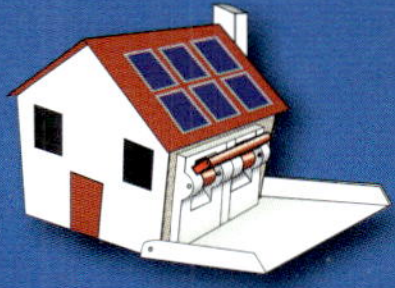

 © Certsure LLP (January 2015)

Electrical equipment outside of the dwelling

13.1 Increased risk of electric shock

There is no specific section in Part 7 of *BS 7671* for installations in gardens or other areas external to the premises. However, the dangerous effects of electric shock are greater for persons in contact with the general mass of Earth. This chapter explains the reason for this increase in risk and deals with the related requirements in *BS 7671* intended to address the risk.

Persons within a building are often insulated from the general mass of Earth by electrically insulating floors such as wood, floor coverings such as carpet, and dry footwear. However, persons in outhouses, garages, sheds or similar locations with earthen or stone floors, and particularly persons outdoors (as in Fig 13.1), are likely to be in contact directly with the general mass of Earth.

When a person is standing on, or otherwise touching, the ground, the resistance of the electrical connection between the person's body and the general mass of Earth is significantly reduced. This results in an increased current through the body to Earth, leading to a greater risk of death or serious injury, in the event of either:

- contact of the person with a live part, or
- contact of the person with an exposed-conductive-part, such as the metallic casing of a Class I appliance, that has become live under single fault conditions.

In addition, the wet conditions to which a person may be exposed outdoors mean that shoes and feet, as well as hands and other parts of the body, could be wet, reducing contact resistance. The person may even be barefoot. The result is that the resistance of the path through the body is further reduced, and the current through the body to Earth in the event of failure of basic insulation or under fault conditions is greater, resulting in increased danger.

Clearly, a person may receive an electric shock from mobile equipment (such as a lawnmower, hedge trimmer or power drill) or from the flexible cable supplying such equipment.

Mobile equipment is electrical equipment intended to be moved while in operation or which can easily be moved from one place to another whilst still connected to the supply.

Published by Certsure LLP © Certsure LLP (January 2015)

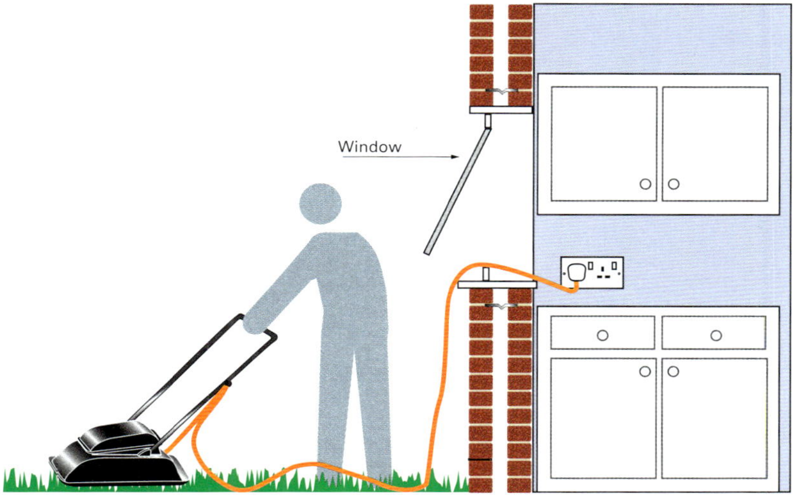

Fig 13.1 A person using electrical equipment whilst standing on the general mass of Earth

13.2 Additional protection by means of an RCD

Regulation 411.3.3 requires **ALL** socket-outlets rated at 20 A or less (with certain exceptions) and mobile equipment with a current rating not exceeding 32 A for use outdoors to be provided with additional protection by means of an RCD having the characteristics specified in Regulation 415.1.

Regulation 415.1 requires the RCD to have a rated residual operating current, $I_{\Delta n}$, not exceeding 30 mA, and a type-tested operating time not exceeding 40 ms at a residual current of 5 $I_{\Delta n}$, as required by the British Standard specifications referred to in that Regulation.

Compliance with Regulation 411.3.3 may be achieved by the installation of RCDs such as RCCBs, RCBOs or socket-outlets with integral RCDs (SRCDs), examples of which are illustrated in Figs 13.2 and 13.3)

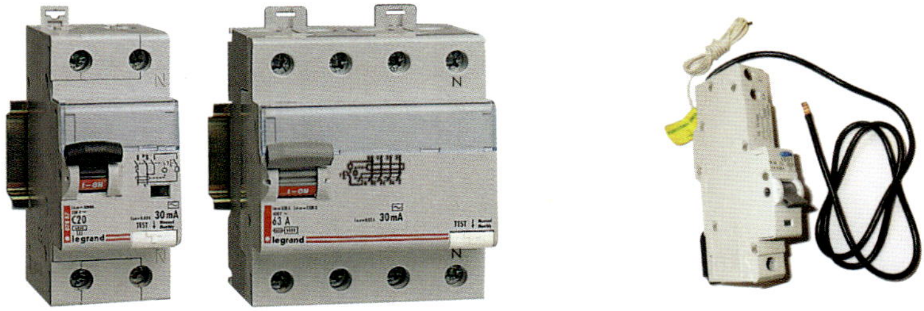

Fig 13.2 Examples of single-phase and three-phase RCCBs, and an RCBO (shown on right)

Photograph courtesy of Legrand Electric Ltd

Fig 13.3 SRCDs (Socket-outlets with RCDs)

Photograph courtesy of Legrand Electric Ltd

A circuit having a current-carrying capacity of 32 A or less supplying mobile equipment for use outdoors, connected other than through a socket-outlet by means of a flexible cable, is also subject to the requirements of Regulation 411.3.3.

Thus, the circuit must be provided with additional protection by means of an RCD having the characteristics specified in Regulation 415.1.

Published by Certsure LLP © Certsure LLP (January 2015)

13.3 Electrical equipment

All equipment installed outside of the premises should be designed for use outdoors and be installed in accordance with the manufacturer's instructions. In some cases, additional measures may need to be taken to protect equipment that is not of itself entirely suitable for installation outdoors. For example, equipment may need to be so placed that it is not directly exposed to the effects of the weather or be placed within an appropriately weatherproof enclosure.

The use of Class II equipment is conducive to electrical safety in such locations and is to be encouraged.

13.3.1 Buried cables

Where cables are buried in the ground, they should be installed in such a manner that they will not suffer damage during the course of any reasonably foreseeable disturbance of the ground above (such as digging over a flower bed or spiking a lawn).

This may affect the choice of cable routes adopted. It will also require the cables to be buried sufficiently deep into the ground. In general, a minimum depth of 600 mm should be acceptable in a domestic garden.

The position of all buried cables should be marked by cable covers or marker tape. (See Fig 13.4). Non-armoured buried cables should be installed in a conduit or duct that provides protection equivalent to armour against mechanical damage (Regulation 522.8.10).

Steel Wire Armoured (SWA) cables and cables having an earthed metal sheath suitable for use as a protective conductor having an outer plastic covering may be buried directly in the ground without further protection.

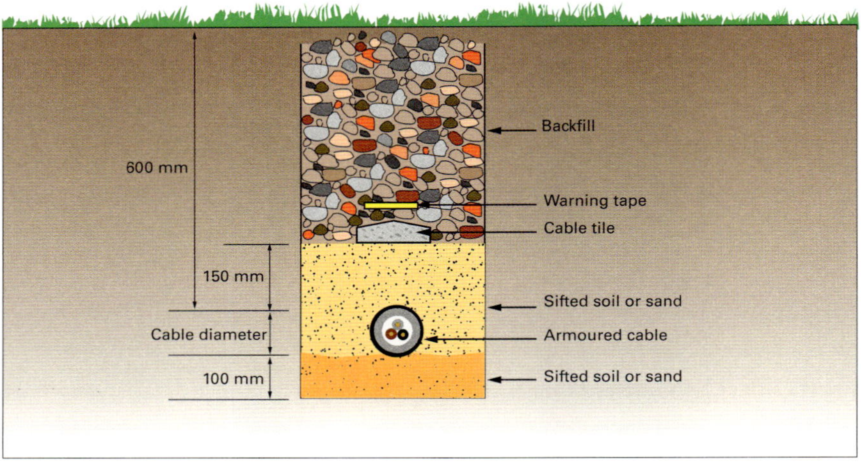

Fig 13.4 Buried cables

13.3.2 Surface-installed cables

Surface-installed cables should be fixed to permanent structures only and should be supported at sufficient height above the ground to avoid accidental contact with footwear and garden tools, which could damage the cable.

Timber fencing is not considered to be suitable for supporting cables for reasons such as:

- wood preservatives could attack the cable sheath,
- timber fencing is unlikely to be sufficiently rigid,
- the life of timber fencing is likely to be less than that of the cable,
- damage likely to occur to the fence due to the high winds (that may present a risk of electric shock).

Surface-installed cables should not be exposed to prolonged sunlight unless they are of a suitable type. Black thermoplastic (PVC) cable sheaths contain carbon black which resists the effects of sunlight. White or grey cable sheaths are likely to deteriorate with prolonged exposure to the sun and should always be shielded to avoid this happening.

 Published by Certsure LLP © Certsure LLP (January 2015)

13.3.3 Armoured cable terminations

Where SWA cables are terminated in a location where they are exposed to the elements, weatherproof glands should be used. In such cases, and where practicable, cables should not be terminated into the top surfaces of enclosures.

A shroud should be installed when terminating an SWA cable, but should not be so tight that it impairs future inspection of the gland.

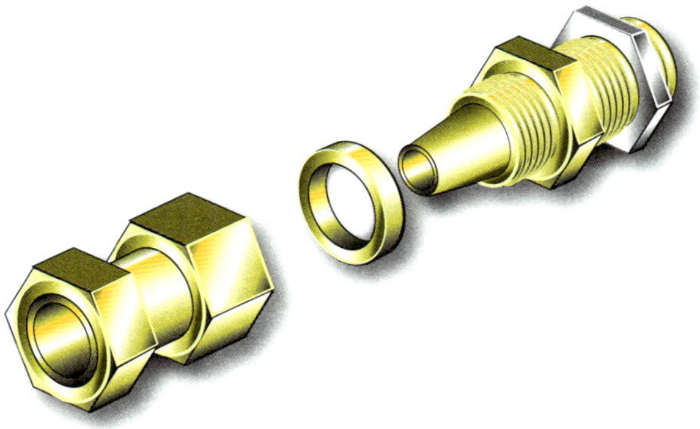

Fig 13.5 Weatherproof SWA gland

13.3.4 Socket-outlets

Socket-outlets may be installed in a garden as a convenient way of connecting luminaires and other equipment.

13 A socket-outlets may be used provided they are designed for use outdoors. Needless to say, 13 A socket-outlets installed in a garden must either incorporate a 30 mA RCD or be supplied from a circuit provided with additional protection by 30 mA RCD.

For domestic installations, only shuttered socket-outlets should be used (see Regulation 553.1.100). Industrial socket-outlets including plugs, connectors and appliance inlets complying with *BS EN 60309-2* are not shuttered and should not be used in domestic premises.

Socket-outlets should not be installed in a position where they may be liable to damage caused by a lawn mower, hedge trimmer or other garden tools.

 © Certsure LLP (January 2015)

13.3.5 Lighting

Section 714 contains additional requirements for outdoor lighting installations. However, as described by Regulation 714.1, Section 714 does not apply to luminaires fixed to the outside building and supplied directly from the internal wiring of that building or to temporary festoon lighting such as Christmas lights. Section 714 does apply to circuits and electrical equipment used for general external lighting and to situations where lighting used to illuminate features in the garden or to provide floodlighting.

Many of the regulations contained in Section 714 relate to street furniture, street lighting, illuminated advertising panels and the like and do not apply to the outdoor lighting of domestic premises. The main requirements of Section 714 that are applicable to the outdoor lighting installations of domestic premises are as follows.

1. It is not permissible for basic protection to be provided by obstacles or protection by placing out of reach in (Regulation 559.10.1).
2. The protective measures non-conducting location and earth-free equipotential bonding are not permitted (Regulation 559.10.2).
3. By necessity enclosures forming part of the outdoor lighting installations must be designed to prevent contact with live parts and where the protective measure is Automatic Disconnection of the Supply, Regulation group 714.411 requires that unless contained in an enclosure that is located where it is only accessible by skilled or instructed persons live parts shall only be accessible by use of a key or a tool. Furthermore Regulation 714.411.2.200 requires that where a luminaire is located at less than 2.8 m above the ground, the lamp should be accessible only after removing a barrier or opening an enclosure requiring the use of a tool.
4. Only lighting equipment designed for external use should be installed outdoors. The requirements applicable to the lighting equipment being used outdoors is summarised in Table 13.1.

Published by Certsure LLP © Certsure LLP (January 2015)

Table 13.1 Summary of external influence requirements of Regulation 714.512.2 applicable to outdoor lighting installations

	Ambient temperature	Relative humidity	Ingress protection		Degree of protection (IP rating) required for enclosure
			Water	Foreign bodies	
Classification (See also Appendix 5 of *BS 7671*)	AA2 to AA4	AB2 to AB4	AD3	AE2	IP33
Description	-40 °C to +40 °C	5 % to 100 %	Resistant to sprays	Small objects (2.5 mm)	Protected against: access to hazardous parts with a tool or spray at an angle of up to 60° of vertical

5. Regulation 714.537.2.1.1 requires that, except as described in Regulation 537.1.2, every circuit shall be capable of being isolated from each of the live supply conductors. Regulation 537.1.2 recognises, that in TN-S or TN-C-S systems the neutral conductor is reliably connected to earth, and need not be isolated. Consequently outdoor lighting supplied by a single-phase TN-S or TN-C-S system can be isolated by a single-pole device in the live conductor but outdoor lighting supplied by a single-phase TT system should be isolated using a double-pole device.

It should be noted that although Regulation 415.1 requires that all mobile equipment with a current rating not exceeding 32 A for use outdoors be provided with additional protection by means of a RCD having the characteristics specified in Regulation 415.1, unless the luminaire is connected to the final circuit by means of a socket-outlet, *BS 7671* does not contain any requirement for outdoor lighting circuits to be provided with additional protection. However, there may be circumstances where due to the characteristics of the supply an RCD is provided for fault-protection.

In addition lighting equipment used outdoors should be securely fixed and protected against accidental damage and attack by rodents. Luminaires installed at low level may require additional mechanical protection. It is advisable that flexible cables used to connect luminaires to the fixed installation should be kept as short as possible.

Festoon lighting, if used, should be adequately supported and securely fixed in accordance with the manufacturer's instructions.

Additional safety measures may be required where luminaires are installed close to a pond.

Submersible luminaires, if used, must always be installed strictly in accordance with the manufacturer's instructions.

Luminaires covered by the following parts of the *BS EN 60598-2* series *Luminaires. Particular requirements* are suitable for use in gardens:

- *BS EN 60598-2-7: 1997 – Portable luminaires for garden use.*
- *BS EN 60598-2-13: 2006 (2012) – Ground recessed luminaires.*
- *BS EN 60598-2-20: 2010 – Lighting chains.*

13.4 Equipment for use in ponds

Only special equipment and submersible cables designed for use in ponds should be used. Risk of damage to equipment and cables will be minimised by careful positioning and routing of cables.

Cables may need additional protection against accidental damage and attack by rodents.

All equipment located close to a pond should be protected against ingress of water and be resistant to corrosion.

Pond pumps should comply with *BS EN 60335-2-41: 2003 (2010) - Household and similar electrical appliances. Safety. Particular requirements for pumps.*

Other equipment for ponds should comply with *BS EN 60335-2-55: 2003 (2008) - Household and similar electrical appliances. Safety. Particular requirements for electrical appliances for use with aquariums and garden ponds.*

Published by Certsure LLP © Certsure LLP (January 2015)

Pond lighting should comply with *BS EN 60598-2-18: 2004 – Luminaires for swimming pools and similar applications*.

All equipment associated with ponds must be installed strictly in accordance with the manufacturer's instructions.

Electrical installations associated with large ponds, which could be used for bathing, should comply with the additional requirements for swimming pools contained in Section 702 of *BS 7671*.

Fig 13.6 Submersible pump with cable

IET WIRING REGULATIONS UPDATED TO: 17TH EDITION BS7671:2008 Amd 3: 2015

Other publications which have been updated to reflect the latest requirements of *BS 7671*: 2008 (Amendment 3): 2015 include -

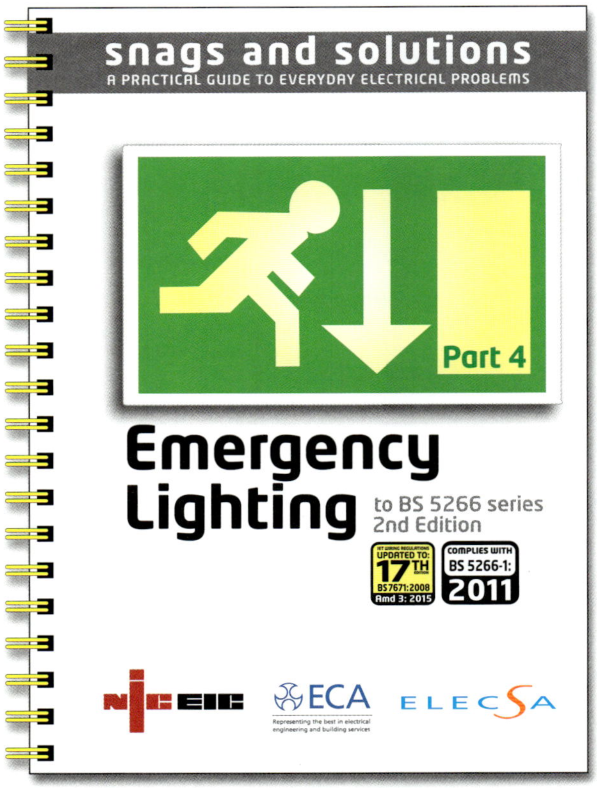

To order this or any other publication contact

NICEIC customers:	0843 290 3485	www.niceicdirect.com
ELECSA/ECA customers:	0333 321 8225	www.elecsa.co.uk

Published by Certsure LLP © Certsure LLP (January 2015)

Chapter

14

Additional sources of supply

 © Certsure LLP (January 2015)

Additional sources of supply

14.1 Introduction

In response to increased concerns over the issue of global warming and climate change, and in order to honour commitments made under the Kyoto Protocol, the UK government enacted a number of measures in the *Climate Change Act 2008*.

Key targets within this Act are:

- to ensure that the net UK carbon account for the year 2050 is at least 80% lower than the 1990 baseline,
- a reduction in emissions of at least 30% against the 1990 baseline by 2020.

At the European level, Directive *2009/28/EC*, contains a national overall target for the UK of 20% for the share of energy from renewable sources in gross final consumption of energy in 2020.

As a result of the above commitments, the UK government introduced Feed-in Tariffs (FITs) to provide a financial incentive to encourage uptake of microgeneration.

Electricity-producing microgeneration systems supplement the conventional large power stations with small-scale embedded generators (SSEGs) located in consumers' premises. These microgeneration systems utilise a range of technologies, including photovoltaic (PV), sterling engine-driven, wind-based and water-based (micro-hydro) systems.

Irrespective of the technology used, microgeneration offers the advantages of zero or extremely low fuel costs and a reduction in the transmission losses that occur in the national transmission of electrical energy.

For microgeneration systems (generally characterised as being rated at up to 16 A per phase) to be connected to the public electricity supply network, the installed equipment must satisfy the requirements of publication *G83/2 – Recommendations for the Connection of Type Tested Small-scale Embedded Generators (up to 16 A per Phase) in Parallel with Low-Voltage Distribution Systems*, issued by the Energy Networks Association. *G83/2* is intended to provide manufacturers and installers with guidance on the technical aspects of connecting SSEGs in parallel with the public electricity supply network.

Published by Certsure LLP © Certsure LLP (January 2015)

In order to access the funds available through FITs, the installer must, amongst other things, supply evidence to the Distribution Network Operator (DNO), within 30 days of commissioning the microgeneration system that the microgeneration system installation complies with *G83/2*.

It should be noted that payments for SSEGs installed under a FITS scheme can only be made if the work is carried out by an installer registered on the Microgeneration Certification Scheme (MCS) and installed in compliance with the guidance published by MCS appropriate to the type(s) of small-scale generation employed.

In recent years, the planning restrictions applying to the installation of domestic microgeneration systems on the outside of buildings have been relaxed, with the installation of some forms of microgeneration system being classed as permitted development.

However, this relaxation is unlikely to apply in conservation areas, or to a listed building or to a building on a world heritage site. The installation of a microgeneration system in one of these situations will require planning permission and may require listed building consent. Even when the work is classed as permitted development, there may be some planning restrictions in force.

The installation of some forms of microgenerator may be subject to planning law - and to non-electrical aspects of the Building Regulations, particularly in relation to structural considerations.

Therefore, before installing a microgeneration system it would be prudent to check with the local planning office as to what restrictions, if any, apply. Depending upon whether the property is in England, Wales, Scotland or Northern Ireland, different legislation will apply. In Scotland a Building Warrant may be required.

In England and Wales it is a statutory requirement that a microgeneration system complies with the relevant parts of the Building Regulations.

Requirements relating to many of the electrical aspects of installing microgeneration systems are included in *BS 7671 (IET Wiring Regulations 17th Edition), BS EN 50438: 2007 - Requirements for the connection of micro-generators in parallel with public low-voltage distribution networks* and, depending on the technology employed, requirements of other standards such as *BS EN 62446: 2009 Grid connected photovoltaic systems – Minimum requirements for system documentation, commissioning tests and inspection*.

 © Certsure LLP (January 2015)

14.2 *BS 7671* requirements for generators to operate in parallel

The general rules of *BS 7671* apply to the provision of small-scale generation for domestic premises (Regulation 110.1.1 (i), (vi) & (xviii) refers). For solar photovoltaic (PV) systems the requirements of Section 712 also apply (See Section 14.4 of this Guide).

Regulation 132.2 indicates that a number of characteristics relating to EACH source of supply need to be determined. This requirement is reinforced by Regulation 551.2.2, which requires prospective short-circuit current and prospective earth fault current to be determined for each source of supply.

Regulation 551.2.2 further requires that the short-circuit rating of protective devices within the installation should not be exceeded for any intended methods of operation of the sources.

Where an installation includes alternative or additional sources of supply, warning notices need to be placed at a number of locations within the installation (Regulations 514.15.1 and 537.1.6 refer). This is discussed in further detail in Section 8.10 of this Guide.

Wherever an installation is supplied from more than one source, Regulation 537.1.6 requires a main switch to be provided for each source of supply, or alternatively, a suitable interlock system shall be provided. (See also Section 7.2 of this Guide.)

Section 551 (Low voltage generating sets) contains a number of requirements applicable to installations containing a means of generation that operates in parallel with a supply taken from a public supply network (Regulation 551.1 refers).

Regulation 551.1.1 clarifies that generating sets driven by power sources such as combustion engines, photovoltaic cells and other suitable sources fall within the scope of Section 551.

A generating set should be installed such that:

- it does not impair the safety or proper functioning of other sources of supply (Regulation 551.2.1).
- any RCDs within the installation installed in accordance with Chapter 41 remain effective for every intended combination of sources of supply (Regulation 551.4.2).

Published by Certsure LLP © Certsure LLP (January 2015)

It remains necessary to provide protection by automatic disconnection of supply in accordance with Section 411, subject to modification specific to the means of operation of the generator (See Regulation 551.4.3.1 and the associated regulations listed therein). In the case of small-scale embedded generation falling within the scope of this Guide, the requirements of Regulation Group 551.7, which relates to generating sets that may operate in parallel with other sources, should be applied. These requirements are summarised below:

The generator should be installed on the supply side of all protective devices for final circuits within the installation.

Alternatively, except for solar PV systems, the generator may be installed on the load side of the all protective devices for a final circuit of the installation, but only if ALL the following conditions are met:

- the current-carrying capacity (I_z) of the conductors of the final circuit is not less than the sum of the rated current of the protective device for the circuit (I_n) and the rated output of the generator (I_g)
- the connection must not be made by plug and socket-outlet
- any RCD providing additional protection of the final circuit must disconnect all live conductors, including the neutral conductor
- there should be no connection between Earth and the live conductors of either the final circuit or the generator
- unless the final circuit protective device disconnects all live conductors, it will be necessary to determine that the sum of the disconnection time for the protective device and the time required for the output voltage of the generating set to fall to 50 V or less does not exceed the appropriate disconnection time required by Regulation 411.3.2 for the circuit in question.

When selecting a generator for use in parallel with a public distribution system, consideration should be given factors such as those listed below to avoid adverse effects to the public distribution system and other installations connected to it:

- power factor,
- voltage changes (variations in rms or peak values),

 © Certsure LLP (January 2015)

- voltage unbalance (differences between voltage deviations caused by differences in phase currents etc),

  Note: voltage unbalance between phases is permitted for single installations where total output does not exceed 16A per phase (see Clause 5.8 of ENA *G83/2*).
- harmonic distortion,
- issues connected with starting,
- synchronising,
- voltage fluctuation (a series of voltage changes or a cyclical variation).

The use of an automated synchronisation system dealing with frequency, phase and voltage is preferred (Regulation 551.7.3).

Automatic switching must be provided to disconnect the generator from the public distribution system in the event of complete loss, specified degrees of variation of voltage or frequency from declared values (see Regulation 551.7.4). Similarly means should be provided, to prevent the connection of a generator to the public distribution system under such circumstances (Regulation 551.7.5).

Means should be provided in a suitably accessible position, to isolate the generator from the public distribution network (Regulation 551.7.6).

For generators falling within the scope of this Guide (having an output not exceeding 16 A) Regulations 551.7.4, 551.7.5 and 551.7.6 all cross-refer to requirements within *BS EN 50438: 2013 - Requirements for the connection of micro-generators in parallel with public low-voltage distribution networks* that should be met.

14.3 Energy Networks Association G83/2

G83/2 - Recommendations for the Connection of Type Tested Small-scale Embedded Generators (Up to 16 A per phase) in Parallel with Low-Voltage Distribution Systems is published by the Energy Networks Association (ENA).

G83/2 contains technical requirements for the design, installation, commissioning and use of such microgeneration systems that must be satisfied before the Distribution Network Operator (DNO) will allow the microgeneration system installation to be connected to the DNO's Network.

Published by Certsure LLP © Certsure LLP (January 2015)

A summary of significant content is given below:

Section 5.2 – The installation between the generator and the point at which the supply is delivered to a consumer's installation (the exit point) is to comply with the requirements of *BS 7671*. The generator should be connected directly to an isolator which disconnects all live conductors. A second isolator may be necessary where an inverter is sited remotely, in a loft for example. This section calls for all isolators forming part of the installation to be capable of being locked in the 'off' (isolated) position, which is over and above *BS 7671* requirements.

Section 5.3 – Requires interface protection to be provided to disconnect the generator system from the DNO's distribution system when operating parameters such as loss of mains, voltage variation and frequency variation exceed the settings shown in Table 1 contained in this section of *G83/2*.

Note: It is expected that Table 1 of *G83/2* will be cited in Annex A of *BS EN 50438* as the specific National settings applicable to the United Kingdom when the standard is next updated.

The generator protection system must prevent its reconnection to the DNO's distribution network until the voltage and frequency on the DNO's network have remained within the limits stated in Table 1 for a minimum of 20 seconds. This is to prevent a generator being damaged by being reconnected when it is out of synchronism with the rest of the network.

Section 6.2 – Virtually repeats the requirement for a warning notice given in Regulation 514.15 of *BS 7671*, calling for the installer to provide labelling at the fused cut-out, meter position, consumer unit and at all points of isolation between the cut-out and the generator.

Section 6.3 – Recommends that periodic testing of the microgeneration system is carried out at intervals suggested by the manufacturer.

 © Certsure LLP (January 2015)

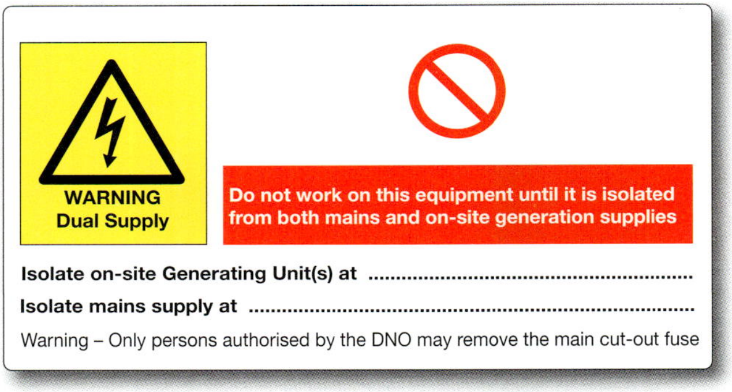

Fig 14.1 Warning notice for installations having more than one source of supply

Section 6.4 – All exposed-conductive-parts shall comply with the earthing requirements of *BS 7671*. There should be no direct connection between the generator current carrying conductors and earth (see also Regulation 551.7.2 (iii)), except where a generator is connected via an inverter, when it is permissible to connect one pole of the d.c. side of the inverter to the DNO's earth terminal if there is at least simple separation insulation between the a.c. and the d.c. sides (for PV systems see also 712.312.2).

Section 7.2 – Installation should be carried out by persons having recognised and approved qualifications relating to general electrical installation work and the type of microgeneration system being installed.

Previous written agreement should be obtained from the relevant DNO prior to any modification of operating criteria relating to the electrical connection.

A functional check of loss of mains protection should be performed as part of the on-site commissioning tests carried out by the installer.

Published by Certsure LLP © Certsure LLP (January 2015)

Section 7.3 – The Installer should advise the DNO of the intention to use a microgeneration system in parallel with the Network no later than 28 days (inclusive of the day of commissioning) after commissioning the microgeneration system. The Installer should also provide the local DNO with all relevant details on the installation.

Section 7.4 – If a component of a microgeneration system is replaced, it is only necessary to notify the relevant DNO where its operating characteristics or those of the interface protection are different from those in place when the system was originally commissioned.

Section 7.5 – The user of the system (the householder) should notify the DNO if a microgeneration system is decommissioned and will no longer be operated as a source of electrical energy in parallel with a DNO's Network.

14.4 Solar photovoltaic (PV) systems

14.4.1 General

Section 712 of *BS 7671* contains requirements applicable to solar PV power supply systems specifically. These requirements are summarised below.

A solar PV system consists of

- PV modules (panels)
- d.c. isolator
- inverter
- a.c isolator
- generation meter
- a.c. isolator

And beyond the consumer unit,

- export meter (usually only provided where the installed capacity of the microgenerator exceeds 30 kW)
- import meter

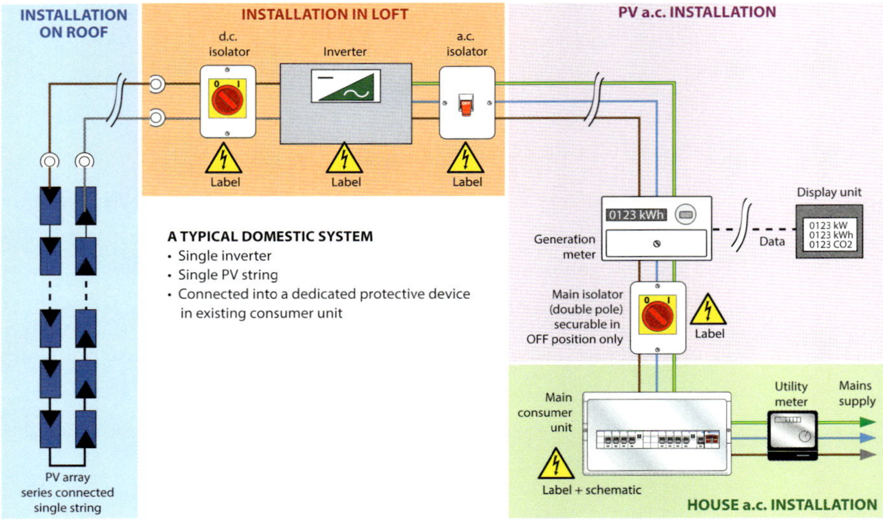

Fig 14.2 Schematic of typical Solar PV microgenerator system

14.4.2 The d.c. side

A solar array is made up from a number of solar panels, or more correctly PV modules connected together. Each module will contain a number of PV cells that generate electricity when exposed to sunlight.

A number of modules will be connected together in series in order to obtain the required output of voltage.

The PV modules should comply with the requirements of a relevant product standard and should be preferably of Class II construction where the open-circuit voltage of the PV string under standard test conditions ($U_{OC\ STC}$) exceeds 120 V d.c. (Regulation 712.511.1). Indeed, Class II construction is preferred on the d.c. side in any case (Regulation 712.412).

The PV modules should be so installed that adequate heat dissipation is ensured for the maximum solar radiation conditions for the location at which they are installed (Regulation 712.512.2.1).

Published by Certsure LLP © Certsure LLP (January 2015)

PV string cables, PV array cables and PV d.c. main cables should be selected and erected such that the risk of earth faults and short-circuits is minimised (Regulation 712.522.8.1). Furthermore, all wiring systems forming part of the solar PV installation should be capable of withstanding the worst conditions of external influence to which they could be expected to be exposed (Regulation 712.522.8.3).

The protective measures of non-conducting location and earth-free local equipotential bonding must not be used on the d.c. side (Regulation 712.410.3.6).

No overload protection is required for PV string and PV array cables where their continuous current-carrying capacity is greater than or equal to 1.25 times the short-circuit current under standard test conditions ($I_{SC\ STC}$) at any location (Regulation 712.433.1).

No overload protection is required for PV main cables where the continuous current-carrying capacity is greater than or equal to 1.25 times $I_{SC\ STC}$ of the PV generator (Regulation 712.433.2).

14.4.3 Isolation and switching

When considering requirements for isolation and switching, Regulation 712.537.2.2.1 states that the public supply is considered to be the source and the PV installation the load. Any equipment on the d.c. side, including isolation and switching devices, must be suitable for use with direct current and direct voltage (Regulation 712.512.1.1 refers).

A means of isolation must be provided between both the PV generator and the inverter, and the inverter and the a.c. side to permit servicing and maintenance (Regulation 712.537.2.1.1). The means of isolation on the d.c. side must be a switch-disconnector (as discussed in Section 7.4 of this Guide) (Regulation 712.537.2.2.5).

Equipment on the d.c. side of the PV installation should be considered to be energised even once it has been disconnected from the a.c. side (Regulation 712.410.3).

Enclosures, junction boxes and the like should comply with the requirements of *BS EN 60439-1: 1999 Low-voltage switchgear and controlgear assemblies. Part 1. Type-tested and partially type-tested assemblies* (712.511.1).

Any junction boxes forming part of the d.c. side of the PV installation should be labelled to warn that parts within will remain live even after isolation from the inverter (Regulation 712.537.2.2.5.1).

The a.c. side

Regulation 712.411.3.2.1.1 states that on the a.c. side, the PV supply cable should be connected to the supply side of any devices providing automatic disconnection for outgoing circuits supplying current-using equipment. This is normally achieved by either connecting the PV supply cable to a dedicated 'way' in the consumer unit, or to provide an additional small consumer unit for the connection of the PV power supply system specifically.

The PV supply cable must be protected against fault current by an overcurrent device at its point of connection to the a.c. installation (Regulation 712.434.1 refers).

If a transformerless inverter has been used, the protective conductor current of its a.c. circuit may at times exceed 10 mA in normal operation. Where this is the case, the relevant requirements of Regulation Group 543.7 will need to be met. See also Section 3.8 of this Guide.

If the a.c. PV supply cable is installed in the fabric of the building at a depth of less than 50 mm from the surface, the requirements of Regulations 522.6.201 or 522.6.202 should be considered, as appropriate. This may require the installation of an RCD meeting the requirements of Regulation 415.1.1. Further information on the additional protection of concealed cables is given in Section 11.5.7 of this Guide. Where an RCD is installed for this purpose it should disconnect all live conductors. So in the case of a single-phase installation, a double-pole RCD would be required to disconnect the line and neutral conductors.

It should be noted that where an inverter not having simple separation is installed, the manufacturer's instructions may require the use of an RCD having a rated residual operating current ($I_{\Delta n}$) of not less than, say, 100 mA.

 Published by Certsure LLP © Certsure LLP (January 2015)

This would mean that a 30 mA RCD could not be installed to provide adcitional protection for a cable concealed in the building fabric. It would therefore be necessary for the designer to meet the requirements of 552.6.201 or 552.6.202 by employing one of the methods described in 552.6.203. Alternatively, using surface mounting of the PV supply cable could be considered. Thought could also be given to using an inverter that does provide simple separation, in which case a 30 mA RCD could be installed.

If the RCD does not disconnect the neutral, the effectiveness of the protection no longer depends solely on the operation of the RCD, but also on the shut-down characteristics of the inverter on loss of the a.c. mains supply. Under *G83/2*, this could be of up to 1 second in duration, in which case the requirements of Regulations 522.6.201 or 522.6.202 would not have been met.

Where the inverter of the PV installation does not provide simple separation between the a.c. and d.c. side, any RCD installed to provide fault (or additional) protection must be of a type that will operate as intended in the presence of d.c. currents in the residual current. Where this is the case, it will not be possible to use a Type AC or Type A RCD. Regulation 712.411.3.2.1.2 states that in such cases any RCD installed must be of Type B to *BS 62423*. This requirement would not apply if the manufacturer's instructions for a particular inverter specifically state that the inverter provides galvanic isolation between the a.c. and dc. sides sufficient to prevent d.c. appearing in the a.c installation.

Any part of the PV power supply system installation requiring maintenance, servicing or the like should be installed such that it remains accessible to allow such activities to be performed safely. (Regulation 712.513.1). This requirement would apply to any junction boxes or inverters placed in, for example, the loft of a house.

Further guidance on the installation of solar photovoltaic microgeneration systems can be found in the *NICEIC Solar PV learning guide*.

14.5 Further information

Anyone involved in the installation of small-scale embedded generator systems should be competent in such work in addition to their basic electrical installation work competency.

In addition to the standards mentioned above, reference should be made to the following sources of information as relevant to the type of system being installed:

Electrical Safety First

Best Practice Guide No 3 (Issue 2) Connecting a microgeneration system to a domestic or similar electrical installation (in parallel with the mains supply).

Energy Saving Trust

CE72 – Energy efficiency best practice in housing. Installing small wind powered electricity generating systems

Microgeneration Certification Scheme Microgeneration Installation Standards

MIS 3002 – Requirements for contractors undertaking the supply, design, installation, set to work commissioning and handover of solar photovoltaic (pv) microgeneration systems.

MIS 3003 – Requirements for contractors undertaking the supply, design, installation, set to work commissioning and handover of micro and small wind turbine systems.

MIS 3007 – Requirements for contractors undertaking the supply, design, installation, set to work commissioning and handover of a heating system containing a micro-cogeneration package.

Published by Certsure LLP © Certsure LLP (January 2015)

Chapter 15

Inspection and testing

Published by Certsure LLP © Certsure LLP (January 2015)

Inspection and testing

15.1 Initial verification

BS 7671 requires inspection and testing of an installation during its construction and on its completion, before a new installation is put into service or an existing installation is returned to service following additions or alterations (Regulation 610.1 refers). Inspection forms a part of the initial verification process and should preferably be carried out before any testing (Regulation 611.1), as defects or signs of significant damage might be found by the inspection that would have made the testing of the installation dangerous to the occupants of the building, or to the person(s) carrying out the inspection and testing. Furthermore, such defects or deterioration might also render any test results obtained invalid.

Wherever possible, the inspection should be carried out with the installation, or that part of it which is under scrutiny, disconnected from the supply. This is in line with the requirements of Regulation 14 of the Electricity at Work Regulations 1989 (EWR) relating to work on or near live conductors.

The human senses of not only sight, but also touch, smell and hearing may be employed as a part of the inspection process.

Whilst the use of sight and touch require little explanation, it should be pointed out that smell and hearing can be usefully employed to identify, for example, the location of arcing at a loose connection or overheating of equipment.

Regulation 611.3 lists items that should be checked during the initial inspection of an installation, and forms the basis of both the Examples of items requiring inspection during initial verification and the Schedule of inspections for domestic and similar premises which are included in Appendix 6 of *BS 7671*.

15.2 Periodic inspection

15.2.1 General

In the case of an existing installation, Regulation 621.1 calls for periodic inspection and testing to be carried out to determine whether the installation remains satisfactory for continued use. This regulation also requires the contents of documentation such as the original Electrical Installation Certificate, or previously issued Periodic Inspection Reports relating to the installation, where available, to be taken into consideration.

 Published by Certsure LLP © Certsure LLP (January 2015)

Regulation 621.1 further states that where no such previous documentation is available an investigation of the electrical installation should be carried out prior to performing any inspection and testing activities.

The periodic inspection should be performed without dismantling, or the minimum of dismantling (Regulation 621.2 refers), in order to reduce the risk of the inspection process actually introducing a fault.

When carrying out a periodic inspection of an existing installation, it is not always possible or necessary to carry out the same degree of inspection and testing as for new installation work. Furthermore, it may not be practicable or indeed physically possible to inspect and test the whole of the installation.

This is recognised by *BS 7671*, which contains a number of requirements relating to the extent of the periodic inspection and testing of an installation, and limitations relating to various aspects of the inspection and testing process.

15.2.2 Extent of the installation to be inspected

The extent of the existing installation to be covered by a periodic inspection should be agreed in advance between the person carrying out the inspection and testing and the client.

A number of factors must be taken into consideration when deciding upon the extent, including:

- the size of the installation,
- the wishes of the client,
- the requirements of third parties, such as insurance providers and licensing authorities,
- the usage of the building and ambient environmental conditions,
- the age and general condition of the electrical installation,
- whether or not it is acceptable for all, or parts of, the installation to be isolated from the supply,
- acceptable durations of any agreed isolation of supply,

 © Certsure LLP (January 2015)

- mutually agreeable times for the inspection and testing to be carried out,
- the time elapsed since the initial verification was completed, or the last periodic inspection was carried out,
- the availability of records relating to the installation, maintenance and previous inspections of the installation
- the effectiveness of any ongoing maintenance as evidenced during the inspection process.

Regulation 621.4 requires that the extent (as well as the results) of the periodic inspection and testing should be recorded. This information has to be described in the Electrical Installation Condition Report (EICR) issued on completion of the inspection and testing process, as required by Regulation 631.2.

15.2.3 Limitations on the inspection and testing

Regulation 631.2 also requires any limitations of the inspection and testing to be detailed on the EICR. Furthermore, Regulation 634.2 requires the reasoning and justification for the limitation(s) to be recorded on the report.

Any limitations should be agreed with the client prior to work starting. However, it is important that neither the client nor the person carrying out the work imposes limitations unnecessarily, as this would result in the report having less validity.

The following are typical examples of limitations.

i) No testing at height where this presents accessibility problems (where, for example, temporary access equipment would be required).

ii) Particular circuits or parts of an installation not tested where disconnection of supply would cause an unacceptable level of disruption to the operations of the client.

iii) Particular circuits or parts of an installation not tested where the implications of an unwanted disconnection would be prohibitively expensive in terms of lost data etc.

Items ii) and iii) above are not generally applicable to installations in domestic premises.

Published by Certsure LLP © Certsure LLP (January 2015)

It should be noted that the following testing activities do **not** have to be listed as limitations.

- Carrying out an insulation resistance test on all circuits connected to a consumer unit or distribution board collectively (Regulation 612.3.2 refers).
- Carrying out an insulation resistance test where all line conductors are connected together and tested to the earthing arrangement where a circuit includes electronic devices that might otherwise be damaged or have an influence on the test results obtained (see Regulations 612.3.1 and 612.3.3).
- Carrying out an insulation resistance test at 250 V d.c. on circuits where surge protective devices or other equipment are likely to be present, which might otherwise be damaged as a result of the testing or have an influence on the test results obtained, subject to a minimum acceptable insulation resistance of 1 MΩ being achieved (Regulation 612.3.2 refers). Such items of equipment should be disconnected prior to carrying out the test where this is practicable.

Although the above items do not need to be listed as limitations of the inspection and testing process, their use is nevertheless noteworthy and so an appropriate description of such should be included in the 'Remarks' column against the appropriate circuit on the Schedule of Test Results.

In terms of the inspection of an installation, it is clearly stated within the 'EXTENT AND LIMITATIONS OF THE INSPECTION' text box on the EICR that:

> ... cables concealed within trunking and conduits, under floors, in roof spaces and generally within the fabric of the building or underground, have **not** been inspected unless specifically agreed between the client and inspector prior to the inspection.

 © Certsure LLP (January 2015)

IET WIRING REGULATIONS
UPDATED TO:
17TH EDITION
BS7671:2008
Amd 3: 2015

Other publications which have been updated to reflect the latest requirements of *BS 7671*: 2008 (Amendment 3): 2015 include -

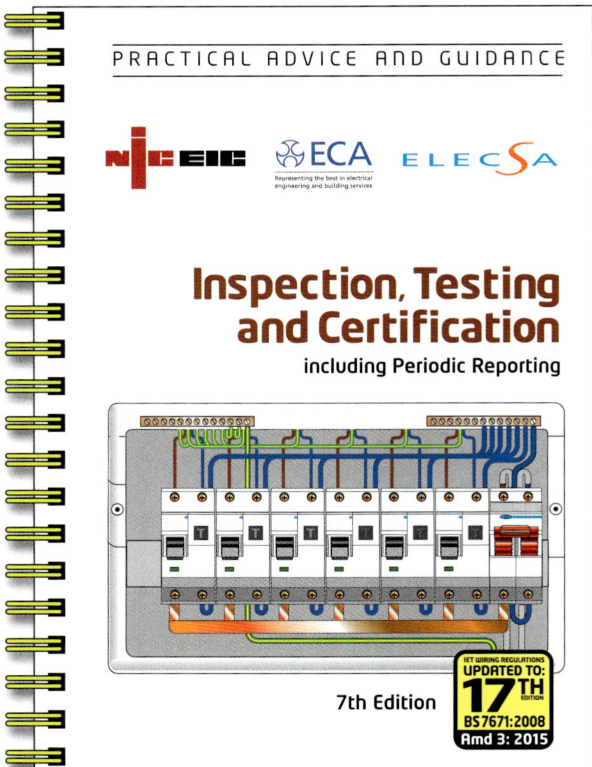

To order this or any other publication contact

NICEIC customers:	0843 290 3485	www.niceicdirect.com
ELECSA/ECA customers:	0333 321 8225	www.elecsa.co.uk

Published by Certsure LLP © Certsure LLP (January 2015)

Testing

Chapter 16

Testing

This section gives guidance on the testing of domestic electrical installations. It should be noted that Regulation 610.1 calls for testing (and inspection) to be carried out, as appropriate, at a number of occasions during the construction of the installation.

In many cases there may be a significant time interval between the initial placement of conductors (sometimes referred to as 'first fixing') and the final handover of the installation. It is possible for damage to have occurred during this time when, for example, cables were plastered over and flooring and ceilings were installed.

It is essential therefore that all the relevant tests are performed as part of the final verification of the electrical installation. In some cases, this will mean repeating a test carried out previously. It is not acceptable to rely solely on test results that were obtained at an earlier stage of the installation process.

16.1 Sequence of tests - initial verification

The following sequence of testing is appropriate when carrying out the initial verification of circuits within a typical domestic installation:

i) Continuity of protective conductors **and** continuity of ring final circuit conductors

ii) Insulation resistance

iii) Polarity by continuity methods

iv) Polarity using a voltage indicator (live polarity check)

v) External earth fault loop impedance **or** Earth electrode resistance

vi) Prospective fault current at the origin (both short-circuit and earth fault)

vii) Earth fault loop impedance of circuits

viii) Prospective fault current of circuits (where necessary)

ix) Tests to verify operation of RCD providing fault protection

x) Tests to verify operation of RCD providing additional protection

xi) Any functional testing deemed appropriate.

Published by Certsure LLP © Certsure LLP (January 2015)

16.2 Sequence of tests - periodic inspection

Whilst no sequence of tests is stated for periodic testing, the following sequence would be appropriate when carrying out a periodic inspection of circuits within a typical domestic installation:

i) External earth fault loop impedance **or** Earth electrode resistance

ii) Prospective fault current at the origin

iii) Continuity of protective conductors **and** continuity of ring final circuit conductors

iv) Insulation resistance

v) Polarity by continuity methods

vi) Polarity using a voltage indicator

vii) Earth fault loop impedance of circuits

viii) Prospective fault current of circuits (where necessary)

ix) Tests to verify operation of RCD providing fault protection

x) Tests to verify operation of RCD providing additional protection

xi) Any functional testing deemed appropriate.

16.3 Test procedures

16.3.1 Continuity of protective conductors

Errors caused by parallel paths

Before carrying out a test to confirm the continuity, or to measure the resistance, of a protective conductor, care should be taken to locate and disconnect (where practicable) any conductive paths which may be connected in parallel with all or part of it. Such parallel paths could be present due, for example, to a connection from a protective conductor to an electrically continuous system of pipework at one or more points along the protective conductor. Such parallel paths could lead to incorrect test results and may even conceal the fact that a protective conductor is not electrically continuous.

Test instrument

The test instrument to be used is an ohmmeter having a low resistance range, or an insulation and continuity test instrument set to the 'continuity' range. It is recommended that the instrument has a short-circuit output current of not less than 200 mA (a.c. or d.c.) and an open-circuit voltage of between 4 V and 24 V. Continuity test readings of less than 1 Ω are common. Therefore, the resistance of the test leads is significant, and should not be included in any recorded test result. If the particular test instrument does not have provision for correcting for the resistance of the test leads, it will be necessary to measure the resistance of the leads when connected together, and for this measured value to be subtracted from all the test readings. See illustration below.

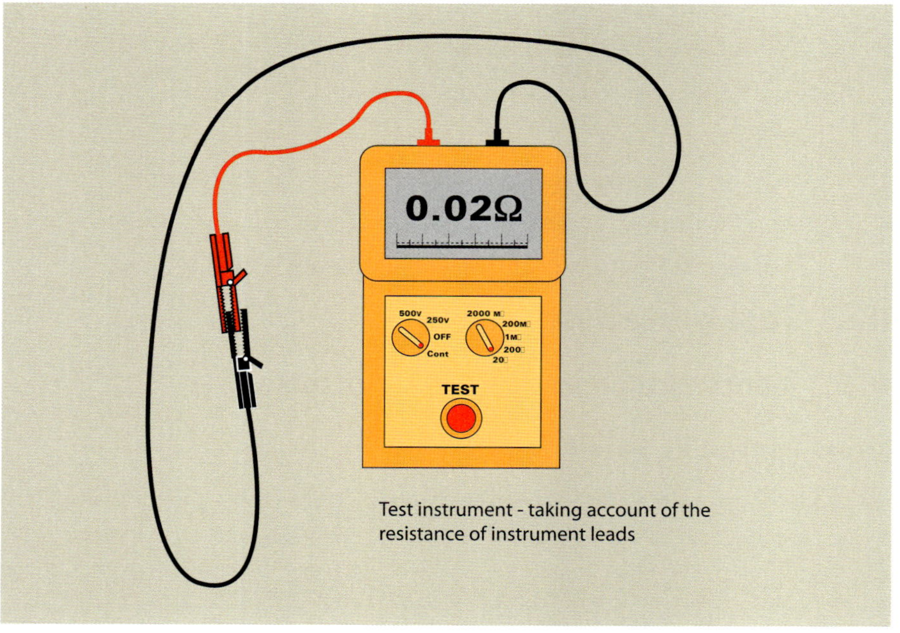

Fig 16.1 Determining the resistance of the test leads

Published by Certsure LLP © Certsure LLP (January 2015)

When carrying out a continuity test using either of the methods described below, remember to either note the resistance of the test leads for subtraction from the overall measured value or use the 'auto-null' facility of the test instrument (if available) so that the test value recorded does not include the resistance of the test leads.

Why do we need to test the continuity of protective conductors?

It is essential to ensure that all circuit protective conductors and bonding conductors are continuous. Otherwise, an exposed-conductive-part, an extraneous-conductive-part or the earthing terminal of a point or accessory could be left without an effective connection to Earth, giving no fault protection in the event of an earth fault.

($R_1 + R_2$) method

This method is applicable to circuit protective conductors and their associated line conductors. It is not applicable to main or supplementary bonding conductors.

The ($R_1 + R_2$) method of testing the continuity of circuit protective conductors has the following advantages:

- The information required to complete the ($R_1 + R_2$) column of the Schedule of Test Results is obtained directly.
- Polarity is verified as each continuity test is performed.
- The method may be more convenient than the R_2 'wander lead' method (see following section).

 © Certsure LLP (January 2015)

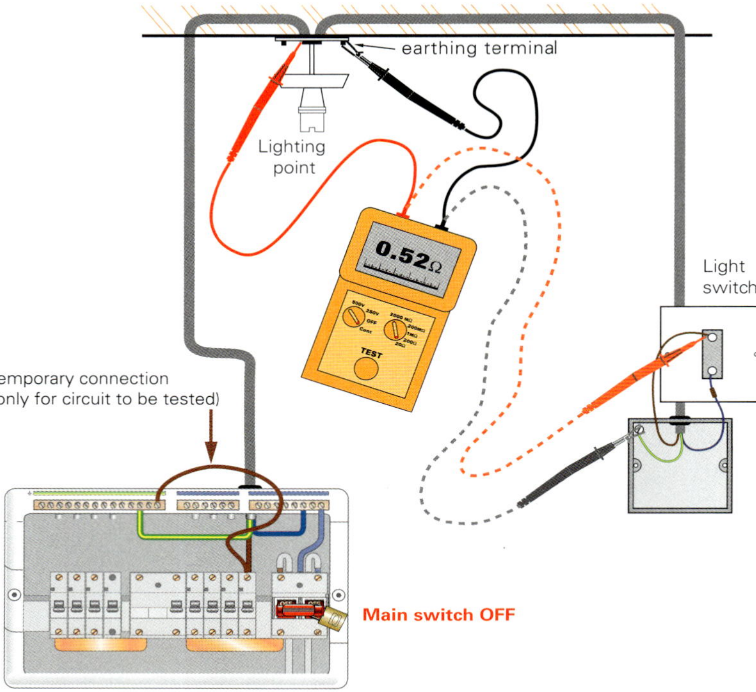

Fig 16.2 Testing continuity of the protective conductor to a lighting point by the ($R_1 + R_2$) method

The test provides a measured value of resistance for the line conductor and the circuit protective conductor of a circuit, in series. The test may be carried out, having first securely isolated the supply, by temporarily connecting together the line conductor and circuit protective conductor at the supply end, and then connecting the test instrument to the terminals of the line conductor and the circuit protective conductor at each point and accessory on the circuit in turn.

The value of ($R_1 + R_2$) measured at the point or accessory electrically most remote from the supply will be the maximum value, and it is this value that should be recorded on the Schedule of Test Results. The test readings at the other points and accessories on the circuit serve to verify that the protective conductor is continuous to each of them, and that the polarity is correct.

Published by Certsure LLP © Certsure LLP (January 2015)

Procedure:

- Securely isolate the supply.
- Disconnect any bonding connections that could affect the test readings.
- Make a temporary connection, at the supply end of the circuit (for example, at a consumer unit) between the line and circuit protective conductor (cpc) of the circuit to be tested.
- Measure the resistance between line and cpc at each point and accessory on the circuit (thereby also confirming correct polarity).
- Any switches should be operated to ensure that all wiring is subjected to testing.
- Record the reading at the electrically most remote* point or accessory (the highest value) of the circuit (and confirm correct polarity for the circuit).
- Re-connect any bonding conductors disconnected for the test.
- Remove the temporary connection.

Whilst the primary purpose of testing for protective conductor continuity is to ensure that such continuity exists, the result of an ($R_1 + R_2$) test can be used to determine the earth fault loop impedance at the point or accessory at which the test is applied. This procedure is explained under the subject heading of 'earth fault loop impedance' in this chapter.

*Note: In the simplified diagram shown, polarity should be verified at both the lighting point (as shown) and the switch. However, the electrically most remote point in this particular circuit will be the switch. The ($R_1 + R_2$) value recorded for this circuit will be that measured at the ceiling outlet between the switch line and cpc.

 © Certsure LLP (January 2015)

R_2 method

This method is used principally for testing protective conductors that are connected to the main earthing terminal (main equipotential bonding conductors, circuit protective conductors and so on). The correct polarity of circuit connections will need to be verified separately. This method is also widely employed during testing forming part of the periodic inspection of an installation.

Where a continuity test involves the opening of enclosures etc, that part of the installation will need to be isolated.

One terminal of the continuity test instrument is connected to the main earthing terminal with a long lead (or 'wander lead') and, with a lead from the other terminal, contact is made with the protective conductor at every position to which it is connected in that circuit, such as at socket-outlets, lighting points, fixed equipment points, switches, exposed-conductive-parts and extraneous-conductive-parts. By this means, provided that no parallel paths are present, the continuity of the protective conductor back to the main earthing terminal can be verified, and its resistance measured.

The wander lead used to carry out this test may be as much as 50 m in length. Therefore the resistance of the lead will be significant. It is essential therefore that the resistance of the wander lead is either 'nulled' prior to testing or is subtracted from the value obtained from testing.

A main or supplementary bonding conductor can be tested by simply attaching the leads of the test instrument to each end of the conductor, having temporarily disconnected one end of that conductor to remove parallel paths.

16.3.2 Continuity of ring final circuit conductors

Why do we need to check the continuity of ring final circuit conductors?

Incorrectly connected, or open circuit, conductors in an installed ring final circuit can lead to overloading of the circuit cables. Testing by the above procedure verifies continuity and correct connection, as well as correct polarity.

Published by Certsure LLP © Certsure LLP (January 2015)

Testing also provides confirmation that both legs of the ring final circuit have been connected into the same protective device. The incorrect connection of a ring final circuit across two protective devices would leave the installation in a dangerous condition particularly when safe isolation of a final circuit was required.

The cables of a ring final circuit start at the outgoing terminals of a protective device within a consumer unit or distribution board, connect to all the points in the ring, and return to the same outgoing terminals. The live (line and neutral) conductors must form a complete unbroken loop without interconnections, as must the circuit protective conductor, unless it is formed by a continuous metal covering or enclosure (such as a steel conduit) containing all the live conductors.

Procedure:

When carrying out this test, it is necessary to either to note the resistance of the test leads for subtraction from the overall measured value or to use the 'auto-null' facility of the test instrument (if available) so that the test value recorded does not include the resistance of the test leads.

Confirm that the circuit to be tested has been securely isolated. Using a low resistance ohmmeter set on its lowest scale (typically 0-2 Ω or similar), carry out the following three-step test procedure:

Step 1

Measure the end-to-end resistance of the:

- line conductor (r_1)
- neutral conductor (r_n)
- cpc (r_2)
  (see Fig 16.3)

The results obtained should be more or less equal (± 0.05 Ω, say) except where the circuit is wired using 'twin and earth' type cables having a cpc of reduced cross-sectional area, where the resistance of the cpc will be higher on account of this.

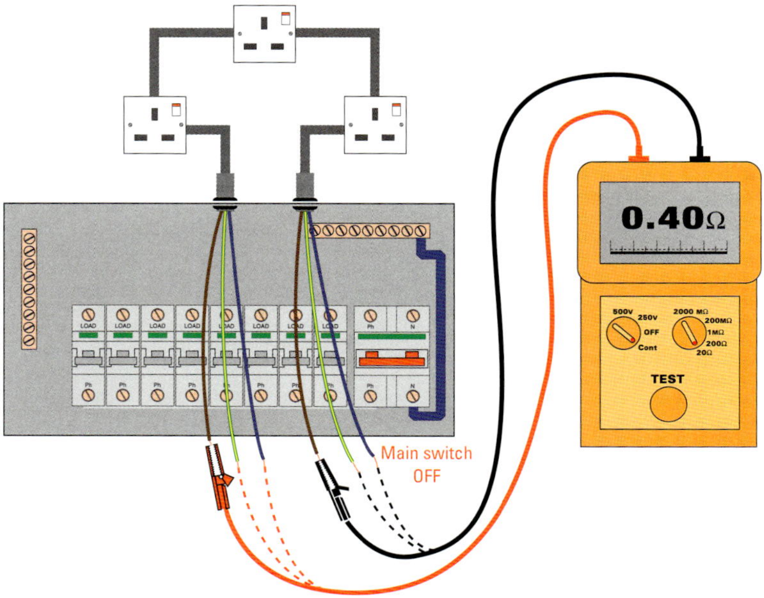

Fig 16.3 Step 1 of ring final circuit continuity test

Step 2

Connect the outgoing line conductor of the circuit to the incoming neutral conductor of the circuit and vice versa at the distribution board or consumer unit, as shown in Fig 16.4.

Measure the resistance between line and neutral terminals at every socket-outlet connected to the circuit. The results obtained should be substantially the same at each socket-outlet and should be approximately one quarter of the combined resistance of the line loop (r_1) and neutral loop (r_n) that is,

$$\frac{r_1 + r_n}{4}$$

Any socket-outlets connected as unfused spurs will have a higher resistance value as a result of the resistance of the spur conductors.

Published by Certsure LLP © Certsure LLP (January 2015)

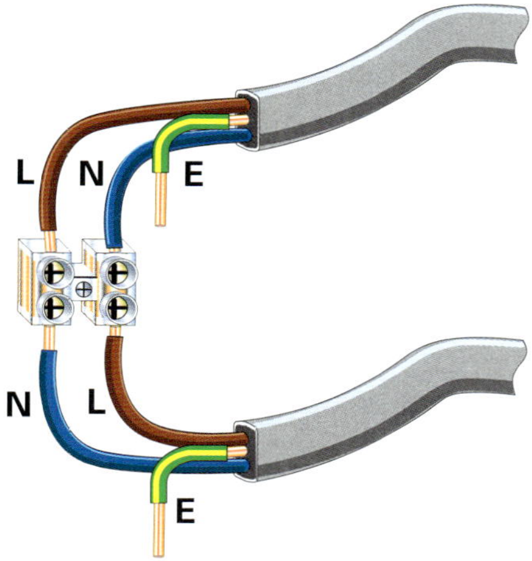

Fig 16.4 Step 2 of ring final circuit continuity test

Step 3

Now connect the outgoing line conductor of the circuit to the incoming cpc of the circuit and vice versa at the distribution board or consumer unit, as shown in Fig 16.5.

Measure the resistance between line and cpc terminals at **every** socket-outlet connected to the circuit under test. The results obtained should be substantially the same at each socket-outlet and should be approximately one quarter of the combined resistance of the line loop (r_1) and cpc loop (r_2), that is,

$$\frac{r_1 + r_n}{4}$$

Any socket-outlets connected as spurs will have a higher resistance value as a result of the resistance of the spur conductors.

The highest value of resistance obtained should be recorded on the *Schedule of Test Results* as the ($R_1 + R_2$) value of the circuit.

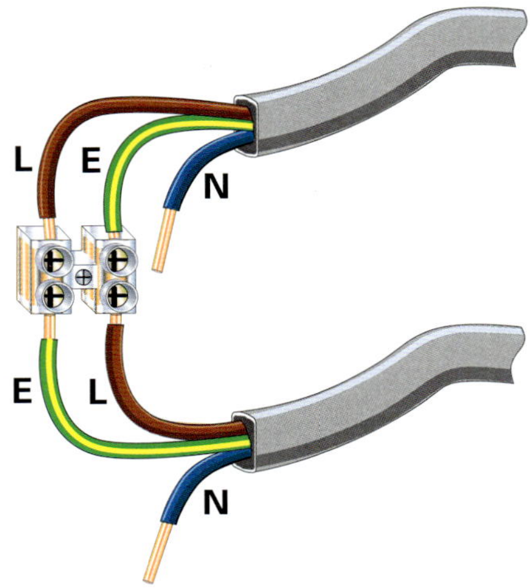

Fig 16.5 Step 3 of ring final circuit continuity test

Note: If, where single-core cables have been used for the circuit wiring, the resistance readings obtained increase as the distance from the distribution board or consumer unit increases, it is likely that the cross-connections have been made to conductors from the same leg of the circuit (i.e. both incoming or outgoing) and not to opposite legs. If this occurs, correctly cross-connect the circuit and start the testing again.

Socket-outlets wired as spurs will give a slightly higher resistance reading depending on the length of the spur.

16.3.3 Insulation resistance

General

Carrying out an insulation resistance test gives an indication of the condition of the insulation of conductors and any equipment to which they are connected. Effective insulation is necessary to provide basic protection and to prevent short-circuits and earth faults.

An insulator should have high insulation resistance, typically many magaohms (MΩ).

The insulation resistance of a conductor is inversely proportional to its length – that is, its insulation resistance decreases as the conductor's length increases and vice versa.

Generally speaking, the insulation resistance of a number of parallel circuits connected to a consumer unit may be tested collectively. So, it is acceptable to carry out an insulation resistance test of a distribution circuit (if any), the consumer unit and the final circuits originating from it, with the protective devices of the final circuits in the ON position and the current-using equipment temporarily disconnected (Regulation 612.3.2 refers).

 Published by Certsure LLP © Certsure LLP (January 2015)

The final circuits connected to the distribution board are in parallel with each other, and so when considering the total insulation resistance, the circuits may be treated as resistors in parallel as shown below.

Example

Three circuits have insulation resistance of 40 MΩ, 40 MΩ and 80 MΩ when tested separately. What is the total resistance if these three circuits were connected in parallel?

$$\frac{1}{R_T} = \frac{1}{R_1} + \frac{1}{R_2} + \frac{1}{R_3} \quad \text{etc}$$

Where:

R_T is the total resistance of the parallel circuits, *and*

R_1, R_2 and R_3 are the individual circuit resistances.

$$\frac{1}{R_1} = \frac{1}{40} + \frac{1}{40} + \frac{1}{80}$$

Using a common denominator (80 in this case);

$$\frac{1}{R_T} = \frac{(2+2+1)}{80}$$

$$\frac{1}{R_T} = \frac{5}{80}$$

$$\frac{R_T}{1} = \frac{80}{5}$$

$$R_T = 16\ \text{M}\Omega$$

To perform the calculation above using a scientific calculator, the following procedure should typically be followed:

40	1/x	+	40	1/x	+	80	1/x	=	1/x

Note: It is essential to press the "1/x" button after pressing the "=".

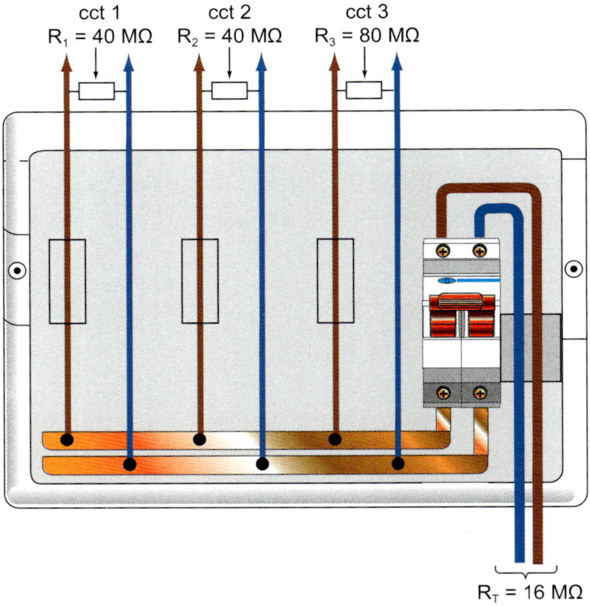

Fig 16.6 The effect of parallel connection on overall measured resistance

Remember:

- the total resistance of any number of resistances in parallel will always be **lower** than lowest individual resistance connected in parallel
- where two identical resistances are connected in parallel, the total resistance will be half that of one of the resistances; for example, the total resistance of two 40 MΩ resistances connected in parallel is 20 MΩ (as would be the case for circuits 1 and 2 in the example above)
- the total resistance of two resistors of any value connected in parallel can be found using the product / sum rule, i.e.

$$R_T = \frac{R_1 \times R_2}{R_1 + R_2}$$

Published by Certsure LLP © Certsure LLP (January 2015)

Preconditions and precautions

Prior to carrying out an insulation resistance test:

Disconnect any equipment likely to

- influence the test results obtained, or
- be damaged by the test voltage

Where this is impracticable or where doubt exists as to whether all such equipment has been disconnected, the following options are available:

- Insulation resistance may be measured between live conductors and protective conductor(s) with all line and neutral conductors connected together. Where this method is used, there is no potential difference between the line and neutral terminals of connected equipment or the components therein (Regulations 612.3.1 and 612.3.3 refer).
- The test voltage applied may be reduced to 250 V d.c. but the minimum acceptable value of insulation resistance remains 1 MΩ (see Regulation 612.3.2).

Testing of low voltage circuits and FELV circuits

Temporarily disconnect all current-using equipment. Remove any lamps from lampholders. Place all switches in the ON position. Two-way and, where fitted, intermediate, switches will need to be operated during the test to ensure that all live conductors are subjected to the testing.

Confirm that the circuit to be tested has been de-energised. Then, using a high resistance ohmmeter set to 500 V d.c. and the highest resistance scale on the instrument, carry out the following test procedure and record the results obtained.

For a single-phase installation, test between line and neutral as shown in Fig 16.7

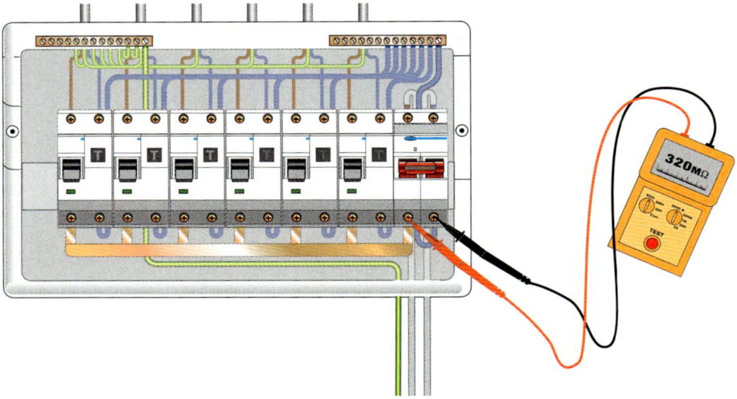

Fig 16.7 Insulation resistance test between line and neutral

Then test between live conductors and protective earth connected to the means of earthing, as shown in Fig 16.8.

However, where the consumer unit has been connected to the energy meter, the test must be carried out on the load side of the main switch in the OFF/isolation position, but with all the circuit protective devices in the ON position.

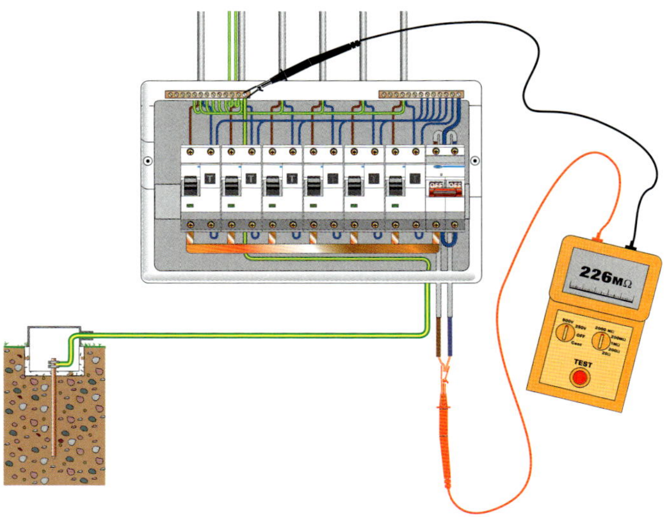

Fig 16.8 Insulation resistance between live conductors and earth (installation forming part of a TT system shown)

Published by Certsure LLP © Certsure LLP (January 2015)

For a three-phase installation, test between:

- line 1 and line 2, *and*
- line 2 and line 3, *and*
- line 1 and line 3, as shown in Fig 16.9, *and*
- lines collectively to neutral. If the reading is acceptable you have saved yourself 2 tests. If the reading is not acceptable, test each line to neutral separately as shown in Fig 16.10
- lines collectively to earth. If the reading is acceptable you have saved yourself 2 tests. If the reading is not acceptable, test each line to earth separately.

When performing an insulation resistance test between live and protective conductors, protective conductors must be connected to the earthing arrangement, that is, the general mass of Earth (as implied by the capitalized word *Earth*) to comply with Regulation 612.3.1.

The connection to Earth is typically achieved by the protective conductor being connected to the main earthing terminal (MET) of the installation, to which the earthing, protective bonding and, where applicable, supplementary bonding also connect, with the MET connected to the earthing arrangement (the distributor's earthing facility or the installation earth electrode as applicable).

Having the protective conductors connected to Earth during the test has the advantage that the test might detect any contact between a live conductor and any 'unearthed' metalwork (such as a concealed part of the building fabric or an isolated section of pipework). If the unearthed metalwork has some relatively low resistance contact with Earth (even hundreds of thousands of ohms), the defect can be identified by the person using the insulation resistance test instrument. Such a dangerous defect might be caused by the penetration of a nail, screw or similar making contact with a live conductor and the unearthed metalwork. If not corrected, the defect would create a risk of electric shock.

The insulation resistance of a FELV circuit, when tested, should meet all of the requirements applicable to a low voltage circuit (Regulation 612.4.4).

The minimum acceptable value of insulation resistance for a distribution circuit with a distribution board or consumer unit and all its final circuits connected is 1 MΩ (See Table 61 of *BS 7671*).

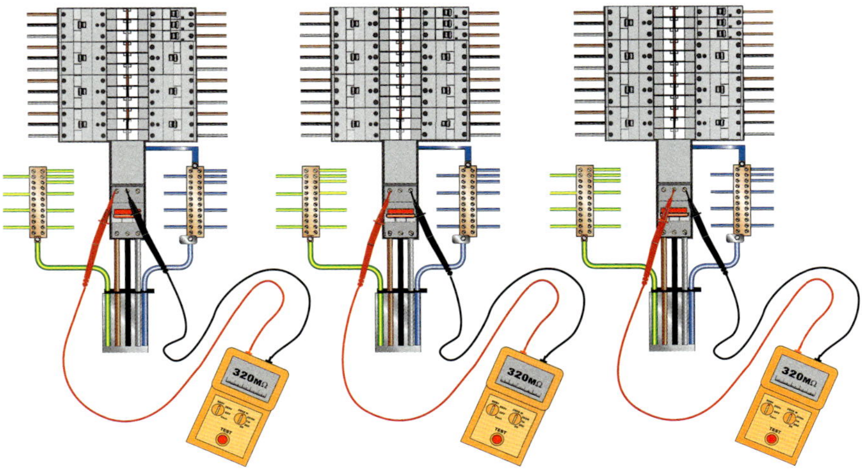

Fig 16.9 Insulation resistance testing between lines

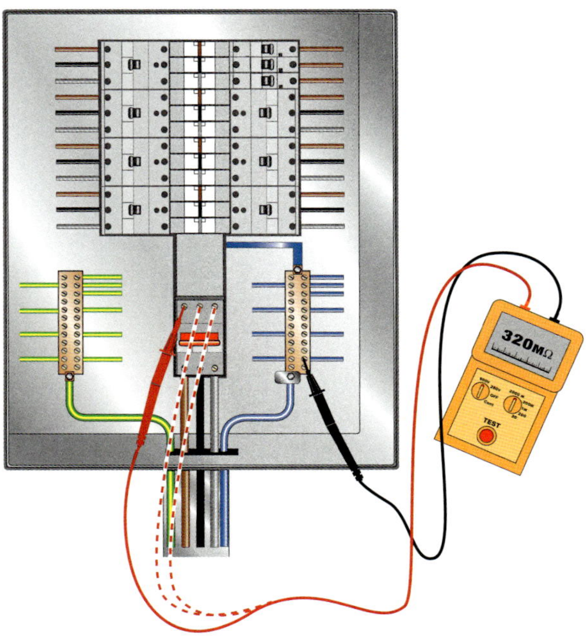

Fig 16.10 Insulation resistance testing between neutral and each line separately

Published by Certsure LLP © Certsure LLP (January 2015)

Regulation 612.3.4 requires that the insulation resistance of functional extra-low voltage circuits shall meet all the test requirements of low-voltage circuits.

Testing of SELV and PELV circuits

Where the protective measure for a circuit is SELV or PELV, it should be confirmed by insulation resistance test using an applied voltage of 500 V d.c. that the live parts so protected are sufficiently separated from the live parts of any other non SELV or PELV circuits within the installation (Regulations 612.4.1 and 612.4.2 refer).

When testing between SELV or PELV conductors or between SELV conductors and Earth, a test voltage of 250 V d.c. should be applied.

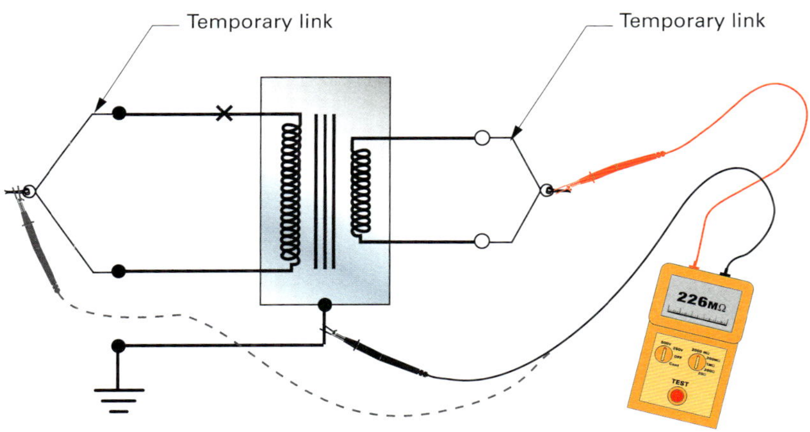

Fig 16.11 Insulation resistance test to confirm separation in a SELV circuit supplied from a double wound transformer

The minimum acceptable value of insulation resistance when confirming the separation of the conductors of SELV and PELV circuits from those of non-SELV or PELV circuits in the same location is 1 MΩ (Regulation 612.4 refers).

The minimum acceptable value of insulation resistance when confirming the separation of the conductors of SELV and PELV circuits from each other, and from Earth, is 0.5 MΩ (Table 61 of *BS 7671* refers).

 © Certsure LLP (January 2015)

16.3.4 Polarity

By continuity methods (installation or circuit de-energised)

It should be noted that a great deal of the verification of polarity may be done by inspection. Further, much of the verification of polarity by continuity methods can be carried out at the same time that the continuity testing is being carried out. In the case of ring final circuits, the continuity of the cpc is verified as a part of the ring final circuit continuity test where the test has been carried out correctly and where acceptable values of continuity were achieved.

Using a low resistance ohmmeter set on its lowest scale (typically 0-2 Ω or similar) carry out the continuity testing in accordance with the $(R_1 + R_2)$ method described in Section 16.3.1. of this Guide, paying particular attention to confirming that any installed single-pole switching devices are correctly connected in the line conductor only.

Other items to be confirmed are that:

- fuses and single-pole circuit-breakers are connected in the line conductor only,
- lampholders (except for those designed for E14 and E27 lamp caps) having a centre contact have the outer or screwed contact connected to the neutral conductor, *and*
- all accessories, such as socket-outlets and fused connection units, have been correctly connected (Regulation 612.6 refers).

Verifying the polarity of an incoming supply (or an existing live circuit)

To ensure that, in service, the polarity of an installation is correct in addition to employing the techniques previously described to check the wiring of the circuit(s) one must check the polarity of the incoming supply.

It should be noted that when checking the polarity of the incoming supply different procedures are required for TT or TN-S and TN-C-S systems.

The results of polarity tests on a correctly connected TT or TN-S system are shown in Tables 16.1 and 16.2 and the results of polarity tests on TN-C-S systems is shown in Tables 16.3, 16.4 and 16.5.

Published by Certsure LLP © Certsure LLP (January 2015)

Table 16.1 Verification of polarity for single-phase TT and TN-S earthing arrangements (using an approved test lamp or voltmeter)

Connections of voltage indicator leads	Required outcome
Line to neutral	Lamp (or 230 V indicator) should light
Neutral to earth	Lamp (or 230 V indicator) should NOT light
Line to earth	Lamp (or 230 V indicator) should light

Table 16.2 Verification of polarity for three-phase TT and TN-S earthing arrangements (using an approved test lamp or voltmeter)

Connections of voltage indicator leads	Required outcome
L1 to L2 L1 to L3 L2 to L3	Lamp should be fully bright or 400 V indicator should light
L1 to N L2 to N L3 to N	Lamp should light or 230 V indicator should light
L1 to E L2 to E L3 to E	Lamp should light or 230 V indicator should light
N to E	Lamp or 230 V indicator should NOT light

Danger of checking the polarity of a TN-C-S system using a two-pole voltage indicator

As shown by Table 16.3 the results of tests of polarity carried out on both a correctly connected TNC-S supply and TNC-S supply with line and CEN conductor reversed are identical. Consequently, a two-pole voltage indicator **can not** be used to verify the polarity of an installation supplied by a TN-C-S supply arrangement. Instead a single-pole voltage indicator complying with GS 38[1] should be used.

[1]Electrical test equipment for use by electricians (downloadable from the HSE website).

Table 16.3 Results of test of polarity on a TN-C-S system using a two-pole voltage indicator

	L-N	L-E	E-N
Correct polarity	230 V	230 V	0 V
Incorrect polarity	230 V	230 V	0 V

Table 16.4 Verification of polarity for single-phase TN-C-S earthing arrangement

Using a suitable single-pole voltage indicator	
Contact to line	Lamp should light
Contact to neutral	Lamp should NOT light
Contact to line	Lamp should light (confirming continued correct operation of indicator)
Connections of voltage indicator leads	**Required outcome**
Line to neutral	Lamp (or 230 V indicator) should light
Neutral to earth	Lamp (or 230 V indicator) should NOT light
Line to earth	Lamp (or 230 V indicator) should light

Published by Certsure LLP © Certsure LLP (January 2015)

Table 16.5 Verification of polarity for three-phase TN-C-S earthing arrangement

Using a suitable single-pole voltage indicator	
Contact to L1	lamp should light
Contact to L2	lamp should light
Contact to L3	lamp should light
Contact to neutral	lamp should NOT light
Contact to any line	lamp should light (confirming continued correct operation of indicator)
Connections of voltage indicator leads	**Required outcome**
L1 to L2	Lamp should be fully bright or 400 V indicator should light
L1 to L3	
L2 to L3	
L1 to N	Lamp should light or 230 V indicator should light
L2 to N	
L3 to N	
L1 to E	Lamp should light or 230 V indicator should light
L2 to E	
L3 to E	
N to E	Lamp should NOT light

16.3.5 External earth fault loop impedance

It is necessary to record the external earth fault loop impedance, Z_e, in the *Supply characteristics and earthing arrangements* section of the Electrical Installation Condition Report.

Z_e is the earth fault loop impedance of that part of the system which is external to the installation. Like the maximum prospective fault current, Z_e can be measured only by testing at the origin of the installation.

 © Certsure LLP (January 2015)

Testing

Before the test, the earthing conductor must be disconnected from the main earthing terminal or otherwise separated from all parallel earth paths such as bonding and circuit protective conductors, as the purpose of the test is to prove that the intended means of earthing is present and of an acceptably low resistance. Any parallel earth paths present during the test would result in a false reading of Z_e being obtained and might perhaps conceal the fact that the intended means of earthing is defective, or even non-existent.

For safety reasons, it is essential that the entire installation is isolated from the supply before the earthing conductor (or, if necessary, any other protective conductors) are disconnected from the main earthing terminal, and that the installation remains isolated for the duration of the testing.

On completion of testing and before the installation is re-energised, the earthing conductor or other protective conductors that were disconnected to facilitate the measurement of Z_e must be reconnected.

The inspector should take particular care during the testing process, as fault conditions are most severe at the origin of the installation, where this test is being performed.

The instrument to be used is a loop impedance test instrument complete with a set of test leads, having two or three probes to suit the particular instrument.

In the two-lead version, connection is made between line and earth of the incoming supply. In the three-lead version it is necessary to make a connection to the neutral of the incoming supply as well as to line and earth.

Some instruments have a facility for polarity indication. Before proceeding with the test, it is necessary to follow the manufacturer's instructions with regard to correct polarity and test procedure. Do not proceed with the test unless the indications on the instrument show that it is safe to do so.

Where the supply is provided with an earth connection from the electricity distributor's network, such as from a TN-S or TN-C-S system, it is unlikely that Z_e will exceed one ohm, and the lowest range of the instrument will be the most appropriate (usually 0 to 20 Ω).

Published by Certsure LLP © Certsure LLP (January 2015)

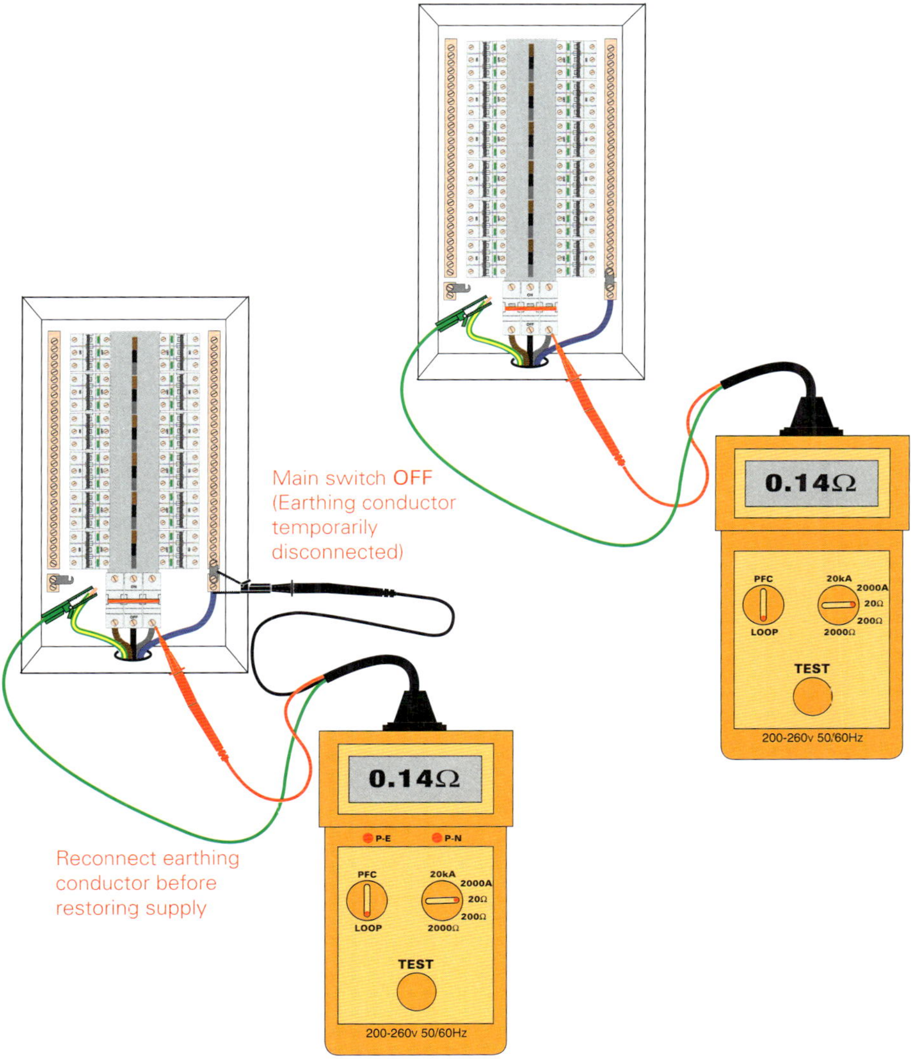

Fig 16.12 External earth fault loop impedance

16.3.6 Earth electrode resistance

General

An installation forming part of a TT system is required to be equipped with an installation earth electrode as its means of earthing. The function of the earth electrode is to make electrical contact with the general mass of earth to provide a suitable path for earth fault current to return to the source (such as via the earth electrode at the distribution transformer).

Measurement of the resistance of the installation earth electrode to the general mass of earth provides information necessary for verifying that the earthing arrangement satisfies the requirements of both *BS 7671* and the particular installation design. The measured resistance value needs to be recorded, together with the type of electrode and its location, in the appropriate boxes in the *'Particulars of the installation'* section of the Electrical Installation Certificate and of the Domestic Electrical Installation Condition Report.

Why do we have to measure the resistance of the installation earth electrode?

Measurement of the earth electrode resistance is required to ensure the resistance is as low as practicable, to aid disconnection time. Generally resistance values less than 200 Ω are desired as values exceeding 200 Ω may not be stable.

BS 7671 recognises the use of the following two types of protective device to provide automatic disconnection of a circuit forming part of a TT system under fault conditions:

a) An RCD.

b) An overcurrent protective device (Regulation 411.5.2).

The former is preferred as the latter may be used only where a suitably low value of earth fault loop impedance (Z_S) is permanently and reliably assured.

Published by Certsure LLP © Certsure LLP (January 2015)

Where an RCD is used for earth fault protection, Regulation 411.5.3 requires the following conditions to be fulfilled:

- 0.2 s maximum disconnection time for a.c. final circuits not exceeding 32 A (Regulation 411.3.2.2) **or**
- 1 s maximum disconnection time for distribution circuits and final circuits exceeding 32 A (Regulation 411.3.2.4), **and**
- $R_A \times I_{\Delta n} \leq 50$ V

Where:

R_A is the sum of the resistances of the earth electrode and protective conductor connecting it to the exposed-conductive-parts (in ohms).

$I_{\Delta n}$ is the rated residual operating current of the RCD.

The requirements of Regulation 411.5.3 are met if the earth fault loop impedance of the final circuit protected by the RCD meets the requirements of Table 41.5 of *BS 7671*.

Where an overcurrent protective device is used, Regulation 411.5.4 requires the following conditions to be fulfilled:

- $Z_s \times I_a \leq U_0 \times C_{min}$

Where:

Z_s is the impedance in ohms (Ω) of the fault loop comprising:

- the source
- the line conductor up to the point of the fault
- the protective conductor of the exposed-conductive-parts
- the earthing conductor
- the earth electrode of the installation, and
- the earth electrode of the source.

I_a is the current in amperes (A) causing automatic operation of the disconnecting device within the time specified in Table 41.1 of Regulation 411.3.2.2 or, as appropriate, Regulation 411.3.2.4.

U_0 is the nominal a.c. rms or d.c. line voltage to Earth in volts (V).

C_{min} is the minimum voltage factor (0.95).

Knowledge of the resistance of the installation earth electrode is therefore essential in order to be able to verify that the installation satisfies these safety requirements.

Two methods of measuring the resistance of an earth electrode are recognised in the NICEIC publication *Inspection, testing and certification*:

- Method 1: using a proprietary earth electrode test instrument.
- Method 2: using a loop impedance test instrument.

In order to use test method 1 it must be possible to install temporary test electrodes in a number of locations up to around 25 m from the electrode under test. This makes it unlikely that an earth electrode test instrument will be used when testing the electrode providing the means of earthing for domestic premises during periodic inspection and testing. As a result, only method 2 (using a loop impedance instrument) is described here.

Details on how to perform testing of earth electrodes using a proprietary earth electrode test instrument are given in NICEIC publication *Inspection, testing and certification*.

Earth electrode resistance using a loop impedance test instrument

A loop impedance test instrument may be used to give a reasonable approximation of the resistance of an installation earth electrode where the electrode under test forms a part of an installation employing RCDs for fault protection, as will typically be the case for a domestic installation forming a part of a TT installation. Although the value obtained will not be particularly precise it will be adequate in relation to the relatively high values of electrode resistance considered acceptable for installations where the circuits are protected by RCDs.

Published by Certsure LLP © Certsure LLP (January 2015)

Leads incorporating fuse protection and/or current limiting resistors should be used when performing this test.

Set the loop impedance test instrument to an appropriate scale (0-20 Ω or similar 'low' range).

With the supply switched off and the earthing conductor of the installation temporarily disconnected from the main earthing terminal, connect a two-lead instrument or a three-lead instrument as shown in the diagrams below. Where any doubt exists regarding the connection of an instrument, the manufacturer's instructions should be followed.

Given that only a small proportion of the overall measured earth fault loop impedance is attributable to those parts of the loop other than the electrode, the result obtained from this test may be taken as the earth electrode resistance.

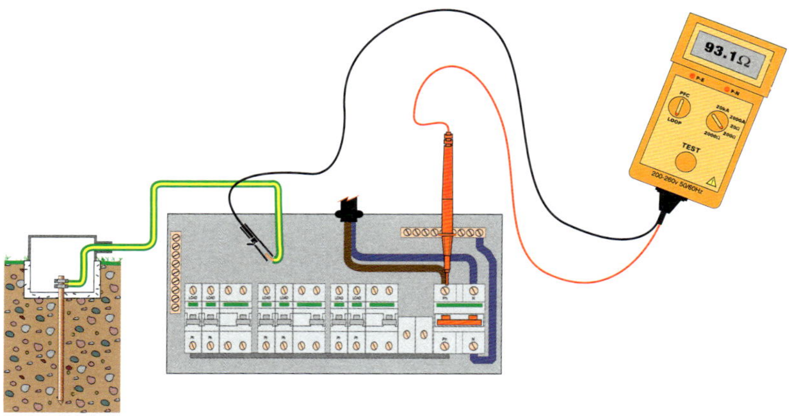

Fig 16.13 Earth electrode testing using a two-lead loop impedance test instrument

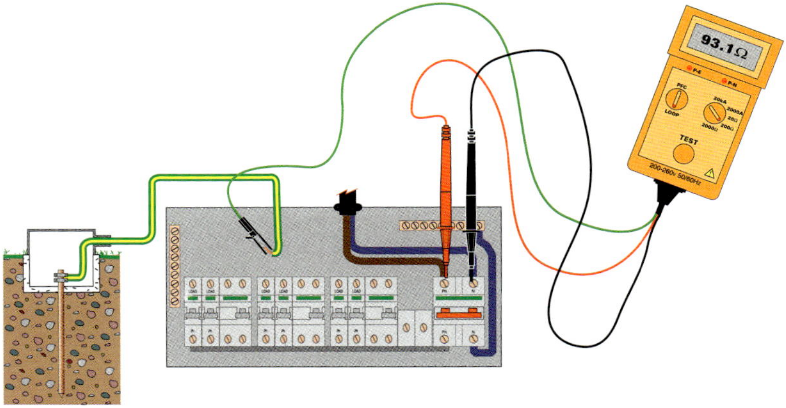

Fig 16.14 Earth electrode testing using a three-lead loop impedance test instrument

Comparing the results of earth electrode resistance testing obtained using different methods

The use of an earth electrode resistance test instrument will provide a considerably more accurate assessment than the use of a loop impedance test instrument.

This can result in some degree of confusion if an earth electrode resistance value obtained using an earth electrode test instrument during the initial verification process is compared to one obtained using a loop impedance test instrument later in the life of the installation. A person not aware of this difference might conclude incorrectly that the electrode had deteriorated dramatically since its resistance was last measured, and recommend a costly improvement to the earth electrode network.

Furthermore, if the resistance of an electrode was found to be in excess of 200 Ω by a small margin when measured using a loop impedance test instrument, the person carrying out the test should either re-test the electrode using an earth electrode test instrument or recommend that such a test is performed before deciding whether or not the installation is unsatisfactory on the grounds of an inadequate (excessively high) electrode resistance.

Published by Certsure LLP © Certsure LLP (January 2015)

16.3.7 Prospective fault current at the origin

General

The maximum prospective fault current is another of the *Supply characteristics and earthing arrangements* that need to be recorded in the 'Nature of supply parameters' section of the Electrical Installation Certificate and the Electrical Installation Condition Report.

This is the current that would flow in the event of a fault at that location, either between live conductors (maximum prospective short-circuit current) or between live conductors and protective earth (maximum prospective earth fault current), whichever is the greater. The value can only be measured by testing at the origin of the installation, which is at the position where the electrical energy is delivered. The tests should therefore be conducted at the main switch or at other switchgear connected directly to the tails from the electricity distributor's metering equipment.

Particular care should be taken during the testing process, as fault conditions are most severe at the origin of an installation, where this test is being performed.

Note that a measurement made at a point further downstream into the installation would not generally be the maximum for the installation. The prospective short-circuit and prospective earth fault current may be determined by an alternative method such as by enquiry or calculation where this is considered appropriate.

The earthing conductor, main equipotential bonding conductors and circuit protective conductors should all remain connected during these tests, because the presence of these and any other parallel paths to earth may reduce the impedance of the fault loop and so increase the prospective fault current.

The instrument to be used is a loop impedance test instrument, with or without a prospective fault current range. A set of test leads is required, having two or three probes to suit the requirements of the particular test instrument.

The diagram below shows a two-lead test instrument connected across the line and neutral of an incoming supply. Note that for measuring a line to earth value, the instrument must be connected across the line and main earthing terminal.

 © Certsure LLP (January 2015)

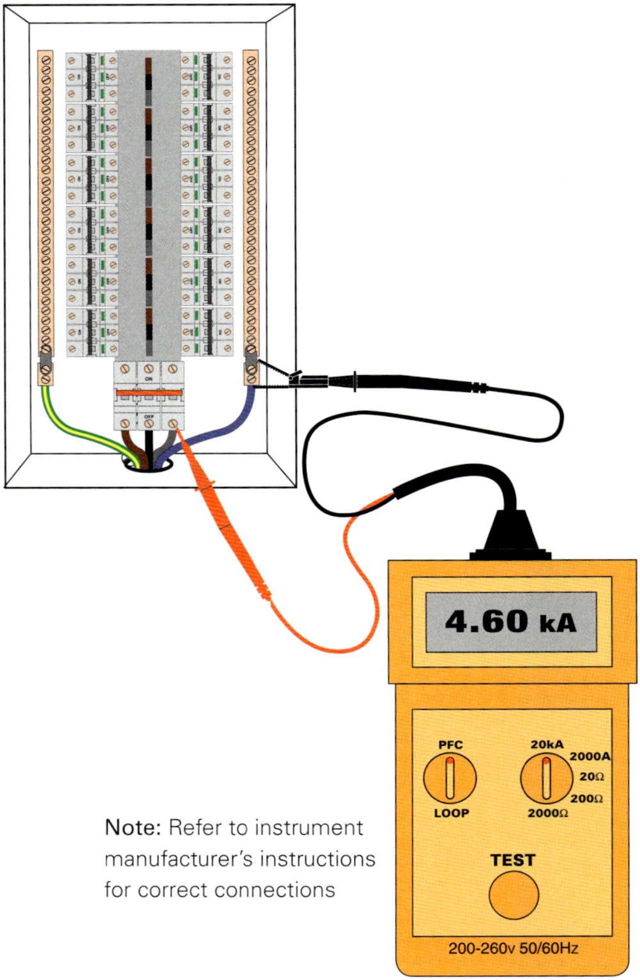

Note: Refer to instrument manufacturer's instructions for correct connections

Fig 16.15 Measurement of prospective fault current using a two-lead instrument

Published by Certsure LLP © Certsure LLP (January 2015)

The figure below shows a three-lead test instrument connected across the line, neutral and earth of an incoming supply. Note that the connections may need to be different for some tests - refer to the instrument manufacturer's instructions.

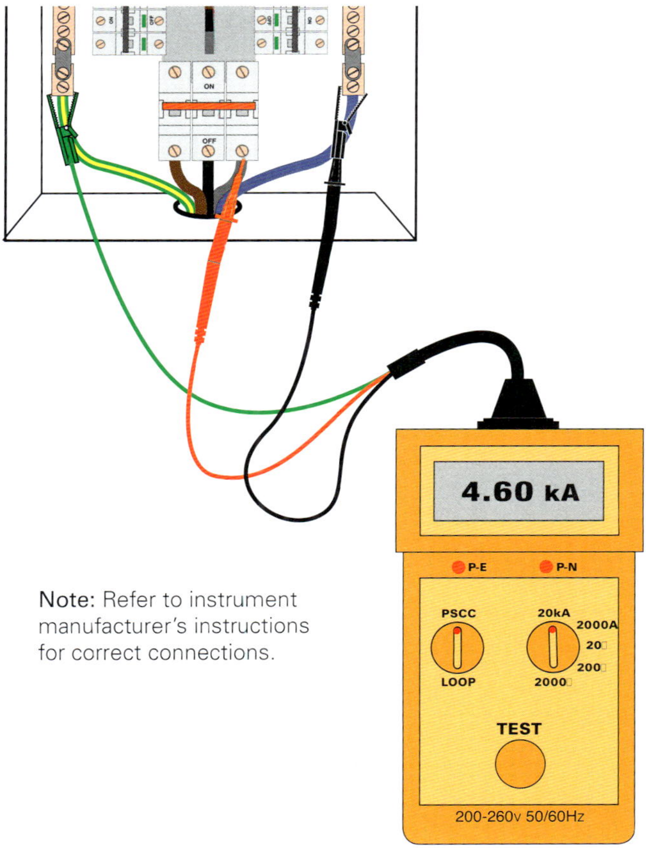

Fig 16.16 Measurement of prospective fault current using a three-lead instrument

Procedure:

- Check that the test instrument, leads, probes and crocodile clips (if any) are suitable for the purpose, and in good serviceable condition.
- Select the appropriate range and scale (for example, for a TN system earthing arrangement, prospective fault current 20 kA).
- Observing all precautions for safety, connect the instrument to the incoming energised supply to measure a line to neutral value.
- Check the polarity indicator (if any) on the instrument for correct connection.
- Press the button.
- Record the reading.
- Repeat the above steps, as appropriate, with the instrument connected for measurement of the line to earth value.

If the test instrument does not have a prospective fault current range, the readings given by the above procedure are fault loop impedances (in ohms). To convert each of these readings into a prospective fault current, divide them into the measured value of line to neutral voltage.

For example, if the voltage measured at the time of the test is 230 V and the measured value of fault loop impedance between line and neutral at the origin is 0.05 Ω:

Maximum prospective short-circuit current (line to neutral)

= 230/0.05 = 4600 A (or 4.6 kA)

(This value would have been given directly if the instrument had a prospective fault current range).

The same procedure is now repeated, taking readings between line and earth to determine the maximum prospective earth fault current.

The higher of the two prospective fault currents (line to neutral or line to earth) should be recorded on the certificate or report.

Published by Certsure LLP © Certsure LLP (January 2015)

Three-phase supplies

Unless a test instrument designed to operate at a nominal voltage of 400 V is available, it will be necessary to calculate the prospective fault current between lines. Where an installation is supplied by two or more phases, the maximum prospective fault current is likely to be between line conductors. If this is found to be the case, then this is the value to be recorded on the certificate or report.

The prospective fault current between lines can be estimated by using the measured value of the line to neutral prospective fault current (obtained as described on the preceding pages).

There is a complex relationship between the line to neutral and the line to line values of prospective fault current, which is beyond the scope of this book.

As a first approximation, which tends to err on the safe side, the prospective fault current between line conductors can be taken as twice that of the prospective fault current line to neutral.

Using the previous example, line to neutral prospective fault current multiplied by two gives:

4.6 kA x 2 = 9.2 kA

(for the calculated value of prospective fault current between lines).

Why do we have to determine prospective fault current?

A fault current protective device, particularly if fitted close to the supply intake position, must generally be capable of successfully interrupting the current which would flow under conditions of short-circuit or earth fault. Otherwise there may be a serious risk of arcing, damage and fire, particularly for circuits having high prospective fault currents.

Accordingly, the short-circuit capacity of a device must be no less than the prospective fault current at the point in the circuit at which it is installed.

The only exceptions to this rule are:

- Where a device having a lower short-circuit capacity is installed in conjunction with what is sometimes called 'back-up' protection (for example, the design might require a circuit-breaker to be backed up by an appropriate HBC fuse) See Regulations 434.5.2 and 536.1.
- Where, as will generally be the case in domestic installations, the protective devices for the circuits of the installation are housed in a consumer unit that meets the requirements of *BS EN 60439-3: 1991 (2001)*. This 'Conditional rating"is discussed later in this section.

The short-circuit capacity of typical devices are as follows:

Circuit-breakers to *BS EN 60898* have a value in a small rectangular box indelibly marked on the device, for example:

6000

This is the 'rated short-circuit capacity' of the device, I_{cn}, assigned by the manufacturer (in amperes, not kA). The value is determined on the basis of type-tests. It is the ultimate short-circuit capacity; and the device may be designed to break a fault of this magnitude only once.

The maximum fault current that the device is designed to break more than once, called the 'service short-circuit capacity', I_{cs}, may be less than the ultimate short-circuit capacity marked on the device, and the manufacturer's data should be consulted for details.

A circuit-breaker to *BS 3871* will have an 'M' number marked on it. This indicates its short-circuit capacity in kA.

For example: M4 denotes 4000 A (4 kA), M9 denotes 9000 A (9 kA).

Fuses are not so straightforward.

Typical values are:

BS 3036 - 1 kA to 4 kA (depending on duty rating)

BS 1361 - 16.5 kA

BS 88-2 - 80 kA (a.c.) 40 kA (d.c.)

BS 88-3 - 16 kA (Type I) 31.5 kA (Type II)

Published by Certsure LLP © Certsure LLP (January 2015)

These values are given only as a guide, and the manufacturer's data or other relevant information for the particular device should be consulted.

Conditional rating of protective devices housed in consumer units.

Where overcurrent protective devices having a rated current up to and including 45 A are incorporated in a consumer unit conforming to *BS EN 60439-3: 1991(2001)* the arrangement is considered to be adequate for a prospective fault current of up to 16 kA, provided the consumer unit is fed by a service cut-out having an HBC fuse to *BS 1361* Type II, rated at not more than 100 A, on a single-phase supply of nominal voltage up to 250 V (Annex ZA of that standard refers).

16.3.8 Circuit earth fault loop impedance

Earth fault loop impedance obtained by testing

The earth fault loop impedance should be measured at the following points within a domestic installation.

- The origin of the installation
- At the furthest point of every distribution circuit (where present)
- At the furthest point of every final circuit where fault protection is provided by automatic disconnection of supply (ADS)

Set the loop impedance test instrument to the appropriate scale as shown in Table 16.6:

Table 16.6 Range selection for earth fault loop testing

System type	Range to be selected on loop impedance tester
TN-S or TN-C-S	0-20 Ω or similar 'low' range
TT	0-200 Ω or similar 'intermediate' range
Where an 'over range' indication is given, the next highest range should be selected until a reading is obtained.	

Testing

With the supply switched ON and the earthing conductor and all main protective bonding conductors connected to the main earthing terminal, connect the instrument as described below.

Where any doubt exists regarding how to connect an instrument, the manufacturer's instructions should be followed.

Two-lead instrument

At the point furthest from the origin, connect

- Red lead to line terminal
- Black lead to earth terminal

Three-lead instrument

At the point furthest from the origin, connect

- Red lead to line terminal
- Black lead to neutral terminal
- Green lead to earth terminal

For fault protection, the limiting values of earth fault loop impedances, Z_S, are given in Tables 41.2, 41.3 and 41.4 of *BS 7671*, for many commonly-used overcurrent protective devices.

The values given in those tables are the limits that apply under earth fault conditions, when the temperature of the conductors can be expected to be higher than when testing is undertaken (usually under no-load conditions).

Consequently, the values of earth fault loop impedance when measured at ambient temperature should be lower than the limits set out in *BS 7671*.

It is generally accepted that, where the measured earth fault loop impedance of a circuit is not greater than 80% of the relevant limit specified in *BS 7671*, the impedance can be expected to be sufficiently low under earth fault conditions to meet the relevant limit specified in *BS 7671*, and for the protective device to automatically disconnect within the time specified.

Published by Certsure LLP © Certsure LLP (January 2015)

Table 16.7 gives the limiting values of earth fault loop impedance for fault protection when measured at ambient temperatures up to 20 °C. The limits on measured values are 80% of the values given in *BS 7671*, rounded down. The boxes marked 'N/A' (Not Applicable) indicate either that the overcurrent protective device is not commonly available or that, by virtue of its characteristics, the device is not generally appropriate for fault protection.

Table 16.7 Limiting values of measured earth fault loop impedance for fault protection

Rated current (A)	Fuses										Circuit-breakers to BS 3871 or BS EN 60898 or RCBOs to BS EN 61009					
	BS 88 (gG) Parts 2 and 6		BS 1361 or BS 1362		BS 3036		BS 88-2 Fuse systems E (bolted) and G (clip in)		BS 88-3 Fuse system C		Type 1	Type 2	Type B	Types 3 and C	Type D	
	0.4 s	5 s	0.4 s	5 s	0.4 s	5 s	0.4 s	5 s	0.4 s	5 s	0.4 s and 5 s				0.4 s	5 s
2	N/A	N/A	N/A	N/A	N/A	N/A	26.48	34.96	N/A	N/A	N/A	N/A	N/A	N/A	N/A	N/A
3	N/A	N/A	12.46	17.63	N/A	N/A	N/A	N/A	N/A	N/A	N/A	N/A	11.64	N/A	N/A	N/A
4	N/A	N/A	N/A	N/A	N/A	N/A	12.48	16.64	N/A	N/A	N/A	N/A	N/A	N/A	N/A	N/A
5	N/A	N/A	7.94	12.48	7.28	13.44	N/A	N/A	7.94	11.64	8.73	4.99	N/A	3.49	1.74	3.49
6	6.47	10.28	N/A	N/A	N/A	N/A	6.24	9.70	N/A	N/A	7.28	4.16	5.82	2.91	1.45	2.91
10	3.88	5.63	N/A	N/A	N/A	N/A	3.71	5.45	3.71	5.45	4.36	2.49	3.49	1.74	0.87	1.74
13	N/A	N/A	1.83	2.90	N/A	N/A	N/A	N/A	N/A	N/A	N/A	N/A	N/A	N/A	N/A	N/A
15	N/A	N/A	2.49	3.80	1.93	4.06	N/A	N/A	N/A	N/A	2.91	1.66	N/A	1.16	0.57	1.16
16	2.05	3.17	N/A	N/A	N/A	N/A	1.93	3.17	1.84	3.12	2.72	1.56	2.18	1.08	0.54	1.08
20	1.34	2.20	1.28	2.12	1.34	2.91	1.34	2.24	1.54	2.56	2.18	1.24	1.74	0.87	0.43	0.87
25	1.08	1.74	N/A	N/A	N/A	N/A	1.02	1.74	N/A	N/A	1.74	0.99	1.39	0.69	0.34	0.69
30	N/A	N/A	0.87	1.39	0.83	2.00	N/A	N/A	N/A	N/A	1.45	0.83	N/A	0.57	0.28	0.57
32	0.79	1.39	N/A	N/A	N/A	N/A	0.79	1.39	0.72	1.24	1.36	0.77	1.08	0.54	0.27	0.54
40	0.62	1.02	N/A	N/A	N/A	N/A	N/A	1.02	N/A	N/A	1.08	0.62	0.87	0.43	0.21	0.43
45	N/A	N/A	0.43	0.72	0.44	1.20	N/A	N/A	N/A	0.79	0.96	0.55	0.77	0.38	0.19	0.38
50	0.45	0.79	N/A	N/A	N/A	N/A	N/A	0.79	N/A	N/A	0.87	0.49	0.69	0.34	0.16	0.34
60	N/A	N/A	0.28	0.52	0.31	0.84	N/A	N/A	N/A	N/A	N/A	N/A	N/A	N/A	N/A	N/A
63	0.34	0.62	N/A	N/A	N/A	N/A	N/A	0.62	N/A	0.54	0.68	0.39	0.55	0.27	0.13	0.27
80	0.23	0.43	0.21	0.37	N/A	N/A	N/A	0.43	N/A	0.40	0.54	0.31	0.43	0.21	0.10	0.21
100	0.17	0.31	0.14	0.27	0.14	0.40	N/A	0.33	N/A	0.29	0.43	0.24	0.34	0.16	0.08	0.16
125	0.12	0.24	N/A	N/A	N/A	N/A	N/A	0.25	N/A	N/A	N/A	N/A	0.27	0.13	0.06	0.13
160	0.09	0.19	N/A	N/A	N/A	N/A	N/A	0.20	N/A	N/A	N/A	N/A	N/A	N/A	N/A	N/A
200	0.07	0.14	N/A	N/A	N/A	N/A	N/A	0.14	N/A	N/A	N/A	N/A	N/A	N/A	N/A	N/A

Table 41.5 of *BS 7671* states the maximum acceptable earth fault loop impedances to ensure RCD operation where an RCD is used for earth fault protection (see Regulation 411.4.9 for TN systems and Regulation 411.5.3 for TT systems).

The values applicable to a nominal voltage to earth (U_0) exceeding 120 V but not greater than 230 V are reproduced below. These are applicable where the supply nominal voltage is 230 V.

Table 16.8 Maximum earth fault loop impedance for RCDs without time-delay

Rated residual current ($I_{\Delta n}$)	Maximum earth fault loop impedance
30 mA	1667 Ω
100 mA	500 Ω
300 mA	167 Ω
500 mA	100 Ω

Note: The resistance of the installation earth electrode should be as low as practicable. A value exceeding 200 Ω may not be acceptable.

Determination of earth fault loop impedance by other means

Regulation 612.9 allows earth fault loop impedance to be determined by means other than measurement. In the case of a design for a new installation it is customary to base the design on the typical 'worst case' value declared by the Distribution Network Operator (DNO). However, where an existing installation is being subjected to periodic inspection and testing, this leaves the person carrying out the testing with the option of deriving the earth fault loop impedance using the measured value of external earth fault loop impedance (Z_e), the measured value of ($R_1 + R_2$), and the formula below:

$$Z_s = Z_e + (R_1 + R_2)$$

Where Z_s = Earth fault loop impedance (Ω)

Z_e = Earth fault loop impedance external to the installation

R_1 = Resistance of line conductor

R_2 = Resistance of protective conductor, or

$(R_1 + R_2)$ = that part of the earth fault loop within the premises

Published by Certsure LLP © Certsure LLP (January 2015)

Example

An installation has an external earth fault loop impedance of 0.5 Ω. Given that the lighting circuit has been wired in 1.5 mm^2 copper conductors having a resistance of 12.1 mΩ/m, and length 30 m, calculate the expected earth fault loop impedance for this circuit at an ambient temperature of 20 °C.

$(R_1 + R_2)$ = length x resistance/m

$(R_1 + R_2) = 30 \times 12.1/1000$

$(R_1 + R_2) = 0.363\ \Omega$.

$Z_s = Z_e + (R_1 + R_2)$

$Z_s = 0.5 + 0.363$

$\mathbf{Z_s = 0.863\ \Omega}$.

16.3.9 Circuit prospective fault current

BS 7671 requires that the prospective fault current is determined at every relevant point within the installation (Regulation 434.1 refers). Regulation 434.5.1 indicates that unless another device installed upstream provides the necessary back up protection, the rated short-circuit breaking capacity of a fault current protective device must not be less than the maximum prospective fault current at the point at which it is installed.

Knowledge of the minimum prospective fault current may be necessary in some cases when considering the degree of temperature rise experienced by a conductor for the duration of a fault, to ensure that cables are adequately protected (Regulation 434.5.2 refers). Where this is the case, it will be necessary to ascertain the fault current at the furthest point of the circuit in question.

Regulation 612.11 requires both prospective short-circuit current and prospective earth fault current to be determined and states that it is acceptable for these to be measured, calculated or determined by another method. Strictly speaking, it is not possible to perform a test to measure prospective fault current except when such a current occurs – which of course would be rather too late if the installed switchgear and other equipment was inadequately fault current rated.

In practice, prospective fault current can be obtained by Ohm's Law as shown below:

$$I_{pf} = \frac{V}{Z}$$

Where

I_{pf} is the prospective fault current (A)

V is the measured voltage at the time of the test (V)

Z is the measured loop impedance (between line and neutral or line and earth, as applicable) at the time of the test (Ω)

The values for voltage and loop impedance used in the equation above are obtained as follows.

With the supply switched **ON** and with the earthing conductor and all main protective bonding conductors connected to the main earthing terminal, connect the instrument as described below.

Where any doubt exists regarding the correct way to connect an instrument, the manufacturer's instructions should be followed:

Three-lead instrument

At the terminals at the point to be tested, connect:

- red lead to line terminal
- black lead to neutral terminal
- green lead to earth terminal

Two-lead instrument to obtain prospective earth-fault current

At the terminals at the point to be tested, connect:

- red lead to line terminal
- black lead to earth terminal

Published by Certsure LLP © Certsure LLP (January 2015)

Two-lead instrument to obtain prospective short-circuit current:

At the terminals at the point to be tested, connect:

- red lead to line terminal
- black lead to neutral terminal

Where a two-lead instrument has been used, whichever is the larger of the prospective short-circuit current and the prospective earth fault current obtained should be taken as the prospective fault current for the circuit under test.

16.3.10 RCD testing

An RCD test instrument is used to confirm the continued effectiveness of RCDs forming part of an electrical installation. The RCD test instrument should be connected at a convenient place in the circuit that the RCD under test protects.

In general, all items of current-using equipment should be disconnected from the circuit under test for the duration of the RCD test.

When testing is not performed using a test lead plugged into a socket-outlet, leads incorporating fuse protection and/or current limiting resistors should be used when performing this test.

RCD testing should not be carried out until it has been confirmed that the circuit protective conductor is electrically continuous (Regulation 612.2.1) and, for a TT system, that the product $R \times I_{\Delta n}$ does not exceed 50 V (Regulation 411.5.3), where R_A is the resistance of the earth electrode and the circuit protective conductor, and $I_{\Delta n}$ is the rated residual operating current of the RCD.

 © Certsure LLP (January 2015)

Typical applications for RCDs in domestic premises

Table 4.7 of this guide summarises the typical applications and rated residual currents for RCDs as required by *BS 7671* that are applicable to installations in domestic and similar premises.

Test requirements where an RCD provides fault protection

Table 16.9 below details the operating times for commonly encountered types of RCD as stated in the relevant product standards. The table includes data for RCDs and RCD protected socket-outlets as these are likely to be encountered when performing a periodic inspection of an existing installation.

Table 16.9 Summary of RCD operating times

Type of RCD (or RCD protected device)	Maximum operating time
Socket-outlet with integral RCD protection to *BS 7288*	Not exceeding 200 ms
General purpose RCD to *BS 4293*	Not exceeding 200 ms
RCD incorporating an intentional time delay to *BS 4293*	From 50 % of rated time delay plus 200 ms to 100 % of rated time delay plus 200 ms
General purpose RCD to *BS EN 61008*	Not exceeding 300 ms
RCD incorporating an intentional time delay (S-type) to *BS EN 61008*	Between 130 ms and 500 ms
RCBO to *BS EN 61009*	Not exceeding 300 ms

Where an RCD has been installed to provide fault protection, the following test procedure should be followed:

Non-tripping test

For instruments with 'trip current selection' test settings.

On instrument, select the

- appropriate RCD residual operating current ($I_{\Delta n}$) rating (i.e. 30 or 100 mA)
- half residual operating current (½ $I_{\Delta n}$) setting

Published by Certsure LLP © Certsure LLP (January 2015)

Perform the test on both positive and negative half-cycles

The RCD should NOT operate for the duration of the test, on either half-cycle.

For instruments with residual operating current range settings only

On instrument, select the range corresponding to half the rated residual operating current (½ $I_{\Delta n}$) of the RCD – that is, 15 mA for 30 mA device or 50 mA for 100 mA device.

Perform the test on both positive and negative half-cycles

The RCD should NOT operate for the duration of the test, on either half-cycle.

Tripping test

For instruments with 'trip current selection' test settings.

On instrument, select the

- appropriate RCD residual operating current ($I_{\Delta n}$) rating (i.e. 30 or 100 mA)
- residual operating current ($I_{\Delta n}$) setting

Perform the test on both positive and negative half-cycles

The RCD should operate within the appropriate maximum operating time stated in the Table that appears earlier in this section on both half-cycles.

For instruments with residual operating current range settings only

On instrument, select the range corresponding to the rated residual operating current ($I_{\Delta n}$) of the RCD

Perform the test on both positive and negative half-cycles

The RCD should operate within the appropriate maximum operating time stated in the Table 16.9 on both half-cycles.

The highest disconnection time, whether occurring in the positive or negative half-cycle test, should be recorded on the schedule of test results.

Test requirements where an RCD provides additional protection

Where an RCD having a rated residual operating current of 30 mA or less has been installed to provide additional protection, the following test procedure should be carried out IN ADDITION TO the testing described above.

For instruments with 'trip current selection' test settings.

On instrument, select the

- appropriate RCD rated residual operating current ($I_{\Delta n}$) (i.e. 10 mA or 30 mA)
- five-times rated residual operating current (5 $I_{\Delta n}$) setting

Perform the test on both positive and negative half-cycles

The RCD should operate in not more than 40 ms (as required by Regulation 415.1.1), on both half-cycles.

For instruments with residual operating current range settings only

On instrument, select the range which is five-times the rated residual operating current

(5 $I_{\Delta n}$) of the RCD – that is, 150 ms for an RCD having a rated residual operating current ($I_{\Delta n}$) of 30 mA.

Perform the test on both positive and negative half-cycles

The RCD should operate in not more than 40 ms (as required by Regulation 415.1.1), on both half-cycles.

The highest disconnection time, whether occurring in the positive or negative half-cycle test, should be recorded on the schedule of test results.

 Published by Certsure LLP © Certsure LLP (January 2015)

16.3.11 Phase sequence

Regulation 612.12 requires a verification that phase sequence has been maintained in a multi-phase installation – that is, that the conductor connected to 'L1', 'L2', 'L3 and 'N' at each point throughout the installation is the same as that connected to 'L1', 'L2', 'L3 and 'N' respectively, at the origin of the installation.

The most effective way of achieving this check at the initial verification stage is to carry out a variation of the (R_1 + R_2) continuity of protective conductors test method as described earlier in this chapter, with the instrument set on its lowest range. Before the supply is connected:

- disconnect the conductors at both ends
- temporarily connect the 'L1' conductor to one end to the protective conductor of the circuit under test
- connect one lead of a low resistance ohmmeter to the other end of the 'L1' conductor, and the other lead of the ohmmeter to the protective conductor of the circuit
- a 'low' reading – that is, close to the zero end of the scale, will indicate continuity
- where necessary, identify both ends of the conductor in accordance with Table 51 of *BS 7671*
- terminate the cable into the corresponding terminals at both ends
- The above procedure should be repeated for each live conductor of the circuit in turn.
- The procedure described above should be carried out for all distribution circuits throughout the installation.

16.3.12 Phase rotation

Even when it has been confirmed that the phase sequence of a multi-phase supply has been maintained throughout the installation, it has been known for internal connections to the terminals of electrical machines to be inconsistent, resulting in seemingly correctly connected equipment operating incorrectly or not as expected.

A phase rotation instrument utilising either a rotating disc or indicator lamps (or both) can be used to confirm that three-phase equipment, including rotating machines, is connected in the correct sequence or, in the case of motors, rotates in the correct direction.

16.3.13 Functional testing

Regulation 612.13.1 requires it to be verified that the integral test button of an RCD functions correctly when pressed. This tests the ability of the mechanical components of the RCD to move freely and confirms that, for example, contacts have not "stuck".

It is also necessary to confirm that installed equipment such as switchgear, controlgear and interlock arrangements is properly and securely installed and has, where applicable, been correctly set up and adjusted ready for operation. (Regulation 612.13.2 refers.)

Although coming under the heading of testing, it is likely that the above functional checks will, in practice, be achieved through inspection.

 Published by Certsure LLP © Certsure LLP (January 2015)

16.3.14 Certification and reporting

Regulation 631.1 requires an Electrical Installation Certificate to be issued on completion of the initial verification (that is, the inspection and testing) of the new electrical installation or of the changes to an existing installation.

Following completion of the periodic inspection of an existing installation Regulation 631.2 requires an Electrical installation Condition Report to be issued.

Both an Electrical Installation Certificate and an Electrical Installation Condition Report should be accompanied by sufficient Schedules of Inspections and Schedules of Test Results to cover the inspection and testing of the installation (see Regulations 632.1 and 634.1) and should be given to the person who ordered the work.

Where the electrical installation work is minor in nature - that is, it does not involve the provision of a new circuit, a Minor Electrical Installation Works Certificate (MEIWC) may be issued instead of an Electrical Installation Certificate (Regulation 631.3 refers). However a MEIWC may only cover work carried out on a single circuit and so where minor works have been carried out on more than one circuit, a MEIWC must be issued for EACH circuit that has been worked on. Alternatively it might be better to issue an Electrical Installation Certificate in such cases.

Electrical Installation Certificates, Minor Electrical Installation Works Certificates and Electrical Installation Condition Reports should be produced and signed or otherwise authenticated by a person competent in such work (see Regulation 631.4).

Detailed coverage on how to complete Electrical Installation Certificates, Electrical Installation Condition Reports and Minor Electrical Installation Works Certificates can be found in the following NICEIC publications:

- *Inspection, Testing and Certification*
- *Domestic Periodic Inspection, Testing and Reporting*

IET WIRING REGULATIONS UPDATED TO: 17TH EDITION BS 7671:2008 Amd 3: 2015

Other publications which have been updated to reflect the latest requirements of *BS 7671*: 2008 (Amendment 3): 2015 include -

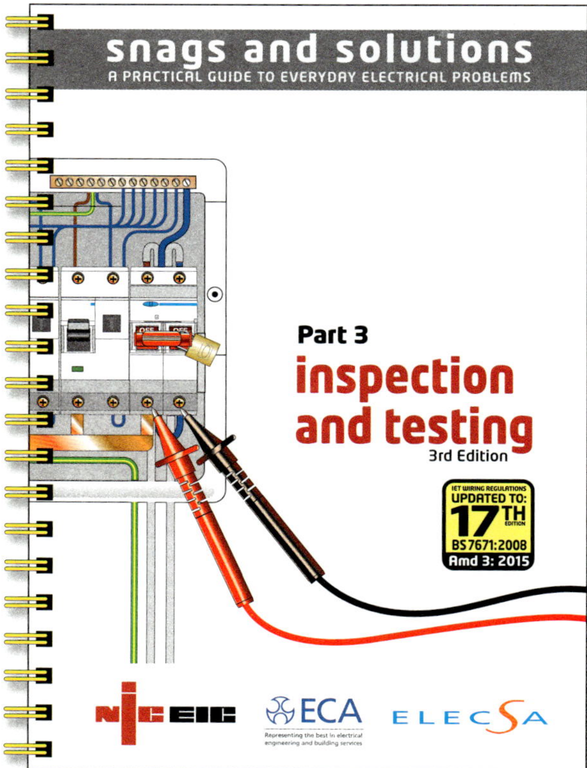

To order this or any other publication contact

NICEIC customers:	0843 290 3485	www.niceicdirect.com
ELECSA/ECA customers:	0333 321 8225	www.elecsa.co.uk

Published by Certsure LLP © Certsure LLP (January 2015)

Appendix A
Final circuit information

A1 General

A2 Floor area served

A3 Maximum demand

A4 Limiting lengths for final circuits

Table A1 Final circuits using *BS 1363* socket-outlets and connection units

Table A2 Radial final circuits supplying lighting

Table A3 Radial final circuits supplying accessories to *BS 1363*

Table A4 Radial final circuits supplying a single load

Table A5 Ring final circuits supplying accessories to *BS 1363*

A5 Minimum permitted protective conductor sizes for energy limiting Class 3 circuit-breakers and RCBOs

Table A6 Minimum permitted protective conductor size for Energy limiting Class 3 circuit-breakers and RCBOs for fault current not exceeding 3 kA, 4.5 kA, 6 kA and 10 kA

Published by Certsure LLP © Certsure LLP (January 2015)

Final circuit information

A1 General

Final circuits, like all circuits of an electrical installation, have to comply with the requirements of *BS 7671*. The guidelines and examples of conventional circuit arrangements given in this Appendix are intended to satisfy the requirements of the following chapters of *BS 7671*:

- **Chapter 43** – Overcurrent protection
- **Chapter 53** – Protection, isolation, switching, control and monitoring
- **Chapter 52 and Appendix 4** – Current-carrying capacities of conductors and voltage drop.

The requirements of the other relevant chapters or sections of *BS 7671* also need to be considered and complied with, including:

- **Chapter 41** – Protection against electric shock
- **Section 434** – Protection against fault current
- **Chapter 54** – Earthing arrangements and protective conductors.

The guidance given in this Guide does not preclude other circuit arrangements where they meet the requirements of *BS 7671*.

A2 Floor area served

The floor area that can be served by a final circuit is dependent on the circuit loads either known or estimated, the diversity of those loads, the voltage drops that occur in the circuit, and the shock protection requirements of the circuit, such as the earth fault loop impedance (Z_S). The floor area served by the circuit is determined by the known or estimated load and should not exceed the value given in Table A1.

A single 30 A or 32 A ring final circuit may serve a floor area of up to 100 m^2. Socket-outlets for washing machines, tumble dryers and dishwashers should be located so as to provide reasonable sharing of the load in each leg of the ring, or consideration should be given to separate circuits. A sufficient number of socket-outlets must be provided as required by Regulation 553.1.7.

Diversity between socket-outlets and permanently connected equipment has already been taken into account in Table A1 and no further diversity should be applied.

Published by Certsure LLP © Certsure LLP (January 2015)

The cross-sectional area of the circuit protective conductor must be not less than that determined in accordance with Regulation Group 543.1.

Table A1 Final circuits using BS 1363 socket-outlets and fused connection units

Type of circuit	Overcurrent protective device Rating (amperes)	Minimum conductor cross-sectional area (mm^2)		Maximum floor area served (m^2)
		Copper conductor thermoplastic (pvc) or thermosetting insulated cables (mm^2)	Copper conductor mineral insulated cables (mm^2)	
Ring	30 or 32	2.5	1.5	100
Radial	30 or 32	4	2.5	75
Radial	20	2.5	1.5	50

Note: Larger cable sizes could be required where the effective current-carrying capacity of the conductor has been reduced by other factors associated with the method of installation or external influences. Section 3 of Appendix 4 in *BS 7671* describes how such factors can be taken into consideration when determining an appropriate current-carrying capacity of a cable for continuous service (I_Z), under particular conditions.

A3 Maximum demand

A final circuit should be designed so that its estimated maximum current demand does not exceed the rated current or current setting (I_n) of its overcurrent protective device, account being taken of the diversity of the loads envisaged. Where there is more than one final circuit serving multiple small loads, the permanently connected equipment and socket-outlets should be distributed amongst these circuits, where practicable, so as to maximize the load capacity available on each circuit for the socket-outlets.

Where a final circuit feeds *BS 1363* socket-outlets or fused connection units, the maximum current for which the circuit may be designed is restricted by the size, type and temperature of conductor that can be accommodated in the terminals of such accessories. *BS 1363* requires the incoming line and neutral terminals to be suitable for the connection, without special preparation, of one, two or three 2.5 mm^2 solid or stranded conductors, or one or two 4.0 mm^2 stranded conductors.

Furthermore, *BS 1363* accessories are designed for the connection of conductors operating at a temperature not exceeding 70 °C.

 © Certsure LLP (January 2015)

Final circuit information

Thermosetting insulated, and some types of mineral insulated, cables can operate with conductor temperatures well above 70 °C. Where such cables are to be connected to socket-outlets and fused connection units complying with *BS 1363*, the cables are to be selected so that the conductor operating temperature is not in excess of 70 °C. In this respect, the conductor size of thermosetting insulated cable must not be less than the size that would have been required for thermoplastic (PVC) insulated cable.

Similarly, the conductor size of mineral insulated cable must not be less than that required for a mineral insulated cable intended to operate at not more than 70 °C (that is, a mineral insulated cable that is bare and exposed to touch or has an overall thermoplastic (PVC) covering). The restriction of conductor temperature to not more than 70 °C may also apply to other equipment in an installation (Regulation 512.1.5 refers).

A4 Limiting lengths for final circuits

Maximum permitted circuit lengths for some common situations are listed as follows:

Table A2 Radial final circuits supplying lighting

Table A3 Radial final circuits supplying accessories to *BS 1363*

Table A4 Radial final circuits supplying a single load

Table A5 Ring final circuits supplying accessories to *BS 1363*

In all cases, the tabulated data relates to the following conditions

- The installation is supplied from a:
  - TN-S system with a maximum external earth fault loop impedance (Z_e) of 0.8 Ω, or
  - TN-C-S system with a maximum Z_e of 0.35 Ω, or
  - TT system with a residual current device for fault protection. The circuit earth fault loop impedance in ohms is not to exceed the applicable value given in Table 41.5 of *BS 7671*, as required by Regulation 411.4.3.
- Maximum circuit cable lengths given for a TN-C-S system may also be applied to a TT system with RCD protection.
- The consumer unit and the main earthing terminal of the installation are located at the origin of the installation.

Published by Certsure LLP © Certsure LLP (January 2015)

- The nominal supply voltage is 230 V single-phase a.c.
- The ambient temperature does not exceed 30 °C.
- 70 °C thermoplastic (pvc) insulated and sheathed flat type cable having copper conductors, conforming to Table 8 of *BS 6004* is used.
- Circuit lengths are measured from the consumer unit to the most distant end of a radial circuit or the total route length for a ring final circuit.
- The maximum circuit cable length has been calculated to satisfy the requirements of *BS 7671* regarding voltage drop limitations and maximum disconnection times.
- In Table A2, a maximum voltage drop of 3 % of the 230 V nominal supply voltage has been allowed in the lighting circuits (Section 525 and Appendix 4 refer). See also Section 10.6 of this Guide.
- In Tables A3, A4 and A5, a maximum of 5 % of the 230 V nominal supply voltage has been allowed in the circuit (Section 525 and Appendix 4 refer). See also Section 10.6 of this Guide.
- Circuit cables are adequately spaced to give a current-carrying capacity (I_z) of at least the rated current (I_n) of the protective device (Regulation 433.1.1 refers). Where the protective device is a *BS 3036* fuse, I_z should be at least I_n divided by the 0.725 factor of Regulation 433.1.101.
- The grouping factors given in Table 4C1 of Appendix 4 in *BS 7671* allow for all the cables in the group to carry their design loads simultaneously and continuously. This is an unlikely event for circuits in household and similar premises, with the exception of cables to water heaters of storage tanks exceeding 15 litres capacity and electric space heating systems.
- With the exception of water heaters of storage tanks exceeding 15 litres and electric space heating, if the following rules are followed, derating for grouping is not necessary
  - I) Cables are not grouped when installed in or under insulation, that is for installation methods 100, 101, 102, or 103.

II) Cables clipped direct (including in cement and plaster) are clipped side by side in one layer, preferably separated by one cable diameter.

III) Cables above ceilings are clipped to joists as per installation methods 100, 101, 102, and 103 of Table 4A2 of Appendix 4 in *BS 7671*.

Reduced cross-section protective conductors

In almost all household and similar circuits using 70 °C (pvc) insulated and sheathed flat cable with protective conductor conforming to Table 8 of *BS 6004*, the protective conductor cross-sectional area will be less than the live conductors. Here the requirement of Table 54.7 will not be met (for line conductors S ≤ 16 mm^2, protective conductors csa to be S mm^2) and so compliance with the adiabatic equation of Regulation 543.1.3 has been taken into account.

Where the protective device is a circuit-breaker to *BS EN 60898-1* or an RCBO to *BS EN 61009-1*, reference should also be made to Section A5 of this Appendix when determining protective conductor sizes.

Maximum disconnection time

A required disconnection time of 0.4 s has been presumed for all circuits having protective devices with a rated current (I_n) ≤ 32 A.

A required disconnection time of 5 s has been presumed for all circuits having protective devices with a rated current (I_n) > 32 A.

Where the rated current (I_n) of the protective device for a circuit ≤ 32 A, cable lengths for a disconnection time of 0.4 s correspond to the maximum values of Z_s given in Tables 41.2 and 41.3 of *BS 7671* (Regulations 411.4.6 and 411.4.7 refer).

Where the rated current (I_n) of the protective device for a circuit > 32 A, cable lengths for a disconnection time of 5 s correspond to the maximum values of Z_s given in Tables 41.2 and 41.3 of *BS 7671* (Regulations 411.4.7 and 411.4.8 refer).

Published by Certsure LLP © Certsure LLP (January 2015)

Where no RCD is presumed (columns 6 and 8), circuit lengths are designed to limit earth fault loop impedance so that disconnection within 0.4 seconds is achieved for fuses (Table 41.2 of *BS 7671*) and instantaneous operation for circuit-breakers (Table 41.3 of *BS 7671*) in the event of a line to Earth fault.

Lighting circuits (Table A2)

The maximum route length of the radial circuit needs to be determined for the part of the circuit supplying the lighting load farthest from the consumer unit. The circuit route length is calculated by adding the appropriate circuit line and neutral conductor lengths (including a line conductors passing through a functional switching device), and then dividing the total by two. The maximum calculated value of circuit route length, between consumer unit and the farthest load is required to be equal to, or less than, the appropriate permitted maximum circuit route length (given in Table A2).

The circuit is assumed to have a load equal to the rated current (I_n) of the circuit protective device evenly distributed along the circuit. Where this is not the case, circuit lengths will need to be reduced where voltage drop is the limiting factor and halved where the load is all at the extremity.

The most onerous installation condition acceptable for the load and the device rating is presumed when calculating the limiting voltage drop. If the installation conditions are not the most onerous allowed (see column 4 of the Tables), the voltage drop will not be as great as presumed in the table.

Radial final circuits supplying accessories to BS 1363 (Table A3)

The circuit is assumed to have a load equal to the rated current (I_n) of the circuit protective device. 13 A of the load is assumed to be at the farthest end of the circuit from the consumer unit, with the remaining load being at 0.75 times L from the consumer unit, where L is the circuit length in metres between the consumer unit and the farthest end of the circuit.

Radial final circuits supplying a single load (Table A4)

Cables supplying whole house heating or water heaters of storage tanks exceeding 15 litres capacity should not be grouped unless appropriately derated.

Published by Certsure LLP © Certsure LLP (January 2015)

Table A2: Maximum total route length for a 230 V radial final circuit supplying lighting loads in household premises using 70 °C thermoplastic (pvc) insulated and sheathed flat cable having copper conductors

	Protective Device	Cable size	Reference method	Maximum length (m)			
1	2	3	4	5	6	7	8
Rating (A)	Type	Line/cpc		$Z_e \le 0.8\ \Omega$ TN-S		$Z_e \le 0.35\ \Omega$ TN-C-S	
				RCD	No RCD	RCD	No RCD
2	BS 88-2.2 and BS 88-6 fuse	1.0/1.0	103, 101, A, 100, 102 C	180	180	180	180
3	BS EN 60898 circuit-breaker / BS EN 61009 RCBO - Type B	1.0/1.0	103, 101, A, 100, 102 C	120	120	120	120
4	BS 88-2.2 and BS 88-6 fuse	1.0/1.0	103, 101, A, 100, 102 C	89	89	89	89
5	BS1361 fuse	1.0/1.0	103, 101, A, 100, 102, C	71	71	71	71
	BS 3036 fuse			71	71	71	71
	BS 88-3 fuse system C			71	71	71	71
5	BS1361 fuse	1.5/1.0	103, 101, A, 100, 102, C	108	108	108	108
	BS 3036 fuse			108	108	108	108
	BS 88-3 fuse system C			108	108	108	108
6	BS 88-2.2 and BS 88-6 fuse	1.0/1.0	103, 101, A, 100, 102, C	59	59	59	59
	BS EN 60898 circuit-breaker / BS EN 61009 RCBO - Type B			59	59	59	59
	BS EN 60898 circuit-breaker / BS EN 61009 RCBO - Type C			59	59	59	59
10	BS 88-2.2 and BS 88-6 fuse	1.0/1.0	101, A, 100, 102, C	35	35	35	35
	BS EN 60898 circuit-breaker / BS EN 61009 RCBO - Type B			35	35	35	35
	BS EN 60898 circuit-breaker / BS EN 61009 RCBO - Type C			32	32	35	35

Published by Certsure LLP © Certsure LLP (January 2015)

Table A2 continued

Protective Device		Cable size	Reference method	Maximum length (m)			
1	2	3	4	5	6	7	8
Rating (A)	Type	Line/cpc		$Z_e \leq 0.8\ \Omega$ TN-S		$Z_e \leq 0.35\ \Omega$ TN-C-S	
				RCD	No RCD	RCD	No RCD
10	BS 88-2.2 and BS 88-6 fuse	1.5 /1.0	103, 101, A, 100, 102, C	52	52	52	52
	BS EN 60898 circuit-breaker / BS EN 61009 RCBO - Type B			52	52	52	52
	BS EN 60898 circuit-breaker / BS EN 61009 RCBO - Type C			47	38	52	50
16	BS 88-2.2 and BS 88-6 fuse	1.5 /1.0	100, 102, C	33	33	33	33
	BS 88-3 fuse system C			33	33	33	33
	BS EN 60898 circuit-breaker / BS EN 61009 RCBO - Type B			33	33	33	33
	BS EN 60898 circuit-breaker / BS EN 61009 RCBO - Type C			19	15	33	28
16	BS 88-2.2 and BS 88-6 fuse	2.5 /1.5	101, A, 100, 102, C	53	53	53	53
	BS 88-3 fuse system C			53	53	53	53
	BS EN 60898 circuit-breaker / BS EN 61009 RCBO - Type B			53	53	53	53
	BS EN 60898 circuit-breaker / BS EN 61009 RCBO - Type C			32	24	53	43

 © Certsure LLP (January 2015)

Table A3: Maximum total route length for a 230 V radial final circuit supplying accessories to BS 1363 in household premises, using 70 °C thermoplastic (pvc) insulated and sheathed flat cable having copper conductors

Protective Device		Cable size	Reference method	Maximum length (m)			
1	2	3	4	5	6	7	8
				$Z_e \leq 0.8\ \Omega$ TN-S		$Z_e \leq 0.35\ \Omega$ TN-C-S	
Rating (A)	Type	Line/cpc		RCD	No RCD	RCD	No RCD
20	BS 88-2.2 and BS 88-6 fuse	2.5 /1.5	A,100,102,C	35	35	35	35
	BS 88-3 fuse system C		A,100,102,C	35	35	35	35
	BS1361 fuse		A,100,102,C	35	35	35	35
	BS 3036 fuse		NP	NP	NP	NP	NP
	BS EN 60898 circuit-breaker / BS EN 61009 RCBO - Type B		A,100,102,C	35	35	35	35
	BS EN 60898 circuit-breaker / BS EN 61009 RCBO - Type C			16	12	35	31
20	BS 88-2.2 and BS 88-6 fuse	4.0/1.5	101,A,100,102,C	59	43	59	59
	BS 88-3 fuse system C		101,A,100,102,C	59	56	59	59
	BS1361 fuse		C	59	40	59	59
	BS 3036 fuse		101,A,100,102,C	63	43	63	63
	BS EN 60898 circuit-breaker / BS EN 61009 RCBO - Type B			59	59	59	59
	BS EN 60898 circuit-breaker / BS EN 61009 RCBO - Type C			26	14	59	36
30	BS1361 fuse	4.0/1.5	C	43	NP	43	10
	BS 3036 fuse			NP	NP	NP	NP
32	BS 88-2.2 and BS 88-6 fuse	4.0/1.5	C	42	9	42	31
	BS 88-3 fuse system C			42	5	42	27
	BS EN 60898 circuit-breaker / BS EN 61009 RCBO - Type B			42	28	42	42
	BS EN 60898 circuit-breaker / BS EN 61009 RCBO - Type C			NP	NP	29	16

Notes: 1) NP = Not permitted 2) Any reference method less onerous than that in column 4 may be used

 © Certsure LLP (January 2015)

Table A4: Maximum total route length for a 230 V radial final circuit supplying loads such as a cooker, shower or heater at the end of the circuit using 70 °C thermoplastic (pvc) insulated and sheathed flat cable having copper conductors

Protective Device		Cable size	Allowed installation method	Maximum length (m)			
1	2	3	4	5	6	7	8
Rating (A)	Type	Line/cpc	Note 2	$Z_e \le 0.8\ \Omega$ TN-S		$Z_e \le 0.35\ \Omega$ TN-C-S	
				RCD	No RCD	RCD	No RCD
15	BS1361 fuse	1.0 /1.0	C	17	17	17	17
	BS 3036 fuse		NP	NP	NP	NP	NP
15	BS1361 fuse	1.5 /1.0	100,102,C	26	26	26	26
	BS 3036 fuse		NP	NP	NP	NP	NP
15	BS1361 fuse	2.5 /1.5	101, A, 100, 102, C	43	43	43	43
	BS 3036 fuse		100,102,C	45	45	45	45
15	BS1361 fuse	4.0/1.5	103,101, A, 100, 102, C	72	72	72	72
	BS 3036 fuse		101, A, 100, 102, C	75	75	75	75
16	BS 88-2.2 and BS 88-6 fuse	1.0 /1.0	C	16	16	16	16
	BS 88-3 fuse system C			16	16	16	16
	BS EN 60898 circuit-breaker / BS EN 61009 RCBO - Type B			16	16	16	16
	BS EN 60898 circuit-breaker / BS EN 61009 RCBO - Type C			13	13	16	16
16	BS 88-2.2 and BS 88-6 fuse	1.5 /1.0	100,102,C	24	24	24	24
	BS 88-3 fuse system C			24	24	24	24
	BS EN 60898 circuit-breaker / BS EN 61009 RCBO - Type B			24	24	24	24
	BS EN 60898 circuit-breaker / BS EN 61009 RCBO - Type C			19	15	24	24
16	BS 88-2.2 and BS 88-6 fuse	2.5 /1.5	101, A, 100, 102, C	40	40	40	40
	BS 88-3 fuse system C			40	40	40	40
	BS EN 60898 circuit-breaker / BS EN 61009 RCBO - Type B			40	40	40	40
	BS EN 60898 circuit-breaker / BS EN 61009 RCBO - Type C			32	24	40	40

 © Certsure LLP (January 2015)

Table A4 continued

Protective Device		Cable size	Allowed installation method	Maximum length (m)			
1	2	3	4	5	6	7	8
Rating (A)	Type	Line/cpc	Note 2	$Z_e \leq 0.8\ \Omega$ TN-S		$Z_e \leq 0.35\ \Omega$ TN-C-S	
				RCD	No RCD	RCD	No RCD
16	BS 88-2.2 and BS 88-6 fuse	4.0/1.5	103, 101, A, 100, 102, C	66	66	66	66
	BS 88-3 fuse system C			66	66	66	66
	BS EN 60898 circuit-breaker / BS EN 61009 RCBO - Type B			66	66	66	66
	BS EN 60898 circuit-breaker / BS EN 61009 RCBO - Type C			51	28	66	50
20	BS 88-2.2 and BS 88-6 fuse	2.5/1.5	A, 100, 102, C	31	31	31	31
	BS 88-3 fuse system C		A, 100, 102, C	31	31	31	31
	BS 1361 fuse		A, 100, 102, C	31	31	31	31
	BS 3036 fuse		NP	NP	NP	NP	NP
	BS EN 60898 circuit-breaker / BS EN 61009 RCBO - Type B		A, 100, 102, C	31	31	31	31
	BS EN 60898 circuit-breaker / BS EN 61009 RCBO - Type C			16	12	31	31
20	BS 88-2.2 and BS 88-6 fuse	4.0/1.5	101, A, 100, 102, C	53	43	53	53
	BS 88-3 fuse system C		101, A, 100, 102, C	53	53	53	53
	BS 1361 fuse		C	53	40	53	53
	BS 3036 fuse		101, A, 100, 102, C	57	43	57	57
	BS EN 60898 circuit-breaker / BS EN 61009 RCBO - Type B			53	53	53	53
	BS EN 60898 circuit-breaker / BS EN 61009 RCBO - Type C			26	14	53	36

Notes: 1) NP = Not permitted 2) Any reference method less onerous than that in column 4 may be used

Published by Certsure LLP © Certsure LLP (January 2015)

Table A4 continued

Protective Device		Cable size	Allowed installation method	Maximum length (m)			
1	2	3	4	5	6	7	8
Rating (A)	Type	Line/cpc	Note 2	$Z_e \leq 0.8\ \Omega$ TN-S		$Z_e \leq 0.35\ \Omega$ TN-C-S	
				RCD	No RCD	RCD	No RCD
	BS 88-2.2 and BS 88-6 fuse		103,101,A,100,102,C	81	69	81	81
	BS 88-3 fuse system C		103,101,A,100,102,C	81	81	81	81
20	BS 1361 fuse	6.0 /2.5	A,100,102,C	81	65	81	81
	BS 3036 fuse			85	69	85	85
	BS EN 60898 circuit-breaker / BS EN 61009 RCBO - Type B		103,101,A,100,102,C	81	81	81	81
	BS EN 60898 circuit-breaker / BS EN 61009 RCBO - Type C			39	23	81	58
	BS 88-2.2 and BS 88-6 fuse			26	20	26	26
25	BS EN 60898 circuit-breaker / BS EN 61009 RCBO - Type B	2.5 /1.5	C	26	26	26	26
	BS EN 60898 circuit-breaker / BS EN 61009 RCBO - Type C			3	3	26	22
	BS 88-2.2 and BS 88-6 fuse			42	23	42	42
25	BS EN 60898 circuit-breaker / BS EN 61009 RCBO - Type B	4.0 /1.5	A,100,102,C	42	42	42	42
	BS EN 60898 circuit-breaker / BS EN 61009 RCBO - Type C			6	3	42	25
	BS 88-2.2 and BS 88-6 fuse			64	38	64	64
25	BS EN 60898 circuit-breaker / BS EN 61009 RCBO - Type B	6.0 /2.5	101,A,100,102,C	64	64	64	64
	BS EN 60898 circuit-breaker / BS EN 61009 RCBO - Type C			9	5	64	41

 © Certsure LLP (January 2015)

Table A4 continued

Protective Device		Cable size	Allowed installation method	Maximum length (m)			
1	2	3	4	5	6	7	8
Rating (A)	Type	Line/cpc	Note 2	$Z_e \le 0.8\ \Omega$ TN-S		$Z_e \le 0.35\ \Omega$ TN-C-S	
				RCD	No RCD	RCD	No RCD
30	BS1361 fuse	4.0 /1.5	C	36	NP	36	10
	BS 3036 fuse		NP	NP	NP	NP	NP
30	BS1361 fuse	6.0 /2.5	A, 100,102,C	53	NP	53	15
	BS 3036 fuse		C	57	19	57	54
30	BS1361 fuse	10.0 /4.0	A, 100,102,C	88	NP	88	25
	BS 3036 fuse		C	93	31	93	89
32	BS 88-2.2 and BS 88-6 fuse	4.0 /1.5	C	33	5	33	27
	BS 88-3 fuse system C			33	9	33	31
	BS EN 60898 circuit-breaker / BS EN 61009 RCBO - Type B			33	28	33	33
	BS EN 60898 circuit-breaker / BS EN 61009 RCBO - Type C			NP	NP	29	16
32	BS 88-2.2 and BS 88-6 fuse	6.0 /2.5	A, 100,102,C	49	15	49	49
	BS 88-3 fuse system C			49	8	49	44
	BS EN 60898 circuit-breaker / BS EN 61009 RCBO - Type B			49	45	49	49
	BS EN 60898 circuit-breaker / BS EN 61009 RCBO - Type C			NP	NP	44	26
32	BS 88-2.2 and BS 88-6 fuse	10.0 /4.0	103, 101, A, 100, 102,C	81	24	81	81
	BS 88-3 fuse system C			81	14	81	72
	BS EN 60898 circuit-breaker / BS EN 61009 RCBO - Type B			81	73	81	81
	BS EN 60898 circuit-breaker / BS EN 61009 RCBO - Type C			NP	NP	75	42

Published by Certsure LLP © Certsure LLP (January 2015)

Table A4 continued

Protective Device		Cable size	Allowed installation method	Maximum length (m)			
1	2	3	4	5	6	7	8
Rating (A)	Type	Line/cpc	Note 2	$Z_e \leq 0.8\ \Omega$ TN-S		$Z_e \leq 0.35\ \Omega$ TN-C-S	
				RCD	No RCD	RCD	No RCD
40	BS 88-2.2 and BS 88-6 fuse	6.0 /2.5	C	40	NP	40	31
	BS EN 60898 circuit-breaker / BS EN 61009 RCBO - Type B			39	23	40	40
	BS EN 60898 circuit-breaker / BS EN 61009 RCBO - Type C			NP	NP	27	15
40	BS 88-2.2 and BS 88-6 fuse	10.0 /4.0	A, 100,102,C	66	NP	66	51
	BS EN 60898 circuit-breaker / BS EN 61009 RCBO - Type B			66	37	66	66
	BS EN 60898 circuit-breaker / BS EN 61009 RCBO - Type C			NP	NP	45	25
40	BS 88-2.2 and BS 88-6 fuse	16.0 /6.0	103, 101, A, 100, 102,C	104	NP	104	78
	BS EN 60898 circuit-breaker / BS EN 61009 RCBO - Type B			104	57	104	104
	BS EN 60898 circuit-breaker / BS EN 61009 RCBO - Type C			NP	NP	72	39
45	BS1361 fuse	6.0 /2.5	C	25	NP	35	18
	BS 88-3 fuse system C		C	14	NP	35	NP
	BS 3036 fuse		NP	NP	NP	NP	NP
45	BS1361 fuse	10.0 /4.0	A, 100,102,C	25	NP	58	NP
	BS 88-3 fuse system C		A, 100,102,C	43	NP	58	29
	BS 3036 fuse		C	62	NP	62	27
45	BS1361 fuse	16.0 /6.0	A, 100,102,C	39	NP	91	NP
	BS 88-3 fuse system C		A, 100,102,C	86	47	91	45
	BS 3036 fuse		C	97	NP	97	41

Notes: 1) NP = Not permitted 2) Any reference method less onerous than that in column 4 may be used

 © Certsure LLP (January 2015)

Table A5: Maximum total route length for a 230 V ring final circuit in household premises using 70 °C thermoplastic (pvc) insulated and sheathed flat cable having copper conductors

Protective Device		Cable size	Reference method	Maximum length (m)			
1	2	3	4	5	6	7	8
				$Z_e \leq 0.8\ \Omega$ TN-S		$Z_e \leq 0.35\ \Omega$ TN-C-S	
Rating (A)	Type	Line/cpc		RCD	No RCD	RCD	No RCD
30	BS1361 fuse	2.5 /1.5	A, 100, 102, C	111	NP	111	34
	BS 3036 fuse			111	41	111	111
32	BS 88-2.2 and BS 88-6 fuse	2.5 /1.5	A, 100, 102, C	106	32	106	106
	BS 88-3 fuse system C			106	18	106	95
	BS EN 60898 circuit-breaker / BS EN 61009 RCBO - Type B			106	97	106	106
	BS EN 60898 circuit-breaker / BS EN 61009 RCBO - Type C			NP	NP	74	56
30	BS1361 fuse	4.0 /1.5	101, A, 102, 102, C	183	NP	183	39
	BS 3036 fuse			183	47	183	137
32	BS 88-2.2 and BS 88-6 fuse	4.0 /1.5	101, A, 102, 102, C	176	37	176	127
	BS 88-3 fuse system C			176	21	176	111
	BS EN 60898 circuit-breaker / BS EN 61009 RCBO - Type B			176	123	176	176
	BS EN 60898 circuit-breaker / BS EN 61009 RCBO - Type C			NP	NP	119	65

Notes: 1) NP = Not permitted 2) Any reference method less onerous than that in column 4 may be used

Published by Certsure LLP © Certsure LLP (January 2015)

A5 Minimum permitted protective conductor sizes for energy limiting Class 3 circuit-breakers and RCBOs

The cross-sectional areas given in Table A6 below have been derived using the following formula from Regulation 543.1.3 of *BS 7671*.

$$S = \frac{\sqrt{I^2 t}}{k}$$

Where

S = cross-sectional area of protective conductor (mm²)

I^2t = applicable energy let-through for type and class of protective device from Annex ZA of *BS EN 60898*

k = factor for type of protective conductor, taking into account

- the nature of the conductor
- conductor material, and
- insulation material.

A value of k of 115 has been used when producing Table A6. This k factor is taken from Table 54.3 of *BS 7671*. It is applicable for a cable having a copper protective conductor bunched with thermoplastic insulated copper conductors – as is the case for the 'twin and earth' type cables commonly used in domestic premises.

It is important that reference is made to the most appropriate part of the table in terms of the maximum prospective fault current that is *likely to be present at the circuit-breaker or RCBO within the installation*. In most cases, this will be significantly lower than the rated short-circuit capacity indicated on the circuit-breaker or RCBO.

It should be noted that the energy let-through values will be typically lower than those quoted in the product standards and, in some cases will give particular values for each rated current of protective device. It follows therefore that use of the manufacturer's data for the particular installed protective device will allow for the selection of a protective conductor of smaller csa than given in Table A6 in many cases.

 © Certsure LLP (January 2015)

Final circuit information

Table A6 Minimum permitted protective conductor size for Energy limiting Class 3 circuit-breakers and RCBOs for fault current not exceeding 3 kA, 4.5 kA, 6 kA and 10 kA.

Rated current (A)	Circuit-breaker/RCBO type					
	Type B			Type C		
	I^2t max (A^2s)	Calculated minimum csa (mm^2)	Minimum available csa (mm^2)	I^2t max (A^2s)	Calculated minimum csa (mm^2)	Minimum available csa (mm^2)
3 kA fault current						
3 to 16	15000	1.064	1.5	18000	1.166	1.5
20 to 32	18000	1.166	1.5	22000	1.289	1.5
40	21600	1.277	1.5	26400	1.412	1.5
4.5 kA fault current						
3 to 16	25000	1.374	1.5	30000	1.506	2.5
20 to 32	32000	1.555	2.5	39000	1.717	2.5
40	38400	1.703	2.5	46800	1.881	2.5
6 kA fault current						
3 to 16	35000	1.626	2.5	42000	1.782	2.5
20 to 32	45000	1.844	2.5	55000	2.039	2.5
40	54000	2.020	2.5	66000	2.233	2.5
10 kA fault current						
3 to 16	70000	2.300	2.5	84000	2.52	4
20 to 32	90000	2.608	4	110000	2.884	4
40	108000	2.857	4	132000	3.159	4

Published by Certsure LLP © Certsure LLP (January 2015)

Appendix B Safe isolation procedures

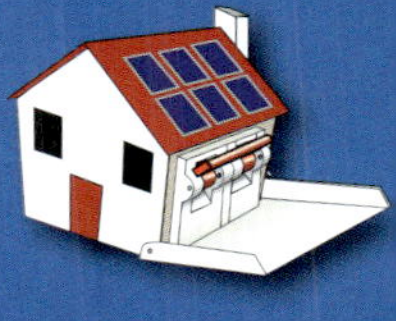

Published by Certsure LLP   © Certsure LLP (January 2015)

Appendix B Safe isolation procedures

All persons carrying out electrical installation or maintenance work must be able to carry out the safe isolation of all or part of an electrical installation.

Regulation 12 of the *Electricity at Work Regulations 1989* deals with means of cutting off the supply and for isolation. The regulation requires that where necessary to prevent danger, suitable means (including, where appropriate, methods of identifying circuits) are made available:

- for cutting off the supply of electrical energy to any electrical equipment, and
- for the isolation of electrical equipment.

Isolation is not simply the operation of an isolating device. It is a procedure, the objective of which is to ensure that the supply is cut off and remains cut off for reasons of safety. The process of isolation can be broken down into a number of steps as necessary for the particular circumstances. As a minimum, the following safe working procedure should be adopted before commencing inspection (*HSG85: Electricity at Work safe working practices* gives detailed guidance on devising safe working practices for people who carry out work on or near electrical equipment).

The example illustrated shows the minimum steps required to isolate the final circuits supplied by a single-phase consumer unit. The consumer unit includes an isolator and circuit-breakers.

When circuits are protected by fuses enclosed in a consumer unit it may be necessary to isolate the whole consumer unit in some cases using the main switch.

Step 1

Check it is safe and acceptable (with the occupier/user) to isolate. If the isolator is an offload device, remove the load.

Open the means of isolation for the circuit(s) to be isolated and secure the isolating device in the open position with a lock or other suitable means.

 Published by Certsure LLP © Certsure LLP (January 2015)

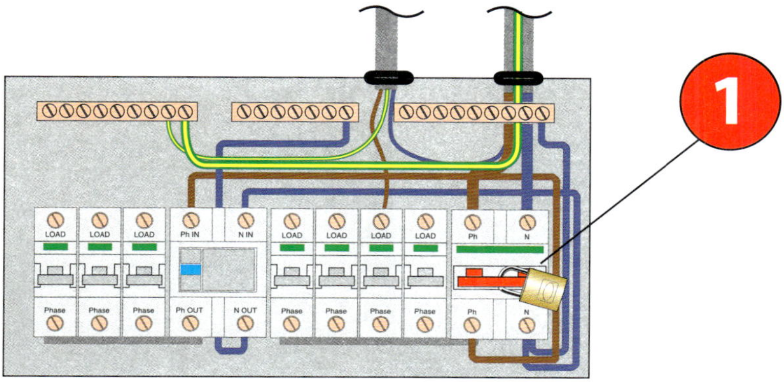

Step 2

Prove the correct operation of a suitable voltage detection instrument against a known voltage source, such as that illustrated. Guidance on voltage detection instruments is given in *HSE Guidance Note GS 38 – Electrical test equipment for use by electricians*.

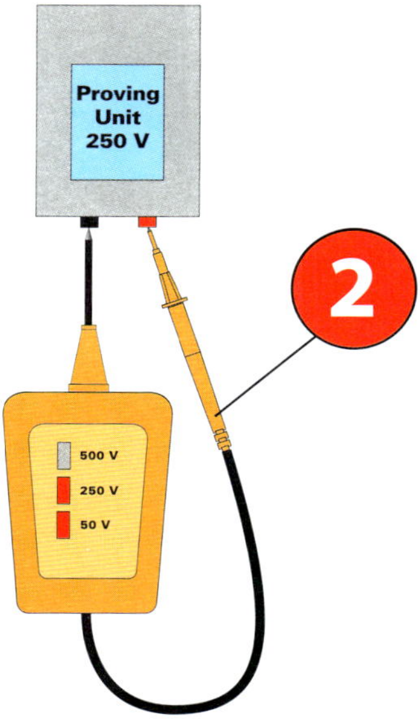

Appendix B Safe isolation procedures

Step 3

Using a voltage detection instrument, check that there is no dangerous voltage present on any circuit conductor to be worked on or near to. It is important to confirm that conductors are **not** energised, for example, due to a wiring fault. Check terminal voltages between: (i) line and earth, (ii) line and neutral (as shown) and (iii) neutral and earth.

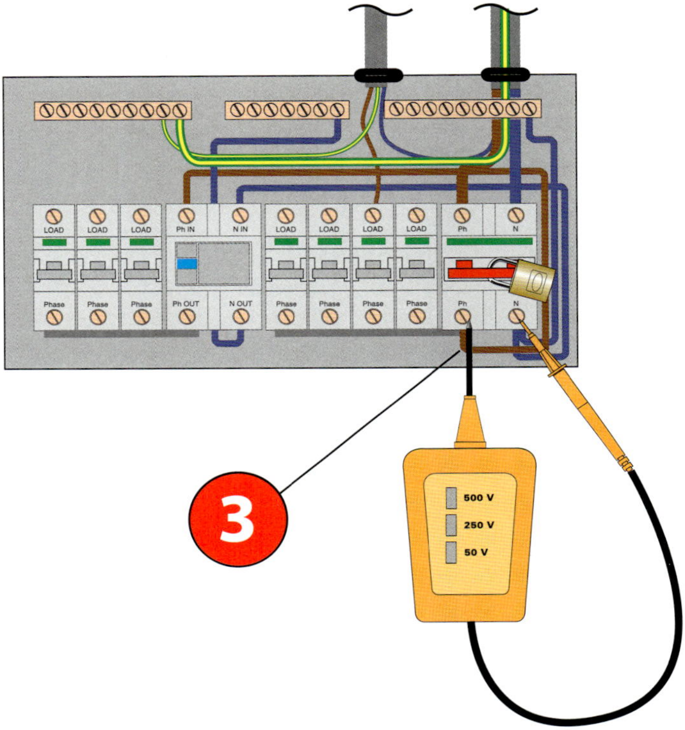

Published by Certsure LLP © Certsure LLP (January 2015)

Step 4

Prove the voltage detection instrument again against the known source to check that it was functioning correctly when the circuit(s) was tested for the presence of voltage.

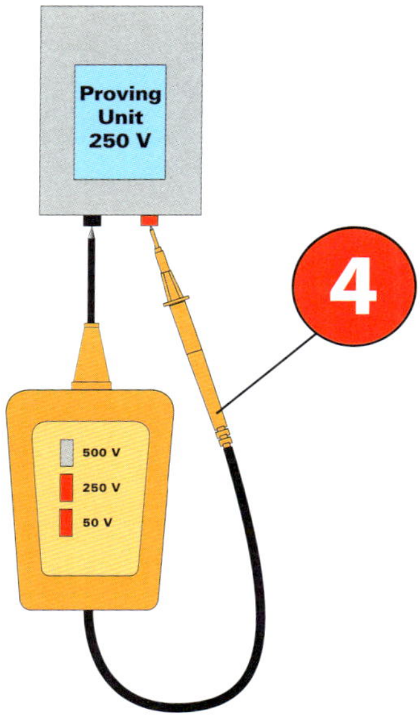

Notes

1. In practice the equipment being worked on is likely to be remote from the consumer unit, for example a socket-outlet located remotely from the means of isolation. In this case it is necessary to check that all the socket-outlet contact terminals are dead.

2. When checking for a voltage between an earth terminal and live (including neutral) terminals, the test probe should make contact with the earth terminal first, to reduce the risk of the remaining probe becoming live.

 © Certsure LLP (January 2015)

Appendix B Safe isolation procedures

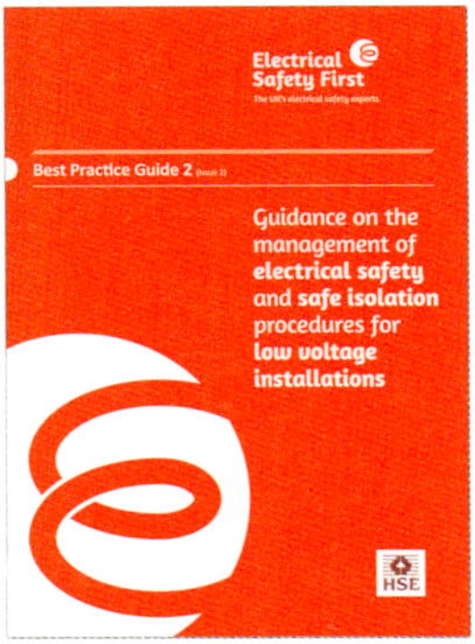

The Electrical Safety First Best Practice Guide 2, *Guidance on the management of electrical safety and safe isolation procedures for low voltage installations* has been produced by Electrical Safety First in conjunction with the Health and Safety Executive (HSE) and other organisations. Its purpose is to provide practical guidance for employers and the self-employed on safe isolation procedures to be followed when working on low voltage electrical installations.

The above guide can be downloaded from Electrical Safety First's website

www.electricalsafetyfirst.org.uk.

ELECSA and NICEIC *Pocket Guide 5 – Guide to isolation procedure* is reproduced in this guide.

All ELECSA and NICEIC Pocket Guides are available to download from the ELECSA and NICEIC website (**www.elecsa.co.uk** and **www.niceic.com**).

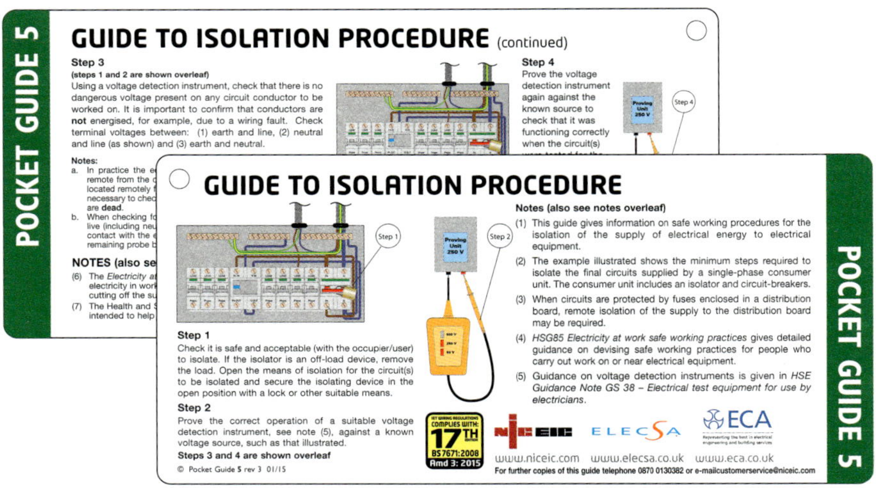

POCKET GUIDE 5

GUIDE TO ISOLATION PROCEDURE (continued)

Step 3

(steps 1 and 2 are shown overleaf)

Using a voltage detection instrument, check that there is no dangerous voltage present on any circuit conductor to be worked on. It is important to confirm that conductors are **not** energised, for example, due to a wiring fault. Check terminal voltages between: (1) earth and line, (2) neutral and line (as shown) and (3) earth and neutral.

Step 4

Prove the voltage detection instrument again against the known source to check that it was functioning correctly when the circuit(s)

GUIDE TO ISOLATION PROCEDURE

Step 1

Check it is safe and acceptable (with the occupier/user) to isolate. If the isolator is an off-load device, remove the load. Open the means of isolation for the circuit(s) to be isolated and secure the isolating device in the open position with a lock or other suitable means.

Step 2

Prove the correct operation of a suitable voltage detection instrument, see note (5), against a known voltage source, such as that illustrated.

Steps 3 and 4 are shown overleaf

© Pocket Guide 5 rev 3 01/15

Notes (also see notes overleaf)

(1) This guide gives information on safe working procedures for the isolation of the supply of electrical energy to electrical equipment.

(2) The example illustrated shows the minimum steps required to isolate the final circuits supplied by a single-phase consumer unit. The consumer unit includes an isolator and circuit-breakers.

(3) When circuits are protected by fuses enclosed in a distribution board, remote isolation of the supply to the distribution board may be required.

(4) *HSG85 Electricity at work safe working practices* gives detailed guidance on devising safe working practices for people who carry out work on or near electrical equipment.

(5) Guidance on voltage detection instruments is given in *HSE Guidance Note GS 38 – Electrical test equipment for use by electricians*.

IET WIRING REGULATIONS COMPLIES WITH: 17TH EDITION BS 7671:2008 Amd 3: 2015

www.niceic.com www.elecsa.co.uk www.eca.co.uk

For further copies of this guide telephone 0870 0130382 or e-mailcustomerservice@niceic.com

POCKET GUIDE 5

Published by Certsure LLP © Certsure LLP (January 2015)

The Briti
Horse Soci

CW01643094

THE WESTERN FELLS ON HORSEBACK

AVAILABLE IN THE "ON HORSEBACK" SERIES

Wiltshire
Westmorland
The Ridgeway Downs
Exmoor
Somerset
Hampshire
Leicestershire & Rutland
Humberside
Northamptonshire
Dorset
Cambridgeshire
The Cotswolds (second edition)
Powys
Buckinghamshire (Circular Routes)
Buckinghamshire (Long Distance)
Yorkshire Dales

First published 1997
by The British Horse Society
Access & Rights of Way Department
British Equestrian Centre
Stoneleigh Park, Kenilworth
Warwickshire CV8 2LR

A catalogue record for this book is available from the British Library

ISBN 1 899016 13 9

All British Horse Society Rights Reserved.
No part of this publication may be reproduced,
stored in a retrieval system, or transmitted,
in any form or by any means, electronic,
mechanical, photocopying, recording
or otherwise, without the prior permission
in writing of the publishers

Copyright © British Horse Society

CONTENTS

ACKNOWLEDGEMENTS

A number of people have given their time and expertise to provide details for this book, or contributed in some other material way.

In particular, the British Horse Society would like to thank John and Pamela Bright, and also David and Helen Kerry, Chris and Hazel Singleton, and Colin and Carole Woodall who surveyed and described many of the trails; Peter and Jenny Myers for their assistance. The Society would also like to thank Marilyn Leech for her unique drawings and Helga Frankland for not only writing the introduction to the book but for her valuable contribution to the text.

But most of all thanks are due to Nigel Redfern, the British Horse Society County Access & Bridleways Officer for Cumbria, who, with his wife Margaret, not only surveyed, developed and described many of the routes, but enthusiastically co-ordinated the whole project. Without him the book would not have been possible.

FOREWORD

When the British Horse Society launched its ARROW Project in 1991, few people could have foreseen the tremendous response and commitment that it would provoke from recreational drivers and riders. That so many guide books have been published, is testament to their dedication and talent. I am delighted, on behalf of all equestrians, to pay tribute to those who have made such a unique contribution towards the achievement of a network of circular and linear trails.

The Society is concerned that little had been achieved for carriage drivers within ARROW: however it is pleasing that some progress has now been made and that a number of driving trails are now available with more to come in subsequent books.

It is a fact that drivers are restricted to Byways and Unclassified County Roads, thus there are fewer chances to provide them with off-road driving opportunities. This calls for a separate approach, with our Rights of Way staff and volunteers working hand-in-glove with drivers and driving organisations, in order to identify and claim lost routes. The Access & Rights of Way Policy Committee, in overseeing this initiative, will do all in its power to gain maximum benefit for drivers from this important partnership.

As it is virtually impossible to produce a circular or linear route without incorporating some metalled highways it is difficult to lay claim to having opened up a given mileage of 'off-road' riding.

What can be claimed however, is that at the end of 1996 details of 350 trails, totalling about 5000 miles, had been published.

With many more books planned to be available by the millenium, the Society can, with some justification, feel proud to have contributed to the safety and the greater enjoyment of those who take pleasure from riding and carriage driving.

E A T BONNOR-MAURICE
Chairman, British Horse Society

PREFACE

Conditioned as we are to the spread of urban development and its supportive system of trunk roads that encroach, inevitably, upon the countryside, it comes as a surprise to reflect that for well over a thousand years after the withdrawal of the Roman legions no public roads were built in Britain, much less new towns and industrial centres. Indeed, the Roman legacy of 5000 miles (8,000 km) of surfaced via strata did not long survive the departure of its builders. Its lapse into decay was to all intents synonymous with the decline and ultimate eclipse of the beleaguered empire itself.

It was not until 1780 that the system of toll roads had reached that figure again. Fifty years later, thanks principally to the efforts of Telford and McAdam, Britain had 20,000 miles (32,000 km) of good roadways underpinning what became known as the Golden Age of Coaching.

Within the past half-century that road system and the myriad acres of developed areas it services has been multiplied more than a hundred times over, whilst the open countryside and, in consequence, the means of access to it, has been eroded commensurately.

Up to the Industrial Revolution and for many years thereafter, the countryside was criss-crossed with tracks, some of them dating from prehistoric times and others relics of the Roman occupation. They provided trade routes for the transport of every sort of commodity as well as being an essential facility for the traveller. John Wesley, for instance, who led the Methodist revival of the 19th century, reckoned to ride 8000 miles on such tracks in the course of a year. There was also a comprehensive system of long-distance drove roads, the equivalent of our modern road system, over which thousands and thousands of cattle, sheep, pigs, geese and turkeys were driven to the main centres of population (cattle were shod for the journey and even geese had their webbed feet protected by a pad of tar and sawdust).

The land enclosures of the 18th and 19th centuries took an obvious toll of all kinds of previously public routes; and industrial development, dependent on railways, roads and canals, made further inroads into the public rights of access. After that the intensification of farming practice and the sheer speed and scope of urban building were both factors in breaking up the old network of tracks, lanes and paths.

Nonetheless, it was possible, just fifty years ago, for Aime Tschiffely, the archetypal long-distance rider who described his 10,000 mile (16,000 km) two and a half year journey from Buenos Aires to Washington DC in his classic The Tales of Two Horses, to take a 'leisurely jaunt' through England on horseback. The book of that 'jaunt' was called simply Bridle Paths and the idea, he said, was to 'jog along, anyhow and anywhere; canter along quiet country lanes, over hills and through dales - sunshine or rain - alone with a horse to see the real England' and he could have done the same in Scotland or Wales.

Twenty years after Tschiffely, the broadcaster Wynford Vaughan Thomas made a TV programme of a ride from one end of Wales to the other over the upland ways once traversed by the sad and shadowy princes of that country. Some of those historic routes are no longer open to horsemen, but Wales can still boast the Pilgrim's Ride, the route followed by the devout in their pilgrimage to Bardsey, the island of the Saints, as well as Glyndwr's Way which traverses the most rugged of the upland country. Elsewhere there are other long-distance routes, the South Downs Way, the Ridgeway and so on, whilst there still remain many shorter routes all over the country that provide the basis for our modern public paths.

Most prominent and active within the environmental lobby seeking to extend and protect the rights of off-road riders is the British Horse Society's Access and Rights of Way Policy Committee, co-ordinating the work of over 100 honorary Access and Bridleways Officers in the UK. Amongst its declared objectives, laid down in its National Strategy for Access is 'the establishment of a basic network of public bridleways and byways in all counties, with cross-country and regional links.' It works towards 'linking long distance bridleways in most areas - so that a rider may travel the country if he so desires.'

This handbook with accurate material supplied by local enthusiasts is just one of a series published by the BHS which in the foreseeable future will cover every region of the country, reflecting and reinforcing the need to preserve an invaluable part of our heritage for as long as men and women find their pleasure 'along country lanes, over hills and through dales - sunshine or rain' along with a horse and like-minded companions.'

ELWYN HARTLEY EDWARDS

INTRODUCTION

History reliably informs us of the invaluable contribution made by horses to the development of mankind. Predicting the future is a much more hazardous business. However, one day modern man might well regret discarding the horse quite so quickly, in favour of the ubiquitous motor car. Only time will tell.

But at least in the British Horse Society's Arrow Project, there has been a concerted attempt to redress matters equine by mapping out an attractive selection of bridleways, byways and minor roads into co-ordinated pleasure rides, so that the countryside can once again be enjoyed from the back of a horse. To all of the volunteers who have thoroughly researched and recorded on paper, their findings, in order that others may enjoy the fruits of their hard work, the BHS owes a huge vote of thanks.

Before selecting any of the rides featured in this book, consider carefully the sort of preparations you need to make. Make sure you and your horse are in good physical condition and used to going on reasonably long rides (say 15-20 miles). And, however placid your horse, there are always imaginary demons lurking just below the surface. So it is no use whistling up a spirit of adventure and then finding your horse goes beserk at the first unfamiliar object on the side of the track.

You may find joining your local BHS Endurance Riding Group helpful. Inexpensive advice is normally available on feeding, fitness and how to use a map while on horseback. Some groups even organise training rides for this very purpose. Remember the Scout's motto: 'Be Prepared'.

FITNESS

Getting a horse to peak fitness is a specialist art. A successful racehorse trainer will, on average, charge £150 per week to get the horses in his care fully wound up. Of course normal pleasure riders are not seeking such lofty status, however the lesson is there for all to see. The more professional you are about bringing your horse on, the better he will go. Study and put into action one of the many available books on horse fitness. Plan well in advance; at least three months. Don't rush your horse. A properly fit horse with well developed muscles will cope ten times better with uneven terrain, sharp inclines and down slopes than one who has been sloppily prepared for only a short length of time.

'Fizzy' horses are no use to man nor beast. Of course some horses get geed up when starting out on an unfamiliar trail. But if properly prepared, trained, and handled, they should quickly settle to the job in hand; i.e. getting the rider from A to B with a minimum of fuss, standing still while gates are being opened and shut, negotiating still and running water, especially when riding in unfamiliar territory. Make sure you and your horse can cope. It's no use hitting the panic button when you are twenty miles from base camp.

Pay close attention to your own personal fitness and stamina before undertaking any long rides. Twenty or thirty miles in the saddle is no laughing matter; your state of health should be taken just as seriously as that of your horse.

MAP READING AND THE COUNTRY CODE

North, south, east or west? It's no use setting out on any trail unless you can read a map and use a compass. Either teach yourself how to use Pathfinder, Explorer, Outdoor Leisure and Landranger Ordnance Survey maps, or get someone more experienced to show you how. It's quite simple and great fun. The maps are all divided into grids. Trail rides are usually charted via grid references. Once you learn how to read a grid reference, in conjunction with a compass to establish the direction to head off in, then most trail rides should be within your grasp.

Roads, bridleways, footpaths, rivers, contours and all major and minor landmarks are featured on Ordnance Survey maps including a comprehensive key to all of the incorporated symbols. You'll go wrong once in a while but practice really does make perfect when it comes to reading maps, and don't forget a plastic map cover is essential for protection against the weather.

The Country Code is something all too rarely abided by these days. How many times have you seen litter strewn by the wayside and gates left open? All of our trails involve using statutory rights of way; make sure you stick to them. It's no use expecting farmers and landowners to co-operate with horse users if they abuse their rights.

SAFETY

Accidents can and do happen. In order to minimise risks and maximise your own safety it is always wise to ride with someone else. Should the worst happen then at least there is help immediately to hand. Whoever the company, before setting off make sure you let a reliable adult know exactly where and when you are going. Approximate start and finishing times as well as an accurate description of your intended route is also essential. Always wear an approved BSI riding hat, correct footwear and carry waterproofs.

TACK

Regular tack inspections are part and parcel of the responsible rider's daily check list. The routine takes on even more importance if you are planning a long ride away from home. If your horse has shown any signs of a sore back, make an appointment with your local saddler to see if the saddle is still a good fit, or broken in any way. Spare girth straps, rope and head collar will also have to fit in your saddle bags along with a basic first aid kit for both horse and rider. A high-pitched whistle is also a good idea for the purpose of alerting a rescue team should you hit difficulties, become stranded, or lay injured in a hidden or hard-to-find location.

INSURANCE

Since we no longer live in a country where it is possible to amble quietly round the back roads and lanes in total safety, Third Party Legal Liability Insurance and Personal Accident Insurance is a must for anyone who opts to travel on horseback these days.

The BHS offers an all inclusive insurance package to cover most eventualities. Don't rely on your own household insurance as this may not provide adequate cover. Loose horses can do untold damage, while the 1995 paralysis of Christopher 'Superman' Reeve from the neck downwards from a seemingly innocuous fall, demonstrated just how freak accidents do very occasionally happen.

PARKING & MONEY

Horsebox and trailer stealing is a fast-growing industry so make sure vehicles are as secure as possible when left at base camp on the start of a day's ride. The engine and bodywork should be etched with the registration mark, mechanical steering locks and alarms fitted where possible. Always park with due consideration to other road users; never block gateways or footpaths. Take sufficient money to cover the day's expenses, plus some extra in the event of an emergency; at least the price of a taxi back to your point of departure.

ACCOMMODATION

If you are setting out on a journey of more than one day, plan your journey even more carefully than usual. The BHS publish a Bed & Breakfast guide for horses - a selection of stopovers where either horse or rider, often both, can be accommodated. The Society does not vet these establishments so always check them out in advance, asking as many questions as possible. For instance some places offer turn out rather than overnight stabling.

Feeding can also be a problem. Colic is all too easily caused by a sudden change of hard feed or a different variety of hay. Ideally you should arrange to drop off food the day befor you ride.

BLOCKED BRIDLEWAYS OR PATHS

If you should encounter blocked, boggy or badly maintained bridleways, mak a note of the exact location and inforn the local Highways Authority by letter sending an additional copy to the BHS to let them know there is a problem This should prompt remedial action One of the only sure-fire ways o ensuring continued access to th countryside is by voluntarily keepin an eye on any bridleways and paths ir your locality, and reporting any problems to the relevant authorities Ultimately this will have the effect o paving the way for your children, anc your children's children, to enjoy the pleasures of our ever diminishing, bu still beautiful land.

The western fells of Cumbria offer the rider some of the most spectacular scenery in England, rugged mountains to the east contrasting with the coastal plain of the western seaboard. This arises from 400 million years of geological activity, sculpted by weather and climatic change, clothed with varying plant and animal life, and finally modified from prehistoric times to the present day by the formative hand of Man.

Geological Structure

Essentially, the Lake District is a dome with a central core of hard volcanic rocks surrounded by circles of sedimentary and wind-eroded deposits. The dome was formed by huge earth movements pressing in, mainly from the south east, and by volcanoes forcing molten rock and ash upwards in the centre. From this dome there evolved a radial pattern of drainage through lakes and rivers. It has been modified several times by further earth movements and glaciation but, as can be seen by a glance at any map, the pattern persists to this day.

Earth movements producing folding and displacement of rock strata, and successive freezing and thawing of glaciers, caused changes in sea level. Erosion, whether by water or wind, and more rapid on the softer rocks, produced vast deposits of sediment, some of them thousands of feet thick, mostly under the sea. It is these sedimentary rocks, once more raised above sea level and ground down by further erosion, which give us the slate, sandstone and limestone rings surrounding the Lake District's volcanic core. It is with the western half of this 'boiled egg with the top cut off' that we are concerned.

Development of Vegetation

The last Ice Age in Britain came to an end about 10,000 years ago, and practically all today's Lake District plant and animal life originated after that. As the ice receded, leaving deeply carved valleys, small hardy plants gained a foothold and, gradually, scrub and woodland crept up the slopes of the fells, leaving only the summits unwooded. At first pine, birch and hazel would predominate, but with a warmer, wetter climate setting in, forests of deciduous trees such as oak, alder, elm and ash took over. Also, importantly, peat accumulated where high rainfall and poor drainage waterlogged the ground preventing the decay of plant remains. The vigorous growth of species favoured by these more favourable conditions stifled many of the original plants, the few remaining ones now being rarities confined to mountain tops and crevices where they escape competition.

As plants re-colonised the land and built up mature communities they were followed by animals, all of which depend ultimately on plants, and a rich fauna found its place in the diversity of habitats. One of these immigrant species, at first few in number and physically rather feeble, but possessing a large brain, was eventually to bring about unprecedented change. Man had taken his place in the history of the Lake District.

Man's Early Influence

The earliest surviving evidence of Man's presence in the Lake District and on the western seaboard dates from the Stone Age about 5000 years ago. Dressed flints have been found near the coast, and stone axes, roughed out from fine-grained scree stones and then polished, are typical of the period. At first, Man would have lived by gathering such food as he could find. Next, he would have begun hunting animals, and eventually herding his own domestic stock. Finally, at the end of the Stone Age, cultivation of crops, notably grain, was pioneered. At this stage Man began to influence his environment significantly.

Grazing herds prevent re-growth of woodland and, to increase the areas of pasture, lightly wooded land could be cleared. Even a stone axe in the hands of a fit, skilled man is a remarkably effective tool. Crop growing would have an even more radical effect. With the coming of the Bronze and Iron Ages, mineral exploration began; a great variety of metals was mined in the western fells until recent times. Much of the present bridleway network had its origin in the carriage of minerals by pack pony from upland mines and quarries.

Remnants of hut circles, ancient field systems, spoil heaps, and those mysterious, probably ritualistic, circles of standing stones remain to this day among the western fells as testimony to well-established human activity. Naturally, the more easily worked ground would be tackled first, and it is no surprise to find that the most ancient settlements occur on the limestone and other soft rocks round the edge rather than in the craggy unyielding heart of the Lake District dome. The alluvial valleys of the interior - heavily timbered and often swampy, though potentially fertile were also left untouched at this stage.

The Roman Occupation
With the Roman invasion of Britain came the building of a quite amazingly extensive series of roads linking military stations. In the western fells these roads served the fort at Hardknott and the stations at Papcastle and Ravenglass as well as others on the coast; but the road system was not so extensive as in many parts of the country, and some of the routes are still not known.

Norse Settlement
Following Roman withdrawal successive waves of Norse settlers came to Britain, and it is primarily their imprint, intertwined with the culture of the native Celts, which gives us today's Cumbrian landscape, and the majority of the County's dialect words and place names. Small farms spread along the dale sides, each with its farmhouse, meadows and home pastures, and above these, on the higher fells, the sheep grazing. Locally this layout predominates over the more usual plan of villages surrounded by strip cultivation and large 'open fields'.

Farming
A dominant feature of Lakeland farming is the many hundreds of miles of dry-stone walls which are so typical of this landscape. In some dales such as Wasdale they are up to six feet thick, serving not only as field boundaries but as somewhere to put the stone which had been cleared from the land. Happily, after a period of neglect, many of these walls are being restored and maintained. Although cattle were kept it was sheep, bred for wool and meat, which were the mainstay of fell farming.

)ne result of centuries of sheep arming has been the decline of voodland and of many moorland plants; heather, for example, is much ess common than it used to be.

'orestry

n the last 70 years or so the Forestry Commission's extensive conifer plantations have replaced some of the ost woodland cover, providing much imber; certain species benefit, such as ed squirrels which are still quite ommon locally even though under rave threat nationally. However, onifer plantations cannot support the vealth of wildlife which was haracteristic of the original woodland.

Modern Changes

'hus we see that landscape is onstantly changing. Over geological ime, huge forces have been at work nd will continue, but on the scale of uman life it is now largely Man who etermines the direction which hanges will take. The most striking xamples of these more recent human nfluences include a shift in aesthetic ppreciation of wild country and a evolution in farming practice.

'ourism

he Cumbrian poet William Vordsworth and his friends were ioneers in opening people's eyes to the eauties of lakes and mountains, itherto scorned and even feared, and f the picturesque farmsteads and amlets ensconced among them. This hange in attitude, together with the rrival of the railway, was the start of a ourist boom which has become a major factor pervading the economy nd culture of the Lake District, which s of course a National Park. Millions f people now enjoy the scenery, often causing serious traffic problems on what used to be quiet country lanes serving only local people. This makes an alternative network of bridleways essential for safe and pleasurable riding.

Modern Farming Practice

Farming methods, having evolved slowly over centuries, were revolutionised after the Second World War, particularly by the introduction of powerful tractors and machinery. Due to changes in demand, dairy cattle were largely replaced by beef breeds, and the fell sheep were crossbred to produce more meat. Some of the traditional steadings are now dominated by huge new all-purpose farm buildings, while others have become holiday homes.

Examples of many of the features described above are referred to in the individual trail guides which follow.

HELGA FRANKLAND

RIDING IN THE WESTERN FELLS

The area covered by this book is the western part of the Lake District, bounde by the trunk roads between Millom, Egremont, Cockermouth and Keswick, an by Borrowdale and Dunnerdale to the east. Nearly all is within the Lake Distric National Park. Fourteen riding routes are described, mostly circular trails, varyin in length from 5 miles (8 km) to 19 miles (30 km) and comprising a total of 16 miles (268 km). Of this total distance 110 miles (178 km) is on public or permissiv bridleways, or unmetalled roads; 11 miles (18 km) on unfenced motor roads and 42 miles (68 km) on other roads, mostly minor roads which are not heavil trafficked.

The western area is the quietest part of the Lake District, with fewer tourists and it is of very special value for this reason; but many of the roads are ver narrow, and riding on those which have no verges requires particular care.

Many of the bridleways in the western area are former packhorse routes, used t carry slate, lead and other minerals down to the ports; and, it is said, sometime returning overnight with loads of contraband goods such as brandy and silk Some of these packhorse trails are included here, but many have had to b omitted because the going is too severe: what had to be acceptable in earlie times for Fell ponies used as pack animals might be unjustifiably hazardous fo horses ridden for pleasure. The principal routes omitted from the book for thi reason are:

Borrowdale to Wasdale by way of Sty Head Pass,
Wasdale to Buttermere by way of Black Sail and Scarth Gap Passe
Honister to Buttermere, south of Fleetwith Pike,
Wasdale to Ennerdale, past Haycock,
Eskdale to Wasdale, past Tongue Moor,
Buttermere to Scarth Gap by way of Red Pike and High Stile,
Buttermere to Floutern Tarn.

Grading

The trails included are graded according to their severity, as follows:

Grade 1: easy going with no problems likely.

Grade 2: including some moderately severe conditions, usually of steep gradients, rocky broken surfaces, soft going, featureless landscap or the risk of mist at high level; but within the scope of any competen rider who is properly equipped and can read a map.

Grade 3: similar conditions to Grade 2 but more severe; many riders might find routes of this grade unsuitable for them or for their horses.

The Maps

Each of the trails has a map which indicates how apparent the track is on the ground:

▬▬▬	Enclosed/Obvious:	this will either be a road or track with a fence or wall on each side, or an obvious unenclosed metalled road or track which can be easily seen.
■ ■ ■ ■	Indistinct:	the line of the route can usually be discerned on the ground because it has some definite feature; but it is not obvious and could be missed.
● ● ● ●	Invisible:	the line of the route cannot be seen.

These maps are not a substitute for the Ordnance Survey maps which it is essential to use when riding these routes.

Safety

Riding on the hills is a serious business: always observe the following rules in order to reduce the risk of mishap or worse:

1. Ensure that your route, destination and expected time of arrival are known, so that you would be missed if you did not arrive - rescuers would know where to search. The Mountain Rescue Service - manned by volunteers - can be called by dialling 999.

2. Always carry the appropriate 1:25,000 Ordnance Survey Pathfinder map and a compass with you, or in the case of the Lake District, the Outdoor Leisure series.

3. Note the weather forecast and do not go if it is unfavourable. The local forecast can be obtained by telephoning the National Park Weatherline on 017687 75757.

4. Not all horses are suitable to ride on some of the routes in this network: think whether yours is likely to be happy on steep slopes and rocky surfaces, or on boggy ground. Native ponies are much more likely to be sensible about bogs than are most other horses.

5. Always ride with a headcollar and lead rope under your bridle, or with a headcollar bridle, so that you can tie up when you stop.

6. Take more warm clothing with you than you think you will need, and a survival bag.

7. Remember that if your horse should become disabled you may have to walk for a long distance over rough country so your own footwear must b suitable for walking as well as riding.

8. Take some emergency rations.

9. Never ride alone, you would be alone when you needed help.

10. If you have to leave an injured person alone while you seek help, make sure that you know where to come back to - not as easy as it may seem when you are leaving!

11. A mobile phone may be useful, but do not expect to depend on it becaus transmission quality is variable, and in many valleys it will not provide service.

Consideration for Others

Although you have a right of way on a Public Bridleway, it is always better t think of that right as a privilege; occasionally it may be tactful not to caus inconvenience to a farmer by pressing on regardless.

Some bridleways, particularly on heavy land, deteriorate rapidly in wet weathe and should be avoided during and soon after heavy rain.

Always ride in a careful and responsible manner, remembering the needs o other users. Walkers, for example, may easily be alarmed by the sudde appearance of horses, particularly on a narrow path. Equally, of course, horse are often alarmed by the sudden appearance of mountain bikes. Ride quietl past farm livestock and fasten all gates which you have opened.

We hope that you will enjoy riding in the Western Fells.

THE WESTERN FELLS
ON HORSEBACK

CODE FOR RIDING & DRIVING RESPONSIBLY

THE BRITISH HORSE SOCIETY

1. **Riders and carriage drivers** everywhere should proceed with courtesy, care and consideration. The British Horse Society recommends the following:

   Care for the Land:

   Do not stray off the line of the path;
   Do not damage timber or hedgerows by jumping;
   Remember that horses' hooves can damage surfaces in bad weather;
   Pay particular attention to protected areas that have significant historical and/or biological value, as they are extremely sensitive to damage.

   Courtesy to other users:

   Remember that walkers, cyclists and other riders may be elderly, disabled, children or simply frightened of horses; whenever possible acknowledge courtesy shown by drivers of motor vehicles.

   Consideration for the farmer:

   Shut the gate behind you;
   Ride slowly past all stock;
   Do not ride on cultivated land unless the right of way crosses it;
   Dogs are seldom welcome on farmland or moorland unless on a lead or under close control.

2. **Observe local byelaws.**

3. **Ride or drive with care on the roads** and take the BHS Riding and Road Safety Test. Always make sure that you can be seen at night or in bad visibility, by wearing the right kind of reflective/ fluorescent aids.

4. **Groups from riding establishments** should contain reasonable numbers, for reasons of both safety and amenity. They should never exceed twenty in total **including** the relevant number of escorts as indicated in BHS guidelines on levels of capability among riders in groups, available on request. Rides should not deviate from the right of way or permitted route and regard must be shown at all times for growing crops, shutting and securing of gates and the consideration and courtesy due to others.

5. **Always obey the Country Code in every way possible:**

   Enjoy the countryside and respect its life and work
   Guard against all risk of fire
   Fasten all gates
   Keep your dogs under close control
   Keep to public paths across farmland
   Use gates and stiles to cross fences, hedges and walls
   Leave livestock, crops and machinery alone
   Take your litter home
   Help keep all water clean
   Protect wildlife, plants and trees
   Take special care on country roads
   Make no unnecessary noise.

LORTON TO BASSENTHWAITE

Trail 1

ᴀN 18 MILE (29 KM) CIRCULAR ᵀRAIL ᴀNTI-CLOCKWISE)

)rdnance Survey Map:
)utdoor Leisure 4 - The English Lakes ᴊorth Western Area (1:25,000).

ᴙoute:
ꞩtanger/Lorton/Boonbeck/ Vhinlatter/Thornthwaite/Wythop Voods.
ᒿ250 feet (685m) of ascent.

ᴾarking & Starting Point:
ʟimited parking is available on the ɩccess road to Stanger (GR.137284). ᴾlease leave room for farm traffic to ɔass.

ᵀrail Grade: 1

ᵀerrain:
ᵀhis route is mostly low level and has ꞩome unavoidable roadwork on it, on ittle-used minor roads.

)f Interest:
ᵀhe buildings at Stanger, dating from ꞁ695, show that farming was a ɔrosperous industry. Stanger Spa, ɲarked as a holy well on the Ordnance ꞩurvey map, was reputed to have healing ɔowers to match any spa in the land, ɩnd attracted Victorian tourists in ɖroves.

ᴙoute Description:

ᶠrom your parking place, follow the ᴡell signed bridleway through the Stanger Farm complex going through two gates, along a short lane, and through a third gate before climbing by the field edge to a trough on the right of the track. *From here you have the first view down Lorton Vale between the bulk of Mosser Fell to the west with Whinlatter and the majestic Buttermere Fells to the east and south.*

Follow the field edge down and then right along the bottom, to turn left into a wetland meadow. *Be prepared for some seasonal standing water.* Keep to the fence on the right, heading across to the ruin of Stanger Spa. *The untouched condition of this meadow with its ancient hedges provides a haven for plants and wildlife.*

Go through the gate and follow the hedge to the left, staying left of Stanger How until you reach a gate by a short length of wall. Go through the gate and keeping by the wall and fence, follow the track until you reach a small footpath gate; bear right, heading south across the field to another small gate. Bear left to reach the wall ahead and keep it to the right, heading to Casshow Wood and the B5292.

Turn right on to the road. *CARE, this is sometimes busy.* At the Y junction bear right on the B5289 towards Low Lorton, and at the next junction take the minor road ahead signposted 'Lorton Church ¼ mile'. Ride on past the church to Cross Gates (GR.156256). *This is where Trail 2 links* *up,* **where you turn left. At the next junction turn left and immediately right, signposted Boonbeck and Scales (3.1 miles: 5 km).**

The yew tree across the beck is the one described by Wordsworth in his poem 'Yew Trees'; in 1653 George Fox, the founder of the Society of Friends, preached under it to a large crowd, as did John Wesley in 1759.

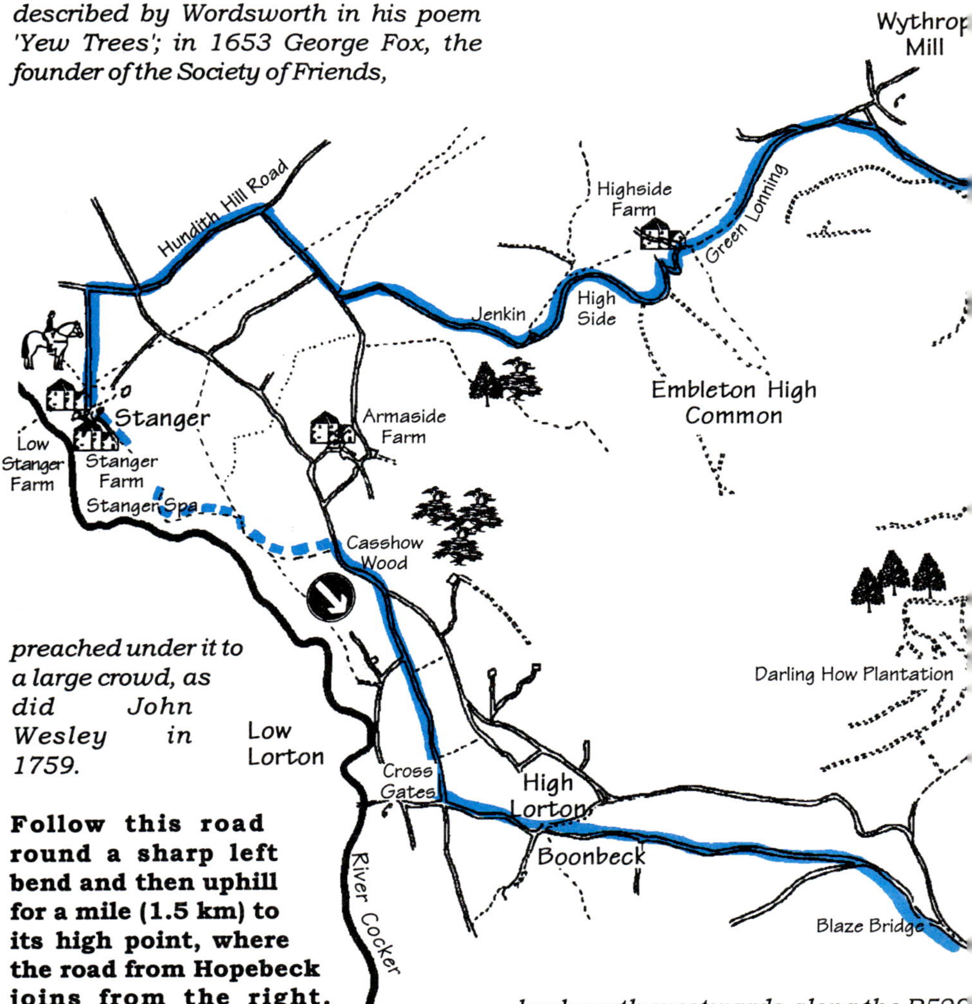

Follow this road round a sharp left bend and then uphill for a mile (1.5 km) to its high point, where the road from Hopebeck joins from the right. *There are impressive views all the way up this road: note the change from soft enclosed pasture to the stark afforestation and the rugged high fells. This road forms part of the Sustrans C2C cycleway.* **Drop down to Blaze Bridge before rejoining the B5292, where you bear right.**

After 600 yards (550m) turn shar left on to a track which rises throug the forest (4.8 miles: 7.7 km). *If th entry should be closed, ride back north-westwards along the B529 for a mile (1.6km) to Junction 31 an enter the forest there.* ***The next 4 miles (7 km) is through Whinlatte Forest which is the property c Forest Enterprise who have kindl given permission for riders to us this route. Please take great car***

take great care and do nothing to interfere with forestry work.

This little-used track rises northwestwards through the forest to reach the 1150 ft (350m) contour, when it starts to swing round

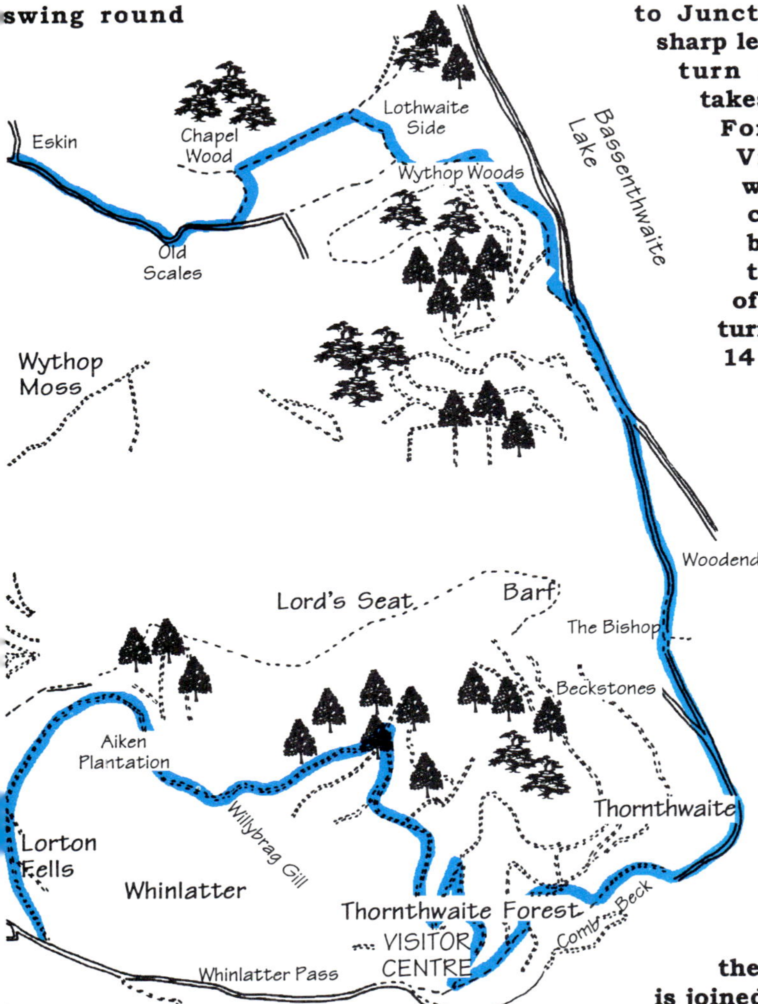

towards Aiken Plantation. Bear right at Junction 27, then ride on to cross Willibrag Gill and Aiken Beck. *Your route is now on the forest roads.* **At Junction 24, near the head of a little valley at 1475 ft (450m), the road turns right to go southwards, and then you bear left at Junction 26.** ***All the junction numbers are marked on posts.*** **Keep straight on at Junction 3, ride down to Junction 2 and turn sharp left. A sharp right turn at Junction 1 takes you down to the Forest Enterprise Visitor Centre where there is a cafe. Join the bridleway here on the road in front of the Centre, and turn left (8.7 miles: 14 km).**

Ride past a cottage on the right and a junction on the left before taking the second junction, bearing left from a hairpin bend (GR.213248). After a few yards the bridleway drops to the right, leaving the forest road, and is joined by a footpath at a blue guide post. There is an awkward approach over some large boulders to ford the beck on the left. Across the beck the bridleway continues to descend, and cuts diagonally across another forest

road, leaving the plantation forest to enter a broadleaved wood.

Take care here, there is a steep drop to the right into Comb Beck, and after 100 yards there is a stretch of slippery bedrock. *Comb Beck has a waterfall and dams which once powered the local lead and zinc mining industry. As the track levels out, look for a metal gate on the left which blocks an old mine entrance, and below that the faint line of a narrow gauge track that used to contour round the hillside above the bridleway.*

Ride on down the track to leave the wood by a gate (GR.220251) beyond which the surface is bedrock for 90 yards (80m) before dropping sharply to the road leading to Thornthwaite. Bear left at each of three minor junctions before bearing left again on to the road near Jenkin Hill Farm. Take the next left towards Beckstones Farm. *The white rock on the hillside ahead is known as th Bishop of Barf, and is traditionall painted by the landlord of the Swa Hotel.* **Your route rejoins the mai road opposite the hotel. Follow thi road past Woodend to just before i joins the A66, where you bear lef on to a disused section of the ol road (11.4 miles: 18.3 km) and rid on to Beck Wythop.** *There are fin views across the broad expanse o Bassenthwaite (formerly known a Broadwater) to the fells of Binsey (146 ft: 447m) and the Skiddaw massif, wit Latrigg (1180 ft: 360m) poised abov Keswick to the south-east.*

Keep the houses of Beck Wythop o the right and join a bridleway whic starts at the edge of the wood ahea and ascends through Wythop Wood to cross diagonally over a wide fores road; *it continues to climb in varyin degrees of steepness and in places ha been cut through the underlying Skiddaw slate, the oldest rocks in the Lake Distric*

Leave the wood by a gate at the top GR.207291) and go straight ahead to the next gate; then bear right along the track to a third gate and he bridleway junction beneath thwaite Side (GR.205291). *To the eft is a shorter route direct to Old Scales.* **Go through the gate and head owards the cleft of a small disused quarry; the grassy track steepens to climb past the quarry on the left and he impressive situation of Lothwaite Side on the right.**

At the top, go through another gate o follow the track down into Chapel Wood. *As you enter the predominantly oak wood, note the number of multi-stemmed trees, the result of coppicing many years ago.* **As the track levels out turn left on to another bridleway eading down to a gate. Go through this and three more gates to reach the tarmac road. Turn right.**

Bear left at the next road junction, at Eskin (GR.185291) (14.5 miles: 23.3 km), and ride for ½ mile (800m) to the road junction above Wythop Mill (GR.177284), which has a working watermill and cafe. Turn left and after 200 yards (180m) bear left on to Green Lonning, a bridleway which leads on to Highside Farm. *From the high point on the track there are views over Cockermouth to the Solway Firth and Scotland, with Criffel in the distance.*

Follow this little winding road for 1½ miles (2.4 km), passing High Side and Jenkin. Turn right at the T-junction (17.6 miles: 28.3 km) and left at the next junction on to Hundith Hill Road.

Follow this road to a crossroads, by the oak trees on the horizon, to cross the B5292. ***CARE here, this is a fast, straight road and traffic from the right comes over a blind brow.***

Take the first left turn back to Stanger and your transport, enjoying the magnificent view of the Lorton Vale.

LOWESWATER TO LORTON

Trail 2

A 13 MILE (21 KM) CIRCULAR TRAIL (ANTI-CLOCKWISE)

Ordnance Survey Map:
Outdoor Leisure 4 - The English Lakes North Western Area (1:25,000).

Route:
Waterend/Loweswater village/ Lanthwaite Green/Hopebeck/Lorton/ Mosser Mains
1015 feet (310m) of ascent.

Parking & Starting Point:
Parking is available in a lay-by near Waterend (GR.118224).

Trail Grade: 1

Terrain:
This is a low level valley ride with an exposed stretch across Mosser Fell; much of it is on little used minor roads, intriguing country lanes with many 16th and 17th Century buildings.

Route Description:

From the lay-by head north-west on the road towards Mockerkin. ***Take care on the narrow road - it can be busy during the summer.*** **After 350 yards (320m), turn left onto the bridleway signposted to Holme Wood which is opposite the Grange Hotel. Climb up to Hudson Place, bearing left at the bridleway junction. In front of the farm bear left through a wooden gate on to a cobbled lane leading down towards the lake.** *The next 1½ miles (2.5km) is shared wit Trail 3, which rides in the opposit direction.*

The gate ahead leads into Holm Wood. *This is a habitat of pie flycatchers, with grebes and over wintering wildfowl on the lake. Note hou woodland management has encourage a mixed range of species, age an density of cover throughout the wood The bridleway continues through th wood, fording Holme Beck and severa smaller streams, with clearings givin tantalising glimpses of Loweswater.*

Leaving the wood by a gate, follow the bridleway through Watergat Farm and onto the farm road t Maggie's Bridge (GR.134210). Rid uphill to turn right at the T-junction towards Loweswater village. Rid downhill again and take the first tur right to the Kirkstile Inn, which ha a tethering rail (2.7 miles: 4.3 km) Go past the Inn and straight ahea downhill, passing the bridleway o the right which is the link with Trai 5. Turn left to go past Muncaste House to the next crossroads an turn right here to cross Scalehil Bridge (GR.149214). As the roa starts to climb, turn right at th bridleway sign into the Nationa Trust Car Park.

Go through the gate at the back o the car park and along a well-use forest road. After 120 yards (110m the bridleway, less heavily used

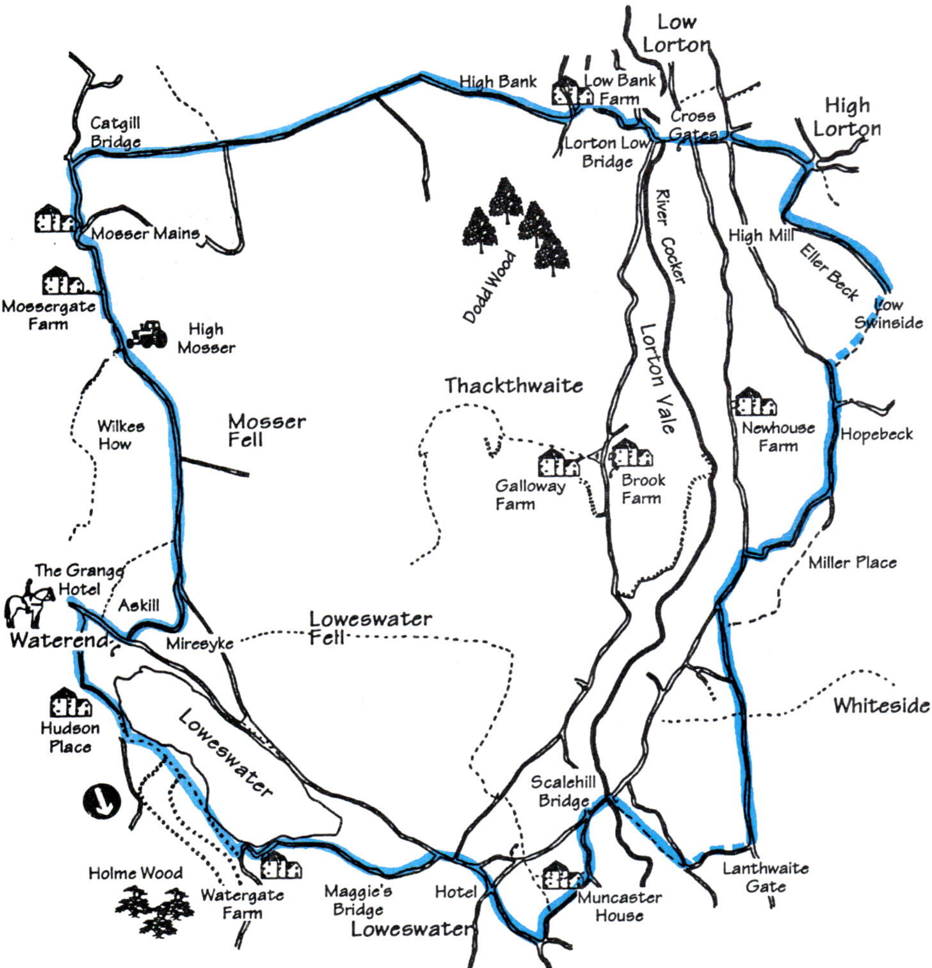

Low Lorton
High Bank
Low Bank Farm
Cross Gates
High Lorton
Catgill Bridge
Lorton Low Bridge
River Cocker
Mosser Maine
High Mill
Eller Beck
Dodd Wood
Mossergate Farm
Low Swinside
High Mosser
Lorton Vale
Thackthwaite
Mosser Fell
Wilkes How
Newhouse Farm
Hopebeck
Galloway Farm
Brook Farm
Miller Place
The Grange Hotel
Askill
Loweswater Fell
Waterend
Miresyke
Whiteside
Hudson Place
Loweswater
Scalehill Bridge
Holme Wood
Watergate Farm
Maggie's Bridge
Hotel
Loweswater
Muncaster House
Lanthwaite Gate

Fell mare and foal

bears left to climb diagonally uphill, crossing a forest road and becoming steeper as it nears the top of the wood. Go through a small gate and follow a broken wall curving to the left before turning right, out of the woodland edge, to another gate and a walled track.

This short length of track gets overgrown, but there is a wide range of wild flowers to identify. You will pass two pairs of gates which are used for sorting sheep when they are brought down from the fell. **Follow the walled track to a small gate and the Buttermere road, B5289, at Lanthwaite Gate (GR.158212).**

Pause here to admire the massive fells of Whiteside (2320 feet: 707m) and Grassmoor (2795 feet: 852 m), with the inviting cleft of Gasgale Gill betwee them carrying the Liza Beck fror Coledale Hause. To the right i Crummock Water, at the foot o Mellbreak (1680 feet: 512m), with Re Pike (2475 feet: 755m) and th Buttermere Fells beyond.

Turn left at the road and ride alon it for 1¼ miles (2 km). ***The bridlewa is obstructed at Miller Place, and s you have to stay on the road.*** **Leav the B5289 at the first right turn (5. miles: 9.3 km) and ride pas Hopebeck on the minor road. Wher the road bears left, take th bridleway to the right towards Lo Swinside (GR.166247).**

Head across the middle of the firs meadow and through a gate, in lin with High Swinside seen over th

trees, staying on this line across the next meadow to another gate before dropping to cross Eller Beck, where the parish boundary wall crosses from one bank to the other. The bridleway then rises to another gate and then goes diagonally across the field into a walled track to Low Swinside. Turn left between the buildings to pick up a narrow lane which meanders down past High Mill to the road junction at Lorton (GR.161255).

Turn left to go past the school to Cross Gates (8.4 miles: 13.5 km). *This short length of road is the link with Trail 1 which rides in the opposite direction.* **Follow the sign ahead to Low Lorton, taking care at the Junction with the B5289, crossing over to turn immediately left to Lorton Low Bridge.**

Lorton Hall is just to the right, behind the formal wall. Parts of the Hall date back to the 10th Century: King Malcolm III and Queen Margaret stayed here in about 1080 during a tour of his kingdom, at a time when Cumbria was part of Scotland. The Hall has two priest holes and a pele-tower; it is said to be haunted by the ghost of a woman carrying a lighted candle. You will find it open to the public by appointment only, telephone 01900 85252.

As you approach the bridge the old Lorton Mill is on the left. **Over the bridge bear right and then first left, to climb by a wood on hairpin bends past Low Bank and High Bank Farms.** *This road rises to 660 feet (200m) and is exposed to the weather, but on a clear day it provides wonderful views across northern Cumbria to the Solway and the Galloway coast beyond.*

Continue along this road for 1¾ miles (2.8 km), eventually dropping to cross Catgill Bridge (GR.118256) and turn left at the next T-junction, over Mosser Beck Bridge to Mosser Mains (11.5 miles: 18.5 km). *At the beck there is a ford to the left where you can water the horses.*

In Mosser Mains turn sharp right and then, curving left, follow an unfenced road, ignoring a steep climb to the right. *This is a County road but it is seldom used, being classed as 'unsuitable for motors'.* **The road is fenced again as it bears right uphill, passing the farms of Mossergate and High Mosser and opening out to moorland as it crests the brow.** *Here the Buttermere Fells appear on the horizon, Mellbreak, Red Pike and High Stile being the most prominent.*

After passing an old quarry track on the left, marking the highest point on this trail at 820 feet (250m), gradually descend for ½ mile (800m) to a signposted bridleway on the right. *This descent opens up incredible views of Loweswater, and Holme Wood nestling under Blake Fell (1880 feet: 573m).* **Go through the gate and head for some mature oak and sycamore trees with Loweswater lying beyond. Ride down through two more gates to a footpath crossing between Askill and Miresyke. Stay on the bridleway still riding downhill and going through two more gates to join the road opposite your starting point.**

ABOVE LOWESWATER

Trail 3

A 6 MILE (9 KM) CIRCULAR TRAIL (ANTI-CLOCKWISE)

Ordnance Survey Map:
Outdoor Leisure 4 - The English Lakes North Western Area (1:25,000)

Route:
Mockerkin How/Burnbank Fell/ Highnook Beck/Maggie's Bridge/ Watergate Farm/Hudson Place/Iredale Place.
590 feet (180m) of ascent.

Parking & Starting Point:
There is parking available for a few vehicles on a hard verge at the start of the bridleway (GR.105226), near Fangs Brow.

Trail Grade: 2

Terrain:
This is a delightful ride and easy going for most of the way. ***In one or two places care is needed on a narrow track along the contour across a steep slope. There would be no access to emergency vehicles between Holme Beck (GR.118212) and Carling Knott (GR.124205).***

Of Interest:
At Fangs Brow, just near the start of the trail, is St Ninian's Well where tradition says that towards the end of the 4th Century AD, Ninian, 'the Apostle of the Picts', one of the early Celtic Saints, preached to, and baptised, his converts.

Route Description:

Take the track across the fell whic is shown on the bridleway sign as 'corpse road'. Follow it down to junction where you take the rou signed 'Loweswater via High Nook going up the hill with the wall o your left. *Where the track bears rig (GR.111220) you have the first view Loweswater, with Crummock Wate beyond. Loweswater is different i character from any of the other lake having a more gentle appearance.* **G through the next gate (GR.113217 where the track divides: take th left hand fork, a wide track goin down the hill and soon running alon the contour across a steep rock slope.**

The bridleway crosses Holme Bec (1.3 miles: 2.1km) on a wide timbe bridge without parapets, and you rid up the hill, past the water intake towards Holme Wood. Continu beside the wood, with the outcrop of Carling Knott (1780 feet: 543m rising steeply to the right.

At the end of the wood the bridlewa turns into the little valley o Highnook Beck, and becomes ver narrow over a short stretch wher you have to be careful. Thereafter i goes down to the valley bottom t ford the beck (GR.124201 continuing down to the farm at Hig Nook where you ride through th farmyard and out onto the farm roa

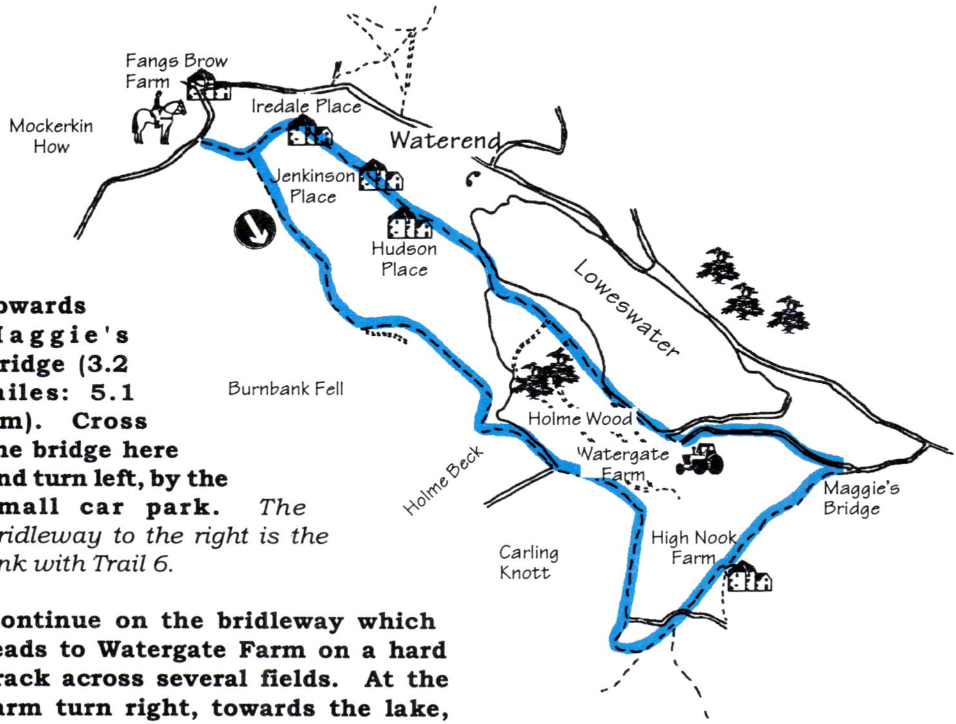

towards Maggie's Bridge (3.2 miles: 5.1 km). Cross the bridge here and turn left, by the small car park. *The bridleway to the right is the link with Trail 6.*

Continue on the bridleway which leads to Watergate Farm on a hard track across several fields. At the farm turn right, towards the lake, and ride into Holme Wood. *Trail 2 follows this part of the route riding in the opposite direction.*

Bear left at the fork (GR.123214), remaining on the main track. *Holme wood is ancient woodland, with some fine mature trees on its lower slopes.*

Leaving the wood the bridleway crosses two fields and then joins a narrow track leading up to Hudson Place. Go through the farm gate, turn sharp right and ride a few yards down the road to a field gate on the left signposted 'Public bridleway Fangs Brow'. Keep the garden wall on your left, go through the next field gate, turn sharp right and continue up the field with the old hedge on your right; then straight across an open field and half-left across the next field, leading onto a hard track at Jenkinson Place.

Leave this farm on the right and ride on along the road. In 50 yards (45m) the farm road bears right and your route along the bridleway rises to the left on a narrow track. Ride past Iredale Place, turn left and ride up the fell with a wall on your left. The next gate leads to your original route, where you turn right and return to your starting point.

BED & BREAKFAST FOR HORSES

AN ESSENTIAL DIRECTORY WHEN PLANNING A RIDING HOLIDAY

£4.95 (inc. p&p)

from:

BHS Book and Gift Shop

Stoneleigh Park, Kenilworth, Warwickshire CV8 2LR

Registered Charity No 210504

BRAITHWAITE TO LOWESWATER

Trail 4

\ 19 MILE (30KM) LINEAR ROUTE SOUTH THEN NORTH-WEST)

)rdnance Survey Map:
)utdoor Leisure 4 - The English Lakes Iorth Western Area (1:25,000)

Route:
3raithwaite/Stair/Swinside/Manesty/ 3range/CastleCrag/Little 3atesgarthdale/Honister Hause/ 3atesgarth/Peggy's Bridge/Burtness Vood/Buttermere/Rannerdale/ ,anthwaite Gate/Scalehill Bridge/ ,oweswater.
2590 feet (790m) of ascent and 'ording several small streams.

'arking & Starting Point:
\lthough there is limited kerbside)arking in the village at Braithwaite,)arking is recommended on a side road unning parallel to the A66 at the north :nd of the village (GR.233242). Iorsebox parking elsewhere on the rail is discouraged because parking)laces are few and the roads are very ıarrow and well used by traffic. ***Remember to ask someone to meet you at the other end of your ride.***

'rail Grade: **2**

'errain:
'he bridleways are generally easy going :xcept for several rocky stretches in 3orrowdale. The roads may be heavily ısed at times during the tourist season.

Route Description:

From your parking place ride into Braithwaite and take the road signposted Newlands and Buttermere, and then, round a corner by the village shop, follow the road to Newlands. *CARE: it is narrow through the village.* After passing the shop ride for 100 yards and on the right is the stone-pillared entrance to Braithwaite Lodge (GR.232235), with a bridleway sign. Follow the wide roadway of hard gravel as it leads uphill through pleasant parkland. *There is a fine view looking back over Braithwaite to the Skiddaw range of fells to the north-east.*

At Braithwaite Lodge the bridleway swings right in front of the Lodge, past the adjoining building with a shed in front of it, then left through a waymarked gate to another gate across the yard. The route continues, on grass, up the right-hand side of the field beside a wire fence to a wicket gate at the top. *From this gate, looking back, Bassenthwaite Lake is in the distance.* **Through the gate the path swings left towards a plantation which is mainly conifers with a few silver birch. This path is quite steep and rough with loose stones. At the top of the rise (GR.233231) the bridleway is signposted to Newlands.**

Follow this track along the edge of the plantation. The track is mainly

earth, not very wide and there is a steep, but not very long slope down to the plantation fence on the left. About 200 yards (180m) from the finger post the path crosses a small outcrop of rock which may be awkward: you are recommended to drop down to the fence here and ride along beside it to rejoin the track when it joins the fence further along.

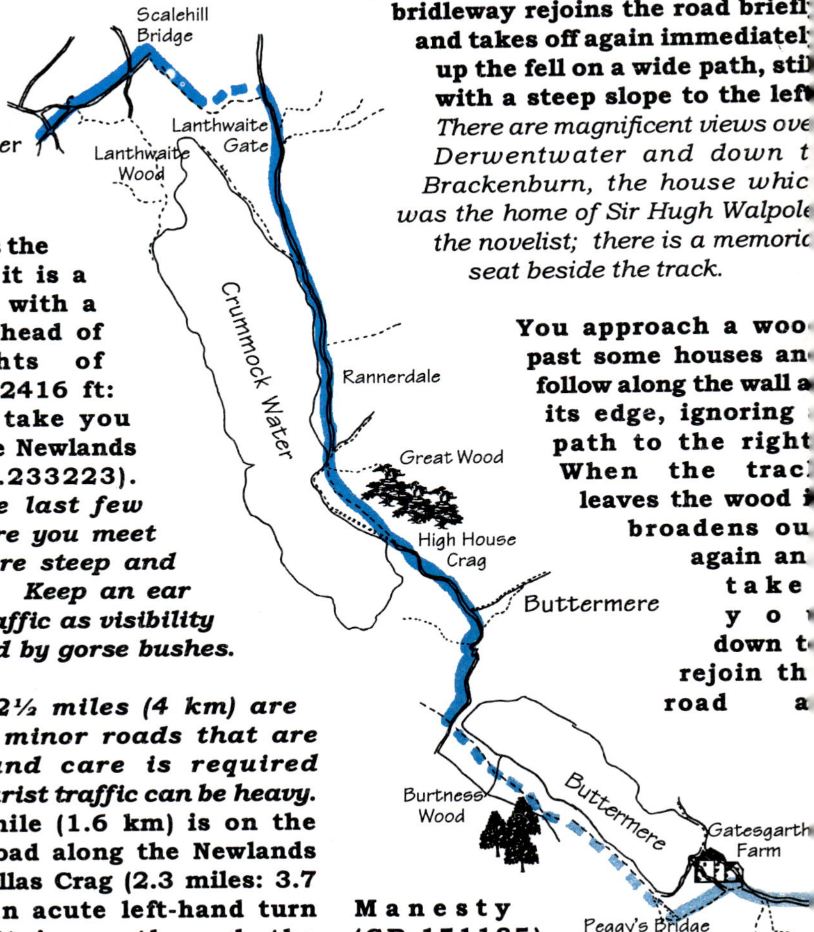

Where the track leaves the plantation it is a wide path, with a fine view ahead of the heights of Robinson (2416 ft: 737m), to take you down to the Newlands road (GR.233223). ***CARE: the last few yards before you meet the road are steep and over shale. Keep an ear open for traffic as visibility is restricted by gorse bushes.***

The next 2½ miles (4 km) are ridden on minor roads that are narrow, and care is required because tourist traffic can be heavy. **The first mile (1.6 km) is on the unfenced road along the Newlands valley; at Ellas Crag (2.3 miles: 3.7 km) take an acute left-hand turn down to Stair; go through the hamlet, across Newlands Beck and turn left to ride up to Swinside. Keep the wood on your left and take the road which swings right. At Hawes End, as the road starts to climb follow the sign on the right whic shows a bridleway. At first this run parallel to the road, but soon rise above it.**

The bridleway meanders southward along the lower reaches of Cat Bell (1480 ft: 451m). *The parallel pat along the ridge above is a popula afternoon walk from Keswick.* **Th bridleway rejoins the road briefl and takes off again immediatel up the fell on a wide path, stil with a steep slope to the lef** *There are magnificent views ove Derwentwater and down t Brackenburn, the house whic was the home of Sir Hugh Walpol the novelist; there is a memori seat beside the track.*

You approach a woo past some houses an follow along the wall a its edge, ignoring path to the right When the trac leaves the wood broadens ou again an take yo down t rejoin th road a Manesty (GR.151185) (5.5 miles: 8.8 km). Ride for ½ mile (800m) southwards past the Borrowdale

ates Hotel into
range-in-
orrowdale.

ust before
he cafe in
range, turn
ight on to a
ignposted
ridleway which is a
etalled road; you
ay meet traffic
long here.

ust beyond
he gate of
ollows Farm
he metalled
oad swings
ight whilst the
ridleway swings
eft along a broad
rack heading for a
ap in a wall and
ontinuing with a wall
n the left and Dalt
Vood on the right.
ollow this to meet
he river. After
ording two small
treams follow the
ignposted
ridleway as it goes
p the hill to the
ight, following the
ank of the second
tream with the wall of a
onifer plantation on the left.

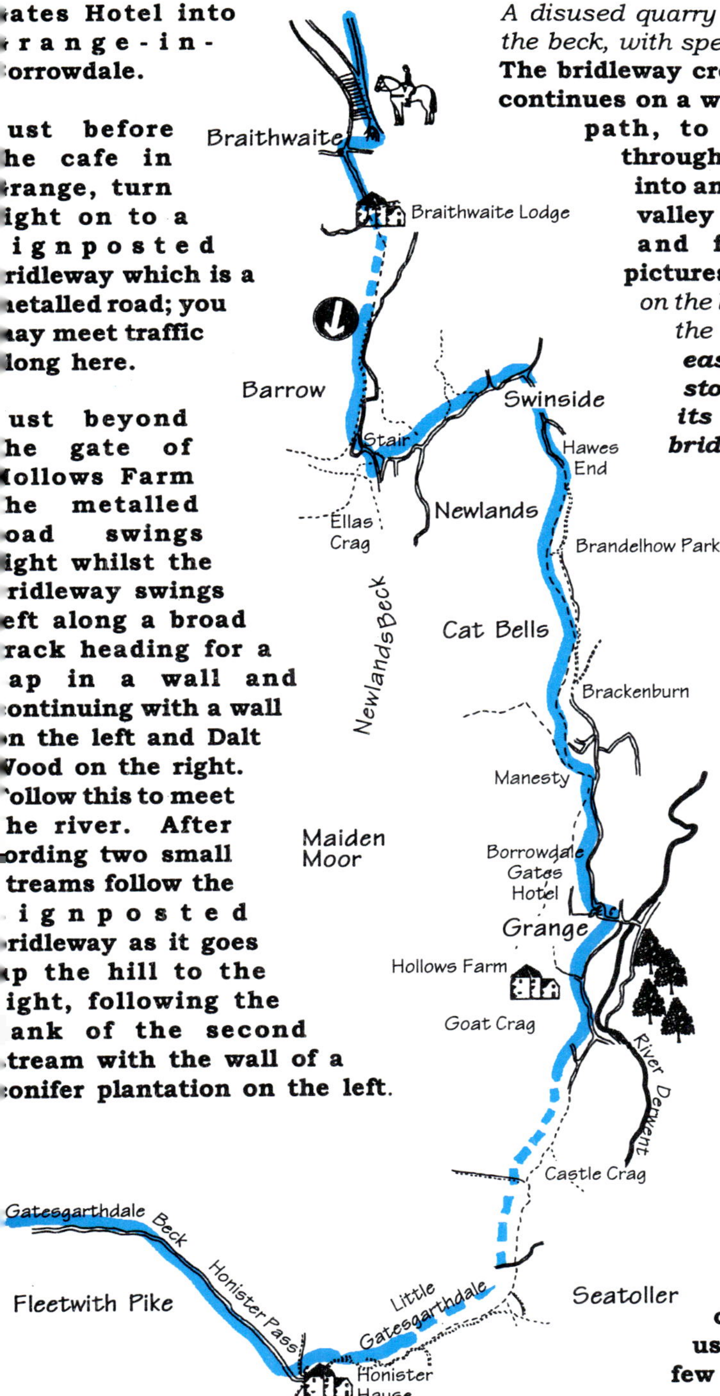

A disused quarry can be seen across the beck, with spectacular slate walls. **The bridleway crosses the beck and continues on a wide, but very stony path, to leave the wood through a gate, continuing into an impressive narrow valley whose steep sides and fallen rocks are picturesque.** *Castle Crag is on the left and Goat Crag on the right.* ***The track is easy to follow but very stony and uneven. At its highest point the bridleway opens out on to the fell, with Rosthwaite in view to the left.***

The best course now is to ignore the signpost ahead and continue to the right on the broad track, crossing two small becks; then leave the track and drop down the hill to the left, making for the footbridge. This bridge is suitable for a horse to be led across and it leads to another smaller bridge. Do not cross this bridge but use the ford which is few yards upstream.

Early tourist at Honister Pass

Beyond these bridges is a bridlegate, and then the track narrows, swinging to the right. ***Ignore the track leading to another gate on a wider track.*** **At the top of the next rise the path widens again, with grass underfoot, and leads on to another bridlegate before dropping down to another bridge with a ford a few yards downstream. Continue along the track as it follows a wall on the left to come to a bridge with a bridlegate at each end.**

At the end of a wall there are two gates (8.6 miles: 13.8 km): take the bridlegate on the right and ride straight on down the track when you will quickly reach the old Honister toll road. This is now a broad track of loose stones but a traffic-free alternative to the motor road. Turn right (GR.241141). It is possible to follow the toll road all the way to Honister Hause, most of the way i runs a short distance north of th motor road, then joins it briefly an further along crosses it, to take short loop to the south. You have t rejoin the road just before reachin the Hause (9.8 miles: 15.8 km).

The buildings on the left at Honist Hause were used for processing the sla from three local quarries. These quarrie were in production from 1643 unt recently and their slate was widely use indeed it was used on the roofs of th Houses of Parliament. The building now house a Youth Hostel.

From Honister Hause stay on th road because the bridleway to th south of Fleetwith Pike is much to rocky for pleasant riding. ***It is 2 miles (4 km) to Gatesgarth Farn through dramatic scenery dow Gatesgarthdale and the road ma***

be busy with tourist traffic. The first part you must ride on the tarmac, and this includes two places where the gradient is very steep, but later the road is unfenced and you may be able to ride on the turf for part of the way. *There are glorious views down the valley as you approach the head of Buttermere, with High Crag (2440 ft: 744m), High Stile (2646 ft: 807m) and Red Pike (2480 ft: 756m) ranged along the lake on the left-hand side.*

Turn left at Gatesgarth Farm (GR.194150) (12.6 miles: 19.6km) on to the bridleway which is signposted for Buttermere and Ennerdale. Follow the track across a stretch of low-lying ground and, after the bridge across the Warnscale Beck, turn right at the bridleway junction on to a good gravel track along the contour. *The bridleway to the left, signposted for Ennerdale via Scarth Gap, is too rugged for pleasure riding.* **After crossing Comb Beck, bear left to go up the fell;** *the right-hand path is a footpath along the lake shore.*

Go through the gate into Burtness Wood. *This is mixed woodland with some oak trees.* **You will come to a Y-junction, where your route follows the left fork. There is a short rocky stretch, which can be avoided by going a few yards downhill through the bracken. At the Y-junction near the end of the wood (GR.173163) the main path leads down towards the lake, where you cross the Buttermere Dubs and ride across another area of low-lying ground to Buttermere village (14.4 miles: 23.2 km).** *This area of silt separates Buttermere and Crummock Water.*

In the village, turn left past the Fish Hotel on the B5289. ***CARE: there is a nasty blind corner before the road rises north-westwards out of the village.*** **After ¼ mile (400m) take a rough track on the right, beside a beech wood. This will avoid a short length of the road. When you return to the road ride for 300 yards (270m) and bear right on a signposted bridleway, and follow a good turf track through the bracken. In ½ mile you will rejoin the road.**

All along here you have wonderful views across Crummock Water to the Mellbreak range beyond.

Your route now follows the road for ¾ mile (1.2 km) before the wall ends and you can then ride much of the way along the verge side. *The fell which looms above the crags to the right is Grassmoor (2793 ft: 852m).*

Turn left on to the bridleway (GR.158212) (17.6 miles: 28.2 km), just past Lanthwaite Gate. *This bridleway is also on Trail 2 and is ridden in the opposite direction.* **Ride along a walled track into Lanthwaite Wood, across a forest road, to join the track which leads down to Scalehill Bridge. Turn left here and ride down to Loweswater and the end of your ride.** ***Remember to ask someone to meet you here!***

COLEDALE

Trail 5

A 7½ MILE (12 KM) CIRCULAR TRAIL (ANTI-CLOCKWISE)

Ordnance Survey Map:
Outdoor Leisure 4 - The English Lakes North Western Area (1:25,000)

Route:
Braithwaite/Coledale/Force Crag Mine/High Moss/Stoneycroft Gill/ Braithwaite Lodge.
1450 feet (440m) of ascent.

Parking & Starting Point:
Although there is limited kerbside parking in Braithwaite village, you will find good parking on a side road that runs parallel to the A66 at the north end of the village (GR.233242).

Trail Grade: 2

Terrain:
This ride is easy going for most of the way, on old mine roads or on turf on the open fell. The patch of featureless hillside up Birkthwaite Beck is best avoided in mist. This ride is only available by kind permission of the National Trust over whose property most of the trail runs. You are not on public bridleways so please take extra care to leave the way as you find it.

Route Description:

Leave Braithwaite village on the Whinlatter road, past the Royal Oak public house. *The roads through the village are very narrow with blind corners, so take great care.* Turn left into a small car park near the top of the hill, then left again to a gate which leads on to the Coledale mine road, signposted 'Footpath to Force Crag and Coledale'. *The road is of vehicle width with a good surface, running along the contour with the bracken-covered fell rising steeply to the right towards Sleet How and Grisedale Pike (2593 feet: 791m) and falling away to the left, down to Coledale Beck.*

The road was built to serve the Force Crag mine which lies two miles up the Coledale valley. Force Crag is a 500 ft (160m) cliff brooding over the head of the valley, and the mine is at the cliff foot. Its deposits were known about in the 16th Century and prospected in 1755, but they were first worked only in 1841. Since then the mine has had a varied history of both success and failure, and eventually closed only very recently. The ores produced have been principally lead, barytes and zinc; small quantities of silver were found in the lead.

During its first 25 years lead was the main attraction and 570 tons was produced during that period. It was carried by horse and cart to Braithwaite and on to Maryport. From 1867 onwards the emphasis changed to barytes, of which more than 5000 tons was produced during the next 14 years. It was carried down from the higher levels by pack pony and then transported to Braithwaite, hauled by horses on a tramway which ran just below the mine road. The mine closed in 1881 when it

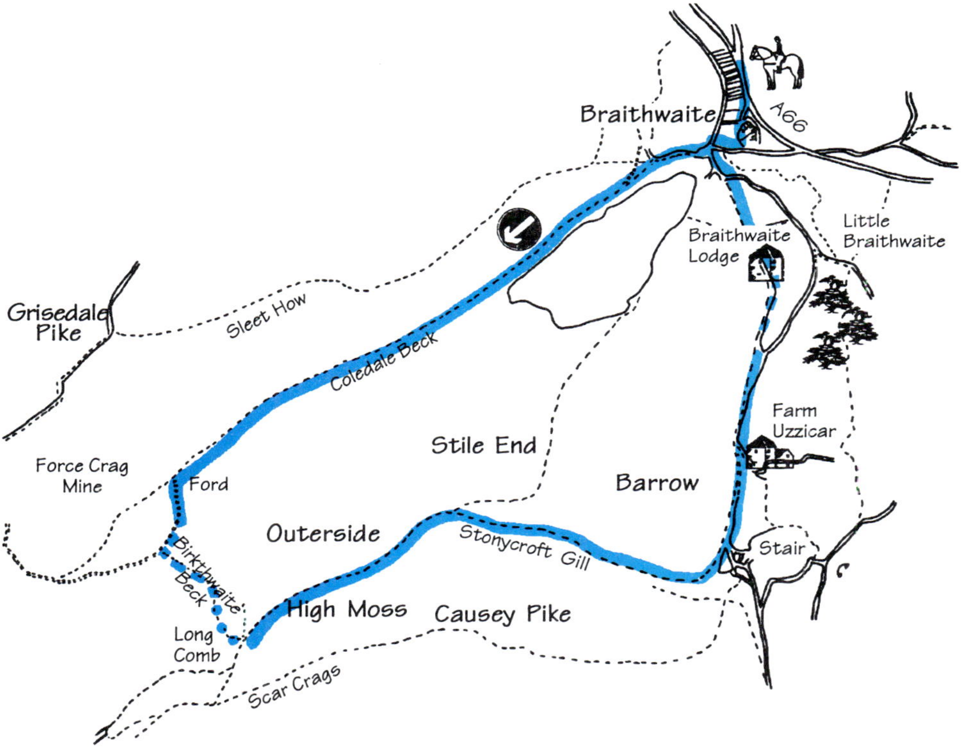

became unprofitable as the price of barytes fell.

After the mine had lain idle for 25 years production restarted in 1906, concentrating on zinc, and this phase lasted until 1922 when once again the mine became unprofitable and had to close. For a few years in the early thirties barytes was mined successfully, and again for two brief periods later; and for five years from 1967 lead and zinc were produced. But modern economic conditions eventually caused the closure of the last working mine in the Lake District. During its working life of 152 years it produced some 60,000 tons of barytes, 1248 tons of zinc and 624 tons of lead, this last containing many ounces of silver.

Just as the mine buildings first come into view, your route leaves the mine road (GR.202218) (2.7 miles: 4.3 km) and drops down to the ford over the Coledale Beck, which can be crossed without difficulty unless the beck is in spate. A rough stony track leads straight up the hill, but most of the way you can ride on the turf alongside. Just before the track bears right there is a cairn which marks the point where you leave it to continue steeply uphill. This track is not easily seen on the ground, but it is just discernible, going straight up the hill towards the col and then taking two S-bends; on the third bend you cross the Birkthwaite Beck, where some care is needed. The track zigzags up the

hill, and at the second cairn you turn sharp left and leave the track, to ride on upwards; here there is no path visible, but the exact route is not critical so long as you keep going uphill.

After a short distance you join a wide track, another old mine road which was built to serve a cobalt mine near Scar Crag, a short distance further up; but you turn left to start riding downhill across High Moss. *As you descend, the fell on your left is Outerside (1862 ft: 568m), and on the right an unusual view of Causey Pike (2089 ft: 637m). Ahead are Stile End (1466 ft: 447m) on the left and Barrow (1492 ft: 455m).*

The route continues down the mine road beside Stoneycroft Gill. ***Most of the way it is a good track, but there are two places where care is needed. The first is on a 100 yard length of loose rock near the top of the gill, and then just above the spoil heaps near the Newlands road where the track crosses rock outcrops.***

You join the Newlands road (GR.232217) (5.2 miles: 8.4 km), and turn left and ride along the road for 550 yards (500m). *The massive bank of scree on the left, 400 feet (120m) high is constantly on the move, causing Barrow to be known locally as 'the whispering mountain'.*

Immediately after the scree you join a signposted bridleway on the left which leaves the road by a narrow path between thick gorse bushes becoming wider up the fell to follow the top fence of the wood. *Trail 4 follows this bridleway ridden in the opposite direction.* **Continue on the bridleway as it leads past Braithwaite Lodge Farm, down the farm road and back into Braithwaite village and your starting point.**

ENNERDALE TO LOWESWATER

Trail 6

A 6 MILE (9 KM) LINEAR ROUTE (EAST THEN NORTH)

Ordnance Survey Map:
Outdoor Leisure 4 - The English Lakes North Western Area (1:25,000)

Route:
Ennerdale (Whins)/Floutern Tarn/ Mosedale/ Flass Wood/ Loweswater
720 feet (220m) of ascent.

Parking & Starting Point:
Parking is available 300 yards (270m) south-east of Whins Farm (GR.101166). This is at the end of the southern leg of the bridleway. ***Remember to ask someone to meet you at the end of your ride!***

Trail Grade: **2**

Terrain:
This is a moorland ride in good condition except for a nasty boggy patch at the head of Mosedale. ***The middle part, from Floutern Cop to the Mosedale Beck crossing, would be inaccessible to emergency vehicles.***

Route Description:

From your parking place take the bridleway which leads up the hill on a hard, narrow track between hedges. *As you gain height there are fine views of Ennerdale Water to the south, with Crag Fell (1715 ft: 523m) beyond.* **Go through the gate on to the open fell (GR.105169), where you can see the track rising steeply at first and then more steadily along the northern side of Gill Beck, with the slopes of Banna Fell (1350 ft: 411m), rising to the left.** ***CARE: where the gradient eases out (GR.117171) there is a short boggy patch.***

For the next stage the track is rather less easily seen. Where the track divides, at a sign asking mountain bikers to dismount, the right fork is the bridleway which you follow.

The bridleway drops towards the wall on the right, and you go through the gate, and then another gate, just cutting off the corner of the enclosure. Beyond the second gate there is a Y-junction, and your route follows the left fork. *The right fork is the bridleway to Buttermere, which is inaccessible across the head of Mosedale because the going is too soft in a large boggy area.*

As the bridleway turns northwards (GR.138175) the going becomes much more boggy, and could give problems particularly in wet weather. *The National Park Authority plan to try and consolidate the surface, but it will always be a boggy area. The worst of it could be avoided by riding along a higher contour on the left, but there is thick bracken on Hen Comb and no track through it.*

Cross Mosedale Beck by a good ford running beside a footbridge

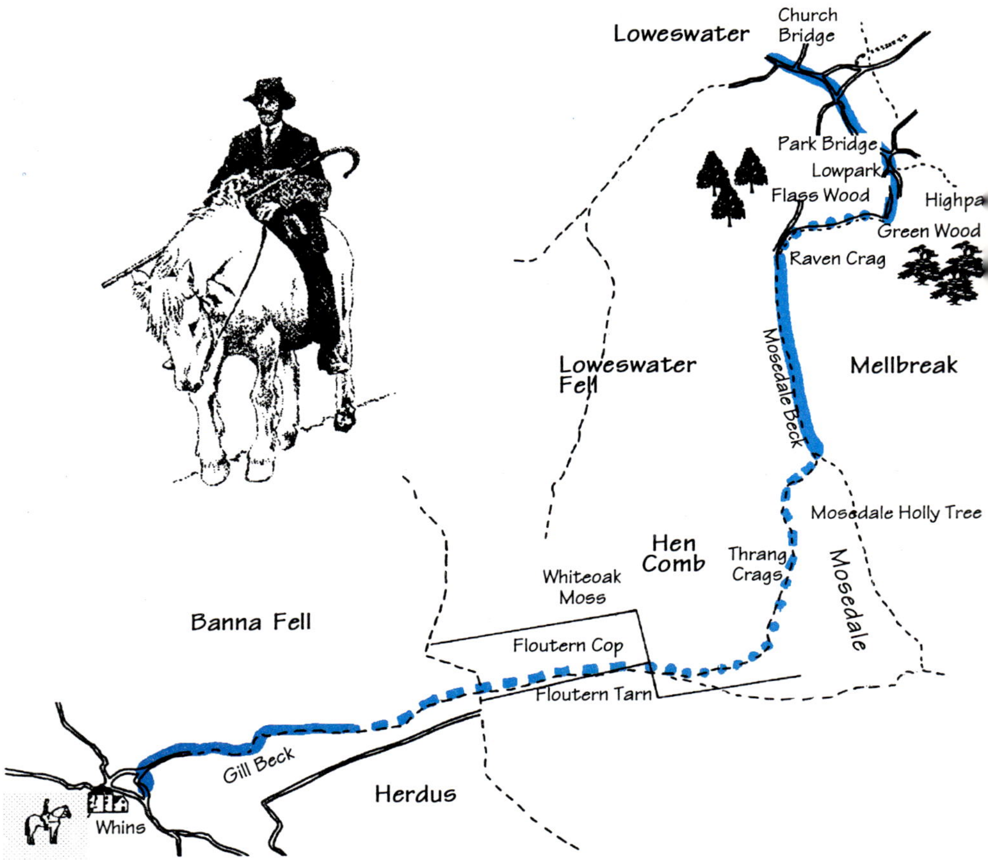

(GR.139181) (3.1 miles: 5 km). The bridleway continues on a good turf track among the bracken, swinging right and then left, along the east side of Mosedale with the mass of Mellbreak (1670 feet: 509m) rising steeply to the right.

At the Y-junction (GR.138199) take the right fork, going above a belt of trees and swinging to the right round the northern end of the Mellbreak Ridge below Raven Crag,. You go into Flass Wood, turn left and ride past Lowpark Farm to join a minor road and cross Park Bridge. *There are impressive views of Crummock Water to the right.* **Turn left over the bridge. The short length of road to Loweswater and the end of your trail, is shared with Trail 2 which is ridden in the opposite direction.**

Remember to arrange for someone to meet you here at the end of your ride.

Disclaimer

Whilst all due care was taken in the preparation of the maps featured in this book, neither the British Horse Society nor their agents or servants accept any responsibility for any inaccuracies which may occur. It should be borne in mind that landmarks and conditions change and it is assumed that the user has a Pathfinder or Landranger Ordnance Survey map and a compass.

The Country Code should be observed by every rider, with great care being taken to keep to the line of the Public Rights of Way particularly when crossing farmland.

Trail 7

ROWRAH TO EGREMONT

AN 18 MILE (29 KM) CIRCULAR TRAIL (CLOCKWISE)

Ordnance Survey Maps:
Outdoor Leisure 4 - The English Lakes North Western Area (1:25,000)
Outdoor Leisure 6 - The English Lakes South Western Area (1:25,000)
Pathfinder 593 (1:25,000)

Route:
Rowrah/Winder/Cleator Moor/ Nannycatch Road/Uldale/Wilton/ Egremont/Parkside/Winder Brow.
1250 feet (380m) of ascent.

Parking & Starting Point:
Parking is available in the cycleway car park at the west end of Rowrah village (GR.055184). Leave the A5086 on a narrow road to the south signposted 'Rowrah Hall'. Cross two bridges and then turn sharp left to go down the hill to the car park.

Trail Grade: **2**

Terrain:
This trail is partly on the cycleway, and partly on 5½ miles (9 km) of little-used minor roads. The rest is on bridleways which are easy going except for a short steep climb above Uldale. The cycleway goes through part of the former industrial landscape of West Cumbria, but the route is attractive in its own way.

Route Description:

From the car park, ride south westwards along the cycleway, goin away from Rowrah village. Jus before the first bridge, bear left t leave the cycleway: ride up the gras slope to a 'horsebox'*, *not up th tarmac path which leads to chicane.*

**The 'horsebox' consists of two sleepe barriers which a horse can step ove quite easily but which prevents acces to the route by motor-cycles.*

You will come out on to a road wher you turn left and then almos immediately right in order to avoi the private road to the quarry. Rid through the little hamlet of Winde continue down the hill, turn left an then right to rejoin the quarry road which is a public road at this point

In a short distance the road to th quarry turns left (GR.052174) an your route continues ahead on a unmetalled track, to circle th quarry which is on the left.

Eskett Quarry produces about 400,00 tons per year of carboniferous limeston products which are used mainly in th local construction industry, a larg proportion going to Sellafield. Blastin takes place about once a week; the roc is then crushed and screened to produc a range of sizes from 9" down to a ver fine dust. The 9" stone is much used b the Environment Agency for gabion construction; other grades are used as filter media in drainage, as concrete aggregate, and in the manufacture of bricks and blocks. The fine dust is spread on the fields as agricultural lime.

NOTE: Blasting Times are posted on a red notice board as being 10.00-10.30; 1.00-1.30; 3.30-4.00. If blasting is taking place at any other time, sentries are posted and a siren is sounded.

Moving away from the quarry the track bears right to lead down the hill to a T-junction, where you turn right on to a minor road (1.9 miles: 3 km).

The next two miles (3.2 km) are on a narrow but little-used lane along the valley of the River Ehen, which is on your left. *The river here forms the boundary of the National Park, and in this valley you are in a narrow strip of land between the harsh industrial landscape of West Cumbria and the western fringes of the Lake District.*

The lane leads to the outskirts of Cleator Moor, where you join the A5086 and turn left. Turn left again after 250 yards (225m) by a pub called Little's Arms (4 miles: 6.4 km) on to a road signposted Ennerdale Bridge to ride down Wath Brow and across the river. Ride for 200 yards (180m) beyond the bridge and turn right to go up Nannycatch Road. The road, which is unsigned, has a small sub-station on the corner.

The road ends beside a plantation and your route continues on a bridleway, an unmetalled track along the field wall. After about ¼ mile (400m) the wall swings away uphill to the left but your route follows the bridleway as it bears right and continues along the contour on Flat Fell, in pleasant moorland country. *The wooded fell on the right is called Dent (1155 ft: 352m).*

At Nannycatch Gate (GR.055130) (6.1 miles: 9.8 km) the track bears away to the left, but your route on the bridleway is through the gate on the right, when it turns right, between the beck and an outcrop of rock, into a narrow valley with bracken-covered fells rising on either side. The going is good, over repeated little fords as the track crosses and re-crosses the beck.

NOTE: The next section of the route involves an awkward steep climb above Uldale Farm. If you wish to avoid this, turn left now to join the forest road sooner.

After the next gate, bear left at the Y-junction, staying on the same side of the beck. Go through the field gate, bear right and ride along between the fence and the beck to Uldale Farm, where you turn left in to the yard. Turn left again in the yard and go through the left-hand of two gates on to a track leading up the fell. The line of the bridleway is impassable at a gully ahead just below the wood so leave the track, turn right and go through a gate at the foot of the slope into the next field.

Bear half-left up the hill and aim for the right-hand end of the wood to find a ridge which runs parallel to the fence a few yards above. At the end of the ridge there is a steep slope up to the gate; it is best to go about 10 yards beyond the gate, where

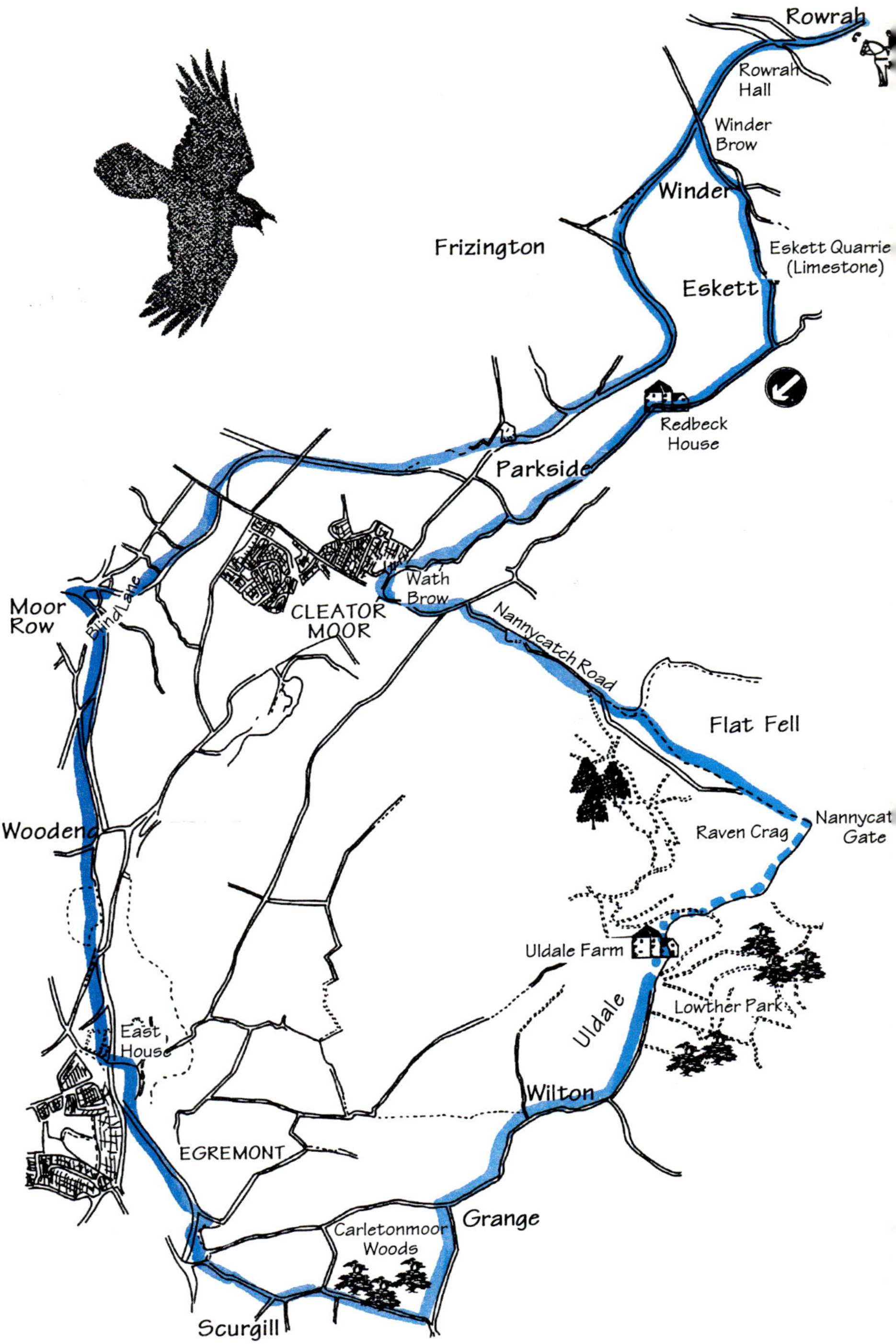
Rowrah
Rowrah Hall
Winder Brow
Winder
Frizington
Eskett Quarrie (Limestone)
Eskett
Redbeck House
Parkside
Wath Brow
CLEATOR MOOR
Moor Row
Blind Lane
Nannycatch Road
Flat Fell
Raven Crag
Nannycat Gate
Wooden
Uldale Farm
Lowther Park
Uldale
East House
Wilton
EGREMONT
Grange
Carletonmoor Woods
Scurgill

here is patch of level ground at the op. Here you rejoin the line of the bridleway. Access through the gate s awkward because there is little room to turn with the steep slope mmediately below.

The gate leads on to a forest road, where you turn right to ride down to the road above Wilton which the bridleway joins on a corner, and you urn right (7.8 miles: 12.6 km) Ride for a mile along this minor road, through the village of Wilton, and turn left at Grange (GR.033104), on to the road towards Haile. *You can ride straight ahead at this point which make your route ½ mile shorter, but it is not such pleasant riding.*

Take the first turn right and ride past Carletonmoor Woods to Scurgill.

On the right is the Florence Mine Heritage Centre which stands on the site of the last working iron ore mine in Europe. The ore, known as haemetite, is found in abundance in the limestone layers of West Cumbria. The red ore is the distinctive colour of the mine, its buildings, and the people who worked there nicknamed 'the Red Men of Cumbria'. Mining began in Roman times and expanded in the 1830s, helped by the advent of the railways. At its peak Florence Mine produced 4000 tons of haemetite each week. The ore was originally used for the production of pig iron, which was made into steel, but demand diminished with the arrival of new technologies. Most of the small amount of ore now produced is annealing ore, used to extract carbon from castings, and it is also used in the manufacture of pigments for paint and cosmetics.

Just past Florence Mine there is a small square sandstone house down the hill on the right (10.3 miles: 16.6 km) Take the path which leads northwards between this house and the by-pass. This path goes up the hill, parallel to the by-pass, then down again to cross the River Ehen over a good timber-decked bridge to the outskirts of Egremont. Bear left, then right, round the car park, and up to a T-junction where you turn right. Ride northwards up the hill, up this fairly quiet street, with little through traffic. At the near edge of the field beside East House, a large early Victorian house, turn left on to a very narrow tarmac path, unsigned, (GR.012114). After 200 yards (180m) this path leads on to the cycleway, which you join by turning sharp right and riding down a long ramp.

This cycleway, which follows one of the many disused mineral railway lines in West Cumbria, was developed by Sustrans in association with West Cumbria Groundwork Trust. It joins the Sustrans C2C route, a cycleway from Whitehaven to Sunderland which will form part of the National Cycle Network. Sustrans (sustainable transport) is a charity which is doing an excellent job in providing cycleways, often by converting disused railway lines as in this case. Most of the routes, but not all, are available to horse-riders. The standard track consists of a tarmac path for cyclists, but there is often a verge alongside which is suitable for horses. The sculptures along the way are a particular feature of Sustrans routes, and you will see several interesting examples between here and Rowrah.

The valuable work which Sustrans is doing to provide cycleways is well worth strong equestrian support. However, please bear in mind that, unlike bridleways, cycleways are provided primarily for cyclists and you should therefore take particular care when riding on them.

The rest of the trail back to Rowrah is mainly a matter of following the cycleway signs. After ½ mile (800m) turn left on to the minor road to Woodend, where you bear right and then left to rejoin the cycleway less than ½ mile (0.7 km) further north (12.8 miles: 20.6 km) At Blind Lane there is a bridge with an overhead frame which provides insufficient headroom. Either dismount and lead across or ride down the ramp alongside.

The junction with the C2C route near Moor Row is a little confusing; bear right and follow the signs to Rowrah.

After 2½ miles (4 km) the landscape opens out and you have a long view up Ennerdale, the most westerly 'spoke' of the Lake District's drainage pattern. **At the next bridge (GR.043169) the easier way is to ride down the ramp and up the other side. The cycleway leads back into the car park at Rowrah and your starting point.**

THE BRITISH HORSE SOCIETY

BHS BOOK AND GIFT SHOP

The largest specialist Equestrian Bookshop in the UK displaying a comprehensive range of equestrian books and videos

The British Horse Society Book and Gift Shop is situated at the British Equestrian Centre on the Showground at Stoneleigh (on the B4113), and is open Monday to Friday 9am-5pm. A full mail order service is available.

Phone now for free catalogues.

Tel: 01203 690676

The British Horse Society

BHS Book and Gift Shop
Stoneleigh Park, Kenilworth
Warwickshire CV8 2LR

Registered Charity No 210504

BLENGDALE

Trail 8

A 12 MILE (19 KM) CIRCULAR TRAIL (CLOCKWISE)

Ordnance Survey Map:
Outdoor Leisure 6 - The English Lakes South Western Area (1:25,000)

Route:
Hurlbarrow/Scargreen/Thornholme/Tongue How/Scalderskew Wood/Brown Edge/Guards Head/Bolton Head/Bleng Bridge/Rowend Bridge/Wind Hall.
1540 feet (470m) of ascent. Your horse must also be willing to be walk through water.

Parking & Starting Point:
Although parking is very limited for this route, there is a hard verge with room for several vehicles on the minor road near the start (GR.071047). Leave the A595 on the road by the Boonwood Garden Centre, near the Red Admiral Hotel.

Trail Grade: 2

Terrain:
This route is fair going for most of its way, but careful map-reading is required in featureless moorland on Tongue How. There are nine fords on the trail, all readily passable except when they are in flood.

Route Description:

Ride northwards along an unmetalled road between stone walls. At Hurlbarrow the road swing left into the farm but you go straigh on through a gate on to a wide gree lane and down the hill to a beck *From here, as from several places o this trail, you have a good view o Sellafield; and in clear weather you ca see the Isle of Man across the Irish Sea* **Ford the little beck, go through th gate and bear left on to the bridlewa signposted Scargreen. After 10 yards turn left on to a hard track (GR.071059).**

The panoramic view of the Sellafiel complex adds, some say, a dramati aspect to the coastal plain; others ar more critical. However, what it does giv the rider is a complete visual history o the nuclear industry. Sellafield is wher the techniques which provide the worl with a safe and secure source o renewable energy have been develope and proved.

To the left lie the Calder Hall nuclea reactors, the first in the world to generat electricity. Their cooling towers are th dominant feature, with clouds of wate vapour being carried towards the fell by the prevailing wind, in the evenin dramatically tinged with pink as the reflect the setting sun. In the centre tw 400 feet (120m) high ventilation tower from the first nuclear reactors ever buil on the site draw the eye. They are slowl being dismantled, but will remain th most visible sign of scientific researc for years to come. To the right the roun dome of the Windscale Advanced Gas

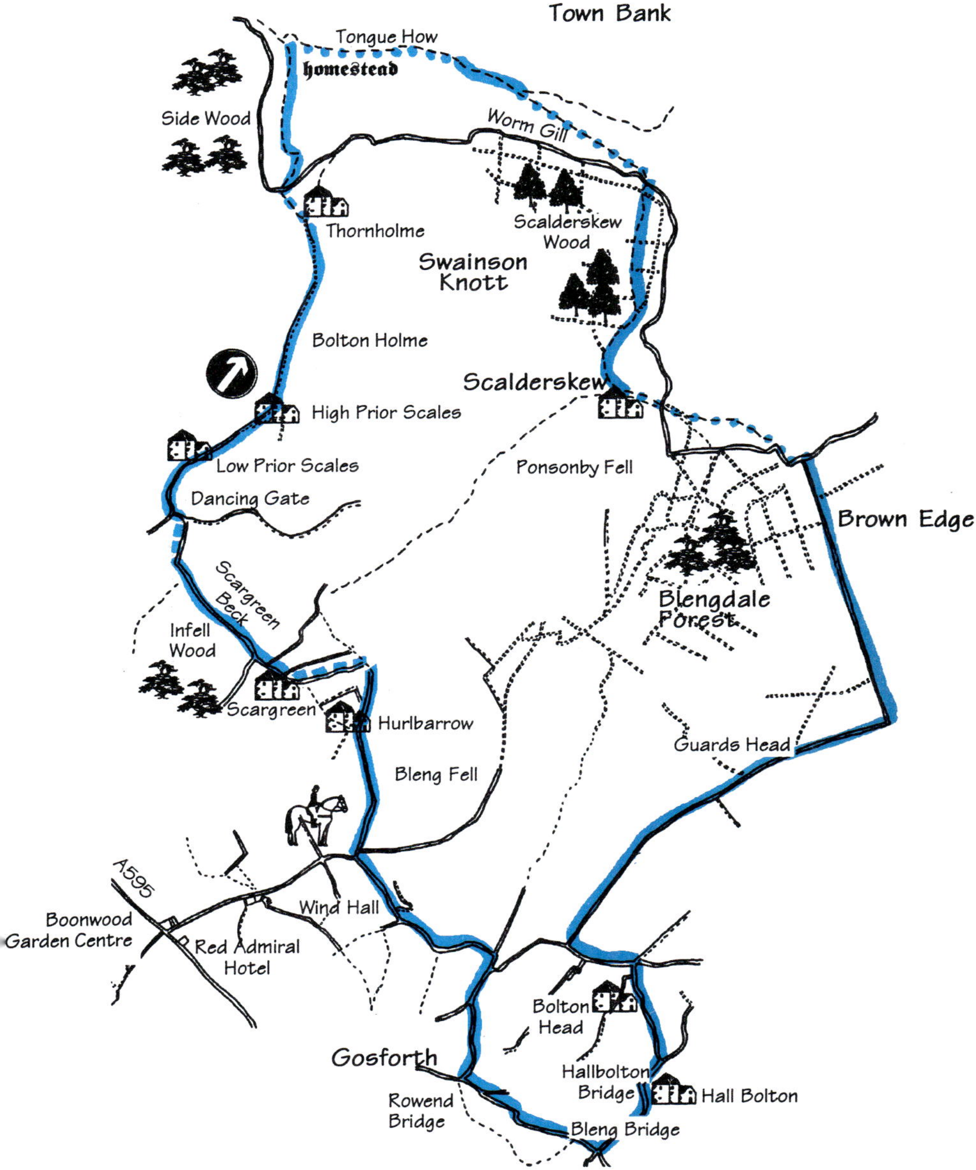

Town Bank
Tongue How
homestead
Side Wood
Worm Gill
Thornholme
Scalderskew
Wood
Swainson
Knott
Bolton Holme
Scalderskew
High Prior Scales
Low Prior Scales
Ponsonby Fell
Dancing Gate
Brown Edge
Scargreen
Beck
Blengdale
Forest
Infell
Wood
Scargreen
Hurlbarrow
Guards Head
Bleng Fell
A595
Wind Hall
Boonwood
Garden Centre
Red Admiral
Hotel
Bolton
Head
Gosforth
Hallbolton
Bridge
Hall Bolton
Rowend
Bridge
Bleng Bridge

Cooled Reactor provides yet another familiar image of the nuclear industry. It houses the first reactor of its type and resulted in 14 similar reactors being built around the country.

However, the main business of Sellafield goes on in the other large buildings that cover the site. It is here that spent nuclear fuel from power stations all over the world is re-processed, with 97 percent of its active ingredients returned to power stations through the world, including that used again to generate up to a quarter of Britain's electricity.

At Scargreen Farm you ford the beck again, go through the farm gate, and turn right on to the road with the farm buildings on your left. *There is a good example of a bank barn, a distinctive Cumbrian feature: the barn is built into the side of the hill with entrances at two levels, at the ground floor for stock at the front and the first floor for fodder at the back.*

Just past Scargreen the road turns sharp left (GR.064060) and there are two tracks to the right. Take the right hand track which continues past an attractive belt of woodland and fords the beck again. After passing the ford, in about 50 yards (45m) leave the track and take a narrow path to the left along by the beck, and across yet another ford; then ride up the steep hill through Infell Wood on a turf track with earth dykes either side.

At the end of the wood the bridleway turns sharp left (GR.060065) but your route continues straight on , fording the beck again and then turning right, going up the hill on a rocky track with a hedge on the left.

This part of the trail is actually a public footpath not a bridleway, but the landowner has kindly given permission for riders to use it — so long as they keep strictly to the path and DO NOT STRAY ON TO THE FIELD. Please therefore take care and observe his request - riders use this track as a concession and NOT as of right!

Turn left on to a farm track at Dancing Gate. Ride the short distance down to the road and turn right. The road goes past two farms then over the fell to Thornholme (GR.067088) (3.5 miles: 5.6 km) where it ends. Turn left before you reach the farmyard onto the bridleway which bears right to cross the Worm Gill. ***The bridge is not very convenient for horses, and riders may be advised to dismount and lead. An alternative is the ford which is just downstream.***

The route, a hard track, swings round to the right and then steeply up the fell to a sharp left-hand bend and round the shoulder of the hill to continue northwards. *This is the valley of the River Calder, with fine views of Side Wood which lies opposite.*

The next stage of the trail needs careful map-reading because the route is not easily apparent on the ground. Just before the bridleway starts to swing to the left, opposite Side Farm, turn right off the track (GR.066098) and, on a bearing of 75 degrees, aim for the 'homestead', an ancient ruin on the crest of the hill where you will soon pick up a track leading eastwards.

Follow this track for ¾ mile (1.2 km) to the Y-junction (GR.081096)

ENTER An Amazing Interactive Experience

The Sellafield Visitors Centre

Enter the Sellafield Visitors Centre, and computerised technology takes excitement all the way into the 21st century.

It's a totally different experience that explores and explains the fascinating world of BNFL.

Designed to inform and entertain the whole family, it features "hands-on" interactive scientific experiments, intriguing shows and fascinating displays of technology. There is a total of ten amazing zones to investigate. Discover all the facts and have your questions answered.

Can you handle all the excitement?

The answer is "yes" - because everything here is just waiting for you to reach out and touch, and admission is free.

It's open every day except Christmas Day 10am to 6pm, April to October and 10am to 4pm, November to March.

Sellafield Visitors Centre, Sellafield, Seascale, Cumbria, CA20 1PG Tel: (019467) 27020

SELLAFIELD VISITORS CENTRE

All the EXCITEMENT you can HANDLE

BNFL

Where science never sleeps

where you leave it to take a rather indistinct grass track leading downhill to the right. There are several boggy places, but these can be avoided by short diversions downhill. Care is needed at an outcrop of rock 50 yards before you reach the gill. Here there are two more fords to cross: the first is Worm Gill, then after a sharp right turn, you will cross a smaller beck. Go through the gate and up into Scalderskew Wood on a stony track.

The track leads on to one of the forest roads, where you turn left. After 40 yards leave the road and bear right on to a grass track between the trees to go southwards. The track bears right after the first ride crossing and goes on through rather desolate woodland to rejoin the forest road (GR.088082).

The road leaves the wood and goes past Scalderskew Farm (6.6 miles: 10.6 km). ***Beware of barking dogs here!*** **Ride on through the next gate and swing south towards Blengdale Forest. On the bend (GR.091076), leave the road and take an indistinct grass track to the left which disappears on the ground after a few yards. Bear diagonally right and make for the wall enclosing the forest. Follow this until it turns sharp right as the River Bleng comes into view. Continue along the top of the bank above the river for about 50 yards, then drop down to cross at the ford beside a set of stepping stones (GR.099073).** *The size of these stones seems to indicate that this crossing was once of some importance.*

Across the river a gate leads to a path going sharply uphill. The forest beyond the ditch on the left is standing timber, to the right, behind

the wall, it has been felled. The path soon joins a hard forestry road where you go straight on to a gate, ignoring another road which comes in from the right (GR.101068).

The road continues straight, leaving Blengdale Forest, crossing an open area where there are fine views of the sea and the estuaries of the Rivers Irt and Esk, and enters another Forest Enterprise wood. After riding for 400 yards (370m) into the wood, the road ends at a T-junction and you go straight ahead on the bridleway, a rough grass track between stone walls but reasonably good going.

At the end of the wood (GR.104056), turn right at the bridleway T-junction, on to a hard track between stone walls which leads down to the minor road 1½ miles (2.5 km) away (GR.084042) where you turn left. After 550 yards (500m) turn right on to the bridleway which is signed Bolton Head and Hall Bolton (10.3 miles: 16.6 km) (GR.088041).

The bridleway is a hard farm track between hedges, with fine views to the left of some of the Wasdale Fells; it becomes narrow and overgrown and leads downhill past a small wood with rhododendrons and some old trees to a T-junction where you turn right on to another bridleway, and go on down the hill to Hallbolton Bridge across the River Bleng. Ride on past attractive parkland and a wooded valley to join the road from Eskdale (GR.086029). Turn right.

CARE - for the next ¾ mile this is a minor road with no verges, and it does carry quite heavy tourist traffic during the summer. Immediately over Rowend Bridge take a farm road on the right (GR.077033). *This road is privately owned but the public have a right of passage.* Follow the road as it leads out to the Wasdale road and turn right. After 300 yards (275m) turn left on to a minor road which takes you up a steep hill back to your starting point.

Ride With:

Care
- For the Land

Courtesy
- To other users

Consideration
- For the Farmer

WASDALE

Trail 9

A 14 MILE (23 KM) CIRCULAR TRAIL (ANTI-CLOCKWISE)

Ordnance Survey Maps:
Outdoor Leisure 6 - The English Lakes South Western Area (1:25,000)

Route:
Forest Bridge, Nether Wasdale/Irton Fell/Miterdale/Low Place/Black Gill/ White Moss/Boot Bank/Burnmoor Tarn/Brackenclose/Wastwater/ Greendale/Ashness How.
2300 feet (700m) of ascent. Your horse must also be willing to walk through water.

Parking & Starting Point:
Parking is possible at the north end of Forest Bridge (GR.128037).

Trail Grade: 3

Terrain:
There are some steep, rocky stretches on this ride. Compass work may be required on one short stretch of moorland. ***Access for emergency vehicles would not be possible from Latterbarrow to Miterdale, or on Boot Bank.***

Route Description:

From your parking place take the bridleway signed 'To Eskdale', to the right of a house called The Flass, *('flass' means swamp)* **at the southern end of the bridge (GR.128037) and follow the garden fence before swinging slightly right to join a farm track coming in from the left. This leads through a gate and follows the wall towards a young plantation. Inside the plantation gate the main track swings right, but your route is shown by a bridleway sign to Eskdale, up the hill beside the wall, along a track which soon becomes steeper, stony and narrow for the most part.** *There are superb views of Wastwater over the wall to the left.*

When the track joins a forest road turn left along it for a few yards and then take the left fork, staying alongside the wall, on a good surface. At the next fork turn right as signed, along a narrow track between the trees. ***This ground is boggy, and the path frequently divides and rejoins. A notice advises caution due to waterlogging of the path but this is placed conveniently at the other end of the track!***

Cross the footbridge, ***CARE: although it is only short, the footbridge is narrow and you are advised to dismount and lead your horse.*** **The clearly-defined path passes between two rails to join a forest road. Turn right, then immediately left between two more rails, up a steep rocky path and out of the wood via two narrow gates (GR.133028).**

You will see your path going south-south-east (164 degrees) up the

hillside ahead. The intervening ground is, however, very wet and you are advised to make a wide detour to the left to avoid the worst area. Rejoin the path where it starts the steep climb of Irton Fell. On the way up the track varies greatly, from grass to steep, narrow and rocky going, and one exceptionally rocky stretch is best avoided by a detour to the right. *As you reach the higher ground the track improves, the trees of Miterdale Forest come into view ahead, and on clear days, the sea can be seen to the right.*

Just before the track reaches the forest it is crossed by a broad footpath, but keep straight on, aiming for a roadway gap in the trees, and enter the forest by a bridlegate (GR.135022).

Ride down the track, cross one gravelled road and at the next, near a junction, turn right then almost immediately left, down a well marked path. After going through a gap in a wall you meet another roadway; cross straight over it and down the path to yet another road, which is again crossed. The track now drops more steeply for about 25 yards (22m) and swings right to cross another path, where you turn left (GR.142012). *Trail 11 passes this crossroads by its other two tracks.* **After about 40 yards (35m) you cross another road, diagonally this time, and soon ford a small beck. The path then widens out into a forest road which takes you out of the wood (GR.146014) (2 miles: 3.2 km).**

Out of the wood continue along the track and when it joins a hard farm road carry straight on along it north-eastwards to Low Place (GR.155018).

At the far end of the farmyard, on the right, is a bridleway sign to Wasdale. Go through the gate. *If you look back here you will see the dialect sign in the wall, for riders going the other way!* **The bridleway ahead which is the direct route to Wasdale is practically impassable, so turn right, cross the River Mite by the ford and follow the main track round to the left.**

At the first wall go through the gate and carry straight on - don't take the right fork. The track meets the wall of a plantation and runs along it to the far end of the wood, where there is a narrow gate and stile. Go through the gate, then leave the path which carries straight on, and turn right up the hill, between Black Gill and the plantation. The bridleway is not obvious, but there is a path of sorts near the plantation fence. At the top of the plantation the path swings right to a stile and a very awkwardly placed narrow gate with a bridleway sign on the far side (GR.166023) (3.5 miles: 5.6 km).

Go through the gate and turn left and follow the indistinct path until it crosses Black Gill. The wall on your left drops down the hill, then climbs again, making a V shape. Make for the place where the wall reaches its highest point (roughly north-east), and when you are within about 100 yards of it (GR.168025) turn right and head off across the moor on a bearing of 110 degrees.

White Moss is very wet and care is needed as there is no obvious track but very soon two stone circles will come into view ahead, to keep you on course.

When you have the circles on your left, one behind the other, make for a rocky outcrop to your right. Ride from the outcrop in an easterly direction and within ¼ mile (400m) you will meet a well-marked narrow path (GR.176022). Turn right along this path, towards a ruined building down the hill.

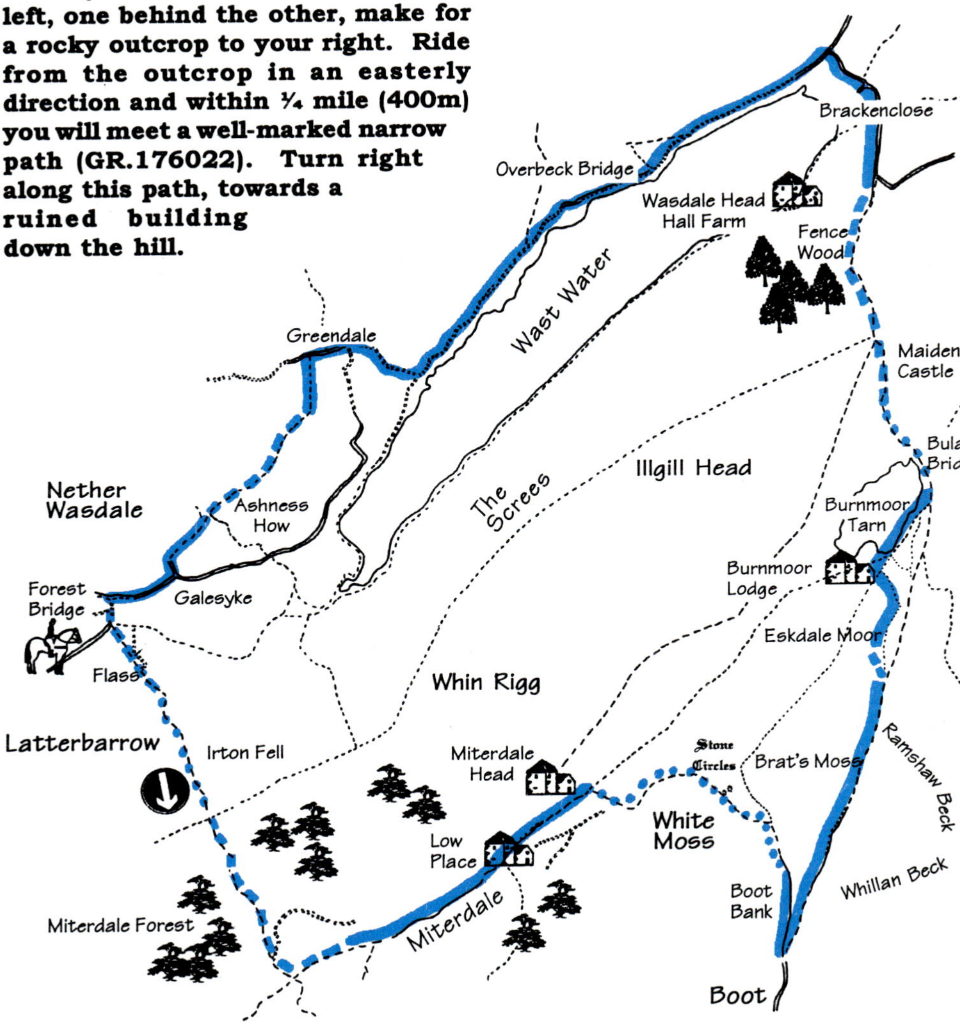

This track becomes increasingly well-defined, passes through a group of half-a-dozen ruined buildings on Boot Bank and runs steeply down, between walls, towards the village of Boot. *In places it is steep and rocky, and care is needed.* *The buildings, peat stores known as 'scales', were simple dry-stone structures roofed with bracken thatch. They were of two types the earlier ones were plain buildings wit a single entrance, on a level patch o ground; the later ones were mor substantial, with an upper and a lowe entrance similar to a bank barn. Eac building in the group held the peat for particular farmhouse. Peat scales wer usually on the farms, but in Eskdale the*

were sited on the fellside just below the lower level of the peat moss. The bridleway was the track on which peat was hauled down to the village on sledges drawn by Fell ponies. Peat was a staple fuel in places like Eskdale for many centuries, but it went out of use nearly 100 years ago.

Ride along this track until you come to a gate on your left at the bottom of a short, pronounced Z-bend (GR.176013). This is the start of the bridleway to Burnmoor Tarn.

The village of Boot can be entered 100 yards further down the track by going through a gate on the left. You will find a shop and pub facilities (5 miles: 8 km). Through the village is the link with Trail 10.

The track to Burnmoor Tarn is very clear on the ground and runs roughly parallel to Whillan Beck most of the way. It is wide and mostly firm, and appears to have been a well used road in former times. Within the enclosed land it forks only once, and you take the right hand fork. Out on the fell the track alternates grassy stretches with stony ones. After leaving the enclosed land you soon cross Ramshaw Beck and at the next significant feature which is a ruined building about 50 yards (45m) to the left of the track, the route swings left round it, in a Z-bend, at the top of which the way is briefly indistinct, but can soon be picked up again going north-north-east.

On the Ordnance Survey map the bridleway actually leaves this track to the right at the corner of the ruined building, and runs closer to Whillan Beck, but it is often invisible on the ground, and is difficult to follow, so it is recommended that the route described here is followed to Burnmoor Tarn where the original bridleway can be resumed.

Beyond the ruined building the track soon becomes a wide, grassy roadway, and as you approach the tarn, and the roof of Burnmoor Lodge comes into view, branch right down a green track towards the north-east end of the tarn, staying fairly close to the water and leading to the place where Whillan Beck leaves the tarn. *It is interesting to note how close together are the inflow and outflow streams of the tarn.* Cross the beck by either the substantial bridge or the good ford alongside it (GR.187046) (7 miles: 11.25 km).

About 75 yards (68m) beyond the bridge the track divides. Take the left fork which swings first towards the end of the tarn and then away from it. The track may not be distinct in wet weather, but there is a clear line of cairns. It meanders a little, but is essentially leaving the tarn in a north-north-west direction. After a few hundred yards there is a large enclosure bounded by collapsed stone walls, and at the end of this you turn right. *Note that the track seems to continue on up the steep slope, so do not be fooled into following it!* You will now be following a clearly defined path, roughly northwards, towards Wastwater. The track soon winds steeply downhill, and Wastwater

comes into view, with Yewbarrow (2055 ft: 627m) towering on the far side.

As you drop down towards a wall you meet another path at right-angles and turn right downhill along it (GR.182063). *This is in fact the same path that you crossed much earlier, just before entering Miterdale Forest.* It takes you towards a small wood and on the right, a ruined settlement. The track is now clear, wide, and in places very stony and rough and it may sometimes be necessary to move a little way up the hillside to find safer footing.

As the track drops down towards the valley it improves and enters the grounds of Brackenclose, the Fell and Rock Climbing Club's Lodge. Inside the grounds follow the wall to the entrance driveway and turn left along it to the wide footbridge, beyond which is a track leading past a car park to join the Wasdale Head road (GR.181076) (9.5 miles: 15.3 km).

Turn left along the road and follow it along the lakeside for about 2½ miles (4 km). *From this road there are excellent views across the lake of the famous Wastwater screes.* ***The road is narrow and twisting, so great care is needed because tourist traffic may be quite heavy. The road is unenclosed but the verges are mostly too rocky to ride on .***

Turn right (GR.151054) (11.9 miles: 19.2 km) and after about ½ mile (800m) you pass Greendale, then a bridge over the Greendale Gill where you turn left along a track marked 'Bridleway to Galesyke and Strands' (GR.143056). This is a very pleasant path, with good surface, along the edge of Roan Wood. At the end of the wood cross the slab bridge, swing right along the wall, and out of the wood by a bridlegate to join a track which comes from the left, a stony track across marshy ground. When the track swings left you carry straight on, along a green road which in turn swings slightly left to a gateway in a wall. The track now becomes a sunken roadway beside a ditch. Ignore both a track from the left and a track which comes in from the right. Keep on round the bottom of the hill and go through another gate onto a wide, clearly defined track which takes you to another gate.

Keep going straight on, towards Galesyke, on a lane enclosed first between fences and then walls. You pass three gates and a cottage before the lane turns left and brings you to a road (GR.133040). Turn right along the road, then take the first turn left to arrive back at Forest Bridge and your starting point (14 miles: 22.5 km).

ESKDALE TO DUNNERDALE

Trail 10

A 10 MILE (15 KM) LINEAR TRAIL (EASTWARDS)

Ordnance Survey Map:
Outdoor Leisure 6 - The English Lakes South Western Area (1:25,000)

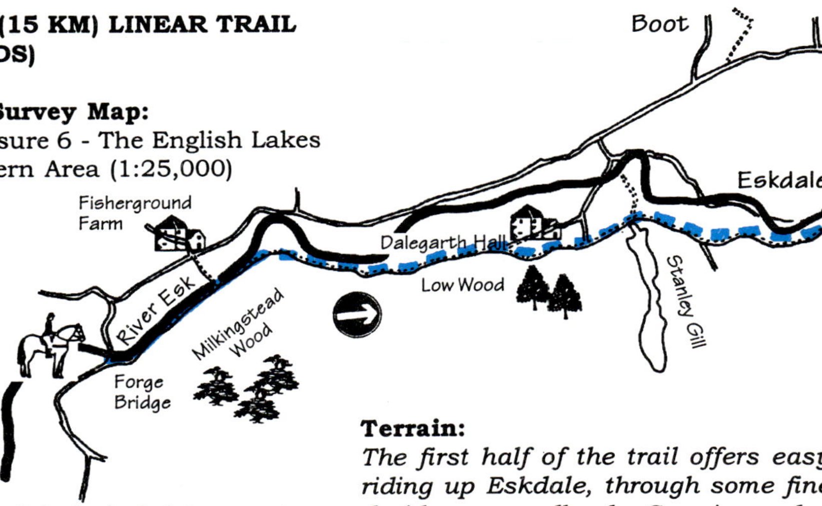

NB: *This trail is included here not so much for use on its own, but to provide a link between Muncaster and the Walna Scar Road, an ancient track across the high fells from Dunnerdale to Coniston.*

Route:
Forge Bridge/Milkingstead Wood/Low Wood/Low Birker/Penny Hill/ Whahouse Bridge/Birker Fell/ Grassguards/High Wallowbarrow/Hall Bridge.
1050 feet (320m) of ascent. Your horse must be able to walk through water on this route.

Parking & Starting Point:
There is a parking place beside Forge Bridge (GR.149995) although this is not recommended as road access in Eskdale is not very suitable for horseboxes.

Trail Grade: **2**

Terrain:
The first half of the trail offers easy riding up Eskdale, through some fine deciduous woodland. Care is needed in two places where there are rock outcrops. Along Harter Fell the going is generally good, but there is a difficult crossing of Grassguards Gill, and rocky stretches between Grassguards and High Wallowbarrow. ***Some of the later parts of the trail would be inaccessible to emergency vehicles.***

Route Description:

Join a bridleway immediately south of Forge Bridge, signposted Stanley Gill, Boot and Upper Eskdale. *The bridleway is a wide track through attractive deciduous woodland, leading upstream along the south bank of the river.* **When you come to two field gates forming a Y-junction, take the right-hand one.**

One and a quarter miles (2 km) after leaving Forge Bridge, just over the wal

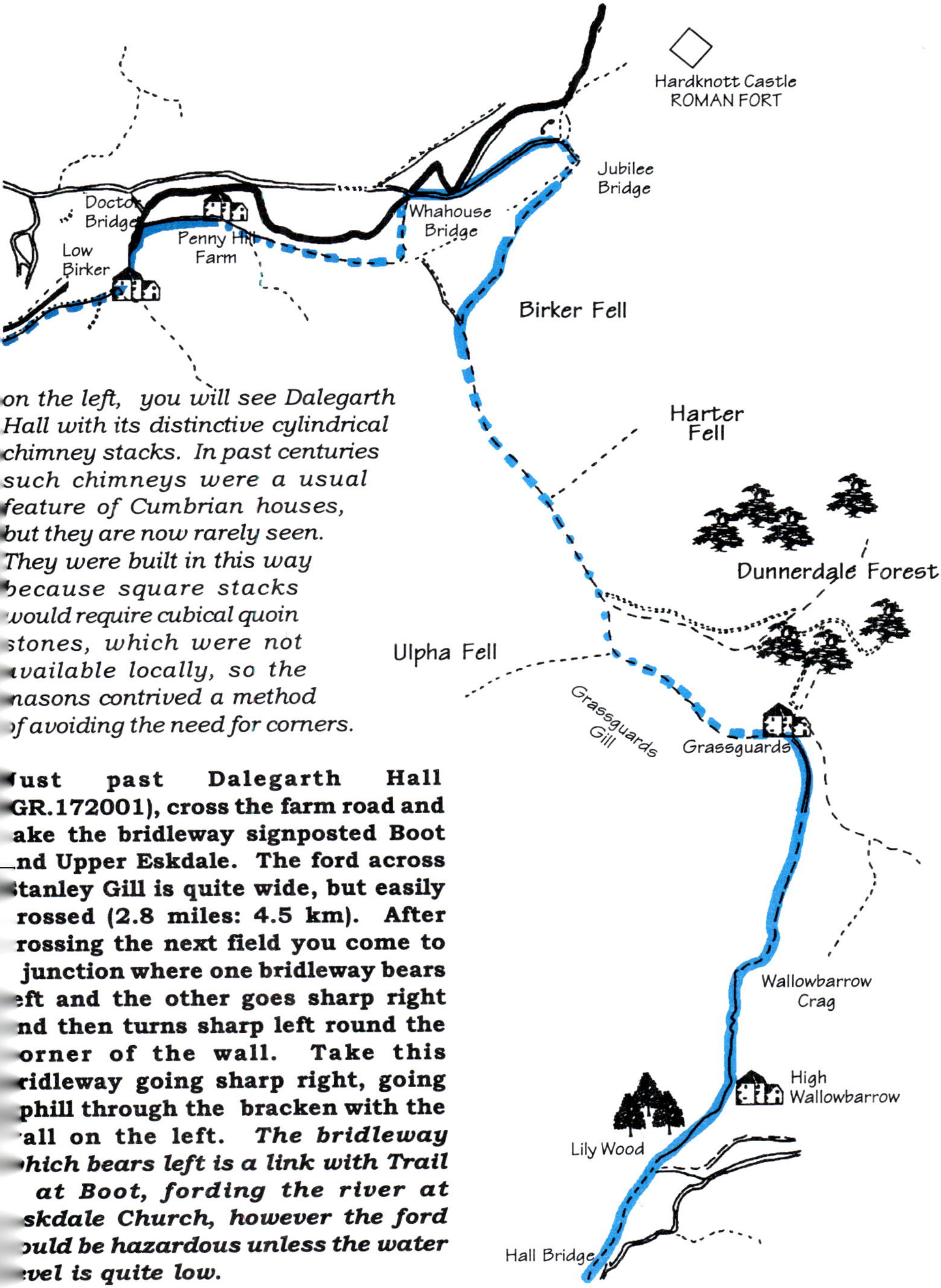

on the left, you will see Dalegarth Hall with its distinctive cylindrical chimney stacks. In past centuries such chimneys were a usual feature of Cumbrian houses, but they are now rarely seen. They were built in this way because square stacks would require cubical quoin stones, which were not available locally, so the masons contrived a method of avoiding the need for corners.

ust past Dalegarth Hall (GR.172001), cross the farm road and ake the bridleway signposted Boot nd Upper Eskdale. The ford across tanley Gill is quite wide, but easily rossed (2.8 miles: 4.5 km). After rossing the next field you come to junction where one bridleway bears eft and the other goes sharp right nd then turns sharp left round the orner of the wall. Take this ridleway going sharp right, going phill through the bracken with the all on the left. ***The bridleway hich bears left is a link with Trail at Boot, fording the river at skdale Church, however the ford ould be hazardous unless the water evel is quite low.***

Your route continues through woodland and fields, and some scrub country. *There is a small pond on the right where water lilies grow (GR.183002).* **Just above Low Birker, bear left at the Y-junction and ride down the hill past the farm house. The bridleway runs beside the river to Doctor Bridge (GR.189007), where you turn right on the road to Penny Hill Farm.** *To the right there looms the rocky cone of Harter Fell (2140 feet: 653m). Your route will follow a bridleway along the base of that cone.*

Bear right in the farmyard and go through the right-hand gate up a track between stone walls. After crossing a field, bear left at the Y-junction ignoring the footpath to the right which goes up to Harter Fell. Continue along the bridleway with the wall on your left and go through a bridlegate into the wood. There is a ford across the beck, it is an easy crossing, but take care because the ford is immediately above a waterfall. At a bridleway junction turn left on to the track signposted Whahouse Bridge and ride down towards the river across another small ford. *Nearby on the right, two becks join, one at a level about three feet higher than the other - an unusual feature.*

The bridleway joins the road at Whahouse Bridge (GR.204009) (4.1 miles: 6.6 km) where you turn right. ***The approach to the road is awkward, up a steep slope with poor visibility. For the next 5/8 mile (1 km) the road towards Hardknott Pass is very narrow, between stone walls, with few verges or passing places: great care is needed because traffic may be quite heavy during the tourist season, and oncoming cars have just completed a hazardous trip over Wrynose and Hardknott Passes.***

Go through the gate by the cattle grid (GR.213011) and turn right on to the bridleway, down to Jubilee Bridge which crosses Hardknott Gill. ***It is a narrow concrete bridge without parapets; it may be better to dismount and lead your horse here.*** **A short, steep stony path leads up from the bridge through two gates, from the second of which the bridleway shows as a green path almost along the contour.**

Ford two becks and the bridleway, which is still wide with a good surface, soon begins to climb and swing left round the shoulder of Birker Fell. *There are superb views of Eskdale to the right and, looking back of Hardknott and the distant heights of the Scafell range.* **Another ford is crossed, near a little waterfall. The track goes through a bridlegate and turns left, away from Eskdale following a small gill and becoming more rocky underfoot. One shor stretch of awkward rock can be by passed by retreating some 30 yard and diverting left, rejoining the trac just above the rock. The pat ascends beside a fence and become narrower and wet as it reaches th flatter terrain. It carries on with th fence on the right, passing throug a narrow gap between the fence an a rocky outcrop with a sma 'balancing stone' on it. The trac widens and generally improves as crosses the plateau, but there a several short boggy stretches whic need care.**

The bridleway enters Dunnerda Forest (GR.211992) (6.2 miles: 1 km). *The Ordnance Survey map m* *appear to be misleading because large areas of the forest have been felled, and new planting carried out on the open fell.* Inside the forest, the track goes straight ahead between the tree stumps, becoming less clear, but leading eventually to a waymarked Y-junction. Take the right fork, which leads to the forest fence.

Immediately through the gate the bridleway drops awkwardly down to a small beck, where the crossing is difficult and great care is needed (GR.214986). After this the path improves as it goes down beside Grassguards Gill, until it reaches a beck which can easily be forded about 30 yards downstream from the footbridge (GR.221981). You then cross a forest road, go through a gate and follow the track with the wall on your right and the gill on your left, which here is a series of rapids and waterfalls, to arrive at Grassguards Farm. Take the small gate to the left of the farm buildings, down to the gill. Go along the building then turn right through the gate into the farmyard. Cross the yard to the far left-hand corner, ride alongside the buildings and through a metal gate into a lane with a wide wall on the right and a fence on the left.

The route is now along a wide farm track, often enclosed by traditional walls of great thickness. *In these dales the purpose of building walls was not only to separate the fields but to get rid of all the stones which littered the land before it was enclosed.* A gate leads the track out on to open moorland with wonderful views over the Duddon valley. After another gate the track begins to descend until the first in-by land is reached. Follow the waymark here to the left and continue as the track drops steeply. ***It is very stony and needs extra care. The surface is often treacherous, with loose stones and larger boulders. The steepness is relieved considerably by a serpentine route, typical of an ancient pack-pony trail. It may be better to dismount and lead for this descent.*** *To the left are the towering Wallowbarrow crags, much used by rock climbers.*

At the foot the waymarked route lies through a gate into a garden. *Yes, this is the right of way!* It then goes out into the yard of High Wallowbarrow (GR.221963) (8.6 miles: 13.9 km). Turn right across the front of the house and on to a driveway. The last mile of the trail is along a minor road. At Hall Bridge (GR.213953) turn right towards Trail 12 and then left towards the Walna Scar Road and your destination.

Insurance

The BHS recommends that before undertaking any of the routes featured in this book, both horse and rider be adequately insured against **THIRD PARTY PUBLIC LIABILITY.** Membership of the BHS gives automatic Third Party Insurance with an indemnity of up to £2,000,000

MUNCASTER FELL

Trail 11

A 13 MILE (21 KM) CIRCULAR TRAIL (ANTI-CLOCKWISE)

Ordnance Survey Map:
Outdoor Leisure 6 - The English Lakes South Western Area (1:25,000)

Route:
Fell Lane/High Eskholme/Muncaster Head/Forge House/Forge Bridge/The Green Station/Foresthow/Irton Road Station/Porterthwaite/Keyhow Coppice/Irton Park/Sandbank/Muncaster Mill.
850 feet (260 m) of ascent.

Parking & Starting Point:
Parking is available in a small lay-by which is a few yards from the end of Fell Lane (GR.099967) down the A595 northbound.

Trail Grade: 1

Terrain:
There is good going all the way on this route using farm tracks or through woodland. The trail goes round the foot of the long ridge of Muncaster Fell, and on its northern side it follows the line of the Ravenglass and Eskdale Railway.

Route Description:

Start your ride from the corner (GR.100968) by taking the public bridleway signposted 'Muncaster Fell' and ride up Fell Lane for ½ mile (800m). *To the right there are fine views across Eskdale of the rock outcrops of Birkby Fell (1450 feet: 442m) and Stainton Fell (1633 feet: 498m). The route of Trail 12 passes by Birkby Fell at the foot of its crags.* **Leave the main track (GR.106976) and bear right on a minor path through the woods, signposted to Lower Eskdale.** *The gardens of Muncaster Castle, just across the main road where you started, are famous for rhododendrons, which have spread into these woods and make an impressive display during early summer.*

Half a mile (800m) along this path, looking down to the right through a gap in the trees, you will see a slender octagonal tower which was built in the 18th century by the first Lord Muncaster. This is to commemorate the visit centuries before of King Henry VI. In May 1464 the King was in hiding after his defeat at the Battle of Hexham, during the Wars of the Roses. He was found by shepherds and taken to the Castle, where Sir John de Penyngton gave him shelter. The tower marks the spot where he was found. In appreciation the King gave Sir John an enamelled glass bowl, the 'Luck of Muncaster', which is still treasured by his descendants.

The narrow path soon turns into a vehicle track, where you bear left to follow the bridleway sign towards Eskdale (1.4 miles: 2.3 km). *Opposite Birks Coppice (GR.132986), there is the site of a Roman tilery just off the track to the right.* **Follow the farm road from Muncaster Head to Forge House and turn left on to the road (GR.147993).** *This road is not usually very busy, and there is a verge to ride on for part of the* *way. The start of Trail 10 is at Forge Bridge.* **Ride past the King George IV Inn (4.1 miles: 6.6 km), and turn left on to the bridleway at The Green Station (GR.146999), which leads down an attractive path towards Bank End Wood.**

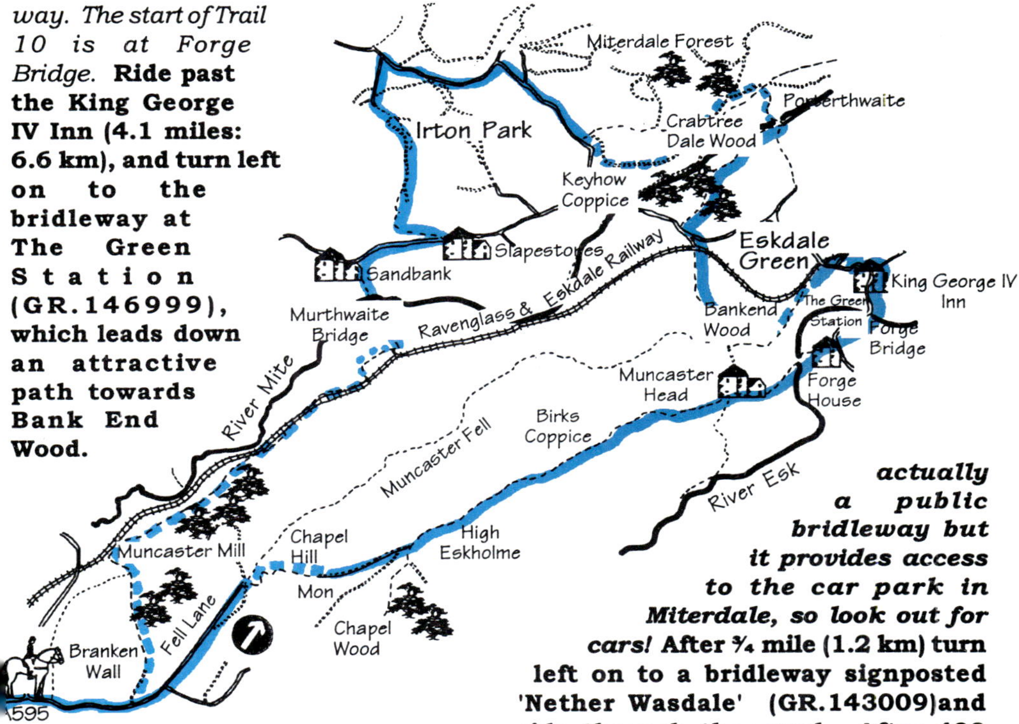

Just before the level crossing, bear left on to a narrower path; ride down to the beck, along a rocky stretch, and up the hill with the wall on your left. At the top, bear right and aim towards the corner of another wall. The bridleway goes between the wall and a large rock outcrop. Where the wall returns to the right, continue across the field to the gate and turn right on to the bridleway signposted to Irton Road and Eskdale Green (GR.139993).

After another ½ mile (800m), cross the bridge over the railway and ride on until you meet the road (5.7 miles: 9.1 km). Turn left. ***This is the road from Gosforth to Eskdale and it has quite heavy traffic during the holiday season.*** **Ride for 150 yards (135m) and turn right.** ***This is actually a public bridleway but it provides access to the car park in Miterdale, so look out for cars!*** **After ¾ mile (1.2 km) turn left on to a bridleway signposted 'Nether Wasdale' (GR.143009)and ride through the wood. After 400 yards (360m) you will come to a bridleway crossroads just before the track rises to join a forest road. Turn left here.**

This is a good track through the wood with a stone wall on the right and the slope down to the River Mite on the left. *The wood is mainly deciduous with oak and beech trees, and there are a few rhododendrons and holly trees.* **Cross a little beck and ride on with the wall on your left. The forest road crosses at an acute angle and you go straight on up the hill. The path leaves the wood to cross a rough field before joining a farm track which leads back to the road. Turn right (GR.129008).**

One mile (1.6 km) along the road, turn left on to a narrow path, a

bridleway signposted for Slapestones (GR.115014). After ¼ mile (400m) you come to a wide forest road and go straight across to a narrow path slightly to the left. The path is clearly seen through the wood, passing close by Parkgate Tarn where water lilies bloom in August. Rejoin the main track and leave it again at the foot of a slight slope where the bridleway follows a path to the right, leading out on to the road at Slapestones. Turn right (GR.119001) and ride along the road for 700 yards (650m) to Sandbank Farm (10.1 miles: 16.2 km).

At Sandbank turn left and ride up the farm road leaving the buildings on your right. *A few yards past the farm, the length of Muncaster Fell looms ½ mile ahead.* **At the end of the second field after Murthwaite Bridge go through the gate and turn sharp right into a small garth with a gate at the end, signposted 'bridleway'. Cross two more fields, turn left and ride up towards the wood with the fence on your left. Turn right (GR.116993) and go along the top of the field to a gate which leads into a small patch of woodland.** ***CARE: for the next 1¾ miles (2.4 km) your route follows almost alongside the line of the Ravenglass and Eskdale Railway. The locomotives are only small but they are still liable to frighten horses.***

This railway, always known as 'La'al Ratty', was built in 1875 to haul haematite from Eskdale and has a history of mixed fortunes because the mineral traffic was never consistently profitable. Originally built to a three foot gauge, it was converted to a gauge of 15 inches in 1915. The line offered a passenger service from the early days which was moderately successful, taking advantage of the expansion of tourism after the First World War. At this stage it was the first miniature railway to be run by a group of enthusiastic amateur railwaymen. But over the longer term its fortunes declined until it was taken over in 1961 by the R & E Railway Preservation Society.

For the past 35 years with increasing success the Ratty on its 7 miles (10 km) of track has been operated as a popular tourist attraction, and its future is now assured. It runs eight locos including the steam locos River Irt, River Esk, River Mite and Northern Rock.

In the patch of woodland the bridleway leads into an open space beside the railway where there is a Y-junction . Take the wider, right-hand track and go along the field with the railway fence on your left. Go through the next gate and turn sharp right through the bracken to a bridleway level crossing (GR.107985). ***Look out for trains this level crossing is an informal affair!***

Turn right and ride on through thick bracken in the wood with the railway not far away on your right. The path, which is waymarked, soon rises to join a forest track; at a crossroads, continue on the main track half-right and slightly downhill. Just above Muncaster Mill Station turn sharp left on a bridleway signposted to the Castle (GR.096977) (12.2 miles: 19.6 km).

Stay on the main forest road, which becomes a Permissive Bridleway by-passing Branken Wall and leads out to a gate at the end of the wood, where you turn left to return to your starting point at the foot of Fell Lane.

Now Available In The

"On Horseback" Series

Wiltshire

Westmorland

The Ridgeway Downs

Exmoor

Somerset

Hampshire

Leicestershire & Rutland

Humberside

Northamptonshire

Dorset

Cambridgeshire

The Cotswolds (second edition)

Powys

Buckinghamshire (Circular Routes)

Buckinghamshire (Long Distance)

Yorkshire Dales

BROAD OAK TO DEVOKE WATER

Trail 12

A 14 MILE (22 KM) CIRCULAR TRAIL (CLOCKWISE)

Ordnance Survey Map:
Outdoor Leisure 6 - The English Lakes South Western Area (1:25,000)

Route:
Broad Oak/Dyke Farm/Birkby Fell/Devoke Water/Crosbythwaite/Bigert Mire/Whitfell/Waberthwaite Fell.
1970 feet (600m) of ascent.

Terrain:
This ride is across attractive fell country. There are recurring boggy stretches on the way where care is needed.

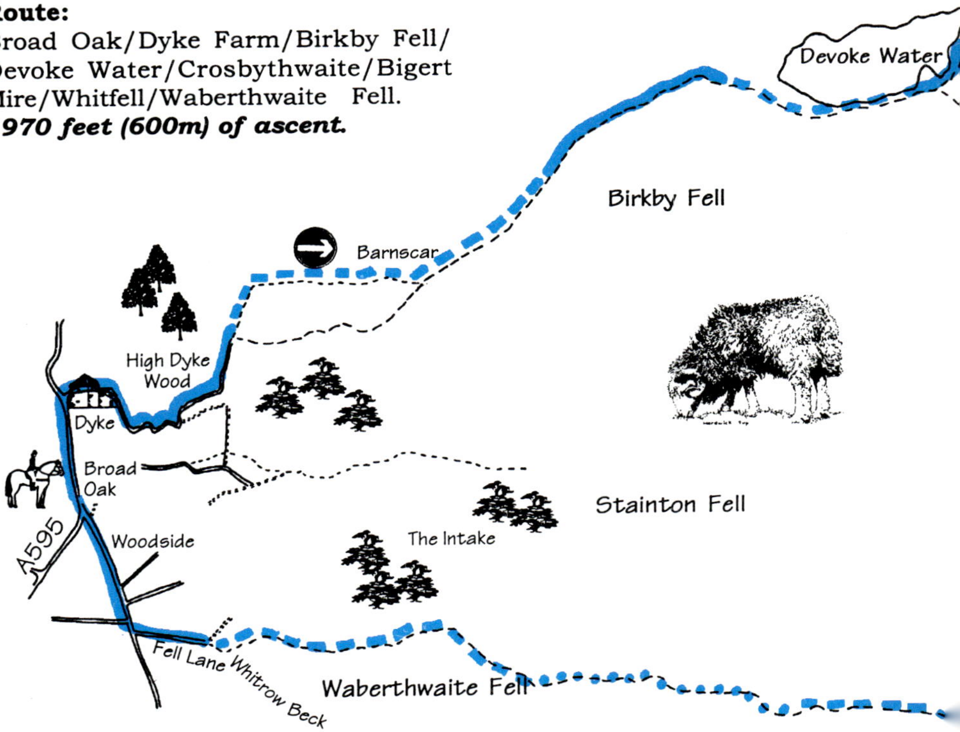

Parking & Starting Point:
There is a good parking place at Broad Oak (GR.114946).

Trail Grade: 2

Route Description:

Ride northwards along the A595 roa for 600 yards (550m). ***Take gre care because this is quite a bus***

trunk road. **Turn right on to a signposted bridleway which goes through the farmyard at Dyke, leading past a pink painted house. The bridleway then climbs steadily upwards on a hard track.** *Look behind for a fine view of the Irish Sea, with the Ravenglass dunes where the now much reduced gull colony is. In the distance is the New Red Sandstone of St Bees Head, the Isle of Man and the Scottish hills. To the right there is a small round building perched on a hill which is known as the pepper pot, which may have been used as a lookout post in the past.*

At the corner of the wood (GR.122954) the bridleway turns right, but this route soon becomes impassable on boggy ground so you have to divert by continuing northwards for 350 yards (320m) on the line of the path to turn right near the far side of the intake and aim for Birkby Fell which you will see ahead. ***NOTE: Riding along the path is permitted because the bridleway is impassable.***

Even here you have to be careful because the going may be boggy; *Eventually the panorama of the Wasdale range comes into view, Great Gable (2948 feet: 899m), Sca Fell and Sca Fell Pike (3207 feet: 978m), the volcanic heart of the Lake District.*

You rejoin the bridleway on the shoulder of Birkby Fell (GR.133957). *Devoke Water soon comes into view, an attractive tarn surrounded by low fells.* **The bridleway rides close to the water, where there is another boggy stretch, and then it joins a good track leading to the road (GR.171977) (5 miles: 8 km). Turn right and ride along the unenclosed road towards Crosbythwaite, a typical lakeland farm. You cross a small packhorse bridge, ride on for 220 yards (200m) and turn right on to a bridleway across the fell (7.2 miles: 11.6 km) when you will see the Kirkby Fells and the Duddon estuary ahead.** *As you gain height the view behind includes the Ulpha Fells, Crinkle Crags and Bow*

Fell (2957 feet: 902m) joining the Sca Fell range. Looking half-left you will see the Duddon estuary with Kirkby Moor in the distance. ***Here, again, the going may be boggy in places.***

The bridleway drops down to Holehouse Gill where you cross the bridge (GR.181932) and ride on past Holehouse Farm, a lime-washed farmhouse with grey slate buildings, towards Bigert Mire. Here you pass several cottages nestling together, and turn left (9.1 miles: 14.7 km) (GR.179927) on to a stony track across the fell which eventually gives way to good going. *Whitfell (1875 feet: 572m) with its pointed cairn rises nearby to the left, and just beyond there is a basin-shaped hollow known as Withe Bottom;* ***the bridleway crosses another boggy patch nearby.***

Waberthwaite Fell comes into view, with the steep gully of Red Gill running down its side, and the bridleway crosses this at the bottom (GR.139935) (11.9 miles: 19.1 km), continuing down to Fell Lane beside the Whitrow Beck. Turn right on to the Corney Fell road which leads on to the main road and back to Broad Oak and your starting place.

BLACK COMBE

A 13 MILE (21 KM) CIRCULAR TRAIL (CLOCKWISE)

Ordnance Survey Map:
Pathfinder: 625 (1:25,000)

Route:
Whitbeck/Fell Cottage/Little Fell/ Black Combe/Kirkbank/Silecroft/ Gutterby
1770 feet (540m) of ascent.

Parking & Starting Point:
There is good parking available in a lay-by on the main road, beside the church at Whitbeck (GR.119839).

Trail Grade: 2

Terrain:
This ride is mostly good going over the open fell, but with a rocky stretch above Kirkbank. Later along the route there is a ride along the shore. Please note that at times of exceptional high tides the beach may not be passable so seek local advice before you set out if you are in any doubt.

Route Description:

Ride up the lane past the church and along behind the houses and cottages. Go through the gate beside the cattle grid, and across the Millergill Beck. *The shoulder of the Combe looms here on the right.* **You pass some cottages on the left.** *On the right there is an old mill with the water wheel still intact on the far side of the building. The track climbs gradually and a view of the sea opens up to show the Isle of Man, St Bees Head and the Scottish coast. As you climb look down to the left and see the village of Bootle and Barfield Tarn.*

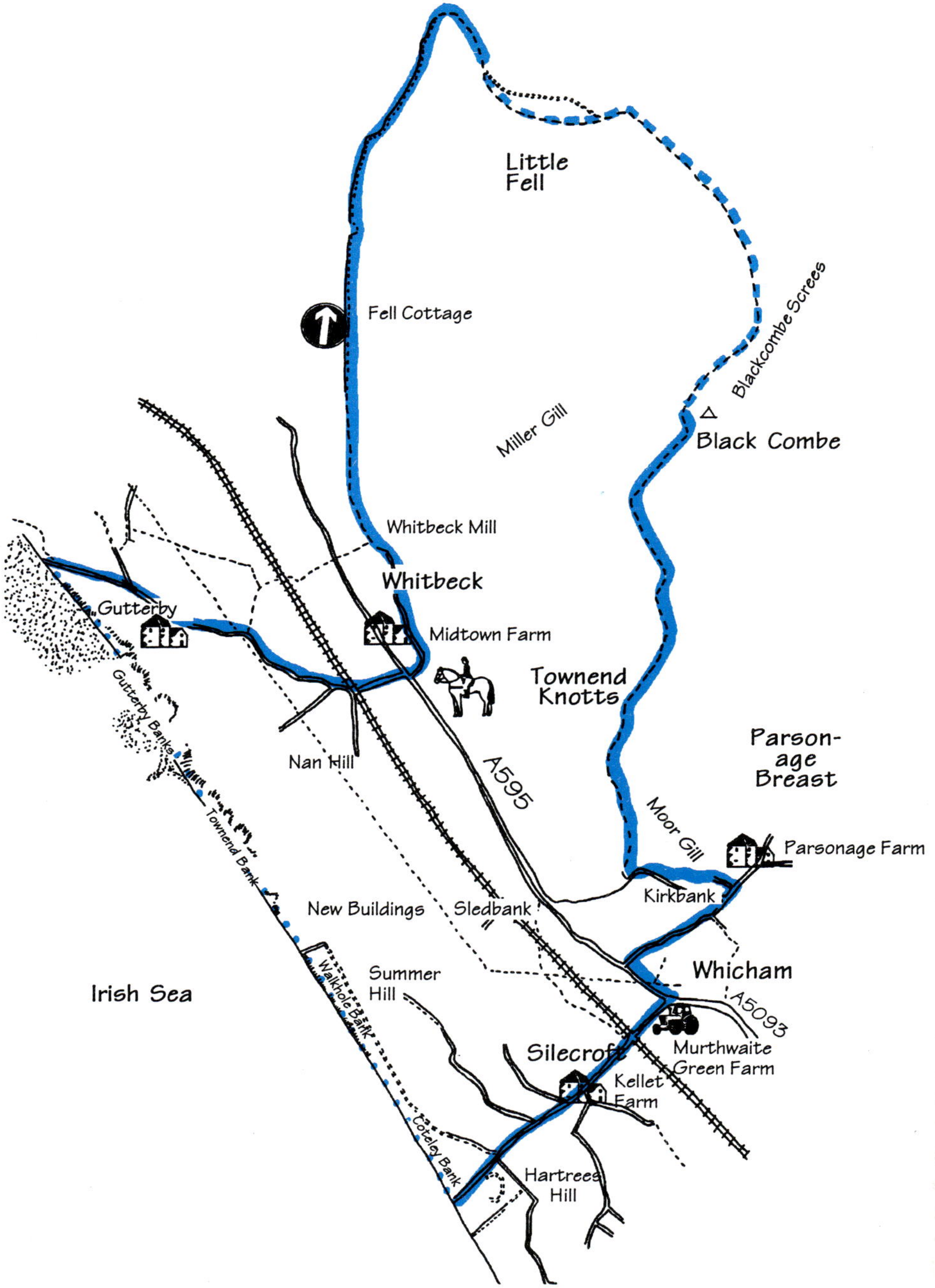

Little Fell
Fell Cottage
Blackcombe Screes
Black Combe
Miller Gill
Whitbeck Mill
Whitbeck
Gutterby
Midtown Farm
Townend Knotts
Gutterby Banks
Nan Hill
Parsonage Breast
A595
Moor Gill
Parsonage Farm
Townend Bank
Kirkbank
New Buildings
Sledbank
Whicham
Irish Sea
Summer Hill
Walkhole Bank
A5093
Silecroft
Murthwaite Green Farm
Kellet Farm
Cotelev Bank
Hartrees Hill

The track becomes steeper as you turn away from the sea. Buck Barrow (1800 feet: 549m) and Corney Fell come into view. *The climb is long and arduous, but the view from the top of Black Combe (1970 feet: 600m) (4.8 miles: 7.8 km) makes it all worthwhile. On a clear day you can see Blackpool and Morecambe to the south and sometimes, if you are lucky, the hills of Snowdonia. Down below the Whicham and Duddon valleys stretch upwards into the Ulpha valley, with the wind turbines ahead on Kirkby Fell.*

The bridleway continues southward on a clear grass track, mainly through bracken. ***There is a steep rocky stretch near Moorgill Beck where care is needed, but this can be avoided by a short detour to the right;*** **and then the track leads on to a very narrow road at Kirkbank (GR.131828). Ride down to the main road and turn right (7 miles: 11.3 km).**

Herdwick tup

The A595 is a single-carriageway trunk road, so take great care. **After less than ½ mile (0.7 km) turn left on to the A5093 towards Millom, which is much less busy. Ride on for 360 yards (330m) and turn right on to a minor road through Silecroft, follow this for a mile (1.6 km) down to the shore (8.7 miles: 14 km) (GR.121811).**

The beach is shingle above high water mark and better avoided, but the foreshore is mostly firm sand and gives very good going. At times of exceptional high tides the beach may not be passable, so seek local advice if in doubt.

After 2¾ miles (4.4 km) turn right up a narrow track in a defile running down to the beach (11.5 miles: 18.4 km) (GR.097847). The track returns at an acute angle and is easily missed, so keep a good look out. It is marked by a post carrying a footpath waymark. A sandy bluff rises from the beach at 45 degrees 350 yards (320m) ahead, with a farm track behind. If the going changes from sand to shingle cobbles, you have ridden too far along the shore.

The track leaving the beach is classified as a Public Footpath, but it has dual status and you are allowed to ride on it. It leads past Gutterby Farm and across an unmanned level crossing back to Whitbeck Church and your starting point.

BROADGATE TO THWAITES FELL

Trail 14

AN 8 MILE (12 KM) CIRCULAR TRAIL (CLOCKWISE)

Ordnance Survey Map:
Pathfinder: 625 (1:25,000)

Route:
Broadgate/Crag Hall/Swinside/Thwaites Fell/Wrayslack/Duddon Bridge/Buckman Brow.
700 feet (210m) of ascent.

Parking & Starting Point:
Parking is available in the wood yard at Broadgate (GR.181867).

Trail Grade: 2

Terrain:
Most of the going is on good tracks across the fell, or on minor roads. Care is needed on a boggy patch between Swinside and the Corney Fell road. The A595 is not heavily trafficked for a trunk road, but care is needed as it is a rather narrow single carriageway.

Route Description:

Ride northwards from your parking place, along the road past an old farmhouse. *The farm buildings are characteristic of an old Lake District style, including a barn that is open on all sides with the main beam supported by cobbled stone pillars.* **Just before Crag Hall turn left on to a bridleway, a stony track leading to Swinside (GR.181873).** *After you have climbed for a short distance, look behind as the view opens up over the Duddon Estuary with Kirkby Moor beyond (1092 feet: 333m). As you continue along the track the Wasdale range comes into view half-right, with Sca Fell and Great Gable looming over the lower fells.*

Two fields before you get to the farm, Swinside stone circle, which is some 4000 years old, is on the right. This consists of 55 stones set in a circle of 90 feet (27.5m) diameter. **At Swinside, turn left and ride past the farm and on to the fell, and then round the shoulder of Swinside Fell (1233 feet: 376m). About 600 yards (560m) further on there is a soft area where some care is needed. This can be avoided by diverting to the left up the fell.**

Merlin

There is a rocky outcrop about 2 miles (3 km) ahead called Buck Barrow (1800 feet: 549m). Keeping this in sight and

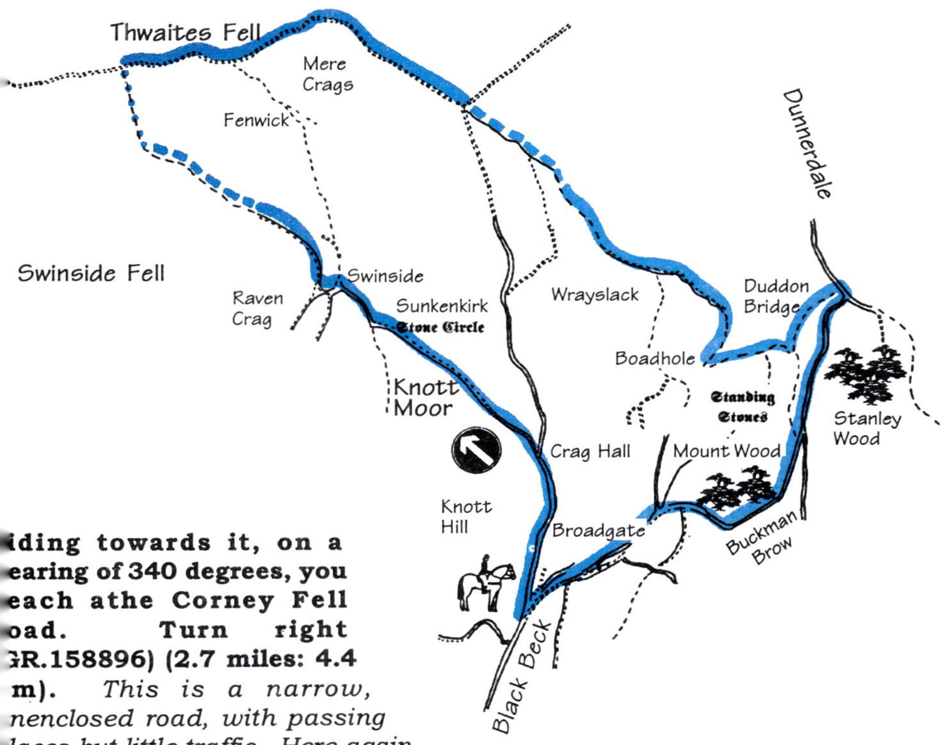

iding towards it, on a earing of 340 degrees, you each athe Corney Fell oad. Turn right ;R.158896) (2.7 miles: 4.4 m). *This is a narrow, nenclosed road, with passing laces but little traffic. Here again iere are marvellous panoramic views f the Ulpha Valley ahead, the Wasdale inge far away to the left and the uddon Estuary to the right with Kirkby loor beyond.*

ide down the hill for 1½ miles (2.4 m) to a Y-junction where the ridleway leading to Boadhole lies raight ahead (GR.177893). Ride long this track as it takes you irough an old slate quarry where ie going is rather rough, and leads i to a fell track through the bracken nd through a gate on the right. ollow the track to the second gate; ear right, ride on for 200 yards 80m) and then turn left, dropping down towards another gate. Go through the gate and follow the track down through an opening in the wall on your left, and through the wood to the old charcoal workings. Ride past these old buildings to the gate on to the road (GR.197883).

Turn right, ride towards the main road, the A595, and turn right again. ***The road past Duddon Bridge Farm is very narrow, so take care.*** **Continue along the road up a steep hill, Buckman Brow, and after 1½ miles (2.4 km) turn right towards the sawmill at Broadgate and so return to your starting place.**

THE BRITISH HORSE SOCIETY

The British Horse Society was founded in 1947 when two separate equestrian bodies - The National Horse Association and the Institute of the Horse and Pony Club - decided to join forces and work together for the good of both horse and rider.

It is a marriage that has proved to be a great success and the British Horse Society has steadily increased its membership from just 4000 in the late 1960's to over 65,000 in the 1990's.

By becoming members of the British Horse Society, horse lovers know they are joining a body of people with a shared interest in the horse. Members can be sure that they are contributing to the work of an equine charity with a primary aim to improve the standards of care for horses and ponies. Welfare is not only about the rescuing of horses in distress (which we do); it is also about acting to prevent abuse in the first place. There are many means to achieving this: by teaching and advising, by looking to the horse's well-being and safety, by providing off-road riding, by encouraging high standards in all equestrian establishments, and fighting for the horse's case with government and in Europe.

The British Horse Society works tirelessly towards these aims thanks to the work of its officials at Stoneleigh and its army of dedicated volunteers out in the field.

Membership benefits the horse lover as well as the horse; the Society can offer something to all equestrians, whether they are weekend riders, interested spectators or keen competitors. The benefits include free Third Party Public Liability and personal Accident insurance, free legal advice, free publications, reductions to British Horse Society events, special facilities at the major shows, and free advice and information on any equine query.

Largely financed by its membership subscriptions, the Society welcomes the support of all horse lovers. If you are thinking of joining the Society and would like to find out more about our work, please contact the Membership Department at the following address:

The British Horse Society
British Equestrian Centre
Stoneleigh Park
Kenilworth
Warwickshire
CV8 2LR
(Telephone: 01203 696697)
Registered Charity No. 210504